RESPONSES TO GOVERNANCE

Governing Corporations, Societies and the World

JOHN DIXON

Assisted by
David Goodwin and Jack Wing

PRAEGER

WESTPORT, CONNECTICUT
LONDON

Library of Congress Cataloging-in-Publication Data

Dixon, John E., 1946 May 9–
  Responses to governance : governing corporations, societies, and the world / John Dixon assisted by David Goodwin and Jack Wing.
    p. cm.
  Includes bibliographical references and index.
  ISBN 0-275-97754-4 (alk. paper)
  1. State, The. 2. Political science. 3. Corporate governance. 4. Globalization. 5. Culture. I. Goodwin, David. II. Wing, Jack. III. Title.
JC11.D59   2003
306.2—dc21   2002022475

British Library Cataloguing in Publication Data is available.

Copyright © 2003 by John Dixon

All rights reserved. No portion of this book may be reproduced, by any process or technique, without the express written consent of the publisher.

Library of Congress Catalog Card Number: 2002022475
ISBN: 0-275-97754-4

First published in 2003

Praeger Publishers, 88 Post Road West, Westport, CT 06881
An imprint of Greenwood Publishing Group, Inc.
www.praeger.com

Printed in the United States of America

The paper used in this book complies with the
Permanent Paper Standard issued by the National
Information Standards Organization (Z39.48–1984).

10 9 8 7 6 5 4 3 2 1

To Alex Kouzmin,

to whom I owe an unrepayable personal and intellectual debt;

for Tina, Piers and Aliki,

Pam,

and

Rhonda and Nicola.

Contents

Preface ix

1. The Governed and the Governors: Demarcating a Quadripartite Reality — 1

2. Cultural Theory: The Articulation of Competing Social Constructs — 17
   Appendix 2.1: The Competing Social Solidarities: Perspectives and Shared Values, Beliefs and Changing Allegiance — 66

3. Corporate Interest and Corporate Governance — 77
   Appendix 3.1: The Competing Social Solidarities on the Corporate Interest and Corporate Governance — 116

4. Public Interest and Societal Governance — 127
   Appendix 4.1: The Competing Social Solidarities on the Public Interest and Societal Governance — 157

5. Global Interest and Global Governance — 167
   Appendix 5.1: The Competing Social Solidarities on the Global Interest and Global Governance — 196

6. Antagonism, Disillusionment and Despair: The Challenges — 205
   Appendix 6.1: The Competing Social Solidarities on Antagonisms, Disillusionment and Despair — 236

7. Conclusion — 241

Bibliography 249

Index 307

Preface

> Sed quis custodiet ipsos Custodes.
>
> Decimus Junius Juvenalis (Juvenal),
> first century AD

To explore the realm of governance is to force the recognition that competing ways of life, and their consequences, are manifestations of particular, and often opposed, sets of beliefs. The quotation from Juvenal, the Roman satirist, with which this Preface is headed can be freely translated as "but who will govern the governors?" It is exemplified by the traumatic events of September 11, 2001, in New York, a chilling reminder of the extremes to which nihilistic acts of rebellion can be carried in the pursuit of beliefs and as responses to what are perceived to be unjust and intrusive processes of governance. That traumatic act, emanating as it did from a singular mutation of the governed, will echo down the ages as a spectacular act of opprobrium. It has provoked a series of retaliatory responses by those attempting to restore the established order, which will have far-reaching consequences for the whole of humanity. History provides many examples of extremist behavior (Breton et al. 2001) that, over the centuries, philosophers, in their quest for the meaning of truth, and, more latterly, psychologists have sought to explain. Any such explanations, if indeed there can be explanations, are beyond the scope of this study.

The focus of this book is to provide a behaviorist perspective on governance. Its concern is with the governed's responses to those who seek to govern them—their governors—and the counterresponses that they induce from the governors. It takes as axiomatic that the governed are not a homogenized and amorphous 'them' in the 'them–us' dichotomy, reduced to what Carlyle called a dead logic formula, and thereby, for the purpose of this study, leaving all the relevant questions begging. The governed are not a disembodied abstraction; they are an aggregate of real and feeling men and women. In a corporation, they are corporate directors (whose governors are those who own or, perhaps, have a stake in that corporation), corporate managers (whose governors are the corporate directors), corporate employees (whose governors are the corporate managers). In a society, they are individuals or groups of individuals, perhaps in corporations, communities, religious organizations, labor unions and other interest groups, located within its jurisdiction (whose governors are members of a society's political and administrative elite). At the global level, they are individuals or groups of individuals in countries, interest groups and corporations within the ambit of international governmental organizations and international regimes (whose governors are those who seek to control those global governance mechanisms). Whether the governed's response to the governance processes of those who wish to exercise dominion over them is one of compliance or antagonism, and how the governors respond to any such displays of antagonism, are issues that have implications for governance capacity, good governance and governability. The objective of this book is to undertake an analysis of the plurality of responses to the governors' differentiated processes.

The broad conclusion drawn is that governance processes must be seen as environments, either where trench warfare takes place between the governed and the governors with whom they disagree, resulting, inevitably, in the victory of one over the other; or where competing governance desires are confronted and integrated. The former means that both the vanquished and the victors are bound: the vanquished are bound, perhaps resentfully, to the victors; the victors are bound to a false governance situation. This may well prove to be unsustainable, leading, inexorably, to a downward spiral in governance capacity, epitomized, at the extreme, by hate and spite, rage and self-pity. The latter means a freeing of both sides, thereby enhancing the prospects of increased governance capacity. Cultural Theory is the analytical construct used to facilitate this analysis.

Cultural Theory was initially conceived by Mary Douglas (Fardon 1999), an anthropologist, in the late 1960s and subsequently developed in the 1970s and 1980s, largely by a clique of European and American scholars, including Richard Ellis, Steven Ney, Steven Rayner, Michael Thompson, and Aaron Wildavsky (Douglas 1999). It began as a neo-Durkheimian typology of cognitive systems ('cultural biases', 'ways of life' or 'social solidarities') derived from people's group engagement preferences. Its theorists are intent, however, on developing this typology into a theory of metacultural differentiation and viability.

This study is firmly based on the early conceptualization of Cultural Theory, and is, avowedly, behaviorist in its orientation. It seeks to minimize reification, an all too obvious inclination of Cultural Theorists, and in so doing addresses the implicit challenge issued by Olli (1999: 59) that "cultural theorists are not entirely clear as to how individuals and solidarities are related" and that they need to "examine the alleged coherence between people's cultural bias, behavioral strategy and social relations" (p. 71). In other words, people are not attracted and repelled by gravitational-like forces from the four corners of their social world. Their adherence to a particular 'social solidarity' in a particular relational situation provides them with a selective screen through which they receive knowledge and interpret the social world and how people behave in it. In making that adherence choice they are committing themselves, perhaps unintentionally and unknowingly, to a set of distinctive and incompatible epistemological, ontological, rationalistic and nomological perspectives, which gives rise to an idiosyncratic set of belief statements—certainties or truths—with which they frame reality. This study explores what those belief statements might be in a governance setting, how firmly they might be held, what is likely to happen if their adherents lose confidence in them, and under what conditions they might change. Most important, what happens if the governed and the governors do not share an adherence to the same set of governance belief statements?

This book is very eclectic, drawing on concepts, frameworks, paradigms and theories from anthropology, economics, management and organizational theory, political science and international relations, philosophy, psychology, and social theory and sociology. It has been written for a very diverse readership: those interested in governance per se; in management, organizational theory and corporate governance; in government and societal governance; in global governance; and, of course, in Cultural Theory and its applications. This has necessitated a distinctive style of book. First, it has copious footnotes. These serve three functions: to define (giving the reader all the technical definitions needed to make the text accessible); to elaborate (giving the reader an appreciation of any nuances); and to contextualize (giving all readers an appreciation of how subject matter sits within a particular academic literature). The footnotes can, however, be ignored, without detriment to understanding the book's line of reasoning. Second, it has summary matrices at the end of Chapters 2 to 6. After reading Chapter 1, these alone can be read to gain a summary of the book's line of reasoning. Third, it has an extensive bibliography. Finally, it has a comprehensive thematic index of both the text and footnotes.

It is most likely that anyone who reads this book will be expert on the subject matter in some sections but not in others, and probably a disinterested reader at times. All readers import something to their reading, which may range along a continuum from innate prejudice to informed criticism, so that they may take away something—hopefully of value—from that reading. Those interested in governance per se, in facing the challenge of reading the entire book cannot fail to ponder on the interactional responses between the governed and the governors. Those interested in corporate governance, societal governance or global governance face the need to read Chapters 1 and 2; then either Chapter 3, 4 or 5; and finally, Chapters 6 and 7. Cultural Theorists will find Chapters 1, 2, 6 and 7 of particular interest, especially the footnotes.

All authors are inevitably intellectual debtors. My debts cannot be adequately expressed, let alone repaid. Foremost, are my personal and intellectual debts to Jack Wing and David Goodwin. These can only be inadequately expressed; and repaid, in part, by granting them associate author status. Without Jack's clarity of expression this book would be less intelligible, and certainly less accessible, than it is. His insightful comments on Chapter 3 reflect his immense knowledge of management and organizational theory acquired over thirty years as an academic. Jack also provided the pertinent quotations from the classics. Without Dave's clarity of thinking, I would have taken many a dead-end turn. His bibliographical and information technology skills enabled me to compile quickly a comprehensive bibliography. He drafted the introductory sections of both Chapters 4 and 5. To both of them go my sincere thanks. I must also thank Rhys Dogan for inducting me into the mysteries of social theory, which have added very considerable value to the end product. Then there are my debts to the thousand or so scholars whose work I have cited. Their individual contributions are clear from the citations in the text and footnotes. I must, however, highlight a few people, only one of whom I have had the pleasure of meeting personally: Mary Douglas, Michael Thompson and Aaron Wildavsky.

I must also thank the editorial team at Praeger, most especially James Sabin, my acquisitions editor, and Lynn Zelem, senior production editor. Their professionalism is evidenced by the end product.

My final, overwhelming and utterly unrepayable debt is the very personal one I owe my wife, Tina, who has, yet again, put up with me writing yet another book, only this time she also proofread the entire manuscript. Indeed the years of marriage she has endured are now exactly the number of books she has endured, which is evidence of something after thirty years.

1

The Governed and the Governors: Demarcating a Quadripartite Reality

INTRODUCTION

Foucault's (1991) concept of governmentality (see also Mitchell 1999) focuses on the two poles of governance[1]—the governed's response to the processes of

---

[1] Governance, which is from the Latin *gubernare*, meaning to rule or to steer (Eilon 1974), is the process of establishing the "conditions for ordered rule and collective action" (Stoker 1998: 17) and applies to all organizations, industries or sectors, as well as to territorial governance units (Hechter 2000: 9) at the local, regional, national and supranational levels. The Commission on Global Governance (1995: 2) defines it as "the sum of many ways individuals and institutions, public and private, manage their common affairs." It constitutes, according to Garland (1997: 174) "the forms of rule by which various authorities govern populations, and the technologies of self through which individuals work on themselves to shape their own subjectivity" (see also O'Malley et al. 1997). Czempiel (1992: 250) emphasizes voluntarism when he defines it as "the capacity to get things done without the legal competence to command that they be done." Rhodes (1997: 46–47) exemplifies the problematic task of defining governance by identifying six separate meanings: as the minimal state, as corporate governance, as the new public management, as good governance, as a sociocybernetic system, and as self-organizing networks. Kooiman (1999) goes further by suggesting (but unfortunately not articulating) that at least double that number are in common usage. He (1999, 2000) has also identified three "governing orders": action contingencies between different partners (problem-solving and opportunity creation); institutional aspects (or conditions); and governance's governing principles (legislation, norms and economic development). Biersteker (1992: 102) asserts, "Governance is essentially purposive and should be distinguished from order ["the presence of regularity or similar patterning"], which does not require conscious purpose or intent. Order can exist without governance, but governance requires some form of order."

those who seek to govern them. Whether the governed's response is one of compliance or antagonism depends upon how they justify, to themselves and to others, the limitations that they tolerate their governors imposing upon them.[2] To understand the implications of this for governance capacity, good governance and governability require an analytical construct that will permit a subtle analysis of the governed's plurality of responses to the governors' differentiated processes. Such responses are the product of the particular *shared meaning system*[3] that they adhere to in any situation, which guides their attitudes and behavior (D'Andrade 1984: 109).[4] Cultural Theory has the capacity to provide such an analytical construct.

---

[2] Flathman (1980: 6) contends, following Gramsci and Arendt, that "power—as distinct from episodic uses of raw force and violence—is impossible in the absence of values and beliefs shared between those who wield power and those subject to it." Lasswell and Kaplan (1950: 95–96) make a similar point. Power is the capacity to produce or prevent change (Morris 1987). It is "the ability to make people...do what they would not otherwise have done" (Allison 1996b: 396; see also Boulder 1990; Dahl 1957, 1968; Champlin 1971; Foucault 1980; Habermas 1986; Hobbs [1651] 1991); Hume [1748] 1920; Riker 1964; Wrong 1979). It remains an essentially contested concept (Gallie 1955, Lukes 1974), one that can only be clarified through discourse. Allison (1996b) offers a five-fold classification of power: *force* (control achieved by using force), *coercion* (control achieved by threats of force that create a situation in which the choice is between doing what is demanded or suffering the unappealing threatened consequences [Wertheimer 1987]), *manipulation* (control exercised by using information, ideas or argument to induce obedience by creating a dependency relationship), *persuasion* (control achieved by using *theoretical* authority—authority over matters of belief—to gain the self-determined and willing subordination of people's judgement or will to those of acknowledged experts, by means of information, ideas and argument), and *authority* (obedience procured by a right to control action, which may be *de jure* (justified) authority or *de facto* (recognized effective) authority [Raz 1990]). French and Raven (1959) offer a power taxonomy from a 'power-over' perspective: *position or legitimate power* (individuals conform because they believe that those exercising power have the right to have power over them), *expert power* (individuals conform because they believe that those exercising power have superior knowledge and skills), *personal or referent power* (individuals conform because they are attracted by, and identify with the person exercising power), *resource or reward power* (individuals conform to receive benefits from the person exercising power) and *physical or coercive power* (individuals conform to avoid punishment). Hales' (2001) power categories are knowledge, economic and normative. Boulder (1990) distinguishes between *destructive threat power*, *constructive exchange power*, and *integrative power*.

[3] A *shared meaning system* is the set of meanings that constitutes "whatever one has to know or believe in order to operate in a manner acceptable to [a group's] members" (D'Andrade 1984: 89). This shared meaning can be *representational* (knowledge and beliefs about the world expressed as true or false propositions), *constructive* (understandings about what people agree counts as what), *directive* (needs or obligations to do something) or *evocative* (distinct and well shared emotional states or feelings that are arousing) (D'Andrade 1984: 96–101).

[4] Thomas and Znaniecki (1918–20) formulated the view that for an individual, there are two sides to the definition of any situation: the objective and the subjective, where an individual "has to take social meaning into account and interpret his [sic] expe-

The purpose of this chapter is to explicate Cultural Theory so that it can be applied, in subsequent chapters, to gain insights into corporate, societal and global governance capacity, good governance and governability. It begins with a discussion of culture and the way it impacts on the attitudes and behavior of its adherents. The premises of Cultural Theory are then laid out, leading to a discussion of their implications for metacultural diversity.

Cultural Theory emphatically rejects the "enlightenment view"[5] that there is one set of "universal laws" or "deep structures" (Shweder 1984b: 27–28), which LeVine (1984: 80) describes as "uniformities of structure and content in human life, culture, and motivation at all times and places" (see, for example, Douglas and Ney 1998). As a theory of metacultural differentiation and viability (Douglas 1978, 1982b, 1992b; Gross and Rayner 1985; Mamadouh 1999a; Schwarz and Thompson 1990; Thompson et al. 1990), Cultural Theory takes as axiomatic that "culture is the selective screen through which the individual receives knowledge of how the world works and how people behave" (Douglas and Ney 1998: 91) and thus can account for various forms of social construction.[6] As

---

rience not exclusively in terms of his own needs and wishes but also in terms of the traditions, customs, beliefs, and aspirations of his social milieu" (p. 230). Merton (1957: 246) built upon this notion the concept of the *self-fulfilling prophecy* ("a *false* definition of the situation evokes a new behavior which makes the original false conception come true").

[5] The enlightenment view posits that man is intentionally rational and scientific and that reason (the intellectual facility to seek evidence for and against potential beliefs, as opposed to blind faith, guessing and unthinking obedience to institutional authority [Moser 1989]) is equally binding regardless of time, place, culture, race, personal desires, or individual endowment and is a universally applicable standard for judging validity and justifying beliefs. From these flow a desire to discover universals: natural laws, deep structures, and progress. There is a struggle between reason and unreason, between science and superstition (Shweder 1984b: 27–28; see also Gergen and Thatchenkey 1998: 16–17).

[6] *Social constructs* are a means of ordering events so as to give clarity of meaning to what would otherwise be an anarchic stream of events (Rayner 1991: 84). They are the product of a discourse—"a framework of thinking in a particular area of social life" (Giddens 2001: 687), or in Foucaultian terms, "the practices that systematically form the objects of which [people] speak," which can be drawn upon to explain or warrant actions (Nightingale and Cromby 1999: 226)—that takes place within a distinctive cognitive structure and can be "tied to specific institutions and actors" (Hajer 1993: 43–46). They provide metanarratives—universal stories—that organize and justify a plurality of different stories; that contain true elements, although they may be incoherent chronologically or contradictory in the messages they transmit; and that can be condensed into icons that constitute the essential elements of a story. All of these become part of the unquestioned stock of taken-for-granted, commonsense or tacit knowledge (or prejudices, to Durkheimians), upon which human activities are based. They "operate through inclusion and exclusion as homogenizing forces, marshalling heterogeneity into ordered realms, silencing and excluding other discourses, other voices in the name of universal principles and general goals" (Storey 1993: 159). They are value oriented and intended to persuade. They have both *cognitive-rational* (objective meaning) and *communicative-rational* (normative meaning) components. They become the social control frameworks "by which

Thompson et al. (1990: 57, see also Wildavsky 1987b, 1991b, 1991c, 1994b) observe, "preferences emerge as an unintended consequence of attempting to organize social life in a particular way." Other people, by making demands, impose ordering on the individual (Douglas and Ney 1998: 98, see also Douglas 1987, 1992a).

Insights into the cognitive processes involved can be gained from Lewin's (1948, 1952, 1972) concept of *life space*. This deals with the world "as the individual sees it" (de Board 1978: 51), and consists of "his [*sic*] conscious and unconscious goals, dreams, hopes and fears, his past experiences and future expectations. The physical and social conditions are also important, limiting as they do the variety of possible life spaces and creating the boundary conditions of the psychological field" (de Board 1978: 53). This *life space* has four dimensions (de Board 1978): *cognitive* (existential or perceptual), *affective* (evaluation), *relational* (or cathartic) and *directive* (intentional), which intermingle and produce an *assumptive world* (K. Young 1979). This has a structure of hierarchically arranged sets of beliefs, values and norms constructed as a result of the interaction of individuals and their environment and categorized as immutable core values, adaptive attitudes, and changeable opinions (Parsons 1995: 375). This *assumptive world* is thus an individual's "cognitive map of the world out there" (K. Young 1979: 33), providing an interface between specific realities and specific assumptions.

This study thus embraces Cutting and Kouzmin's (1999: 480) proposition that "social conduct should...be seen as the product of the synthesis between personal orientation or motivation of the individual and the demands of the social system (culture and authority)." Where there is congruity there is harmony, consistency and, apparently, rational, acceptable behavior. Where there is incongruity, there is dysfunction or tension.[7] And it acknowledges Rosaldo's

---

we justify our actions to others and call them to account to us for theirs" (Rayner 1991: 84). *Social constructionism* (Gergen 1999, 2001) embraces those social theories that emphasize that social life is socially created (Marshall 1998: 609). It relates to the psychological concept of *social contructivism*, the proposition that all knowledge is derived from the mental constructions of those in a social system (Reber 1995: 157). It also relates to the philosophical concepts of *cognitive pluralism*, the proposition that there are a various ways that people individually and in groups can go about the business of reasoning (Wilson 1979), and *epistemic relativism*, the proposition that one system of reasoning may be best for one group, perhaps in terms of reflective equilibrium or truth-generating capacity, while a quite different system might be best for another group (Goodman 1965).

[7] Cutting and Kouzmin elsewhere (1997: 86) note: "it can be seen that the individual's sense of identity and values and beliefs run deep and are likely to be very stable held together by strong interconnecting patterns of neuronal processes [see Edelman 1992]." Beliefs and values can thus be the prime determinants of individual motivation. Any patterns of behavior that can be identified as forming around these prime determinants of motivation are powerful aids in understanding how societies operate. D'Andrade (1984: 113), however, makes the very pertinent point that shared ideas, values, and attitudes that an individual has to know in order to behave appropriately as a member of society constitute a culture (see also Friese and Wagner 1999: 105), whereas the same values and attitudes, if idiosyncratic, constitute a personality. This study is concerned

(1984: 142) distinction between *thoughts*, which are the product of neuronal processes, and *emotions*, which are "about the ways in which the social world is one in which *we* are involved." He goes on (p. 142, see also Hochschild 1979): "The stakes, solutions, threats, and possibilities for response are apt, in every case, to take their shape from what one's world and one's conception of such things as body, affect, and self are like. Feelings are not substances to be discovered in our blood but social practices organized by stories that we both enact and tell. Our forms of understanding structure them."

This study, then, is about better understanding the plurality of cultural beliefs—"the ideas and thoughts common to several individuals that govern interaction" (Greif 1994: 915)—and their impact on the mode of governance and governance capacity of corporations, societies and the world.

CULTURE

Schein (1991) depicts culture at three levels: basic assumptions about existence, shared norms, and language and symbols. It consists of "a 'tool kit' of rituals, symbols, stories, and world-views" (Johnston and Klandermans 1995: 7) or "mental products" (Pye 1968: 218) that organizes ideas (LeVine 1984: 73) and provides a conceptual structure that is used by groups of people to construct their reality (D'Andrade 1984: 115), so they can inhabit the world they imagine (Geertz 1983).[8] This reality is not just shared; it is "intersubjectively shared, so that everyone assumes that others see the same things they see" (D'Andrade 1984: 115).

Culture thus designates a cognitive system, which, according to Spiro (1984: 323), is "a set of 'propositions,' both descriptive...and normative...about nature, man and society." He adds (p. 323), "cultural propositions are developed in the historical experience of social groups...[and they] are encoded in the *collective*, rather than private, signs. [They] include propositions referring to social structure, social organization, social behavior, and the like...[which are] noncultural situational, ecological, economic, political, biological, emotional etc.) as well as cultural (ideational) determinants." Thus, as Shweder and Bourne (1984: 142) point out, "what one thinks about (e.g. other people) and how one thinks (e.g. "contexts and cases") may be mediated by the world premises to which one is committed (e.g. holism) and by the metaphors[9] by which one lives."

A cognitive system thus provides the knowledge that constitutes the perceptual filter guiding the attitudes and behavior of its adherents (D'Andrade

---

with the diversity of shared ways of thinking, ideas, beliefs, values, and attitudes—cultures—not personalities.

[8] In this situation, as postmodernist standpoint epistemologies would suggest, "the criterias [sic] for 'truth' depends on what group you belong to" (Dahl 1999: 181).

[9] Metaphors, figures of speech that involve comparison, can be classified as *poetic* (which hint at relationships between the known and unknown), *evocative* (which transfer a principle from one context to another), and *structurally identical* (which relate two similar objects) (see Draaisma 2000, Lakoff and Johnston 1980, Sacks 1979).

1984: 109) by appropriately *framing*[10] the social situations they encounter (Johnston and Klandermans 1995: 8, see also Wildavsky 1989b).[11]

Culture, then, is "a description of a particular way of life" (Williams 1965: 57).

CULTURAL THEORY

Cultural Theory,[12] which has its origins in anthropology, is a framework[13] that permits the classification of different types of cultures (cognitive systems)

---

[10] "Framing is a way of selecting, organizing, interpreting, and making sense of complex reality to provide guideposts for knowing, analyzing, persuading, and acting. A *frame* is a perspective from which an amorphous, ill-defined, problematic situation can be made sense of and acted on" (Rein and Schön 1993: 146; see also Goffman 1974: 10–11).

[11] Fisher (1988: 1) talks of "culturally-established mental frameworks or mindsets."

[12] Cultural Theory has been applied, for example, to *risk perceptions and management* (Brickman 1984; Douglas 1983, 1985; Douglas and Wildavsky 1982; Drake 1991; Drake and Wildavsky 1991; Jenkins-Smith and Smith 1994; Kunreuther et al. 1983; Rayner 1984, 1986, 1987, 1992; Rayner and Cantor 1987; Tansey and Riordan 1999; Thompson 1983a, 1983b, 1993; Thompson and Gyawali 2001; Thompson and Rayner 1998a; Thompson and Raynor 1998c; Wildavsky and Drake 1990); *the environment* (Dixit 1997, Douglas 1972, 1991;, Douglas et al. 1997; Ellis and F. Thompson 1997a, 1997b; Grendstad and Selles 1997, 2000; Gyawali 1999, 2000a, 2000b; Linnerooth-Bayer 1999; Linnerooth-Bayer and Fitzgerald 1996; Ney and Thompson 2000a; Prakash 1998; Price and Thompson 1997; Rayner 1987; Thompson 1982a, 1984, 1989b, 1997a, 1998; Thompson et al. 1986; Verweij 2000); *politics, public policy, budgeting and the state* (Bale 1999; Coughlan and Lockhart 1998; Coyle and Ellis, 1994; Eckstein 1988; Edvardsen 1997; Ellis 1992a, 1992b; Grendstad 2000; Grendstad and Selles 1995; Hendriks 1994; Hendriks and Zouridis 1999; Hoppe 1999, 2000; Laitin and Wildavsky 1988; Lockhart 1998; Mamadouh 1999b; Molenaers and Thompson 1999; Ney and Molenaers 1999; Ney and Thompson 1999; Olli 1999; Schwarz and Thompson 1990; Shackelton 1991; Thompson 1997b; Thompson et al. 1986, 1992, 1999a, 1999b; Veries 1999; Wildavsky 1984, 1988, 1998; Wildavsky and Chai 1994); *human behavior and attitudes* (Chai and Wildavsky 1994; Lockhart 1997; Owen 1982); *management and organizational theory* (Altman and Baruch 1998; Coyle 1997; Douglas 1986a, 1992b, 1995; Ellis 1991; Hood 1998; Mars 1982; M. Thompson 1992; Thompson and Wildavsky 1986a); *consumption styles* (Drake and Thompson 1993, 1999; Mars and Mars 1993); *developmental issues* (Rayner 1992; Roe 1996; Wildavsky 1994a); *social policy and development* (Douglas and Calvez 1990; Jensen 1999; Thompson and Wildavsky 1986b; Wildavsky 1982, 1993; Thompson 2000a); *technology assessment and choice* (Hoppe and Grin 1999; Rayner and Cantor 1987; Tranvik et al. 2000); *history* (Ellis and Wildavsky 1989, 1990; McLeod 1982; Polisar and Wildavsky 1989); *biblical exegesis* (Atkins 1991); *conflicts and international relations* (Crider 1999; Grendstad 1999, 2001; Montgomery 2000; Richards 1998, 1999; Spalding 1996, 2000; Verweij 1995, 1999) and *scientific method* (Bloor 1982; Rudwick 1982).

[13] Ostrom and Ostrom (1997: 82) have argued persuasively that Cultural Theory is not a 'theory' but rather a 'framework' (which "provides a way of looking at a complex set of phenomena [and helps] to identify the elements that should be included in the theories that elucidate frameworks as applied to a more confirmed set of phenomena"); and that the typology it spawns is a model (which "specifies all working parts [of a theory] in

according to the amount of autonomy[14] preferred by individuals (see particularly Douglas 1978, 1982a, 1982b, 1982c, 1989; Douglas and Ney 1998; Ellis and M. Thompson 1997a; Thompson and Rayner 1998a; Thompson et al. 1990, 1998). By so doing it embodies the epistemological[15] and ontological[16] dichotomies.

---

the most simplified form so as to assess the implications of particular assumptions about the working part of the theory"). They argue that to be a theory, Cultural Theory "requires assumptions about motive power or forces that lead to particular processes and likely outcomes. A theory generates explanations of observed behavior in some realm of the world." This issue is specifically addressed in Chapter 2.

[14] Defined as sovereignty over oneself or self-determination subject to the exercise of reason and the rational scrutiny of action-driving desires and values (Dworkin 1988).

[15] Epistemology is concerned with the contentions about how the world can be known. A person can know a fact only if he or she has a true belief about it (that is, if he or she holds a belief, as a propositional attitude or intentional state, that a factual proposition is true, which, then, when combined with desire or some other mental state, gives rise to behavioral dispositions). However, only some true beliefs are knowledge (as distinct from, for example, from lucky guesses). The conversion of a true belief into knowledge requires a criterion or standard by which judgements can be made about what is and is not genuine knowledge—what is knowable—or, in other words, what constitutes sufficient justification to warrant a true belief being treated as knowledge. There are many such criteria. A true belief can be justified, for example,

- on the evidence of sensory experiences, so becoming *a posteriori* knowledge (*naturalized epistemology*) (Kant [1781-87] 1963);
- if there are sufficiently good justification reasons that are, themselves either in need of no further supporting reasons (*foundationalism*) or are mutually supporting (*coherentism*) (Lucey 1996);
- if it is a product of a psychological process that produces a high proportion of true beliefs (*reliabilism*) (Alston 1989);
- if its prima facie justification cannot be made defective, as a source of knowledge, by being overridden or defeated by evidence that the subject does not possess (*epistemic defeasibility*) (Shope 1983); or
- if the degree of belief held in a true belief, which is a measure the believer's willingness to act in accordance with that belief, conforms to the axioms of probability theory (*probabilism*) (Rosenkrantz 1977).

Within the social sciences, the epistemological debate is on the question of whether knowledge is to be understood individualistically (true beliefs should be justified by reference to individual experience or reason) or socially (true beliefs should be justified by reference to testimony, consensus or received wisdom) (Hollis 1994, Natanson 1963). At its heart is the relationship between the objective and the subjective. Truth, in line with the Kierkegaardian dichotomy, can be characterized as objective—"If I know that twice two is four...I need not struggle to make it my own; it is a reliable piece of lumber in my mental attic" (Barrett 1958: 152), or subjective—"a truth that must penetrate my own personal existence, or it is nothing; and I must struggle to renew it in my life each day...it is not a truth that I have, it is a truth that I am" (Barrett 1958: 153). There are two broad epistemological approaches (Hollis 1994): *naturalism* and *hermeneutics*.

[16] Ontology is the philosophical investigation of existence or being (Nozick 1981). What does and can exist? What it is for something to exist? What are the conditions necessary for its existence? What might be the relations of dependency among things that exist? The ontological debate within the social sciences considers the relationship be-

Adherence to a particular pattern of social relationship generates a distinctive way of looking at the world, which legitimizes a corresponding type of social relations (Thompson et al. 1990: 1). Its foundation is the proposition that people can choose how (or even whether) to engage with other people in any relational situation.[17] Indeed, they can choose to engage differently in different relational situations (Thompson 1996, Thompson et al. 1990). In making their group-engagement process choice, they are committing themselves, perhaps unintentionally and unknowingly, to a number of other choices, for each group-engagement process embodies a set of distinctive epistemological, ontological, rationalistic[18] and nomological[19] propositions. This gives rise to a set of shared values and beliefs, which, in turn, give rise to an idiosyncratic set of truth propositions,[20] or truths, with which they *frame* reality, defined as "patterns of culture" (Schwarz and Thompson 1990: 69).[21] If they choose to be social beings, and thus to engage with their social environment, they can choose to do so by building networks (individualized or egocentric social groups) or by joining collectives (collectivized social groups).[22] Each of these group-engagement processes can be bifurcated according to whether the individual accepts or rejects

---

tween the external (*structuralism*) and internal (*agency*) dimensions of human behavior (Giddens 1984).

[17] This can range from families and clans; to for-profit and non-profit corporations; to social, economic and political networks; to societal governance and governmental organizations at the tribal, village, local community, regional or national levels; through to international organizations and regimes at the global level. The relational situations that can be mapped in accordance with the Cultural Theory framework may, according to Douglas (1982b: 20), "be ever so large, so that all members cannot possibly know each other well, [however] there would have to be in all parts of it a pressure from face-to-face situations to draw the same boundaries and accept the alignment of insiders and outsiders." Some Cultural Theory applications (see, for example, Atkins 1991, Grendstad 2001, Gross and Rayner 1985, Montogery 2000) have categorized societies (and other social units) in accordance with the Cultural Theory framework. The behaviorist orientation of this study requires that individuals, rather than groups of individuals, be the unit of inquiry.

[18] Rationality as concerned with contentions about the forms of reasoning that should be the basis for thought and action.

[19] Nomologicality is concerned with contentions about how people behave, or are prone to behave, in given situations (Weber [1915] 1947, [1904] 1949).

[20] For a discussion of the concept of truth and its relationship to meaning, see Davidson 1984, Kirkham 1992, Lepore 1986.

[21] Bhaskar (1979: 48) points out that social structures are not independent of people's perception of what they "are doing in their activity." Cultural Theory's "patterns of culture" constitute what he calls (p. 48) a "theory of these activities."

[22] The *engagement style* construct in social psychology, which deals with the way individuals construe their world and their place in it, analogously dichotomizes the way in which individuals experience their interaction with the social environment (McKinney 1981): as an *active (or influencing) agent*, which "implies an engagement with an environment by 'doing' or acting in it" (p. 359), or a *passive (or reactive) patient*, which "implies 'being done to' ["being acted upon" or "being chosen" (p. 360)] by the environment" (p. 359).

inequality as the "relationship-arranging principle" (Thompson and Taylor 1986: 3). Thus, a set of four group-engagement forms emerges: *collectivized social groupings patterned on the principle of inequality* (denoted as *hierarchist* group engagements involving asymmetrical transactions and fettered competition); *collectivized social groupings patterned on the principle of equality* (denoted as *egalitarian* group engagements involving symmetrical transactions and fettered competition); *individualized social groups patterned on the principle of inequality* (denoted as *fatalistic* group engagements involving asymmetrical transactions and unfettered competition); and *individualized social groupings patterned on the principle of equality* (denoted as individualist group engagements involving symmetrical transactions and unfettered competition).

In making personal choices about appropriate relationship-arranging principles, Cultural Theory assumes that people are rational but inherently relational, and thus fully empowered to make choices about how to live in a society. These choices "sum up a lifetime, past hopes dashed or expectations fulfilled," and abandon them according to circumstances (Douglas and Ney 1998: 184; see also Elster 1985a: 6, Thompson 1996). A basic premise of Cultural Theory is that *agency* is produced by, and produces, *structure*.[23] While organizing precedes and conditions action (Altman and Baruch 1998: 780), actions change social relations. These are, according to Wuthnow et al. (1984: 128), malleable, like clay:

We mold them this way or that way as we make, and shape, our society, our social order, class structure, state apparatus, or mode of production. But whatever the shape, however

---

[23] Cultural Theory engages with the ontological synthesis debate (see, for example, Archer 1982, 1990, 1995, 1996; Bourdieu 1998; Giddens 1979, 1981, 1984, 1993; Mouzelis 1989). In contention is whether the relationship between *structure* and *agency* is distinguishable, analytically, from what is related by it (Archer 1996: 680). Giddens' *structuration theory* (1979, 1981, 1984) asserts that there is an identity (duality rather than (analytical) dualism) relationship between *structure* and *agency*. He argues that social structures exist "only in so far as forms of social conduct are reproduced chronically across time and space" (1984: xxi); and that human agents "have, as an inherent aspect of what they do, the capacity to understand what they do while they do it" (1984: xxii). "The reflexive capacities of the human actor are characteristically involved in a continuous manner with the flow of day-to-day conduct in the contexts of social activity" (Giddens 1984: xxiii). He thereby conflates them. By dissolving of the difference between *structure* and *agency*, *structuration theory* does not permit, according to Archer (1990: 78–79), any examination of the circumstances that give people more or less freedom from the constraints of structure, that enable actors to change structure, or that cause structural constraints upon agency to vary. To address these issues requires a *poststructurationist* dualist explanatory methodology, which permits the variable relations between agency and structure to be investigated. Archer's *morphogenesis theory* (or *analytical dualism* or *methodological interactionism*) (Archer 1982, 1990, 1995; see also Parker 2000) conceptualizes *agency* and *structure* "as both distinct and different, but also as interdependently related to each other" (Parker 2000: 70). The yet to be resolved issue, then, is whether *agency* and *structure* are identical or are they distinct, different, although interdependent?

redistributed the rights, power, and the surplus value, there is still some kind of social order—still some clay—and that clay is reaffirmed and reproduced by ritual, regardless of the shape it is in.

On the basis of these relationship-arranging principles, Cultural Theory postulates a "comparative classification of individuals' social environments as generators of different 'patterns of culture'" (Schwarz and Thompson 1990: 69; see also Benedict 1935, Geertz 1973, Smircich 1983)—a typology[24] derived from a *grid-group* space.[25] This space—in effect, a *grid-group* social-control space or *social map*—is defined by two polythetic variables[26] that incorporate "fundamental cultural constraints" (Gross and Rayner 1985: 5):[27] a *group* dimension of bonding,[28] identity and self-definition that involves constitutive norms[29]—"the outside boundary that people erect between themselves and the outside world"

---

[24] Cultural Theory's typology is an example of McKinney's (1966: 18, also 6) "constructive-type typology:" "a purposive, planned selection, abstraction, combination, and (sometimes) accentuation of a set of criteria with empirical referents that serve as a basis for comparison of empirical cases," which are heuristic devices intended for comparative and predictive purposes. On his *ideal-extracted* typology continuum (p. 24), it falls toward the *extracted* pole, where typologies are "based upon the notions of average, common, and concrete."

[25] Gross and Rayner (1985) considered that this space is continuously differentiable, but this perspective has lost favor among Cultural Theorists, who have generally accepted Ellis and Thompson's (1997a) dichotomizing of the *grid* and *group* dimensions.

[26] The relationship between the *grid* and *group* variables is associational rather than causal; thus, one does not presume the other.

[27] Thompson et al. (1999a: 3, 22–23, n. 3) and Ellis and Thompson (1999: 5) have questioned the original formulation of the typology (Douglas 1979, Thompson et al. 1990) on two grounds: whether these two dimensions are orthogonal, and thus, ipso facto, whether they can define a two-dimensional space within which four discrete *patterns of culture* categories can be demarcated; and whether the demarcation of such categories is possible in such a space (see also Altman and Baruch 1998: 781, Jeffcutt 1994). This led Cultural Theory in a new direction, which will be explicitly discussed in Chapter 2.

[28] The *group* dimension is the social incorporation dimension (Douglas 1978), embracing the characteristics of networks, interactions, boundaries and shared activities (Rayner 1987), which Wuthnow et al. (1984: 126) consider to emphasize "the well-boundedness of group life, [and] seems to represent a more highly corporate order than grid" dimension of the typology. Alternatively, it means: "the extent to which an individual is incorporated into bounded groups. The greater the incorporation, the more individual choice is subject to group determination" (Thompson et al. 1990: 5); "the extent to which people are driven by or restricted in thought and action by their commitment to a social unit larger than the individual" (Altman and Baruch 1998: 771); and "individualism" (Hofstede 1991: 325). Where the *group* pressures are high, people are increasingly controlled by other people's pressure—thus, fettered competition prevails—"the individual store is constantly raided for group purposes" (Douglas and Isherwood 1979: 42), which represents the "collectivist end of the scale" (Hofstede 1991: 325). As *group* pressures lessen, they are subject to less external controls, and thus they increasingly engage in unfettered competition.

[29] Constitutive norms define identity (Searle 1995).

(Douglas 1982b: 138)—and a *grid* dimension[30] of constraints and rules[31] that involve regulatory norms[32]—"all the other social distinctions and delegations of authority [used] to limit how people behave to one another" (Douglas 1982b: 138).

The dimensions of *grid* and *group* represent two different ways in which a collective can "grip" its members (Wuthnow et al. 1984: 122)—by the imposition of individual behavior constraints (*grid* grip) or by the subjugation of individual choice to group determination (*group* grip). Schwarz and Thompson (1990: 69) argue that these dimensions not only control people's basic choices, as social beings, about whom they interact with and how that interaction takes place, but also define "the limits against which social behavior can be mapped." The resultant *social map* can, itself, be construed as a social construct, for its external boundaries are the upper and lower limits to which people, if they wish to become or remain engaged with others in a particular relational situation, are

---

[30] The *grid* dimension is the individuation dimension (Douglas 1978), embracing the characteristics of accountability, specialization, role allocation and resource allocation (Rayner 1987), which Wuthnow et al. (1984: 126) consider to be "an intermediary stage of corporate organization where the collectivity exists as a structuring of individuals rather than as a single corporate actor." Alternatively, it means "the degree to which an individual's life is circumscribed by externally imposed prescription. The more binding and extensive the scope of the prescription, the less of life that is open to individual negotiation" (Thompson et al. 1990: 5); "the rules which relate one person to another on an egocentric basis" (Douglas 1970: viii); "the complementary bundle of constraints on social interaction—a composite index of the extent to which people's behavior is constrained by normative role differentiation" (Altman and Baruch 1998: 771); and "uncertainty avoidance" (Hofstede 1991: 325). When the *grid* pressures are high, there is a "system of shared classifications" (Hofstede 1991: 325) and individuals are accepting of "their allotted station in life" (Douglas and Isherwood 1979: 40). This imposes "moral and normative prohibitions which limit or highly structure individual interactions" (Wuthnow et al. 1984: 120; see also Douglas 1994: 178)—thus, asymmetrical transactions prevail (Ostrander 1982)—and creates strong group boundaries through which entry is difficult (Douglas 1994: 178). As grid pressures lessen, individuals increasingly engage in symmetrical transactions, as they "have more scope to deal with one another as they wish. The move away from the insulation of strong *grid* is not necessarily a move to disorganization and the lack of rule" (Douglas and Isherwood 1979: 39). Rather, it is, using Falk Moore's (1983) terminology, a movement away from *external rules* (those that are formally dictated by institutions) to *internal rules* (those that are self-made as a result of spontaneous interpersonal interaction).

[31] "Rules are human artifacts used to proscribe, prescribe, and encourage particular actions" (Cornett and Caporaso 1992: 232). All social practices are regulated by rules. This does not mean that people blindly follow them. Generally people choose whether to follow a rule on the basis of the perceived consequences of that choice. Thus, people must learn not only rules but also what is involved in using different types of rules, which is important because of the centrality of rule-accepting and rule-guided behavior in social relationships. Onuf (1989) identifies three functional categories of rules: *instructive, directive* and *commitment*.

[32] Regulatory norms describe the collective expectations of what constitutes proper behavior of actors with a given identity (Katzenstein 1996).

expected to accept the subjugation of their individual choice to collective determination (the *group* boundary points) and the collective imposition of individual behavior constraints that limit their individual interactions (the *grid* boundary points). Together, these boundary points define the extremities of the *social map* that apply to people in that relational situation. People may, of course, choose not to tolerate even the most minimal level of either collective engagement or social behavior constraints in that relational situation, so taking themselves off the *social map* by becoming, in Cultural Theory terms, *hermits*[33] (Schwarz and Thompson 1990: 79, n. 14; see also Thompson 1982c).

Upon this *social map* can be imposed a pair of *grid* and *group* divides to demarcate four types of social beings, on the basis of their preferred forms of group engagement, which, in turn, demarcate four viable *social solidarities*[34]

---

[33] A *hermit* is a person who "by definition, isolates himself [*sic*] from both the processes of group dynamics and the imposition of prescriptions on himself and on others" (Schwarz and Thompson 1990: 79, n. 14). Cultural Theorists have long agonized over where to place the *hermit* within the *grid-group* framework. Douglas (1978: 42) originally seemed to locate the *hermit* at the minimum *grid-group* grip point, oxymoronically co-located with those who are willing to tolerate only the most minimal level of either collective engagement or social behavior constraints. She subsequently preferred (1982b: 11) "to leave the hermit off the map of social controls, crediting him [*sic*] with full escape." This became the orthodoxy, because there is "no place for autonomy in the grid-group scheme" (Thompson et al. 1999a: 21, n. 3; see also Schwarz and Thompson 1990: 78; Thompson 1982a, 1982b; Thompson et al. 1990; Thompson and Wildavsky 1986b). This perspective, however, changed with the new direction in which Cultural Theory has taken. Thompson et al. (1999: 22, n. 6) first considered that "autonomists [hermits]…are also captured [by the Cultural Theory], even though the position they end up at—rather like Wordsworth's station in the cloud—is not pin-pointed by the grid-group scheme." Then Thompson and Ellis (1997a: 6) placed them at the center, and the heart, of the revised Cultural Theory's dynamic model, which puts them back on the *social map*. This issue is discussed further in Chapter 2.

[34] Cultural Theory's *social solidarities* should *not* be viewed as Weberian ideal-types (Weber ([1904] 1949, 1962, 1968a) that capture a "particular core and logic of reality against which actual examples of reality can be compared in a meaningful way" (Cutting and Kouzmin 2000: 502, n. 1). They are certainly not, as Douglas et al. (1997:128) clearly stated, "culture groups." Rather, they represent "a point of view [alternatively, a way of life, a cultural bias, a cultural dialogue, or a cosmology], with its own framing assumptions and readily available solutions for standardized problems." They are "the cognitive containers in which social interests are defined and classified, argued, negotiated and fought out" (Douglas and Ney 1998: 12). The *social solidarities*, both individually and collectively, contribute to a person's *assumptive world* (K. Young 1979: 33), which comprises a hierarchically arranged set of beliefs, information, values and norms. A *community-of-assumptions* embraces all those who share the same *assumptive world* as the basis of their view of the world and themselves, views usually held without awareness of their hypothetical nature and with the presumption that the world really is the way their internalized and institutionalized images depict it (Etzioni 1968: 178–79). Indeed, scattered individuals may well share similar cultural biases (Douglas et al. 1997: 128). Any of the *social solidarities* may manifest as: *a policy community*: "a special type of stable network which has advantages in encouraging bargaining in policy

that are applicable across time and place;[35] a *grid-group* typology[36] (Douglas 1982b: 200, Douglas and Ney 1998: 102, Thompson et al. 1990), namely: *hierarchist* (high *group*/high *grid*), *enclavist* (high *group*/low *grid*), *fatalist* (low *group*/high *grid*) and *individualist* (low *group*/low *grid*).[37] These discrete *social*

---

resolution. In this language the policy network is a statement of shared interests in a policy problem: a policy community exists where there is an effective shared community of views on the problem" (Jordan 1990: 327); *a discourse coalition*: "a group of actors who share a social construct" (Hajer 1993: 43) that does battle in the public sphere for legitimacy (Douglas and Ney 1998: 126), as a culture in dialogue (Douglas and Ney 1998: 126); *an epistemic community*: "a community...composed of professionals (usually recruited from several disciplines) who share a commitment to a common causal model and common set of political values. They are united by a belief in the truth of their model and by a commitment to translate this truth into public policy, in the conviction that human welfare will be enhanced as a result" (Haas 1990: 41); *an issue network*: "a shared-knowledge group having to do with some aspect (or, as defined by the network, some problem) of public policy" (Heclo 1978: 103); or *an advocacy coalition*: comprising "people from a variety of positions (elected and agency officials, interest group leaders, researchers etc.) who share a particular belief system—that is a set of basic values, causal assumptions, and problem perceptions—and who show a nontrivial degree of coordinated activity over time" (Sabatier and Jenkins-Smith 1993: 25; see also Sabatier 1986, 1987, 1988, 1991, 1993).

[35] A belief in a *social solidarity* is an end in itself, rather than a means to an end. It can be considered a stable orientation for action (Eckstein 1988: 790) or *habitus* (the mental and social conditioning that comes about through the acquisition of patterns of thought, behavior and taste, which links *structure* and *agency*) (see Bourdieu 1998, Douglas 1994: 134). However, it is naïve to believe that any *social solidarity* can be "self-stabilizing and capable of endlessly competent accommodation" (Perri 2001a). Finally, "the beliefs must be treated as part of the action and not separated from it" (Thompson et al. 1990: 199).

[36] This *social map* constitutes a set of polythetic categories formed in accordance with a number of properties such that no one property is to be present for every member of that category. Gross and Rayner (1985: 58) explain: "[Designation to a particular polythetic class is] according to a set of properties subject to the following general conditions: 1) Each individual possesses a large but unspecified proportion of the chosen properties; 2) Each property is more commonly found among individuals in the class than among individuals outside the class but in the same domain. It is not required that any property in the set must occur in every individual in the class." People in a particular category may well have differing proportions of its defining properties; and individuals in different categories may well have properties in common. Schmutzer and Bandler (1980; see also Schumtzer 1994) inadvertently proved Cultural Theory's impossibility theorem, postulated by Thompson et al. (1990), which limits the number of viable categories to five—four based on the prescribed relationship-arranging principles, with the fifth premised on an individual choosing not to engage with other people—by the application of a transaction matrix based on the notions of the degree of social relationship openness (the *grid* dimension) and of connectedness (the *group* dimension) (see Rayner and Malone 1998: 6, Thompson and Ellis 1997a: 6–7). Coughlin (1994), by simultaneously measuring the *grid-group* dimensions and the four discrete *patterns of culture*, has established that there is a reasonable correlation between the dimensions and the patterns.

solidarities, Schwarz and Thompson (1990: 68) argue, are the only "morally justifiable" institutionally induced perceptions. Thompson and Taylor (1986: 23) explain the viability of each of these *social solidarities* in terms of the credibility of their worldview and the capacity of their truths to deliver on the expectations that flow from their system of knowledge. However, as Olli (1999: 59) correctly observes, "cultural theorists are not entirely clear as to how individuals and [social] solidarities are related" (see also Selles 1991a, 1991b; Thompson and Rayner 1998c; Wildavsky 1991a).[38]

The *social map* of any particular relational situation permits people to be categorized by *social solidarity* in accordance with the limitations that they permit other people to place on their autonomy (Schwarz and Thompson 1990: 73, Thompson et al. 1999b, Thompson and Wildavsky 1986b; see also Hofstede 1991: 325, Ostrander 1982).[39] Each *social solidarity*'s concomitant *social construct* is used by its adherents to *frame* reality in a way that justifies the imposition of constraints on their autonomy by other people in a particular relational situation (Douglas 1994: 187; see also Wildavsky 1989b).

CONCLUSION

Since governance is the interaction between the governors' processes and the governed's responses, an analytical construct is needed that will permit a subtle analysis of this interaction. Cultural Theory is such a construct.[40] It is a theory of cultures[41]—more precisely, a theory of metacultural differentiation

---

[37] Somewhat facetiously, these four social beings have their counterparts in Burton's ([1621] 2000) human temperaments typology: the *phlegmatic* (the *hierarchist*), the *sanguine* (the *individualist*), the *melancholic* (the *fatalist*), and the *choleric* (the *enclavist*).

[38] Indeed, Olli (1999: 71) further urges Cultural Theory empiricists to "examine the alleged coherence between people's cultural bias, behavioral strategy and social relations." This issue is explicitly discussed in Chapter 2.

[39] Social psychologists concerned with people's perceptions of the relative importance of *endogenous* (internally derived) and *exogenous* (externally imposed) sources of control over their behavior refer to the *locus of control,* as measured along a dimension extending from *high internal* (those who tend to accept responsibility for their actions and consider that they are in control of their lives and destinies, largely through their own personal effort, ability, and initiative), to *high external* (those who tend to see control as external to themselves, residing in powerful others or social structures, or in luck or fate) (Levenson 1981: 49–52, O'Brien 1984: 7, Reber 1995: 423). It can be postulated a priori that *individualists* would be located toward the *high internal* end of the dimension, followed by *enclavists* and *fatalists*, with *hierarchists* located toward the *high external* end of the dimension.

[40] Altman and Baruch (1998: 783) suggest that a typology should be judged by "its ability to organize information and sharpen distinctions, and thus enhancing the understanding of the phenomenon under study." By these criteria, Cultural Theory's *gridgroup* typology stands in good stead, for it facilitates the organization of information and it sharpens distinctions, as will become apparent in the next chapter.

[41] By reflecting on Cultural Theory as a theory of cultures, Schwarz and Thompson (1990: 2) draw an important and insightful conclusion that may well explain why Cul-

and plurality—based on the proposition that people can choose whether to engage with other people, and thus become either antisocial beings (or *hermits*) or social beings. If they choose to be social beings, they can do so by either building their own ego-centered network or joining a collective. Each of these forms of social engagement can be bifurcated, depending upon whether the individual accepts or rejects inequality as the relationship-arranging principle. This demarcates four viable *social solidarities*, each of which relate to the preferred form of group engagement—*hierarchist, enclavist, fatalist* and *individualist*. Each offers their adherents a distinctive set of truths with which to *frame* reality. Attention is turned in the next chapter to the articulation of these contending truths, and to the processes by which *social solidarity* allegiances can change.

---

tural Theory has long remained a cult theory: "Cultural Theory itself is surprisingly simple; the difficulties arise, not in understanding it, but rather in accepting it and in grasping its import for the conceptions of politics, technology and social choice to which we have long been accustomed. Indeed, the very idea of a theory of culture is perhaps the main obstacle to the easy assimilation of our [Cultural Theory] arguments."

2

Cultural Theory: The Articulation of Competing Social Constructs

INTRODUCTION

Cultural pluralism, the notion of social units as configurations of *social solidarity* adherents, is essentially a way of coming to terms with the dilemma of the interrelationship *structure* and *agency* in a particular relational situation. The plurality of *social solidarities* posited by Cultural Theory represents a confined set of viable patterns of interpersonal (or social) relations and a shared set of sociocognitive propositions (Thompson et al. 1990: 1). Each *social solidarity* contributes to the construction of an identity for its adherents.[1] Each offers criteria for deciding what is truth and what is rational (Thompson et al. 1998: 352, citing Grauer et al. 1985). Each offers a reasonable, characteristic solution to specific organizational [social unit] problems, which, in turn, have a cumulative

---

[1] The way in which adherents to a *social solidarity* attempt to define its inherently ambiguous—and potentially dangerous—periphery enables them to better grasp what constitutes their key values. Sarup's (1996: 11–12) observations on group boundaries and their maintenance are insightful: "because the range of human behaviors is so wide, groups maintain boundaries to limit the type of behavior within a defined cultural territory. Boundaries are an important point of reference for those participating in any system. ...Within the boundary, the norm has jurisdiction....Each time a deviant behavior is punished, the authority of the norm is sharpened, the declaration is made where the boundaries of the group are located. This is the way in which it can be asserted how much diversity and variability can be contained within a system before it loses its distinct structure. In short, deviants and agencies of control are boundary-maintaining mechanisms."

effect on that organization" (Douglas and Ney 1998: 147).² But, as Thompson et al. (1990: 272) point out, a *social solidarity* "rules out certain courses of action as incongruent with a way of life," although it "does not necessarily rule in a specific alternative."

The purpose of this chapter is twofold. First, it enunciates, for each of the four *social solidarities*—hierarchist, enclavist, fatalist and individualist—both the philosophical and sociocognitive premises and the shared values and beliefs that underpin the idiosyncratic set of truths (or truth propositions) their adherents use to frame reality. Second, it explores the possible processes by which an individual's *social solidarity* allegiance changes. This is now a contestable domain within Cultural Theory.

HIERARCHIST SOCIAL SOLIDARITY

People who embrace hierarchy as their relationship-arranging principle are subscribing to an ascribed and pattern-maintaining hierarchy (Douglas 1982b, Thompson and Wildavsky 1986b). Its social order is based on positional authority, expressed through orderly differentiation, the rules for which establish a sense of identity. Status graduations are based on explicit characteristics, such as age, gender, educational attainment and professional rank (Douglas et al. 1998: 327). These institutionalized, hierarchical classifications not only keep people apart but also regulate their interactions (Douglas 1982b: 191), which are immune to change by individual effort. Its members, having been socialized on the basis of an "affirmative attitude to power and authority" (Hoppe 2000: 19, n. 10), are thus subject to the control of others and the demands of roles that are socially imposed (Thompson et al. 1990: 6; see also Douglas 1994: 142–44). Hierarchists have acquired the habits of self-control³ and obedience to command.⁴

Homo hierarchus (Dumont 1970) has many group-defining and group-identifying regulations, plus many constraints on how to act (Douglas 1982b).⁵ Their personal security is achieved at the expense of overt competition and so-

---

[2] Cultural Theory insists only that a *social solidarity* in a particular relational situation that does not manage to get enough of its adherents to behave and to justify their behavior enough of the time in accordance with its premises and values will inevitably cease to exist. "Genericity...not total compliance is what the theory predicts" (Schwarz and Thompson 1990: 79, n. 11).

[3] Hierarchists would accept that reason has to struggle to regulate and resolve contrary and conflicting emotions in a person in order for that person to be well-ordered and, in Aristotelian terms, have a right set of emotions (Ackrill 1981).

[4] To hierarchists, voluntary obedience is grounded in a sense of obligation to obey a sanctioned command. This sense of obligation may be unquestioning, which is considered a virtue in some social units (such as certain religious and military organizations) but morally reprehensible in others. It may be constrained by any limits they are willing to impose unilaterally upon the command-issuing authority.

[5] Vroom (1960) has documented that authoritarians (Adorno et al. 1950) and people with weak independence needs are unaffected—receive no positive attitudinal or motivational outcomes—when given opportunities to participate in decision making.

cial mobility (Altman and Baruch 1998: 772). The all-too-evident stratified ranks are, of course, subsumed within the overreaching collective that contains them (Douglas 1994: 224–25; see also Wildavsky 1989a). Axiomatically, according to Douglas (1994: 225):

the hierarchy is maintained by claims accepted on behalf of the whole community; because claims over-riding those of individual members are accepted, authority can be exerted on behalf of the community; its member persons perform public ceremonies, invest in public goods, and justify a high degree of organization in order to strengthen the public claims they cherish. One result is that a well-run hierarchy has a lot to offer its members, and in consequence it is not worried lest they secede. Loyalty being secure, the main concern is that the up-down structure be not weakened.

Hierarchists, needless to say, trust authority (Molenaers and Thompson 1999: 191).[6]

Hierarchists are inclined toward ritualism and sacrifice (Schwarz and Thompson 1990: 66, which they use to support both their hierarchical social structures and deontological moral codes[7] (Douglas 1970, Schwarz and Thompson 1990: 66).

Hierarchist Perspective on Motivation

The social context for hierarchists is one where everyone knows his or her place. Interpersonal relationships are governed by a set of entrenched social norms (Hart 1961, Raz 1975) that constitute individually accepted rules by which people conduct themselves and their affairs. Insights into the motivations of people operating in such an environment can be gained from an exploration of enneagramic motivational ideal-types.[8] Hierarchists would dominate the enneagramic ideal-types that are governed by the "mental center"—"the mind." This cultivates in them a need, according to Cutting and Kouzmin (1997: 90–91), for "safety and security in well-defined organizations and systems." External authority is thus accepted as the principal determinant of what is expected of people. To attain the Platonic self-controlled and well-ordered self (Plato

---

[6] Giddens (1990: 35) defines trust as "confidence in the reliability of a person or a system." Powell (1990: 205) observes: "Trust reduces complex realities far more quickly and economically than prediction, authority, or bargaining."

[7] Deontological ethics emphasize duty and obligation and are premised on ethical propositions about certain kinds of obligations or duties being intrinsically good and thus right (Fried 1978). Such duties and obligations justify reasons for action. They are binding normative requirements among those who accept their ethical underpinnings. They thus must be performed; not to do so justifies criticism and condemnation from fellow adherents (Zimmerman 1996).

[8] The enneagram is concerned with the motivations of people operating in external environments. It is based on the perception that patterns of personal motivation can be derived from three primal centers: the "heart" (the *emotional* center), the "head" (the *mental* center) and the "gut" (the *instinctive* center) (see Narango 1990; see also Cutting and Kouzmin 1997).

[c380s] 1952) is a highly valued aspiration, achieved by the application of logical and impersonal reasoning that strives for order and clarity.[9] Riso (1987: 25) concludes that these enneagramic ideal-types are "out of touch with [their] ability to act on [their] own without the approval of an authority figure of some sort." Thus it would follow that their primary source of self-esteem[10] (Baumeister 1993) is authority figure approval, on the basis of their loyalty and conformity, and thus their recognition as a member of the hierarchy. On this basis it would follow that the hierarchist's metalife-goal is to win approval by authority figures, so as to be recognized as a member of the hierarchy that promises to give them physical and psychological safety and security. As Starr (1992: 134) observes "for [privileged members of the community] to be unclassified would result in their being unrecognized."

Hierarchist Perspective on Rationality

Hierarchist culture encourages a rationality that is functionally analytical (Hoppe 2000), albeit a *bounded rationality* (Simon 1957, 1960, 1976). They would consider the intellect (reason and rational calculation) to be rightly constrained by hierarchically determined affects (values and beliefs), thus producing decisions that are satisfactory. They are also preoccupied with a *procedural rationality* that is more concerned with who does what than with any outcomes that might be achieved (Schwarz and Thompson 1990: 7). Epistemologically, hierarchists embrace *naturalism*;[11] ontologically, they embrace *structuralism*;[12]

---

[9] In terms of Riesman's (1950) *inner-other directedness* dichotomy, hierarchists would have an *other-directedness* orientation, preferring to seek approval and acceptance from others. The needs they emphasize would be Maslow's (1970) physiological, safety (security), social (affiliation) and esteem needs; Ardrey's (1967) identity, security and stimulation needs; Alderfer's (1938) power needs; White's (1959) competence needs; and McCelland's (1961) achievement, power and affiliation needs (see also McCelland et al. 1953).

[10] Douglas (1994: 192) long ago called for a Cultural Theory of esteem.

[11] *Naturalism* grounds social knowledge in material forces, such as economic and biological processes. It proposes two types of knowledge: the *analytic* and the *synthetic* (Hempel 1966). *Analytic statements* contain *a priori* (non-empirical) knowledge derived from deductive logic, which offer a profound and strong demonstration of cause and effect and explanation. However, this form of reasoning only produces definitive knowledge of mathematical and linguistic relationships. *Synthetic statements* contain *a posteriori* (empirical or sensory experience-based) knowledge derived through inductive inference, which offer a weak and contingent correlation of cause and effect (Williams and May 1996: 25). There are two key traditions within *naturalism* (Dixon and Dogan 2002): *positivism* ("the world as it is given to observation...is the way the world actually is" [Nightingale and Cromby 1999: 227]), which rejects unobservables and requires an agent ontology; and *realism* ("that reality exists independently of our representations of it" (Nightingale and Cromby 1999: 228), which allows unobservables and a structuralist ontology. *Naturalism* embraces, inter alia, (see Alexander 1982, Baert 1998; Giddens 1990, 1991; Hollis 1994) *empiricism, positivism* and *logical positivism*. *Naturalism's* dilemma is that while it might be able to offer reasonably reliable predictions, it cannot identify unambiguous causal relationships (Williams and May 1996).

and thus, methodologically,[13] they embrace naturalist structuralism.[14] They thus presume an objective social world, knowable by the application of the scientific method, in which structures exercise power over agency, which makes human behavior predictable. Thus, social action proceeds on the assumption that social reality can be identified through the observation of patterns in, and correlation between, forms of materially based social behavior, and that social action strategies can be developed on the presumption that hierarchical and institutional structures are able to influence the material basis of human behavior in a predictable manner (Dixon and Dogan 2002a).

Hierarchists are, therefore, continually striving for the objective reality, knowable as objective truths derived from 'objective facts.' Any statement that cannot be verified by abstract thinking using the scientific method is relegated the status of expressions of emotion or belief (metaphysics, theology, aesthetics, or ethics).

Hierarchist Perspective on Learning and Knowledge

Hierarchists have a learning style that focuses on "anticipation" (Schwarz and Thompson 1990: 66) and knowledge, which is the product of a slow, patient, accumulating, collective effort (Douglas 1994: 108) is considered authoritative only when it is complete, organized (Schwarz and Thompson 1990: 66), and verified by the application of abstract thinking using the scientific method. They are thus one of March's (1999) slow learners.

---

[12] *Structuralism's* central proposition is that social structures ["the ordered social interrelationships, or the recurring patterns of social behavior that determine the nature of human action" (Parker 2000: 125)] impose themselves and exercise power upon agency, which means structures (order) governs action (Robey 1973). Social structures are regarded as constraining in that they mold people's actions and thoughts, and in that it is difficult, if not impossible, for one person to transform these structures (Baert 1998: 11). It embraces, inter alia, *anthropological structuralism, functional structuralism, historical materialism, linguistic structuralism, hermeneutic phenomenology, symbolic interactionism, language games, poststructuralism* and *postmodernism*. Structuralism's dilemma is that it might be able explain the empirically strong correlation between individual behavior and social cohort, but it cannot unambiguously explain outliers derived from acts of choice by free individuals (Williams and May 1996).

[13] *Methodologies* determine how investigations are conducted, how evidence is assessed, and how what is true or false—factual knowledge—is to be decided (Lucey 1996). Methodological families are a set of *methodologies* that embody the very particular combinations of consistent epistemological and ontological assumptions that give rise to philosophically coherent enquiry agendas and methods (see Hollis 1994: 19).

[14] *Naturalist structuralism* embraces, inter alia (Williams and May 1996, Dogan 2001), *anthropological structuralism* (concerned with how members of a society relate to social organizations and societal structures), *functional structuralism* (concerned with explaining the existence of a phenomenon or the carrying out of an action in terms of its consequences), *historical materialism* (concerned with explaining how particular forms of society come into existence by reference to socioeconomic processes and relations), and *linguistic structuralism* (concerned with the basic set of rules that govern the combination of sounds that produce meaning, so describing a language).

Hierarchists are self-protective toward their system of knowledge (Douglas 1994: 32). They are loyal to their management information system procedures (Schwarz and Thompson 1990: 134). Their information handling is characterized by normality and appropriateness (Hendriks and Zouridis 1999: 123). They are, certainly, prone to information asymmetries (Hood 1998). They believe that information must be tightly controlled so as to avoid worrisome contradictions and incompatibilities being known about by other adherents to this *social solidarity* (Douglas 1982b). This, according to Douglas and Ney (1998: 183), "may be dangerous for hierarchy because of the danger of not knowing when times have changed and administrative formulas are outdated."

Hierarchist Perspective on Problem Solving and Decision Making

Hierarchists prefer problems to be defined in a highly structured way (Hoppe 2000). They consider problems to be decomposable into relatively independent, or essential, constituent parts (Popper [1962] 1969). This facilitates, not only causal and evaluative information gathering for impact and risk assessment, but also the search for alternative solutions that can be prioritized by their importance, urgency and values contestability. Decision making is thus focused on working out a satisfactorily efficient and effective solution. Pugh and Hickson (1996: 134) describe the satisficing decision-making process as envisaged by Simon (1960):

In this process decision-makers are content with gross simplifications, taking into account only those comparatively few relevant factors which their minds can manage to encompass. 'Most human decision making whether individual or organizational, is concerned with the discovery and selection of satisfactory alternatives; only in exceptional cases is it concerned with the discovery and selection of optimal alternatives.'

Any solutions so identified are presumed to be amenable to collective intervention, involving the manipulation of control, constraint and leverage factors that can be built into a set of action plans for organizational implementation. Hierarchists subscribe to the belief that efficiently ordered and appropriate actions will lead to the right results.

Hierarchists prefer to presume a high degree of certainty of both problem-relevant knowledge and agreement on ends. This is because they prefer to avoid conflict over contested objectives or values standards,[15] for it might provoke major disagreement, and thus turbulent social processes. They prefer, instead, to comply with hierarchically determined objectives and values standards. Any judgments that they might be expected to make they would prefer to be focused on what Vickers (1983) identifies as reality judgments: What is out there? What is the problem? What predictions can be made?

---

[15] Hirschman (cited in Messner 1997: 374, n. 31) distinguishes between divisible *more-or-less* conflicts, which are resolvable through compromising and bargaining, and indivisible *either-or* conflicts, which are less easily resolvable.

Any decision outcome would be judged by hierarchists to have been agreed upon by the application of a natural (or other ideal) standard, by reference to some extrapersonal ideal such as 'divine right,' 'the queen's pleasure,' or 'the national interest' (Schwarz and Thompson 1990: 132). This makes consent[16] hypothetical, on the basis of what someone ought to agree with under an idealized standard (Schwarz and Thompson 1990: 67). This, in turn, presumes, of course, that such a standard can be met (Schwarz and Thompson 1990: 133), and that, in terms of Weber's ([1915] 1947) nomological perspectives, human behavior is predictable because a person's choice decisions are made on the basis of reasoned and rational thought processes constrained by the known, hierarchical norms of group behavior.

Hierarchist Perspective on Risks and Risk Taking

Because hierarchists see the world as being "conditionally benevolent," and thus as a positive-sum game within limits (Thompson and Taylor 1986: 22), high risks can be taken (Douglas and Ney 1998: 136) provided the critical choices about how risks should be defined, measured and evaluated is made by experts without the need to accommodate moral or political issues. Societal risks (human-caused hazards [Rescher 1983]) can be involuntarily imposed once the powers that be have decided upon their ethical acceptability. But the management of risk must be left to experts unencumbered by moral or political considerations. The risk environment is thus presumed to be knowable within an acceptable degree of probability. Success in the face of risk is expected by hierarchists (Douglas and Wildavsky 1982, Thompson et al. 1990). Their risk-handling style is one of "rejection and absorption" (Schwarz and Thompson 1990: 67).

The salient risk facing hierarchists, which stems from explanatory weaknesses of the naturalist-structuralist methodology, is the loss of control or public trust (Schwarz and Thompson 1990: 67).

Hierarchist Shared Values and Beliefs

On Human Nature. People are, to hierarchists, sinful,[17] with a basic instinct for seeking pleasure and avoiding pain, but they can be redeemed by good institutions (Thompson et al. 1990).

On Power, Rules and Compliance. Hierarchists prefer to exercise French and Raven's (1959) legitimate or expert power, Boulder's (1990) threat power, or Hales' (2001) knowledge power, and so are inclined toward directive rules.[18] Or, as Mamadouh (1999b: 143) characterizes it, "they decide what we should do,"

---

[16] Consent is the removal of moral or legal objections to, or liability for, the performance of an act, an arrangement or an expectation, thereby justifying or legitimizing them (Beran 1987).

[17] "Men are always more ready for evil than for good" (Machiavelli [1513] 1977: 306).

[18] Directive rules "ask, command, demand, permit [and] caution" (Onuf 1989: 86).

which Jensen (1999: 174; see also Jensen 1998) reverses: "*we* are entitled to decide what *they* must do." This is expected to solicit voluntary compliance on the basis of a cognitive commitment derived from rational calculations made in the context of structural processes, such as rules and procedures prescribed by those in or with authority.

On Blame.[19] In the event of failure, hierarchists blame deviants because they refuse either to accept their place in the social order or to operate within its rules (Thompson et al. 1990).[20]

On Apathy. Apathy is taken by hierarchists to mean consent, since participation is constrained within a hierarchy, so as to ensure that individuals only act within the sphere of competence assigned to them (Thompson et al. 1990).

On Freedom.[21] The hierarchists' primary paternalistic concern is with constraining *negative* freedom, for the good of those whose liberty has been restricted, perhaps against their will, in order to achieve collectively determined goals; *positive* freedoms are threatening, as they permit greater individual autonomy.

On Time and the Future. Hierarchists perceive a balance between the short and the long term (Schwarz and Thompson 1990: 67). They see a continuity of the past, present and future, which they do not expect to be seriously threatened, although they consider that the future cannot be left to its own devices; it must be protected (Douglas and Wildavsky 1982).

---

[19] For a discussion of the Cultural Theory of responsibility see Wildavsky 1987a: 283–93; see also Polisar and Wildavsky 1989.

[20] Blaming those whose behavior violates shared behavior expectations is justified on the grounds that conformity is a moral obligation on everyone reconded to be in a social order, who are expected to know and accept its socially affirmed values and norms.

[21] Berlin (1969) drew a distinction between *positive freedom* (freedom to take control of one's life, identified with Rousseau's notion of moral self-government) and *negative freedom* (freedom from control, interference or exploitation, identified with the Hobbesian idea of the absence of constraint or obstacles) (see also Miller 1991). *Positive freedom* is the ability to do, choose and achieve outcomes—optionality—attained by empowerment, which is inherently a collective, rather than an individual, pursuit. It is based on three premises (Hyde and Dixon 2001). The first is that all individuals have capacities or latent, but desirable, qualities. The second is that *positive freedom* consists of the realization of these capacities, which may therefore be conceptualized, in the broader sense, as individual autonomy. The third is that social conditions are the decisive influence on the realization of these capacities. *Negative freedom* is the right of self-determination—autonomy—the absence of external constraints on individual action. It is also based on three premises (Hyde and Dixon 2001). The first is that individuals require the private space to identify appropriate personal goals and ambitions. The second is that personal goals and ambitions have value only if they are freely chosen. The third is that voluntary action—choice and personal responsibility—enables individuals to meet important spiritual needs.

On Nature.[22] Nature is bountiful within limits yet perverse and vulnerable; nevertheless tolerant of intervention. Hierarchists thus have a tendency to conserve resources (Schwarz and Thompson 1990, Thompson et al. 1990).

On Technology and Engineering.[23] High-technology virtuosity best describes the hierarchists' position (Schwarz and Thompson 1990: 66). Technology has instrumental value to the expert, especially when it encourages a command system (Douglas and Ney 1998: 182). Information technology, however, is a dual-edged sword: while it is a means by which the behavior of individuals and groups of individuals can be regulated, it can also threaten the legitimate, expert and knowledge power-base of the hierarchy, necessitating tight controls over the spread of contradictory and incompatible information.

On Economic Growth. Wealth creation is desirable to hierarchists, provided any sacrifice made by the collective in the accumulation process leads to collective gain (Thompson et al. 1990).

On Scarcity. To hierarchists, scarcity justifies administrative allocation by direct bureaucratic fiat, so as to ensure that the collective has adequate resources (Thompson et al. 1990).

On Reconciling Human Wants with Scarce Resources. The hierarchy, with its predilection for conspicuous displays (Douglas 1994: 227), prefers to identify the wants that should be met from available resources, which are perceived as scarce (Schwarz and Thompson 1990: 66). It expects individual sacrifices to be made in the collective interest (Douglas 1994, Thompson et al. 1990). The hierarchist, "who anchors his stratified collectivity in the weight of history," has a traditionalist consumption style (Douglas et al. 1998: 255).

On Inequality and Envy. As inequality is institutionalized in a hierarchy, equality is generally threatening.[24] This is not true, however, of either rank-order equality[25] or equality before the law, which is sacrosanct (Schwarz and Thompson 1990: 66). Hierarchists thus consider that envy must therefore be controlled, for ostentation is reserved only for the collective (Thompson et al. 1990).

On the Market Sphere.[26] To hierarchists the marketplace is a strange and isomorphic realm that is perverse but tolerant of public intervention. Hierar-

---

[22] For a discussion of the myths of nature in Cultural Theory, which draws upon Hollis 1984; see Thompson et al. 1990; see also Grendstad and Selles 2000, Thompson 1997, and Thompson and Reyner 1998a.

[23] For a discussion of Cultural Theory and technology see Douglas and Ney 1998: 180–83.

[24] Hierarchists would reject the principles of equality of opportunity, equality of objective outcome, equality of outcome taking into consideration need or 'just desert,' or equality relative to individual contribution (Eckhoff 1974).

[25] Rank-order equality)is achieved when the allocation of rewards follows a set of normative expectations to avoid felt injustice (Eckhoff 1974).

[26] Cantor et al. (1992: 21–24) suggest that a market has five characteristics: (1) a process that determines property rights, which "define control over goods and services;" (2) a desire for an exchange to take place, based on differences in "tastes, endowment, or both;" (3) a condition that the transaction costs (exchange identification, negotiation and enforcement costs) "do not exceed the perceived gains from completing the exchange;"

chists, by institutionalizing status differences, place constraints on competition (Thompson et al. 1998: 331). Market forces should thus be mapped and managed, not only by contractual sanctions, but also by public intervention strategies in the collective interest, so as to ensure that market behavior and outcomes remain within an acceptable range, thereby avoiding unbridled entrepreneurial behavior that is experimental and exuberant.

On Organizing.[27] Hierarchists seek out "rule-bound" (Hood 1998: 9) "nested bounded groups" (Schwarz and Thompson 1990: 66; see also Thompson and Taylor 1986: 3–5). These are preferably large, although with "controllability (through inherent orderliness)" (Schwarz and Thompson 1990: 66). They must have embedded as organizational values that loyalty is rewarded and positional status is respected (Schwarz and Thompson 1990: 75), and that correct procedures and discriminated statuses are supported (Schwarz and Thompson 1990: 66).[28]

On Sacrifices for, or Voluntary Contributions to, the Collective.[29] Hierarchists, who are dominated by a sense of duty, would be willing to make the expected voluntary sacrifices for the collective because such sacrifices would receive the approval of authority figures, thus minimizing any threat of their being

---

(4) a condition that choice exists "over trading partners, trading periods, or both;" and (5) a level of trust that ensures the "transaction [being] completed in an atmosphere of noncoercion." They argue (pp. 23–24) that all market processes are governed by exchange structures—the rules that govern demand, supply, and the transaction costs for a particular set of transactions.

[27] For a discussion of Cultural Theory and organizations, see Altman and Baruch 1998, Coyle 1997, Douglas 1995, Douglas and Ney 1998, Hood 1998.

[28] Jaques (1976: 13) makes the point: "Bureaucracy is not only a rational and efficient type of human organization, as Weber emphasizes, but it has the potential to provide the setting both for constructive human relationships and for individual creative expression and dissatisfaction." Du Gay (2000) highlights bureaucracy's continuing relevance to the achievement of social order and good government in liberal democratic societies.

[29] A differentiation needs to be made between *other-regarding helping behavior*, which involves no sacrifice, and *altruism*, which does (Reber 1995). Rushton and Sorrentino (1981: 427) provide a useful definitional starting point: "Altruism is behavior directed towards the benefit of others at some cost to the self where no extrinsic or intrinsic benefit is the primary intent of the behavior." The concept of *altruism* is contestable (Campbell 1972, R. Cohen, 1972, Dawkins 1976, Hobbs [1651] 1991); at issue is the degree of definitional latitude that should be permitted in relation to motivation (the furtherance of self-interest, whether as a primary or secondary motivational source) and the nonmaterial rewards (the furtherance of self-satisfaction). Hobbes ([1651] 1991: 231) observed that people are naturally self-seeking and thus show concern for others only because of a desire to avoid a life that is "solitary, poor, nasty, brutish and short." Bourdieu (1999: 73) argues that the sacrificing of selfish interest in the collective interest is induced by offering "material or symbolic" profits to those who make such sacrifices. For a discussion of how different types of collective behavior are related to different values or norms, see Smelser 1963. For a discussion of Cultural Theory and altruism, see Wildavsky 1993, Wildavsky and Lockhart 1998. For a discussion of Cultural Theory and voluntary cooperation, see Wildavsky and Lockhart 1998.

excluded from the collective. They would, similarly, be willing to make the expected voluntary contributions to collective action (Wildavsky and Lockhart 1998: 122), even if they might be excluded from receiving valued benefits from that collective action.

ENCLAVIST SOCIAL SOLIDARITY

Enclavists constitute communities of unranked natural groupings of people who are inspired by common objectives (Douglas 1994: 184). These common ends are robust and quite definitely not merely congruent private ends. To enclavists, a significant constituent of their identity—their sense of who they are—is their awareness of themselves as belonging to such groups. This form of social order is based on personal authority, "expressed through egalitarian homogeneity, that is, by operating rules of equality that keep each participant at the same status" (Douglas et al. 1998: 327). It is a community that is characterized by voluntarism, in that members are free to leave at will (Douglas 1994: 184); by exclusivism, for it has strong barriers identifying and separating its members from outsiders[30] (Douglas 1982b), which are protected by ritual (Douglas 1970); by egalitarianism, which means that they want their community to have no leaders and no rules or protocol telling people how to behave[31] (Douglas 1982b, Rayner 1988, Wildavsky 1989a); and by their "burning thirst for justice and their anger against injustice"[32] (Douglas and Ney 1998: 145; see also Wildavsky

---

[30] These are akin to Scharpf's (1991: 297) "boundaries of distrust and irrelevance." Collins (1981: 944) gives insights into the processes involved:

The actual structures in the social world, especially centered on the network upholding property and authority, involve continuous monitoring by individuals of each other's group loyalties. Since the social world can involve quite a few lines of authority and sets of coalitions, the task of monitoring them can be extremely complex. How is this possible, given people's inherently limited cognitive capacities?

The solution must be that negotiations are carried out implicitly, on a different level than the use of consciously manipulated verbal symbols. I propose that the mechanism is emotional rather than cognitive. Individuals monitor others' attitudes towards social coalitions, hence towards the degree of support for routines, by feeling the amount of confidence and enthusiasm there is towards certain leaders and activities, or the amount of fear of being attacked by a strong coalition, or the amount of contempt for a weak one. These emotional energies are transmitted by contagion among members of a group, in flows which operate very much like the set of negotiations which produce prices within a market.

[31] Enclavists would have empathy with that branch of *anarchism* (Slevin 1996a) that seeks the creation of a spontaneous order on a voluntary, cooperative basis without recourse to force or coercion.

[32] Enclavists would endorse the Hegelian proposition that nothing great is ever done without passion or emotion (Taylor 1975). They would no doubt base their impassioned sense of injustice on deontological ethical arguments that emphasize social rights and obligations. They may well accept that they are *utopians*, with a disposition to embrace the vision of a society from which all the social evils have been removed and in which there exists the complete human fulfillment and wellbeing that come with the attainment of freedom, equality and perfect justice (Kateb 1963; More [1516] 1989; Taylor 1982,

1991d). Their bias is toward fundamentalism[33] (Schwarz and Thompson 1990: 66) and millenarianism[34] (Schwarz and Thompson 1990: 66; see also Rayner 1982b), as they are ever in search of the perfect world. The three pillars that typify an enclavist culture are thus the protective boundary, the threat of defection, and the principles of equality and nondiscrimination, with ambiguity a consequence.

Enclavist groups are dissidents (Douglas 1982b, Sivan 1995, Thompson and Wildavsky 1986b) and, as they lack any internal role differentiation, relations between group members are ambiguous. No individual has the authority to exercise control over another, which makes internal conflicts difficult to resolve according to Thompson et al. (1990: 6; see also Rayner 1988). This makes them intrinsically factional (Douglas and Ney 1998: 118). Schism is part of their reality, as they have no way to settle disputes except by expulsion (Douglas 1982b). Because enclavists give their leaders no authority, they are inclined to blame the corruption of the outside world for their difficulties.[35] As a consequence, the more defiant is their posture toward the outside, the less they gain external recognition. Thus, compromise becomes more unthinkable; negotiations become less possible. This "whirls them more and more speedily toward complete closure" (Douglas and Ney 1998: 150). Their main anxiety is the fear of secession by the faithful, which weakens authority and encourages a tendency to invoke the principle of equality (Douglas 1994: 225). This places enclavist communities at the mercy of defectors (Douglas 1994: 138). Such a group generates a facade of invulnerability and inherent morality, a close-mindedness that manifests itself in collective rationalizations and outsider stereotyping, and strong pressure toward uniformity "through self-censorship, illusions of unanimity, direct pressure on potential dissenters, and self-appointed mind guards" (Hoppe 2000: 11). Enclavists have, according to Douglas and Ney (1998:102), an inclination toward conspiracy theory. They trust only those who have not been corrupted by power-

---

1996b). However, they would resist the idea that they are *idealists* in pursuit of unattainable objectives (Jones 1996a).

[33] This is the strict maintenance of traditional orthodox doctrines, which may be political or religious. *Islamic fundamentalism* "denotes any movement to favor strict observance teaching of the *Qur'an* and the *shari'a* (Islamic law)" (Robertson 1996: 251–52). It emerged as a response to Islamic reform movements that sought to modernize or Westernize Islam, especially by incorporating some of the characteristic elements Western rationalism and values. It has evolved a political ideology that has the express aim of replacing "the sovereignty of the people expressed through parliamentary legislation, with the 'sovereignty of God' as revealed, in its perfection and finality, through the *Shari'a*" (Ruthven 1997: 5). Its intention is to connect Islam with state power in some Islamic societies (Rashid 2001). *Christian fundamentalism* denotes any movement that adheres to the literal truth of biblical history and the status of Scripture "as direct and unchallengeable revelation of the word of God" (Wood 1996: 67–68). It has evolved political agendas and populist lobbies in some Christian countries.

[34] Millenarianism is "the belief . . . that cataclysmic changes will occur in the near future, heralding the arrival of a new epoch" (Giddens 2001: 694), and especially the hope that oppressive governments will be overthrown (Reeve 1996d).

[35] This is akin to Scharpf's (1991: 297) "opportunism for guile."

hungry and inequitable institutions, whether they be markets or hierarchies (Molenaers and Thompson 1999: 192).

Enclavist groups are greedy institutions that "try to pre-empt the total personality of their members, their time and their resources" (Douglas and Ney 1998: 146, citing Coser 1974) and that generate hostility to outsiders, which leads to intolerance, a refusal to negotiate, threats of expulsion, and even violence (Douglas and Ney 1998: 146). They create a social context in which the external group boundary is, typically, the dominant consideration. The social experience of the individual is shaped by the 'we' versus 'them' mentality. The suspicion of outsider infiltration or of insider betrayal is rampant (Altman and Baruch 1998: 773). Socialization is based on passively and actively resisting all types of power and authority. (Hoppe 2000: 19, n. 10).

Enclavist Perspective on Motivation

The social context for enclavists is one where no one has a place but everyone belongs and is committed. This gives rise to a negotiated set of jointly affirmed social norms (Hart 1961, Raz 1975) that constitute the rules by which members of a social group should conduct themselves and their affairs. They dominate the enneagramic ideal-types that are governed by the "emotional center"—"the heart"—which cultivates the need for "approval and acceptance by others. It is about the achievement of...relationships so that they are recognized and acclaimed by others." There is a dependence on being popular, liked and trusted, and thus belonging[36] (Cutting and Kouzmin 1997: 90–91). Riso (1987: 26) concludes that these enneagramic ideal-types are "out of touch with [their] feelings, projecting an image which substitutes for genuine feelings." Thus, it would follow that their primary source of self-esteem is recognition and acclaim by like-minded others. This is attained on the basis that they place high value on personal relationships, being seen as trustworthy, dependable and popular, and that they are very committed to a common ensemble of precepts, concepts, ideas and values derived from public discourses, persuasive discourses with targeted individuals, and consciousness-raising discourses with fellow participants engaged in collective action. On this basis it would follow that the enclavist's metalife-goal is to be recognized and acclaimed by like-minded people.

---

[36] In terms of Riesman's (1950) *inner-other directedness* dichotomy, enclavists would have an *other-directedness* orientation, preferring to seek the approval and acceptance of others. The needs emphasized by enclavists would be Maslow's (1970) social (affiliation or acceptance), esteem and self-actualization (distinctive psychological potential) needs; Ardrey's (1967) identity, security and stimulation needs; Alderfer's (1972) existence, relatedness and growth needs; and McCelland's (1961, 1967; see also McCelland et al. 1953) achievement, power and affiliation needs.

Enclavist Perspective on Rationality

Enclavists prefer to engage in reasoning that is values-based and intersubjective, and informed by critical theory.[37] This involves processes in which all committed actors are empowered and enabled to make and question arguments. This makes good argument and the validity of normative judgments the final authority (Bakhtin 1981, Foucault 1978, Gergen and Thatchenkey 1998), which involves the use of intersubjective communications to construct agreed mutual understandings (de Haven-Smith 1988: 85). Enclaves create a *critical rationality* that emphasizes the importance of sororal and fraternal cooperation (Schwarz and Thompson 1990: 7). Hoppe (2000) describes this as communicative-value rationality. Epistemologically, enclavists embrace hermeneutics;[38] ontologically, they embrace structuralism and thus, methodologically, they embrace hermeneutic structuralism.[39] They thus presume a subjective social world, knowable

---

[37] Critical theory holds that reason is concerned exclusively with the choice of effective means for achieving, through human action, arbitrary (tacit) ends, as distinct from inherently rational (instrumental) ends (Held 1980). Criticism must be 'internal' or 'immanent,' always seeking to demonstrate the ways that society is losing its legitimacy by failing to live up to its own tacit claims about how it allows its members to lead a good life. Such claims, it is argued, can be identified from the beliefs, cultural artifacts, and forms of experience present in society.

[38] *Hermeneutics* ("the science of interpretation [which] maintains an interest in the content as well as the form of what is being interpreted" [Marshall 1998: 327]) has as its central proposition that "the social world must be understood from within, rather than explained from without" (Hollis 1994: 16; see also Baert 1998; Giddens 1990, 1991; Hollis 1994). It contends that knowledge (justified true beliefs) rests on interpretations embedded in day-to-day expressions or forms of life derived from cultural practice, discourse and language (Winch 1990). Thus, both reasoning and morality are relative, across time, societies and individuals (epistemic and moral relativism, respectively), which means that people in different societies have very different beliefs and belief systems (social relativism). There is, therefore, no 'best' or most justified mode of reasoning or morality (Davidson 1984, Goodman 1965, Hollis and Lukes 1982, Mackie 1977). Human knowledge is generated by acts of ideation that rest on intersubjectively shared symbols, or typifications, that allow for reciprocity of perspectives (Schutz [1932] 1967). However, this pre-acquaintance is active, and the indexicality or context dependency (Perry 1993) of social life requires acts of reflexive interpretation to ensure the appropriate contextualization of meaning (Blumer 1969, Garfinkel [1967] 1984). It embraces, inter alia, *linguistic philosophy, epistemological hermeneutics, existentialism,* and *hermeneutic* and *transcendental phenomenology.* Hermeneutics' dilemma is that the knowledge that is derived is culturally specific and subject to severe relativism, which makes explanation contingent on culture. It is also dynamic and open to constant revision, which makes prediction problematic (Dixon and Dogan 2002a).

[39] Embracing, inter alia (Williams and May 1996, Dogan 2001), *symbolic interactionalism* (meaning emerges through the interaction of language, identity and society and thus "the self-society relationship [is] a product of symbolic communications between social actors," with society being the product of those interactions [Nightingale and Cromby 1999: 229; see also Blumer 1969, Mead 1934]); *language games* (the complex of interwoven speech and action that are ordered in praxis in a way that makes sense to the participants), and *poststructuralism* ("the meaning of signs (words)...[is] always

only as it is socially constructed, with people's action being determined by their collective interpretation of this reality.[40] Thus, social action proceeds on the assumption that social reality can be identified through the interrogation of expressions or forms of life: the attempt to understand the interpretative framework of the individuals or groups that are the subject of the social activity, which enables their behavior to be predicted. Further, appropriate forms of social action can be developed only within the terms of the appropriate discourses, based on the existing symbolic interaction of the social actors, with specific social action strategies being utilized after extensive consultation involving mutual engagement by the social actors (Dixon and Dogan 2002a).

Enclavists are continually striving to unearth what Cutting and Kouzmin (2000b: 528–29) call the socially determined sensible and practicable good, achieved by a group consensus[41] through discourses on contestable values and standards.

---

changing and contestable" [Nightingale and Cromby 1999: 228; see also Foucault [1966] 1970]).

[40] Enclavists would accept the proposition that "notions of truth, objectivity, reason and other grand narratives have been superseded by notions of diversity, instability, fragmentation and indeterminacy" (Nightingale and Cromby 1999: 228; see also Delanty 2000). They would identify with the underpinning notions of *multiculturalation of meaning* (the multiplicity of interpretation of meaning that reflect a diversity of cultural contexts [Gergen and Thatchenkey 1998]); *narrative knowledge* (knowledge in the form of story-telling, perhaps involving myths and legends, which both explains and legitimates knowledge) [Lyotard 1979, Tsoukas 1998]); *relativism* ("the belief that there are no grounds for postulating or investigating a reality independent of the knower; that there is no ultimate truth and, therefore, no grounds for presuming that any one truth claim is 'better' than any other" [Nightingale and Cromby 1999: 228]); *perspectivism* ("the external world is interpreted through alternative systems of beliefs and concepts and that there is no means of establishing that one view is necessarily any 'better' than another" [Nightingale and Cromby 1999: 227]); and *indexicality* (words and phrases whose interpretation are dependant on the context of their use, which allow expression of beliefs about one's subjective place in the world and about beliefs that are the immediate antecedents of action [Forbes 1989]). They would also take comfort from postmodernism. Post modernists, as critical theorists who see human systems as self-reflexive and able to construct and maintain meaning and values (Harvey 1992), and who have a penchant for philosophico-historical reductionism (Ermarth 1992), have developed "a sharp, subtle, and derogatory account of modern consciousness which undermines much we believe by showing us the influences which have molded our beliefs." This permits the identification of "the structure and irrational origins of our 'patriarchal' or 'industrial' thought" (Allison 1996a: 119; see also Hutcheon 1989, White 1991). Postmodernists argue that societies are no longer governed by history or progress. They would find challenging, however, the proposition that research should be concerned with "investigations of potentially mutually shaping (dialectical) interaction between agency, structure and social chance" (Sibeon 2000: 290; see also Sibeon 1999, M. Smith 1993).

[41] Janis (1972) argues that while group consensus builds loyalty to the group's viewpoint—*groupthink*—it suppresses dissenting viewpoints that may blind decision makers to the 'realities.'

Enclavist Perspective on Learning and Knowledge

Enclavists have a learning style that focuses on "trial without error" (Schwarz and Thompson 1990: 66), and knowledge is considered "imperfect but holistic" (Schwarz and Thompson 1990: 66). Axiomatically, they give no authority, for information to be treated as objective truth, simply because it is derived by experts. Instead, they prefer it to be thoroughly discussed so as to construct appropriate mutual understandings.[42] They are thus among March's (1999) slow learners.

Enclavists demand that all information on their external environment should be openly and readily available, so that the errors 'they' make can be exploited to win converts. As Douglas and Ney (1998: 183) point out, however: "Enclavists can afford to indulge in creationism and flat-earth science and in primitivism in doctrine. If it boasts an original, esoteric revaluation, it can make a virtue of its strict control of knowledge about the internal environment. How else but by censorship can it preserve its legacy." Undoubtedly, enclavists deal with information according to whatever criteria are appropriate for their egalitarian relationships (Schwarz and Thompson 1990: 134; see also Hendriks and Zouridis 1999: 124).

Enclavist Perspective on Problem Solving and Decision Making

Enclavists prefer problems to be defined in a moderately structured way (Hoppe 2000). They prefer to presume a moderate degree of certainty of problem-relevant knowledge, but they anticipate intense disagreement about ends. Indeed, they prefer to contest objectives and values standards, as this gives them an opportunity to convert outsiders to their point of view, with the inevitable conflict shaped by socially constructed notions of distributive justice, equality and fairness. They thus place stress on the valuative problem dimension—the desirability of the impact of means on ends—at least to the extent that it overlaps collectively agreed values with respect to who gets what, when and how. Causal and evaluative information gathering, impact and risk assessment, and the search for alternative solutions are all constrained by the commonly accepted values framework. Enclavists subscribe to the belief that socially endorsed ends are so crucial that they inevitably justify the means used to achieve them, after having fully rationalized and justified any moral or ethical risks involved. Indeed, any judgments they might be expected to make they would prefer to be focused on what Vickers (1983) identifies as value judgments: What social values and norms are best? What ought to be?

To enclavists, decision-making involves forcing 'them' to give up their 'wrong' values by accepting 'our' values and thereby agreeing with 'our' decision. Whether any decision outcome has been agreed to can only be determined by the application of the expressed preferences standard involving direct consent (Schwarz and Thompson 1990: 67), which means that a decision is justifiable

---

[42] Enclavists would be sympathetic to Lerry and Taket's (1994) death-of-the-expert proposition

only if everyone concerned agrees with it (Schwarz and Thompson 1990: 131). This presumes that those who need to give their consent are sufficiently engaged socially to know their preferences (Schwarz and Thompson 1990: 132), and that, nomologically, human behavior is predictable because a person makes preference decisions on the basis of known understandings that have been mutually constructed as regulatory norms.[43]

Enclavist Perspective on Risks and Risk Taking

Because enclavists see the world as hostile, and thus as a negative-sum game (Thompson and Taylor 1986: 22), risks create a sense of anger and righteousness, with risk takers cast as evil doers (Douglas and Ney 1998: 137). Societal risks should be defined, measured and evaluated by those with an interest in or concern about the risk environment. They should not have societal risks involuntarily imposed upon society, rather they should be able to specify the conditions, if any, under which it is ethically acceptable to do so. Risks are thus to be minimized and highly politicized. The existing authorities tolerate unacceptably high risks, so enclavists assert, because they ignore the welfare of people. Failure in the face of risk is expected (Douglas and Wildavsky 1982, Thompson et al. 1990). Their risk-handling style is "rejection and deflection" (Schwarz and Thompson 1990: 67).

The salient risks facing enclavists are that, given the inherent relativism of the hermeneutic-structuralist methodology, people may not come to an agreement on a course of action (Schwarz and Thompson 1990: 67) and that, given the presumed structuralist ontology, voluntary compliance by free individuals to any agreed course of action cannot be assured.

Enclavist Shared Values and Beliefs

On Human Nature. Enclavists consider human nature to be circumstantial, a product of their social formations. People are born good,[44] with a capacity for real moral progress, only to be corrupted by the power exercised by people in evil institutions in markets and hierarchies (Douglas 1982b, Thompson et al. 1990).

On Power, Rules and Compliance. Enclavists prefer to exercise Boulder's (1990) integrative power, French and Raven's (1959) personal or referent power, or Hales' (2001) normative power; thus they prefer instructive rules.[45] Or, as Mamadouh (1999b: 142) characterizes it: "We should decide what we want to

---

[43] Regulatory norms describe the collectively agreed expectations of what constitutes the proper behavior of actors with a given identity (Katzenstein 1996). For a discussion on how highly cohesive groups make decisions and enforce norms, see Janis 1972.

[44] "It is clear that there is in man a natural aptitude to virtuous action" (Aquinas [1264] 1974: 127).

[45] Instructive rules state beliefs that are intended to be accepted (Onuf 1989: 85; but see also 120).

do." This is expected to solicit voluntary compliance on the basis of moral commitment (Etzioni 1961).

On Blame. In the event of failure, enclavists blame 'outsiders' or the 'traitors within' (Thompson et al. 1990).[46]

On Apathy. Apathy can be justified only if participation, which is highly desirable to enclavists, is intended to support the established order rather than to be real and meaningful (Thompson et al. 1990).

On Freedom. The primary concern of enclavists is with enhancing *positive* freedom, a prerequisite for which is equality of outcome, which is taken as a value in its own right and justifies constraints being imposed on *negative* freedom.

On Time and the Future. To enclavists the long term dominates short term (Schwarz and Thompson 1990: 67). They perceive a discontinuity between the past, present and future. Moreover, the future is expected to undergo a radical change for the worse (Douglas and Wildavsky 1982).

On Nature. Enclavists are catastrophists (Thompson and Rayner 1998a: 157) who see nature as ephemeral, fragile and unforgiving (Schwarz and Thompson 1990, Thompson et al. 1990). This means that resources must be diligently and carefully managed.

On Technology and Engineering. "Frugal and environmentally benign" (Schwarz and Thompson 1990: 66) characterizes the enclavists' view. Technology is a source of unacceptable risks. Information technology is a dual-edged sword: it threatens group solidarity by making values-disconfirming information more readily available, but it also facilitates both intragroup communications and the conversion of 'outsiders.'

On Economic Growth. Wealth creation is of little interest to enclavists. This is because abundance makes the maintenance of outcome equality problematic by creating interpersonal differences (Thompson et al. 1990).

On Scarcity. Scarcity justifies, according to enclavists, collective action to change inegalitarian lifestyles in order to ensure that resources last as long as possible (Thompson et al. 1990).

On Reconciling Human Wants with Scarce Resources. Since enclavists consider that resources are fixed and thus are depleting over time, they believe that they cannot be managed (Schwarz and Thompson 1990: 66). Thus, the only acceptable option is to decrease wants to a level below that which can be resourced (Thompson et al. 1990). The enclavist, to whom "thrift is more elegant, more appropriate than vulgar display" (Douglas 1994: 228), has a naturalist consumption style (Douglas et al. 1998: 255).

On Inequality and Envy. Distinctions between people are not legitimate to enclavists. Therefore they consider the principles of equality of results and of

---

[46] Blaming outsiders and traitors within is justified on the ground that anti-social behavior deserves to be blamed and punished (Sher 1987).

need and 'just desert' to be right (Schwarz and Thompson 1990: 66).[47] Envy must thus be controlled (Thompson et al. 1990).

On the Market Sphere. The market sphere is an inhospitable realm to enclavists, one that threatens equality of condition. Enclavists constrain competition to avoid status distinctions (Thompson et al. 1998: 331). The market should thus be held strictly accountable for its processes and outcomes by means of full and effective public disclosure, so as to ensure that any social costs incurred are the subject of a group-norming and -forming values discourse before being addressed.

On Organizing. Enclavists seek out highly participative "egalitarian bounded groups"[48] (Schwarz and Thompson 1990: 66; see also Hood 1998: 9, Thompson and Taylor 1986: 3-5) in which respect is identified with agape, a special kind of fraternal or sororal love. These organizations are small (Schwarz and Thompson 1990: 66). They have a negotiated order[49] and a moral fervor, which gives rise to a collective affirmation of opposition to the outside world (Schwarz and Thompson 1990: 66).[50] This protects their members from the external hostile world (Schwarz and Thompson 1990: 75).[51] Such organizations thus achieve "sustainability (through [their] inherent fragility)" (Schwarz and Thompson 1990: 66).

On Sacrifices for, and Voluntary Contributions to, the Collective. Enclavists, as collective activists,[52] would expect to make voluntary sacrifices for the col-

---

[47] Enclavists would, of course, reject the principles of equality of opportunity, equality relative to individual contribution, and rank-order equality.

[48] That there is a third organizational form—networks—between the rational-bureaucratic model (Weber [1915] 1947, [1904] 1949) and transactional-market model (Williamson 1973, 1975, 1979, 1985, 1986, 1994; Williamson and Ouchi 1983) has long been postulated (Francis et al. 1983, Ouchi 1980, Rothschild-Whitt 1979). However, as Schwarz and Thompson (1990: 79, n. 13) point out, what these third organizational forms have lacked is a set of social dimensions that can generate a proper typology, which can be provided by Cultural Theory.

[49] A negotiated order, according to Strauss (1978: 56) is "something at which members of any society, any organization, must work. For the shared agreements...are not binding for all time...review is called for...the bases of concerted action (social order) must be constituted continually, or 'worked out'."

[50] When this is the dominant ethos, Hood's (1998: 135) radical egalitarian organization with a transformational agenda is created (see also Bittner 1963, Wildavsky 1991d). These may be manifest as *social movements*, which are "characterized by a departure from conventional methods of political organization and expression, and experimentation with new forms of social relations and cultural meanings and identities...[that] reflect the multiple contradistinctions within social systems (based on racial, gender and cultural dichotomies, as well as class)" (Skinner 1996: 343). These seek to coordinate and organize collective behavior as a response to problematic circumstances and situations.

[51] When this is the dominant goal, Hood's (1998: 133) sequestered egalitarian organization is created, in which seclusion and isolation are of paramount importance.

[52] Social psychologists using the *locus of control* construct (Levenson 1981: 49–52) argue that social activists are more likely to be at the *internalist* end of the *locus of control* spectrum—those who tend to accept responsibility for their actions and consider they

lective; to do otherwise would be to suggest that they are not trustworthy and dependable, which would threaten their attainment of group recognition and acclaim. Because they value warm and supportive interpersonal relations, enclavists would similarly expect to make voluntary contributions to collective action (Wildavsky and Lockhart 1998: 121), even if they could not be excluded from receiving valued benefits from that action.

FATALIST SOCIAL SOLIDARITY

The fatalist *social solidarity* is a reaction to existence that results in self-chosen isolationism (Douglas 1982b, Thompson and Wildavsky 1986b). It is attractive to anyone who is intent on standing apart from the struggle with a sense of fatalism, and thus in isolation (Douglas and Ney 1998: 102; see also Friere 1972, McMahon 1979, Ortega y Gasset 1970).[53] This *social solidarity* is characterized by the absence of any desire to explain or influence events, and by a freedom from any ideological commitments (Douglas 1994: 225). This is not, however, freedom from responsibility: "freedom is not an escape, but a life sentence: to exist is to be responsible for oneself, to choose oneself and to face the consequences of choosing. Freedom is therefore always accompanied by anguish"[54] (N. Thompson 1992: 23). Fatalists do not necessarily approve of their condition; rather, they judge it to be unalterable because human choice and action can have no influence on future events.[55] They are people who have been alienated[56] and marginalized from social life, and who find social cooperation

---

are in control of their lives and destinies, largely through their own personal effort, ability and initiative (see, for example, Gore and Rotter 1963, Strickland 1965; but see also Blanchard and Scarboro 1972, Evans and Alexander 1970, Gootnick 1974)—which is, arguably, where enclavists can be placed.

[53] This sense of aloneness, which can generate the detachment and disconnection that focuses awareness of the existential human condition, is captured in the writings of Albert Camus and Jean-Paul Sartre, is replete in the music of Gustav Mahler and Dimitri Shostakovich, and is echoed in both the fiction of Iris Murdoch and John Fowles and the poems of Thorm Gunn and José Ortega y Gasset.

[54] Sartre ([1943] 1957) situated freedom in the context of *facticity* (facts about a person that cannot be changed, such as age, gender and race) and *situation* (the given set of circumstances that have a past and that set the expectations of self and others). Thus, individual free choice is constrained by personal history and contemporaneous circumstances, both of which condition options.

[55] Oscar Lewis, in his *Children of Sanchez* (1961: 171), gives a poignant example of the fatalist when he describes Manuel Sanchez's ruminations about the failure of his shoe manufacturing venture:

To me, one's destiny is controlled by a mysterious hand that moves all things. Only for the select, do things turn out as planned; to those of us who are born to be tamale eaters, He sends only tamales. We plan and some little thing happens to wash it all away....God gives us just enough to go on vegetating, no?

[56] The concept of *alienation* describes the "sense that our own abilities, as human beings, are taken over by other beings" (Giddens 2001: 683). Feuerbach [1841] 1893) refers to it as giving causal power to the gods or divine forces distinct from people. It is a

difficult because they lack the prerequisite interpersonal skills and attributes (Schmutzer 1994; see also Pizzorno 1966). They would have an enduring belief that events in their life are not under their control.[57] This may well be a true belief in external control or it may be a belief that enables them to blame luck, fate or the powers that be for any undesirable outcomes they experience.[58] They perceive their behavior to be regulated by others, leaving little scope for personal choice, "providing instead a set of railway lines with remote control points for interactions" (Douglas 1978: 16). Thus fatalists are subject to the rules made by those who are determined to put some rational coherence into their lives (Douglas 1982b, Wildavsky 1989a). Inevitably, then, they are people who are the subject of binding prescriptions but who are excluded from group membership (Thompson et al. 1990: 7).[59] As a result, "fatalists are 'fickle isolates,' convinced that people are not to be trusted" (Molenaers and Thompson 1999: 192).

Insights into the fatalist culture can be gleaned from Durkheim's (1952) concept of anomie (see also Passes and Agnew 1997), the normlessness caused by the breakdown of, or confusion or conflict in, the social norms[60]; from Sztompka's (1996: 38) "syndrome of distrust," whereby social relations are

---

feeling of estrangement, separation and externalization, of individuals from each other; from specific situations and processes; and from their beliefs and values, thereby undermining their attachment to, and identification with, them. Marshall (1998: 14) identifies its dimensions: existentialism, powerlessness, meaninglessness, isolation, normlessness and self-estrangement. *Existentialism* ("the systematic investigation of the nature of human existence, giving priority to immediate experiences of aloneness, death, and moral responsibility" [Marshall 1998: 213]) stresses "the alienation of a person from him- or her-self. This separation of the individual from the presumed 'real' or 'deeper' self is assumed to result from preoccupation with conformity, the wishes of others, the pressures from social institutions, and other 'outer directed' motivations" (Reber 1995: 24). Marxists argue that "a direct consequence of man's alienation from the product of his work, from his life's activity, and from his species-existence, is the alienation of man from man" (Marx 1967: 295). Blauner (1964) found that feelings of powerlessness, isolation and self-estrangement were experienced by workers associated with machines and the assembly-line production processes. Reeve (1996a: 7) concludes that alienation "describes the sometimes debilitating effects of life in modern, large-scale societies."

[57] In his analysis of suicide, Durkheim ([1897] 1952: 34) defines a fatalistic situation as one where the future is "pitilessly blocked and passions violently choked by oppressive discipline."

[58] On the *locus of control* spectrum (Levenson 1981, O'Brien 1984, Reber 1995) fatalists would certainly be among the *externalists,* who willingly see the hand of fate in whatever happens to them. They believe that they have no control over their life, instead just let it passively wash over them.

[59] Camus captures this in his Afterword to his *The Outsider* ([1942] 1982: 118), where he sums it up in one paradoxical sentence: "In our society any man who does not cry at his mother's funeral is liable to be condemned to death." His hero, Meursault, "is condemned because he does not play the game. In this sense he is an outsider to the society in which he lives, wandering on the fringe, on the outskirts of life, solitary and sensual" (p. 118).

[60] Fatalists would deny the validity of both deontological moral arguments and consequentialist ethical propositions, which are used to justify their exploitation or exclusion.

dominated by insulation; and from Sartre's ([1946] 1973: 32) idea that "man is condemned to be free."[61] At the extreme, individual autonomy is minimal, with little scope for personal transactions (Altman and Baruch 1998: 772). Fatalists "expect conspiracy, but it does not shock or surprise them" (Douglas 1994: 110). They are prone to put a brave face on hopelessness, allowing them to embrace a genial fatalism (Douglas and Ney 1998: 114; see also Douglas 1996). Their bias is toward "inconsistent eclecticism" (Schwarz and Thompson 1990: 66). Their socialization is based on emotive values, described by Sartre ([1938] 1948) as magical transformations. In Nietzschean terms, emotion and reason stand not in opposition but in complementariness (Schacht 1983). They are both passively and actively resistant to all types of power and authority (Hoppe 2000: 19, n. 10). Fatalists look to ritual to support them in a competitive group setting (Douglas 1970).

Fatalist Perspective on Motivation

The social context for fatalists is one where everyone has a place but no one belongs or cares. Interpersonal relationships are governed by a set of sanctioned social norms that constitute the ingrained rules by which they must conduct themselves and their affairs (Hart 1961, Raz 1975). They dominate the enneagramic ideal-types that are governed by the "instinctive center"—"the gut"—which cultivates a need for "survival, for both the individual and the group [most notably the family]," and for "permanency and fixed, long-term associations. Justice and doing what is right is a big issue, particularly if survival is at stake," and generates a "strong adherence to traditions and customs" (Cutting and Kouzmin 1997: 90–91).[62] Riso (1987: 26) concludes that these ideal-types are "out of touch with [their] ability to relate to the environment as an individual." Thus it would follow that a primary source of self-esteem for fatalists is their capacity to survive against fate's odds. On this basis it would follow that the fatalist's metalife-goal is to be a survivor despite the odds that fate decrees.

Fatalist Perspective on Rationality

Fatalists' culture encourages nonrationality (Shweder 1984a: 38; but see also Elster 1985b, Popkin 1979, Portes 1972), "where the canons of rationality, validity, truth, and efficiency are simply beside the point—irrelevant!"[63] (Shweder

---

[61] Existentialists, for example, Sartre ([1946] 1973), argue that people are all that there is, and, because they are cursed with freedom, they must make their own way in the world as responsible agents willing and able to determine their own development through acts of will.

[62] In terms of Riesman's (1950) *inner-other directedness* dichotomy, fatalists would have an *inner-directedness* orientation, preferring to act independently and in accordance with their personal moral code. The needs they emphasize would be Maslow's (1970) physiological and safety (security) needs.

[63] Fatalists would, no doubt, be comfortable with Heidegger's assertion that "thinking only begins at the point where we have come to know that Reason, glorified for centuries, is the most obstinate adversary of thinking" (cited in Barrett 1958: 184).

1984a: 38). Statements about an unknowable world cannot be confirmed or disproved, as no evidence or experience can possibly be considered as proof.[64] Thus what an individual believes to be real is the basis for reasoning.[65] Fatalists engender a *fatalistic rationality* in which outcomes are to be enjoyed or endured, never sought (Schwarz and Thompson 1990: 8). This is described by Hoppe (2000) as inspirational-strategic rationality.[66] Epistemologically, fatalists embrace hermeneutics; ontologically, they embrace agency;[67] and thus, methodologically, they embrace hermeneutic agency.[68] They therefore presume a subjec-

---

[64] At the extreme, fatalists may well embrace the radical form of *solipsism* that holds that nothing at all exists apart from one's own mind and mental states (Russell 1948: Part III, Ch. 2).

[65] Sartre ([1946] 1973: 23, 26, 44) saw the doctrine of *existentialism* as being based "upon pure subjectivity—upon the Cartesian 'I think [therefore I am]'," "which is the absolute truth of consciousness as it attains to itself." Thus "we must begin from the subjective." "Existence comes before essence." Individuals simply exist and it is up to them to decide their own fate, for which they alone are responsible, and to define their own identity, or essential characteristics, in the course of living out their lives in the most authentic and fulfilling way possible, which means they must face up to and take over their own existence with clarity and intensity. Nietzsche, according to (Stack 1977: 17), saw the central conception of *nihilism* (an extreme form of skepticism, which maintains that nothing in the world is real, and which asserts that moral or religious principles have no validity, and that life is devoid of meaning) is that "existence must not be interpreted in terms of 'purpose', 'unity', 'Being', or 'truth'." For the Nietzschean nihilist there is no 'true' world at all. Kierkegaard's related propositions were that "in regard to every other reality external to the individual it can only be known through 'thinking it'" (Stack 1977: 197, n. 19), and that "existence, in its true or authentic form, is a subjective teleological activity for man, an activity characterized by dialectical tension and an intensification of subjectivity" (Stack 1977: 199, n. 40).

[66] To quote Sartre ([1946] 1973: 36): "If values are uncertain, if they are still too abstract to determine the particular, concrete case under consideration, nothing remains but to trust in our instincts."

[67] *Agency's* central proposition is that "individuals have some control over their actions and can be agents of their actions (voluntarism), enabled by their psychological and social psychological make-up" (Parker 2000: 125). Thus "people actively interpret their surrounding reality, and act accordingly" (Baert 1998: 3). Such actions are the product of a person's mental states of, say, hope, belief and desire that focus his or her mind's capacity to direct itself on objects, which need not necessarily exist (Brand and Walton 1976, Donagan 1987, Searle 1983). For people to be moved to action thus requires a belief about the way things are, about the actions possible given the way things are, and about the likely effects of those actions on the way things are; and a desire to change the way things are by a course of action in the hope that it brings about the intended change (Marks 1986). Agency embraces, inter alia, *rational choice theory, social phenomenology, dramaturgical analysis* and *ethnomethodology*. Agency's dilemma is that it can apparently explain the empirically strong correlation between individual behavior and free choice, but it cannot explain outliers that are the product of a correlation between individual behavior and social cohort (Williams and May 1996).

[68] Embracing, inter alia (Williams and May 1996, Dogan 2001) *social phenomenology* (how people construct, on the basis of their undifferentiated experiences, objects and the knowledge of those objects); *dramaturgical analysis* (the use of theatrical metaphors

tive social world that is contestably knowable as what people believe it to be, with agency constrained by their subjective perceptions of social reality, which makes human behavior unpredictable. Thus, social action proceeds on the assumption that the social world is subjective, unknowable and unpredictable (Dixon and Dogan 2002a).

Fatalists continually strive to deal with the real by discerning the true reality as it is, which includes all that which forms a part of what an individual believes to be real; as there are few objective truths.

Fatalist Perspective on Learning and Knowledge

Fatalists have a learning style that focuses on trial and error (Schwarz and Thompson 1990: 66). They give no credence to any information purporting to consist of 'objective truths' derived by 'experts,' which they consider to be irrelevant (Schwarz and Thompson 1990: 66). They are thus among March's (1999) fast learners.

Fatalist Perspective on Problem Solving and Decision Making

Fatalists see problems as existing in a risky, unstable and unknowable environment. Problems should neither have a structure imposed upon them nor have their causation presumed. All possible solutions should be kept open to maximize opportunities for escaping fate by at least preventing the worst outcome or minimizing damage. They should be viewed as problem-coping strategies, perhaps in the hope that the problem will go away of its own accord.

Fatalists prefer to presume no certainties and to avoid contesting problem knowledge, ends or means by reference to their unknowability assumption. Thus, surprise dominates. Intelligence cannot improve ignorance and goals and values are luxuries. Only nondecisions or incremental decisions make sense (Hoppe 2000: 9). The nomological assumption is that human behavior is unpredictable because preference decisions are made on the basis of what a person believes to be 'real,' constrained as little as possible by any group norms.

Fatalists would undoubtedly subscribe to the belief that what is important is to make sense of reality, assuming that human behavior is unpredictable. They would thus subscribe to Weick's (1995) perception that sense making involves rolling or serial hindsight and is driven by plausibility rather than accuracy. Pugh and Hickson (1996: 124–25) describe the Weickian sense-making process: "It is a continual weaving of sense from beliefs, from the implicit assumptions,

---

to study social interaction [Giddens 2001: 688]); *ethnomethodology* ("directed to the tasks of learning how [a group's] members' actual, ordinary activities consist of methods to make practical actions, practical circumstances, commonsense knowledge of social structures, and practical sociological reasoning analyzable" [Garfinkel [1967] 1984: 4], thereby enabling a discerning of "the ways in which people construct the world" [Nightingale and Cromby 1999: 227] and "make sense of what others say and do" [Giddens 2001: 689]); and *reflexivity* ("the connection between knowledge and social life" [Giddens 2001: 697]).

from tales from the past, and from ideas about what will happen as a result of what can be done. The whole sense-making process gives ostensible orderliness to what has gone on, and, indeed, is going on." Thus, any judgments they might be expected to make they would prefer to be focused on what Vickers (1983) identifies as action judgments: What to do? How to do it? What action to take?

Decision making to fatalists involves random search behavior, inspiration, risk minimization, and perhaps even a lottery (Hood 1998). It does not matter to fatalists whether decisions are agreed to, for they consider that decisions are made for them, whether they agree or not (Schwarz and Thompson 1990: 133).

Fatalist Perspective on Risks and Risk Taking

Because fatalists see the world as being random and disordered, and thus as a zero-sum game (Thompson and Taylor 1986: 22), risks are unknowable and thus cannot be measured or evaluated. Whether societal risks should be involuntarily imposed or not is beside the point, for the powers that be will decide what they will do, and exercise the necessary coercive or threat power to do it. All that can be done is to avoid if possible, or otherwise shrug off, any risks (Douglas and Ney 1998: 137), on the grounds that the chances of gain are negligible, making failure inevitable (Douglas and Wildavsky 1882, Thompson et al. 1990). Their risk-handling style is "acceptance and deflection" (Schwarz and Thompson 1990: 67).

The salient risk, which stems from the contestable-subjectivity premises of the hermeneutic-agency methodology, is that the social world may be knowable and predictable, making their isolation no longer necessary for survival (but see Schwarz and Thompson 1990: 67).

Fatalist Shared Values and Beliefs

On Human Nature. People are unpredictably capricious, as far as fatalists are concerned.[69] Some may be benevolent, but most are malevolent and can be neither trusted[70] nor changed (Thompson et al. 1990).

On Power, Rules and Compliance. Fatalists expect people to exercise Boulder's (1990) destructive threat power or French and Raven's (1959) physical or

---

[69] As Sartre ([1946] 1973: 28) reflects: "there is no human nature, because there is no God to have a conception of it. Man simply is. Not that he is simply what he conceives himself to be, but he is what he wills, and as he conceives himself after already existing—as he wills to be after that leap toward existence. Man is nothing else but that which he makes of himself."

[70] Banfield's (1958) study of a southern Italian village's quasi-feudal relationship structures explores the boundaries of trust in a fatalist social *milieu*, which he characterizes as amoral familialism. He observes: "trust and cooperation within the family coexisted with complete distrust and morally unrestrained cheating among individuals not belonging to the same family" (p. 162; see also Bott 1957, Luhmann 1988). As Machiavelli ([1513] 1961) remarked: "men are wretched creatures who would not keep their word to you" (p. 100), and they will "always do badly by you unless they are forced to be virtuous" (p. 127).

coercive power over them. They thus expect directive rules to be imposed upon them. Or, as Jensen (1999: 174) characterizes it: *"they* decide what *I* must do." They deny any voluntary compliance obligations, which means they comply only under coercion, so giving rise to alienative compliance (Etzioni 1961).

On Blame. In the event of failure, fatalists blame fate[71] (Thompson et al. 1990), because there is no discernible causation pattern to the events surrounding failure.

On Apathy. Apathy, which is the conscious, rational way in which fatalists deal with life's anxieties (Thompson et al. 1990), which is justified on the grounds that the individual cannot make a difference.

On Freedom. The primary worry of fatalists is that whatever *negative* freedoms they have attained are not retainable, which inclines them to believe they are suffering, or to anticipate suffering, greater external control, interference and exploitation. They are instinctively skeptical of *positive* freedom, as fate would inevitably frustrate any steps they might take toward greater self-determination.

On Time and the Future. Fatalists have "involuntary myopia" (Schwarz and Thompson 1990: 67), believing that the future is unknowable and that chance and fate determine the sequence of events.

On Nature. Nature is erratic and capricious (Schwarz and Thompson 1990, Thompson et al. 1990), which makes the conservation and management of resources problematic to fatalists.

On Technology and Engineering. Fatalists see technology as yet another means of their exploitation by the powers that be. Information technology is a source of social control, but it can also facilitate their preference for privacy (Douglas and Ney 1998: 182).

On Economic Growth. Wealth creation is acceptable to fatalists, although they do not expect to benefit from its accumulation (Thompson et al. 1990).

On Scarcity. Scarcity is a capricious burden that must be borne as fate decrees, and so, to fatalists, it justifies no societal response (Thompson et al. 1990).

On Reconciling Human Wants with Scare Resources. Since neither wants nor resources can be managed, fatalists live in the hope of good fortune, but they survive by coping as best they can (Thompson et al. 1990). They view accessing resources as a lottery. As far as they are concerned the world operates without rhyme or reason, so there is no point in trying to manage needs and resources (Schwarz and Thompson 1990: 66). They have an isolated consumption style (Douglas et al. 1998: 255).

On Inequality and Envy. Equity, to fatalists, is unachievable (Schwarz and Thompson 1990: 66). Inequality is thus inevitable; envy is thus pointless (Thompson et al. 1990).

On the Market Sphere. A capricious and inhospitable realm is how fatalists see the marketplace, which they believe exploits individuals and is indifferent to

---

[71] Blaming fate is justified on the premise that no one can be a free agent and thus no one has free will, which means that no one can be held responsible, morally or otherwise, for their actions (Cicero [44 BC] 1991, Strawson 1986).

their needs. Fatalists face unfettered competition with status differences (Thompson et al. 1998: 331). Fatalists would like to see the market made less capricious, so that other people have less control over their lives. They are, however, without expectations in this regard.

On Organizing. Because fatalists exist only on the margins of the social world (Schwarz and Thompson 1990: 76),[72] they see social cooperation as problematic, they neither give nor expect respect. Thus their organizational expectations are limited to "copability (through inherent chaos)" (Schwarz and Thompson 1990: 66).

On Sacrifices for, and Voluntary Contributions to, the Collective. Fatalists, dominated by a concern for their own survival, would not willingly make sacrifices for the collective unless those sacrifices were perceived to be a means of deriving a future reward of some good fortune against fate, and provided they did not compromise the fatalists' self-chosen degree of isolation from an untrustworthy collective. With their estrangement being reinforced by their ignorance (Wildavsky and Lockhart 1998: 116), they would similarly not be willing to make any voluntary contributions to collective action unless they believed that they could otherwise be excluded from receiving any benefit produced that they value.

INDIVIDUALIST SOCIAL SOLIDARITY

Those who emphasize the importance of the individual, and his or her interests, freedom and choice, adhere to the individualist *social solidarity* (Douglas 1982b, M. Thompson 1992, Thompson and Wildavsky 1986b, Thompson et al. 1990). They see the self-determining self[73]—*homo economicus* (Douglas and Ney 1998: 22–23, 32–43)—as preliminary to any social-role engagement. Individualists are "isolated psycho-physiological entities"[74] (Schwarz and Thompson

---

[72] Some Cultural Theorists are prone to portray fatalists as "excluded at the level of institutional interaction" (Schwarz and Thompson 1990: 76; see also Thompson et al. 1990), but fatalist employees have been identified by Eilstein (1995: 71) as "closet fatalists," by Mars (1982:70) as isolated "cheats," and by Leonardi (1995: 171–73) as "criminal capitalists."

[73] Granovetter (1985: 483, 487) identifies the economist's undersocialized conception of human action.

[74] Individualists would embrace the propositions of *sociobiology* (the study of biological basis of social behavior), notably the work of Wilson (1975, 1978) and Dawkins (1976), which has its historical roots in the nineteenth-century biological determinism that followed Darwin (Degler 1991). Its central biological reductionist-essentialist proposition is that social behavior is predominantly the product of the material processes of genetics and natural selection, which generates the need for a new synthesis between evolutionary biology and the social sciences (Wilson 1978; but see Lumsden and Wilson 1981; and see also Caplan 1978, Kitcher 1885, Lewontin et al. 1984). Its premises are that the human mind, human behavior and human nature are all essentially biologically determined (Wilson 1975, 1978), and that individuals, as organisms, are survival machines with 'selfish' genes that instruct them to be selfish and inhibit their propensity to be cooperative, although cultural parameters can mediate this propensity (Dawkins 1976). The search for

1990: 68; see also Thompson and Taylor 1986: 5), bound by neither group incorporation nor prescribed roles, both of which they consider to be negotiable (Thompson et al. 1990: 6). A market-based social order is characterized by competition that involves individual consumption choices and contractual relationships (Douglas et al. 1998: 327).

People in an individualistic collective would demand maximum freedom to negotiate among themselves. They would accept no effective group boundaries and no constraints on private transactions[75] (Douglas 1982b, Wildavsky 1989a). Indeed, an individualist is "an assiduous builder of networks for private gain" (Douglas 1994: 47). The individualist *social solidarity* has a bias toward "pragmatic materialism" (Schwarz and Thompson 1990: 66).

An individualist's social context is dominated by individual autonomy, strongly competitive conditions, and thus volatility (Altman and Baruch 1998: 772). They trust others until given reason not to (Molenaers and Thompson 1999: 191).[76] Personal responsibility is based upon honor, shame, guilt, and luck (Douglas and Isherwood 1979: 40). Socialization is based on affirmative attitudes to authority and power (Hoppe 2000: 19, n. 10).

The individualist *social solidarity* is thus distinguished by the weakness of collective claims over its members (Douglas 1994: 225), who are disinterested in rituals because there is no need to reaffirm the collective reality of group life (Douglas 1970).

Wilson's new synthesis has spawned *evolutionary psychology* (the proposition that Darwinian forces of variation and natural selection shape both the human mind and human behavior; see Barkow et al. 1992); *evolutionary epistemology* (the evolutionary-based theory of knowledge; see Campbell and Cziko 1990, Fetzer 1985, Hahlweg and Hooker 1989); *evolutionary ethics* (Hurd 1996, Rachels 1990, Ridley 1986, Richards 1987, Rolston 1995, Ruse 1986, Singer 1981, Thompson 1995) embracing the genetic basis of *altruism* (Alexander 1987, Axelrod 1984, de Waal 1996, Ridley 1997, Trivers 1985, Wynne-Edwards 1986) and of *human nature* (Arnhart 1998, Blank 1995); and *evolutionary politics* or *biopolitics* (the biological and evolutionary basis of political institutions; see Beckstrom 1993, Johnson 1995; Masters 1989; Schubert and Masters 1991; Somit and Peterson 1995, 1997; Vanhanen 1992). *Evolutionary economics* does not fall under the rubric of the sociobiological new synthesis, for its starting point is the proposition that economic change must be viewed as a developmental or evolutionary process within a historical-cultural or institutional context (Andersen 1994, Nelson and Winter 1982, Witt 1993.

[75] Vroom (1960) argues that, when given opportunities to participate in decision-making, people with strong independence needs develop positive attitudinal or motivational outcomes.

[76] Arrow (1984: 104) recognizes that relations of trust and confidence may bind actors so strongly together that they "will not cheat even though it may be 'rational economic behavior' to do so." Gambetta (1988a: 9) considers "the claim that cooperation can evolve without trust...is inconceivable in relation to humans without at least a disposition to trust." Later, he soberingly concludes: "If distrust is complete, cooperation will fail among free agents" (1988b: 219). Thus, negotiations over property rights are presumed to take place within a collectively determined set of rules of the law of property, tort and contract (Mènard 2000; see also Fukuyama 1995, Pejovich 2001).

The Individualist Perspective on Motivation

The social context for individualists is one where no one has a place and commitment is only to one's self. Interpersonal relationships are governed by personal moral codes that determine how each person conducts his or her self and his or her affairs. Individualists dominate the enneagramic ideal-types that are dominated by the "emotional center"—"the heart"—which cultivates the need for "the achievement of things...so that they are recognized and acclaimed by others. There is a dependence on being popular; on being liked and trusted" (Cutting and Kouzmin 1997: 90–91).[77] Riso (1987: 26) concludes that these ideal-types are "out of touch with [their] feelings, projecting an image which substitutes for genuine feelings."[78] Thus, it would follow that their primary source of self-esteem is recognition and acclaim by the materially successful.[79] On this basis it would follow that the individualist's metalife-goal is to be recognized and acclaimed for achieving a high level of material success.[80]

---

[77] In terms of Riesman's (1950) *inner-other directedness* dichotomy, individualists would have an *inner-directedness* orientation, preferring to act independently and in accordance with their personal moral code. The needs they emphasize would be Maslow's (1970) physiological, safety (security) and esteem needs, and Riesman's (1950) and Packard's (1959) prestige needs (see also Furnham 1984, Porter and Lawler 1968).

[78] The psychological characterization of *narcissists* by Lasch (1978) is insightful (see also Baumeister 1993, Bushman and Baumeister 1998). Their pervasive, narrow-minded and overly indulgent obsession with self is promoted by their emphasis on developing and expressing characteristic attributes and potentials in a way that enables the attainment of achievements they judge to be good, thereby comprehensively disclosing their real nature. They are often successful in the outside world, because they have confidence and do not fear failure. They respond well in a crisis, because it gives them a chance to bring glory upon themselves. They are forever seeking adoration. They need parasitic relationships to reinforce their self-love, which means they want to be associated with people who reinforce their self-image. They have a low tolerance of frustration, inadequacy and strong emotional feelings, due to a lack of ego development. They are inclined to violence in the face of perceived insulting provocation. They want to punish those who threaten their favorable views of themselves. They thus feel an inner emptiness, fluctuating as they do between self-love and self-hatred.

[79] This proposition is consistent with presumptions of methodological individualism (Arrow 1994), because their utility functions would contain an element reflecting a strong preference for conspicuous consumption. For a discussion of the economics of the mind, see Rizzello 1999.

[80] Douglas (1994: 151; see also Douglas and Isherwood 1979) makes the point: "Put crudely, the reason anyone wants anything (physical needs apart) is for sharing with or showing or giving to someone else in recognition of similar gestures, gifts or services received in the past."

Individualist Perspective on Rationality

The individualist culture encourages a formal rationality that is teleological,[81] synoptical, and instrumental,[82] which serves as the basis of reasoning. People thus make purposive and predatory decisions on the basis of self-interest,[83] so as to maximize their satisfaction, given their idiosyncratic set of consistently ordered and prioritized preferences that are unconstrained by any group norms[84] (Douglas and Ney 1998: 75). For individualists, according to Schwarz and Thompson (1990: 6), "the bottom line is what they care for, not the relational niceties of the people who happen to have come together to achieve that result." [85]

---

[81] Teleological reasoning focuses on the achievement of purposes, goals and ends (*intrinsic teleology*) (Woodfield 1976).

[82] Instrumental reasoning is *practical reasoning* (O'Neill 1989), concerned with applying neo-Kantian rationalism to identify ways of achieving ends and to determine which ends or norms of human activity should provide the basis for ethical judgments on the rightness of actions (*consequential ethics*).

[83] Three justifications can be given for the proposition that people act in their self-interest: that people should act to maximize their own good (*ethical egoism*); that people actually seek to maximize their own good (*psychological egoism*); and that people who act in their own self-interest will largely or exclusively behave virtuously because that behavior enhances their wellbeing in the broadest sense (*egoistic moral motivation*) (Scheffler 1992).

[84] Individualists would view most favorably the *contractarian* proposition that moral principles, indeed even all morality, can be construed in terms of rational bargaining among self-interested individuals (Hampton 1986). Thus they can be deduced from the rational choices made, behind a veil of ignorance, by self-interested rational contractors deprived of information about their talents and attributes (Rawls 1972).

[85] Individualists are, axiologically, ethical pragmatists, rejecting dogmatic attitudes to moral precepts and principles and advocating that moral conflicts be resolved by an assessment of their consequences (Gouinlock 1972, Meyers 1986). Thus they are *ethical consequentialists* in that they prefer to judge the rightness of their actions by the value of their actual, or even intended, effects in terms of producing the most good (ethics:*act-consequentialism*, or, in utilitarian terms, *act-utilitarianism*), even if this is not the intention, which, perhaps, it should not be (a precept of indirect act-consequentialism). Moreover, actions can also be right, they assert, if they follow a set of rules general acceptance of which would best promote the most good (*rule-consequentialism* or, in utilitarian terms, *rule-utilitarianism*) (Scarre 1996, Scheffler 1988). The acceptance that the rightness of action can best be judged by the goodness of consequence is in accord with two versions of both *situational ethics* (Fletcher 1966) and *teleological ethics* (Muirhead 1932). *Empirical situationism* holds that when making a judgment on the rightness of action a morally decisive weight should be assigned to actual consequences. *Mournful realism* argues that action can be right, even if it compromises moral ideals, when it improves matters in ways a given a situation makes viable. *Teleological ethics* defines right action by reference to ethical values grounded in some conception of final purpose or good (such as *utilitarianism*). In essence, there are facts—moral facts about actual consequences, improvements, goodness of action—and rules for action that should determine what is right action (*moral realism*) (Brink 1989).

To individualists, any statement that is not empirically verifiable is relegated to the status of an expression of irrational emotions,[86] values or beliefs, and thus endogenized and assigned to a residual category of tosh, or nonsense (Williamson 1994). Hoppe (2000) describes this as functional-strategic rationality.[87] Epistemologically, individualists embrace naturalism; ontologically, they embrace agency; and thus, methodologically, they embrace naturalist agency.[88] They thus presume an objective social world, knowable by the application of the scientific method,[89] in which people are agents of their actions, with their behavior made predictable by their unconstrained self-interest. Thus, social action proceeds on the assumption that social reality can be identified through the observation of patterns in, and correlation between, forms of social behavior, viewed as assessments of material self-interest by individuals. Similarly, appropriate forms of social action must be developed on the presumption that individuals will participate only to the extent that they offer clear and unambiguous personal, material advantage (Dixon and Dogan 2002a).

Individualists continually strive to discover objective truths, those empirically measurable and verifiable observations that will unearth the objective reality, most notably, the market will, as derived from revealed preferences.

Individualist Perspective on Learning and Knowledge

Individualists have a learning style that focuses on luck (Schwarz and Thompson 1990: 66); they are forever exploring their external environment, optimistically hoping to come across new opportunities for possible exploitation.

---

[86] The proposition that emotions are primitive, dangerous or irrational has its intellectual antecedents in elements of *stoicism*. This holds that moral goodness and happiness are only achieved if people are the embodiment of perfect rationality, and avoid emotions or passions (the source of vices), which are, at root, false value judgments (Sandbach 1975).

[87] Modernists would identify with the underlying propositions of *the individual rational agent, systematic empiricism, language as representation, the idealizing of the narrative of progress* (Gergen and Thatchenkey 1998) and *propositional knowledge* (Tsoukas 1998).

[88] Embracing, inter alia (Williams and May 1996, Dogan 2001), *essentialism* ("the nature of objects [including people] is determined by their internal properties or essences" [Nightingale and Cromby 1999: 226]); *reductionism* ("complex phenomena may be explained by reference to or as a consequence of less complex processes or phenomena" [Nightingale and Cromby 1999: 228]); *materialism* ("everything that exists either is 'matter' or depends on matter for its existence" [Nightingale and Cromby 1999: 227]); *rational choice theory* (explanations of, and perhaps justifications for, the collective results of the actions of individuals premised on self-interested rational behavior in the context of a set of the transitivity and consistency preferences [see, for example, Shughart and Razzolini 2001, and for a discussion of values in rational choice theory, see Hechter 1994]); and *game theory* (a theory of rational decision making under conditions of uncertainty).

[89] These are the procedures for attaining scientific knowledge, including the formulation of theories and their testing against observation or experiment (Hanson 1958).

They are thus among March's (1999) fast learners. They value knowledge, for the market rewards new knowledge that discredits old knowledge (Douglas 1994: 32). Their information handling is "highly pragmatic and utilitarian" (Hendriks and Zouridis 1999: 123), so information must be openly and readily available for culling in the search for exploitable opportunities.

Individualist Perspective on Problem Solving and Decision Making

Individualists prefer problems to be defined in a moderately structured way (Hoppe 2000), with stress placed on means rather than goals. They prefer to presume a modest degree of agreement on ends, achieved by reference either to their 'feasibility' or 'achievability' or to their 'universality' or 'superrationality,' so as to avoid contestable objectives and values standards, the resolution of which would delay action by initiating pointless values discourses. Thus, they subscribe to the belief that these 'unexceptionable' ends (such as maximizing material wellbeing) are so crucial that they inevitably justify the means used to achieve them, despite any moral or ethical risks involved. Individualists do, however, anticipate disagreement on the certainty of problem-relevant knowledge, arguing that usable knowledge—that which satisfies self-selected aspiration levels—is best gained from the common sense and practical knowledge derived from personal networks rather than from scientific and professional experts (Hoppe 2000).

Decision analysis for individualists involves the selection from among all the alternative feasible means the one that creates the best opportunity for improvement (conceived as the most cost-effective or cost-efficient, or as generating the greatest net benefit). These feasible means determine, not only which problems are solvable, but also which goals are worth considering. Indeed, any judgments they might be expected to make they would prefer to be focused on what Vickers (1983) identifies as action judgments: What to do? How to do it? What action to take?

In terms of decision making, individualists would be inclined to shift the vital decisions onto the "old boy network" (Schwarz and Thompson 1990: 134) and a decision outcome is considered to be agreed upon only by the application of the revealed-preferences standard, involving implicit consent (Schwarz and Thompson 1990: 67). This means that if a decision is made (such as to purchase a product made by child labor), then consent is implied (in this instance, for the use of child labor in the production of that product), thereby presuming that if someone accepts a decision, it is because he or she has chosen to accept it (Schwarz and Thompson 1990: 131–32). This also means that, nomologically, human behavior is predictable on the basis of rational choice.

Individualist Perspective on Risks and Risk Taking

Because individualists see the world as benevolent, and thus as a positive-sum game (Thompson and Taylor 1986: 22), risks are perceived as creating opportunities to be exploited for personal reward. The spread of news of risk opportunities, however, must be minimized (Douglas and Ney 1998: 137), so as to avoid the possible imposition of constraints on *negative* freedom. Success is expected, as entrepreneurial talent and new technology are believed to be capable of mitigating any unforeseen consequences of risk taking (Douglas and Wildavsky 1982, Thompson et al. 1990). Societal risks need to be defined, measured, evaluated and their ethical acceptability judged by reference to the consequences of (or the good produced by) the activities giving rise to such risks. Their risk-handling style is "acceptance and absorption" (Schwarz and Thompson 1990: 67).

The salient risks facing individualists are that, given the incapacity of the naturalist-agency methodology to identify causal relationships, contractual relationships may be incomplete because of uncertainty and opportunism, and that social actions that presume agent ontology may be unable to overcome problems derived from structural imperatives, which constitute threats to market functioning (Schwarz and Thompson 1990: 67).

Individualist Shared Values and Beliefs

On Human Nature. People are, universally,[90] seen by individualists as self-determining, with the necessary hopes, beliefs and desires needed to take self-interested and self-seeking actions, which means that they are malleable. Their efforts can thus be focused and channeled by appropriate inducements (Thompson et al. 1990).

On Power, Rules and Compliance. Individualists prefer to exercise Boulder's (1990) exchange power, French and Raven's (1959) resource or reward power, or Hales' (2001) economic power, and thus have a preference for commitment rules.[91] As Mamadouh (1999b: 142) characterizes it: "*I* decide what *I* want to do." This is expected to induce instrumental compliance, based on an economic calculation of the compliance costs and benefits involved (Etzioni 1961).

On Blame. In the event of failure, individualists blame either bad luck[92] or rogues[93] (Thompson et al. 1990).

On Apathy. Apathy implies consent, as far as individualists are concerned, for participation is justified only if the benefits of participating exceed the costs of so doing (Thompson et al. 1990).

On Freedom. The primary concern of individualists is to maximize their *negative* freedom, so as to maximize their autonomy. They are hostile to any

---

[90] Individualists would gratefully accept the sociobiological proposition that there is a universal human nature—biologically determined (Wilson 1978)—that underlies psychological mechanisms (Barkow et al. 1992), which can be characterized as selfish and self-serving (Arnhart 1998, Richards 1987, Wilson 1978).

[91] Commitment rules specify commitments, promises and offerings that entail rights and duties (Onuf 1989: 87; but see also 197, 217).

[92] Blaming bad luck is justified on the premise that retrospective responsibility for the consequences of an action should be limited to that which is under the control of the action taker (Lucas 1993, Zimmerman 1988).

[93] Such blame is justified on the utilitarian grounds of the consequential reduction in happiness cause by the behavior of rogues (Klein 1990).

positive freedoms that constrain freedom of choice, because they deny people the right to exercise personal responsibility.

On Time and the Future. To individualists the short term dominates the long term (Schwarz and Thompson 1990: 67). The future is forever changing, but the continuity of the past, present and future is never seriously threatened. It abounds with opportunities awaiting entrepreneurial exploitation that will leave it better off (Douglas and Wildavsky 1982).

On Nature. Individualists are cornucopians (Thompson and Rayner 1998a: 157), who see nature as benign and forgiving (Schwarz and Thompson 1990, Thompson et al. 1990), and thus see resources as there to be exploited.

On Technology and Engineering. "Appropriate (as cheap and as cheerful as possible)" (Schwarz and Thompson 1990: 66) characterizes the individualist's view. Technology is a source of exploitable opportunities and a means of mitigating unforeseen consequences. Information technology promises reduced costs.

On Economic Growth. Wealth creation is most desirable to individualists, because there will be more material wellbeing for all, but mostly for them (Thompson et al. 1990).

On Scarcity. Scarcity justifies, in the eyes of individualists, the use of the marketplace to allocate the available scarce resources, so as to ensure that the maximum achievable level of material welfare is generated (Thompson et al. 1990).

On Reconciling Human Wants and Scarce Resources. While wants are unlimited and resources are abundant (Schwarz and Thompson 1990: 66), both are manageable as far as individualists are concerned, as is the gap between them (Thompson et al. 1990). Wants are presumed to have their exclusive origin within the individual who is able to value, rank, and trade off wants so as to be able to express them as consistent preferences (Thompson et al. 1998: 340). Thus, individualists would disapprove of sumptuary laws, or indeed, any controls whatever on individual freedom of choice. Consumerism is rampant within an individualist culture (Douglas 1994: 228).[94] Individualists, who see the world as their oyster, have a cosmopolitan consumption style (Douglas et al. 1998: 255).

On Inequality and Envy. To individualists, inequality is the product of some people being more able to appropriate the benefits of risk taking. Achieving "equality of opportunity" is appropriate (Schwarz and Thompson 1990: 66), and they would readily accept the principle of equality relative to individual contribution (Eckhoff 1974).[95] Envy thus spurs ambition and encourages risk taking (Thompson et al. 1990).

---

[94] "Human appetites are insatiable for by nature we are so constituted that there is nothing we cannot long for" (Machiavelli [1519] 1970: 268).

[95] Individualists would, of course reject the principles of equality of objective outcome, equality of outcome taking into consideration need and 'just desert,' or rank-order equality.

On the Market Sphere. The market is benign and exploitable by those who are enterprising, provided they have the necessary skills, because it is presumed to be knowable within an acceptable degree of probability. To the individualist, the market knows best, for only it can produce the most wealth from the limited resources available. It should thus be subject only to minimal public intervention. Some would argue that that should involve simply the creation of a legal framework to establish market rules under the laws of property, tort and contract.

On Organizing. Individualists create "ego-focused groups"[96] (Schwarz and Thompson 1990: 66; see also Thompson and Taylor 1986: 3–5) in which respect is based on merit. They are free to negotiate relationships on the basis of contractual exchanges (Schwarz and Thompson 1990: 75). They decide on the most appropriate institutional arrangements in the light of the relative costs and benefits of executing contracts or joining an organization.[97] As Messner (1997: 176) notes: "There is in principle no difference between contract and organization: organizations are interpreted as the sum of contractual arrangements." A feature of these groups, as far as individualists are concerned, is their "exploitability (through inherent fluidity)" (Schwarz and Thompson 1990: 66). They can be of any appropriate scale (Schwarz and Thompson 1990: 66).

On Sacrifices for, and Voluntary Contributions to, the Collective. Individualists, who are dominated by their own self-interest, would only make sacrifices for the collective if the personal costs they would incur were offset either by the intangible benefits (such as enhanced recognition and acclaim) they were likely to receive or by the expectation of reciprocity[98] in the future. Individualists, with their egoistic and hedonistic motivations, would similarly not be willing to make any contributions to collective action (Wildavsky and Lockhart 1998: 118,

---

[96] They would readily agree with the sociobiological proposition that collaboration is built only on the foundations of exploitation, selfish (or reciprocal) cooperation or nepotism (Johnson 1995). They would, of course, also agree with Bentham's remark (cited in Etzioni 1988: 5): "The community is a fictitious body, composed of…individual persons."

[97] The marketplace is the most efficacious transactional mode when all necessary and sufficient information that needs to be conveyed to all the parties concerned is contained in a price. If, however, there are quasi-moral elements in a transaction, or if a transaction requires much more information, or involves much less certain information, then a hierarchy brings together the inadequately informed parties concerned, under a degree of control (Pugh and Hickson 1996: 27; see also Williamson 1973, Williamson and Ouchi 1983). Organizations are thus devices for reducing the transaction costs—the cost of negotiating and concluding contracts and monitoring their execution (including the costs of asymmetrical information, deception, irresponsibility, risk, and unstable expectations) (Williamson 1975, 1979, 1986, 1994)—associated with uncertainty and opportunism (Hood 1998: 102, n. 3).

[98] For a sociobiological discussion of *reciprocal altruism*—the proposition that unrelated organisms that engage in mutual aid are more likely to prosper than those that do not—see Trivers 1985.

Wildavsky 1991b).[99] Their concern for their own self-interest—based on the personal costs and benefits involved in collective action—discourages collective participation so as to minimize the personal cost of the collective provision (Weimer and Vining 1992: 51).

CHANGING SOCIAL SOLIDARITY ALLEGIANCES

The legitimacy of each *social solidarity* is built on the foundations of its 'truths,' which contradict the 'truths' of each of the other *social solidarities*. They are thus self-defining adversarially, which enables their adherents to know who they are and what they stand for. They thus stand in opposition to each other (Olli 1999: 73, n.1). They are forever disorganizing and manipulating their competitors (Schwarz and Thompson 1990: 79, n. 12; see also Thompson 1983a). With their contending 'truths,' they compete for converts. They thus stand in essential contestation, which gives them, in any relational situation, a contingent temporariness.[100] Cultural Theory thus has a dynamic dimension.

There are two competing explanations of the allegiance change process. One is Ellis and Thompson's (1997a) behaviorally unsophisticated *homing-in process*, whereby each *social solidarity* is a magnet-like attractor. The alternative presented here is a *process of modest changes in incremental preference weightings* that shifts the boundaries of a person's *social-control comfort zone*[101] on the *social map* (or *social control space*) of a particular relational situation.

ELLIS AND THOMPSON'S HOMING-IN PROCESS

Ellis and Thompson (1997a: 5–7, 9, 18) have recast Cultural Theory, building on Rayner's (1992) stability hypothesis, in an attempt to transform it into a theory that seeks to explain observed behavior. In so doing they postulate a new Cultural Theory *social map*. To derive this *social map*, they have transformed the *grid* and *group* dimensions into dichotomies. For the *grid* dimension, they demarcate symmetrical and asymmetrical transactions by offering "the bold hypothesis" that social situations generate a relatively even mixture of symmetrical and asymmetrical transactions that would not be viable, which allows for a third possibility: no transactions at all (pp. 5–6). For the *group* dimension, they demarcate unfettered and fettered competition, offering "no involvement" as the

---

[99] This is rational choice's *free-rider* (nonexcludability and joint consumption) dilemma associated with collective action, which demonstrates the fallacy of composition (see Olsen 1965; but see also Marwell and Ames 1981). Ridley and Dawkins (1981: 29) cast a natural selection orientation on this dilemma: "A population of suckers (unconditional altruists) would be vulnerable to invasion by 'cheats' who accept help but do not reciprocate; cheats take the benefits but do not incur the costs and so are favored over suckers by natural selection." For a Cultural Theory perspective on this dilemma, see Douglas 1994: 129–32, Wildavsky 1993.

[100] Bhaskar (1979: 48) observes: "Because social structures are themselves social constructs, they are themselves possible objects of transformation and so may be only relatively enduring."

[101] This is analogous to Barnard's (1938) *zone of indifference*.

Cultural Theory 53

third possibility (pp. 5–6): "If you are busy bidding and bargaining with whomsoever it pleases you to bid and bargain with [that is, unfettered competition], then you are not going to be able to devote yourself to the restraining of that sort of behavior, and vice versa" (pp. 5–6). They utilized Schmutzer and Bandler's (1980) transformation matrix to establish the five *singularities*—hierarchist, enclavist, fatalist, individualist and hermit. These are the focal points of the five *basins of attraction*—four of which are defined by the configurations of symmetrical-asymmetrical transactions and the unfettered-fettered competition dichotomies, which give rise to the four group-engagement forms that constitute its *watersheds* (pp. 6–7), namely *hierarchist* (fettered competition and asymmetrical transactions), *enclavist* (fettered competition and symmetrical transactions), *fatalist* (unfettered competition and asymmetrical transactions) and *individualist* (unfettered competition and symmetrical transactions), with the residual central *basin of attraction* being the *hermit* or isolate (no involvement and no transactions). The product is "a plane [on a morphogenetic field] that contains five points, each of which is altogether different from any of the other points on that plane" (p. 7).

This recasting of Cultural Theory's *social map* enables Ellis and Thompson (1997a: 8–9) to argue that the five *singularities* provide people who move toward them with more and more shared meaning, making them magnet-like attractors engaged in a competitive *homing-in*, polarizing process. They explain this magnet-like process by drawing on Barth's (1966) transactional process. This postulates that an actor with "a ragbag of disparate values," entering into transactions with other actors with a "differently constituted ragbag," will, inevitably, experience "a perceptual mismatch between what he expects to happen and what actually happens." This mismatch initiates in him a rearranging of his values "in the hope of doing rather better next time." Over time, and following endless transactions with other actors, "his ragbag of values" gradually becomes more systematic, more internally consistent, and more like those held by the people with whom he conducts transactions. They add: "Of course, we do not all stay where we end up—there is always some movement of people between these destinations—but social life is absolutely not a one-way journey to a single destination" (p. 8). In other words, people come in thrall of a different singularity. Each singularity thus endeavors to bring people into their thrall, so as to encourage them to cross the *watershed* into its *basin of attraction*.

In Ellis and Thompson's (1997a) *homing-in process*, the *hermit zone*—the central *basin of attraction* on Cultural Theory's new *social map*—plays an important new role. It acts, they argue, as a competitive 'attractor,' as it is only by moving toward this *singularity* that people learn what they want and do not want (p. 18, n. 3). Indeed, it is the only zone "within which each of the four patterns of relationships is sufficiently dismantled to allow it then to be built up into one of the other three" (p. 9). They even go as far as to argue that if the central "hermit zone…was not there, then there would be no transactional niche where the four engaged social beings could pause to change their spots, recharge their batteries, lick their wounds, or do whatever it is that has to be done if they are to go from one corner to another" (p. 9).

THE SOCIAL-CONTROL COMFORT-ZONE CHANGE PROCESS

An alternative *social solidarity* change process builds upon Rayner's (1992) mobility hypothesis, and perceives a shifting allegiance as a series of modest incremental changes to preference weightings (Coyle and Ellis 1994: 220). These can be derived from the behavioral implications of the inherent logic of the *social map* of any relational situation. They can be used to demarcate changes in a person's *social-control comfort zone*[102] upon that *social map*, and thus changes in *social solidarity* allegiance. The theory of surprise, developed a decade or more ago, most notably by Thompson (Thompson et al. 1990, Schwarz and Thompson 1990), provides a process that explains changes in the boundaries of a person's social-control comfort zone.

Three premises underpin the proposition that people change their *social solidarity* allegiance by making incremental changes to their social control preference weightings. The first is that the only way people can change their *social solidarity* allegiance is by changing the social constraints that lead them to give credence to a particular set of moral principles (Schwarz and Thompson 1990: 7).[103] The second is that inside each person are four possible, competing sets of social proclivities (*social solidarities*), each of which is striving for dominance as he or she seeks the best way of organizing a relational situation (Douglas and Ney 1998: 93). The final premise is that individuals do not have a coherent attitude toward the *social solidarities*, which means that they can combine support, indifference and rejection of a *social solidarity* with relative ease, thus their support for one does not require the rejection of the other three (Olli 1999: 70).

Social-Control Comfort Zones

The idea that a person's social-control comfort zone can be demarcated on the *social map* of any relational situation is based on the proposition that within each person there is a cognitive system, informed by his or her preferred *social solidarity*, that provides the perceptual filter that he or she uses to frame social relationships in that relational situation. The contest taking place within each person is between competing sets of epistemological, ontological and nomological assumptions and normative values and beliefs, the outcome of which determines the tolerable limitations that he or she permits to be placed on his or her

---

[102] This proposition is consistent with Gross and Rayner's (1985) interpretation of grid-group space being continuously differentiable. Its heuristic value is not diminished by the current inability to devise interval scales that will permit the precise measurement of this space and the precise demarcation on it of a person's social-control comfort zone.

[103] Thorngate (2001: 95–105) argued that 80 years of psychology research suggests that attitudes can be formed and changed in at least four ways: *direct experience* ('hands-on' learning); *functional experience* (social pressures and conformity, whether the product of normative influences, derived from attempts to avoid embarrassment, censure or ostracism, or information influences, generated by publicly expressing a behavior or opinion); *interpersonal communications;* and *thought* (whether deductive, inductive, or imaginative. The first two, experiential factors, he considers, are more powerful than the other factors.

autonomy by others with the power to do so—that is, the *tolerated* degrees of circumscription of individual behavior by externally imposed prescription (tolerated *grid*-grip) and the tolerated degrees of subjugation of individual choice to group determination (tolerated *group*-grip). The upper and lower limits of a person's tolerated behavior circumscription (or *grid*-grip limits) and tolerated choice subjugation (or *group*-grip limits)—expressed as a set of *grid-group* coordinates on a *social map* of a particular relational situation—demarcates a person's social-control comfort zone for that relational situation. Thus in a particular relational situation people only willingly tolerate the behavior circumscription and choice subjugation that is within their *social-control comfort zone*. Insights into the nature of these comfort zones can be gleaned from Olli's (1995 and 1999) three plausible models of the individual, which allow the exploration of the relationship between people and the *social solidarity* to which they adhere.

Olli's (1995: 60) first model is the *coherent individual*, who is "consistent, solid and single-minded," and who adheres to only one *social solidarity* in all relational situations. To such a person, this dominant *social solidarity* comes "very close to becoming a permanent trait of the individual, almost like a personality." Olli argues (p. 60) that there are different degrees of coherence: strong support for one *social solidarity* and strong rejection of the other three; or strong support for one and indifference to the other three. The coherent individual's social-control comfort zone would always fall exclusively within his or her chosen *social solidarity* segment on any *social map*, and would have restricted boundaries that reflect his or her intolerance of widely differing degrees of *group*-grip and *grid*-grip.

Olli's (1999: 60) second model is the *sequential individual*, who has the ability to switch between *social solidarities* as if they were roles. Such a person can "quickly adapt by changing their biases to a new set of values and attitudes thereby still being internally coherent;...a rejection of one bias follows the acceptance of another bias depending on the context." The sequential individual's social-control comfort zone in any relational situation would also fall exclusively within limits defined by his or her preferred *social solidarity* on that *social map*. It would have expansive boundaries that reflect his or her adaptability, and thus ability, to accommodate wide degrees of *group*-grip and *grid*-grip in different relational situations.

Olli's (1999: 60–61) third model is the *synthetic individual*, who is capable of learning about different *social solidarities* in a manner that makes them "almost turn into schemes or versatile jigsaw pieces of knowledge." Such people who are not "internally coherent in terms of cultural biases, but they display an individual stability and consistency across different contexts...[and] they have a greater repertoire of ways of acting (and justifying) in a given situation." The synthetic individual's *social-control comfort zone* would have expansive boundaries within their preferred *social solidarity* segment of a *social map*, which reflect his or her ability to combine rejection of and support for different *social solidarities* in different ways. Thus he or she would be able to cope with ambiguity, and therefore with very wide degrees of *group*-grip and *grid*-grip.

To explain what causes people to redefine their social-control comfort zone boundaries is to explain the process by which they shift their *social solidarity* allegiance.

The Theory of Surprise

Cultural Theorists have long drawn upon a theory of surprise[104] to explain shifting *social solidarity* allegiances in a particular relational situation (Thompson et al. 1990; see also Grendstad and Selles 1999; Price and Thompson 1997; M. Thompson 1998a, 1992). Thompson and Taylor (1986: 1) argue that people consider changing their *social solidarity* allegiance[105] as a result of being surprised by the unexpected outcomes of events.[106] This occurs when certainties are in conflict with the expectations that flow from a socially constructed system of knowledge.[107] They then postulate three surprise axioms (p. 2): "an event is never surprising in itself"; "it is potentially surprising only in relation to a particular set of convictions about how the world is"; and "it is actually surprising only if it is noticed by the holder of that particular set of convictions."

The occurrence of unexpected outcomes of events may be surprising but, as Festinger (1957) found, facts that disprove belief may, indeed, initially reinforce people's beliefs, making them prone to Hirschman's (1991: 168) "rhetoric of intransigence." There is, however, a point reached—a disillusionment threshold—where the cumulative effect of belief-disconfirming facts serves to disconfirm or disprove beliefs, so initiating a cognitive dissonance[108] (Festinger 1957). This emotional state demands, in the first instance, that the validity of their chosen *social solidarity's* worldview be questioned, because it would seem no longer to be capable of delivering on its expectations. Ultimately, however, it would necessitate the instigation of the value and attitudinal changes needed to

---

[104] The Cultural Theory of surprise has its origins in the literature on ecology (see Holling 1986).

[105] Grendstad and Selles (1999: 50, citing M. Thompson 1992) argue that Cultural Theory cannot predict who becomes a fatalist, a hierarchist, an individualist or an enclavist. They argue that it can, however, predict what sorts of defectors will tend to arise as a result of what sorts of surprises are encountered. This proposition is explored subsequently.

[106] What Bhaskar (1979: 47) speaks of as "historically significant events."

[107] Thompson and Taylor (1986: 32) also argue, at the metaphysical level, that a surprise can be "queerer than we imagine" (when what is not yet known but is knowable in the future—the knowable future certainties—could, in the future, be in conflict with what that future knowledge is now imagined to be on the basis of a contemporaneous, socially constructed system of knowledge); or perhaps even "queerer than we could imagine" (when what is not now known and is unknowable in the future—the unknowable future certainties—could, in the future, be in conflict with what we could imagine that future knowledge to be on the basis of a socially constructed system of knowledge in the future).

[108] Cognitive dissonance is "the emotional state set up when two simultaneously held attitudes or cognitions are inconsistent or when there is a conflict between belief and overt behavior" (Reber 1995: 134).

modify belief patterns so as to bring them into alignment with their perception of reality. Or, as Young expresses it: "messages [about the assumptive world] travel 'up the line' and may lead to some adjustment in assumptions" (K. Young 1979: 350).

The point at which *social solidarity* adherents become disillusioned enough to begin questioning their assumptive world depends on how committed they are to remaining in their social-control comfort zone; that is, to maintaining their current patterns of interpersonal relationships (reflected in their degree of toleration of *grid-grip*) and their shared values and attitudes (reflected in their degree of toleration of *group-grip*). This depends on four factors: first, how important those interpersonal relationships and shared values and attitudes are to the maintenance of their self-esteem; second, how important their current metalife goal is to them; third, how much they are out of touch with those aspects of their character that would come to the fore if they were to embark on a *social solidarity* allegiance change; and finally, the extent to which an alternative *social solidarity* not only can enhance the degree to which they value themselves but also can give them an acceptable and achievable new metalife goal.

If Olli's coherent individuals are confronted with a surprise then they may well choose not to notice it, or if it is noticed, it may well reinforce their faith in their chosen *social solidarity*, thus making them more intransigent. In either case there would be no incentive for them to change their *social-control comfort-zone* boundaries and thus, ultimately, their *social solidarity* allegiance. If, however, the cumulative effects of a long sequence of surprises moves them to their disillusionment threshold, then their *social-control comfort-zone* boundaries would have to change in order to dissipate the effects of the cognitive dissonance they are experiencing. If these boundary changes take them across a *grid* or *group* divide toward another *social solidarity* on a *social map*, then their *social solidarity* allegiance will have changed in that relational situation, albeit only with considerable reluctance. Because they have explicitly and consciously rejected, or, at least, are quite indifferent to, the truth propositions of the alternative *social solidarities*, they would expect, essentially, to have to effect a personality change in order to permit them to accept, as their own, a new set of beliefs, values, attitudes, practices and standards that are in better alignment with their perception of reality.

If Olli's sequential individuals are confronted with a surprise, they will notice. They would quickly become disillusioned with their chosen *social solidarity*. They would then expect to adapt by changing their social-control comfort-zone boundaries, so as to dissipate the effects of the cognitive dissonance that they are experiencing. Should this expectation not be realized immediately, then further surprises and disillusionment will compel them to continue changing iteratively their social-control comfort-zone boundaries until the cognitive dissonance they are experiencing is diminished to a tolerable level, even if this takes them across one of the *grid* or *group* divides, thereby requiring them to accept the truth propositions of another *social solidarity*.

If Olli's synthetic individuals are confronted with a surprise, then it will be noticed but, because of their ability to cope with internal incoherency, they would be flexible enough to deal with its ambiguities.[109] They would expect to be able to reduce their cognitive dissonance to a tolerable level by drawing upon the narratives of more than one competing *social solidarity* to redefine their social-control comfort-zone boundaries, and so reconceptualize their cognitive map of reality. Should this expectation not be immediately realizable, then further surprises and disillusionment will insist that they change their *social solidarity* allegiance, iteratively, until the cognitive dissonance is diminished to a tolerable level.

What, then, are the surprises—the unexpected outcomes of events—that could give rise to a state of cognitive dissonance in adherents to particular *social solidarities*?

Hierarchists' Salient Surprise. Hierarchists will be surprised if experts are repeatedly unable to understand a sequence of events and its outcomes, and thus unable to understand the nature, causation and consequences of problems or to determine their solutions. This would mean that reality and its risks are not knowable to within an acceptable degree of probability by experts, and thus cannot be effectively managed by experts.

Enclavists' Salient Surprise. Enclavists will be surprised if they cannot repeatedly negotiate an inclusive consensus on the causes and consequences of a sequence of events and its outcomes, and thus are unable to build a consensus on the nature, causation and consequences of problems and their solutions. This would mean that the set of mutual understandings that provide the basis for determining mutually acceptable joint perspectives cannot be generated by a group consensus, achieved through norming and forming discourses on contestable values standards. Thus, reality and its risks are not knowable to an acceptable degree of probability, and therefore cannot be effectively managed by them.

Fatalists' Salient Surprise. Fatalists will be surprised if anyone is repeatedly able to understand a sequence of events to the point that they can explain why, how and with what consequences events occurred, and thus are able to understand the nature, causation and consequences of problems and to determine their solutions. This would mean that the world they thought to be capricious is, indeed, knowable to an acceptable degree of probability, and thus can be effectively managed.

Individualists' Salient Surprise. Individualists will be surprised if law abiding buyers and sellers, with a sense of personal responsibility, find that they are repeatedly unable to understand a sequence of events and their outcomes in terms of market forces, and thus are unable to understand the nature, causation and consequences of problems or to determine their solutions. This would mean that reality and its risks are not knowable to within an acceptable degree of probability by market operators using new technology, and thus cannot be effectively managed by them.

---

[109] Sociologists speak of a person having a *dual consciousness*, and thus being able to simultaneously hold two apparently inconsistent sets of beliefs that are derived from a dominant and a subordinate culture or value system (Marshall 1998: 174).

From Surprise to Disillusionment: On Crossing the Divides

It is difficult to predict when people will abandon their adherence to one *social solidarity* and move toward another. Whenever that decision is made, however, it suggests that they are confronting their disillusionment threshold in that particular relational situation, because the cumulative effect of the surprises they have experienced has disillusioned them enough to want to question their *social solidarity* allegiance. They must then decide which of the competing *social solidarities* they should move toward in order to dissipate the effects of the cognitive dissonance that they are experiencing. Of crucial importance here are their perceptions of adherents to the other *social solidarities*, and what they perceive to be the self-esteem and metalife-goal implications of the disillusionment they are experiencing.

Hierarchists on Enclavists. Hierarchists consider that enclavists belong to cliquish, self-absorbed, and faction-ridden groups, with no respect for the authority of the collective. Both have a commitment to a social unit larger than the individual, but the issue in contention is the enclavist's demand for equality in his or her social relationships. This would require hierarchists to tolerate, at least, a weaker *grid*-grip.

Hierarchists would be attracted to the enclavist *social solidarity* if it becomes apparent to them that their physiological and psychological safety and security needs are at risk of not being met by the hierarchy. Then they would have to be willing to express their concerns about the hierarchy's limitations and to engage with like-minded people to construct mutually acceptable joint worldview perspectives that evoke moral commitment. This must be achieved through norming and forming discourses on contestable values standards. This would require them to disengage from their structured, orderly and paternalistic group and engage with people who share their concerns, which would, in turn, require them to negotiate their relationship with other people as equals, and to demonstrate continually their commitment to the common cause. As a result, they would have to confront both their reluctance to determine their interpersonal relationships without reference to authority figures, and their willingness to value the recognition and acclaim of those who are committed to their new common cause more highly than the approval of authority figures.

Hierarchists on Fatalists. Hierarchists consider fatalists to be deviant (Schwarz and Thompson 1990: 79, n. 15), for the hierarchy must be all-inclusive, with no outcasts (Thompson et al. 1999b: 23, n. 14) and no one is permitted to violate the established norms. Fatalists are considered deviant because they existentially "emphasize human limitations and the tragic dimensions of experience" (Yalom 1980: 247), and because they question the collective's motivation and capacity. Both have their social relationships circumscribed by externally imposed prescriptions, but the issue in contention is the fatalists' indifference to the paternalistic protection offered by the collective. This would require hierarchists to tolerate, at least, a weaker *group*-grip.

Hierarchists would be attracted to the fatalist *social solidarity* if it becomes apparent to them that their future is in the hands of unknowing experts who are too innovative and take too many risks, which means that their safety and security needs are at risk of not being met. Their destiny has, thus, become a matter of fate. This would require them to abandon their structured, orderly and paternalistic group, and become loners and survivors who are indifferent to authority. As a result, they would have to confront both their reluctance to act without the approval of authority figures, in fear of being excluded from the paternalistic protection offered by the collective, and the need to accept that seeing themselves as survivors despite the odds that fate decrees is more important than gaining the approval of authority figures.

Hierarchists on Individualists. Hierarchists consider individualists to be self-interested and self-centered people who place too little value on either the collective or its authority. The issue in contention is fundamental: the individualist's insistence on commitment to the self and self-interest and to equality and reciprocity in his or her social relationships. This would require hierarchists to tolerate both a weaker *grid*-grip and a weaker *group*-grip.

Hierarchists would be attracted to the individualist *social solidarity* if it becomes apparent to them that, because their physiological and psychological safety and security needs are at risk of not being met by the hierarchy, they must now be permitted to negotiate freely their own contractual relationships, as they see fit. This would require them to abandon their structured, orderly and paternalistic group, and become networking risk takers, seeking conspicuous material success. As a result, they would have to confront their reluctance to determine their interpersonal relationships without reference to the authority figures, their fear of being excluded from the paternalistic protection of the collective if they act without authority-figure approval, and their need to accept that the recognition and acclaim of materially successful people is more important than the approval of authority figures.

Enclavists on Hierarchists. Enclavists consider that hierarchists belong to entrenched hierarchical citadels of privilege that are forever seeking to exercise control over people. Both have a commitment to a social unit larger than the individual, but the issue in contention is the hierarchist's acceptance of externally imposed circumscription of his or her social interactions. This would require enclavists to tolerate, at least, a stronger *grid*-grip.

Enclavists would be attracted to the hierarchist *social solidarity* if two matters become evident to them. One is that they cannot negotiate the mutually acceptable solutions to value-important problems that will win them the recognition and acclaim they expect. The other is that hierarchical experts can, after all, understand such problems, and indeed have found appropriate solutions that involve socially imposed constraints on behavior that are compatible with their values framework. This would require them to disengage from their personally negotiated relationships, as equals, with committed people and to engage with others in a structured, orderly and paternalistic hierarchy. As a result, they would have to confront both their true feelings in support of inequality and differentiation, which have been suppressed by their need to retain membership in their egalitarian communities of interest by maintaining an image of being likable, trustworthy and committed to a common cause, and their need to accept that the approval of authority figures is more important than the recognition and acclaim of those who are similarly committed to the common cause.

Enclavists on Fatalists. Enclavists consider fatalists to be downtrodden (Schwarz and Thompson 1990: 79, n. 15) and fatalistically preoccupied with the human condition. They question the point of engaging in values discourses for group-forming and -norming purposes. They also do not reciprocate their "love for the oppressed" (Thompson et al. 1999b: 23, n. 14). The issue in contention is fundamental: the fatalist's unwillingness to become engaged with any collective while being willing to accept externally imposed circumscription of his or her social interactions. This would require enclavists to tolerate both a stronger *grid*-grip and a weaker *group*-grip.

Enclavists would be attracted to the fatalist *social solidarity* if two matters become evident to them. One is that they could not negotiate the mutually acceptable solutions to value-important problems that will win them the recognition and acclaim they are seeking. The other is if they consider their future to be in the hands of those in authority who are too innovative and take too many risks because they do not share their values. Their destiny has, thus, become a matter of fate. This would require them to disengage from their personally negotiated relationships, as equals, with committed people and become loners and survivors who are detached from any values discourse. As a result, they would have to confront both their suppressed true feelings in support of not being committed to anyone, including themselves, or any cause; and their need to accept that seeing themselves as survivors, despite the odds that fate decrees, is more important than the recognition and acclaim of those committed to the common cause that they had previously valued.

Enclavists on Individualists. Enclavists consider individualists to be self-interested and self-centered people who place too much value on exploiting opportunities without reference to values discourse for group-forming and -norming purposes. Both reject externally imposed circumscription of their social interactions, but the issue in contention is the individualist's commitment only to self and to self-interest. This would require enclavists to tolerate, at least, a weaker *group*-grip.

Enclavists would be attracted to the individualist *social solidarity* if it becomes apparent to them that they could not negotiate the mutually acceptable solutions to value-important problems that will win them the recognition and acclaim they expect; and if they are convinced that the only solution is to be permitted to negotiate freely their own contractual relationships. This would require them to abandon their personally negotiated egalitarian relationships with committed people, and become networking risk takers seeking conspicuous material success. As a result they would have to confront both their suppressed true feelings in support of their commitment to themselves and to self-interest, and their need to accept that the recognition and acclaim of materially successful people is more important than the recognition and acclaim of those committed to the common cause that they had previously valued.

Fatalists on Hierarchists. Fatalists consider that hierarchists belong to entrenched hierarchical citadels of privilege that are forever seeking, perhaps conspiratorially, to dominate and marginalize the individual. Both have their social relationships circumscribed by externally imposed prescriptions, but the issue in contention is the hierarchist's commitment to a social unit larger than the individual. This would require fatalists to tolerate, at least, a stronger *group*-grip.

Fatalists would be attracted to the hierarchist *social solidarity* if it becomes apparent to them that they no longer need to survive in isolation, because the world and its risks are knowable, after all, by the hierarchical experts; and that they must now embrace socially imposed roles and rituals in order to be included as recipients of whatever benefits (including costs avoided) are to be derived from being a member of an hierarchy. This would require them to abandon their isolationism and indifference to authority, and become members of a structured, orderly and paternalistic hierarchy. As a result, they would have to confront both their inability to engage personally with an hierarchically ordered social environment, and the need to accept that gaining the approval of new authority figures is more important than seeing themselves as survivors despite the odds that fate decrees.

Fatalists on Enclavists. Fatalists consider that enclavists belong to cliquish, self-absorbed and faction-ridden groups that are perpetually protesting and proselytizing in their search for converts. The issue in contention is fundamental: the enclavist's demand for both group engagement and equality in their social relationships. This would require fatalists to tolerate both a stronger *group*-grip and a weaker *grid*-grip.

Fatalists would be attracted to the enclavist *social solidarity* if it becomes apparent to them that they no longer needed to survive in isolation, because the world and its risks are knowable, after all, by people engaging with like-minded, committed others in the construction of mutually acceptable joint perspectives on the world and its risks that evoke moral commitment, achieved through group-norming and -forming discourses on contestable values standards. This would require them to abandon their isolationism and indifference to values discourse and to engage with like-minded people who share their concerns, and negotiate their relationships with them as equals; and to demonstrate continually their commitment to the common cause. As a result, they would have to confront both their inability not only to engage personally with an egalitarian social environment, but also to relate to their human environment closely enough to engender a commitment to any cause; and their need to accept that gaining the recognition and acclaim of those who are committed to their new common cause is more important than seeing themselves as capable survivors, despite the odds that fate decrees.

Fatalists on Individualists. Fatalists consider individualists to be self-interested and self-centered people who are forever seeking to exploit hapless others. Both reject group engagement, but the issue in contention is the individualist's insistence on equality and reciprocity in his or her social relationships. This would require fatalists to tolerate, at least, a weaker *grid*-grip.

Fatalists would be attracted to the individualist *social solidarity* if it becomes apparent that they no longer needed to survive in isolation, because the world and its risks are, after all, knowable by those operating in the marketplace, and thus that they must now be permitted to negotiate freely their own contractual relationships. This would require them to abandon their isolationism and indifference to material success, and become networking risk takers seeking material success. As a result, they would have to confront both their inability to relate personally to their human environment closely enough to identify exploitable entrepreneurial opportunities, and their need to accept that gaining the recognition and acclaim of materially successful people is more important than seeing themselves as survivors despite the odds that fate decrees.

Individualists on Hierarchists. Individualists consider that hierarchists belong to entrenched hierarchical citadels of privilege that are forever seeking to constrain their negative freedom. The issue in contention is fundamental: the hierarchist's insistence on group engagement on the basis of hierarchically determined inequality and differentiation in their social relationships. This would require individualists to tolerate both a stronger *grid*-grip and a stronger *group*-grip.

Individualists would be attracted to the hierarchist *social solidarity* if it becomes apparent to them that their need to gain power and to be recognized and acclaimed by materially successful people can no longer be met because the market is now going to be governed by hierarchical experts who have demonstrated their understanding of the market, its problems and their solutions, which means that they must now accept the imposition of constraints on their behavior and socially imposed roles and rituals. This would require them to abandon their actively self-interested preference for networked, spontaneous exchange relationships and become members of a structured, orderly and paternalistic hierarchy. As a result they would have to confront both their true feelings in favor of unequal engagements with people, which have been suppressed by their need to maintain an image of being likable and trustworthy opportunists who establish relationships for mutual benefit; and their need to accept that gaining the approval of authority figures is more important than gaining the recognition and acclaim of materially successful people.

Individualists on Enclavists. Individualists consider that enclavists belong to cliquish, self-absorbed, and faction-ridden groups that are too intent on winning converts by means of protests and values discourses. Both reject group circumscription of their social relationships, but the issue in contention is the enclavist's demand for group engagement with a concomitant values commitment. This would require individualists to tolerate, at least, a stronger *group*-grip.

Individualists would be attracted to the enclavist *social solidarity* if it becomes apparent to them that their need to gain power and to be recognized and acclaimed by the materially successful cannot be met because market operators are unable to take risks that are consistent with their values framework. This means they must express their concerns about inappropriate risk taking in the marketplace, and must be willing to engage with like-minded people to construct mutually acceptable joint perspectives on the world and its risks that evoke a moral commitment, which is achieved through discourses on contestable values and standards. This would require them to abandon their actively self-interested preference for networked, spontaneous exchange relationships and engage with people who share their concerns and continually demand that everyone demonstrate commitment to the common cause. As a result, they would have to confront both their suppressed true feelings in favor of making the necessary commitment to a socially contracted set of values, and their need to accept that gaining the recognition and acclaim of those who are committed to their new common cause is more important than gaining the recognition and acclaim of materially successful people.

Individualists on Fatalists. Individualists consider fatalists to be unmotivated (Schwarz and Thompson 1990: 80, n. 15) and preoccupied with the human condition, forever questioning the point of participating (Thompson et al. 1999b: 23, n. 14) or of taking risky initiatives. Both reject group engagement, but the issue in contention is the fatalists' willingness to accept externally imposed circumspection on their social relationships. This would require individualists to tolerate, at least, a stronger *grid*-grip.

Individualists would be attracted to the fatalist *social solidarity* if it becomes apparent to them that their need to be recognized and acclaimed for their material success could never be met because the marketplace is so discredited that they no longer have any autonomy to determine their own standing in it. Thus, their future is in the hands of both the privileged in authority, who are forever seeking to enforce collective choices and circumscribe social interactions, and hostile dissidents, who are forever demanding that innovative and risky courses of action be taken. Their destiny has, thus, become a matter of fate. This would require them to abandon their actively self-interested preference for networked, spontaneous exchange relationships and to become loners and survivors who are indifferent to material success. As a result they would have to confront both their suppressed true feelings about no longer being committed to themselves, and their need to accept that being perceived as a survivor, despite the odds that fate decrees, is more important than gaining the recognition and acclaim of materially successful people.

Beyond Disillusionment, Toward Despair

A surprise may be serious enough to overwhelm all the *social solidarities.* They are all flawed because their epistemological and ontological foundations are fundamentally flawed. Thus, the cognitive dissonance being experienced cannot be diminished to a tolerable level by changing *social solidarity* allegiance. Disillusionment would then accumulate further until a despair threshold is reached. At this point, the disillusioned would be willing to acknowledge that no *social solidarity* can provide them with the truth propositions that allow their cognitive map of reality to deliver on their expectations.

Insights into the behavioral responses that might flow from crossing this despair threshold can be gleaned from Merton's (1957) analysis of individual adaptation to anomic situations. He identified five behavioral responses that individuals adopt in situations where the socially constructed cultural goals that a society considers worth striving for are judged not to be within their reach: *conformism* (continuing to seek those goals in the generally accepted way, anyway, in the hope of eventual success, because that is what is expected of them), *ritualism* (adhering to the generally accepted rituals surrounding the seeking of those goals, so as to be seen to be goal seeking, but without any hope of success), *innovation* (finding unconventional ways of achieving those goals), *retreatism* (abandoning all hope of achieving those goals by any means) and *rebellion* (abandoning the desire to achieve those goals and substituting other personal goals in their stead).

CONCLUSION

Cultural Theory posits four *social solidarities*, one associated with each of the four types of social beings. Each has a distinctive set of sociocognitive and motivational perspectives, with a concomitant set of shared values, beliefs and attitudes. Each thus has an idiosyncratic set of truth propositions, which inevitably stand in contradistinction to the truths posited by the other *social solidarities*. Each stands opposed as competitor, forever seeking converts with their contending truths.

Both the attractiveness and repulsiveness of these competing truth propositions determine people's allegiance to a particular *social solidarity* in a particular relational situation. The two competing explanations of the *social solidarity* allegiance change process are Ellis and Thompson's (1997a) behaviorally unsophisticated *homing-in process*, invoking the metaphor of a magnet; and *an incremental social control preference weightings change process*, invoking the metaphor of a gradually changing zone of indifference (Barnard 1938).

The nature of the truth propositions accepted by adherents to each of the *social solidarities* will now be articulated for corporate governance (in Chapter 3), for societal governance (in Chapter 4) and for global governance (in Chapter 5). Then the implications of the antagonisms between adherents to *social solidarities* for the governance capacity, and governability will be explored (in Chapters 6 and 7).

Appendix 2.1
The Competing Social Solidarities: Perspectives and Shared Values, Beliefs and Changing Allegiance

Dimension	Hierarchist	Enclavist	Fatalist	Individualist
Grid-group balance:	Strong *group*/strong *grid*.	Strong *group*/weak *grid*.	Weak *group*/strong *grid*.	Weak *group*/weak *grid*.
Group-engagement preference:	Collectivized with inequality (nested, bounded groups that are large and controllable because of their inherent orderliness). Loyalty expected and given.	Collectivized with equality (egalitarian bounded groups that are small and sustainable because of their inherent fragility). Voice expected and given.	Individualized with inequality (at the margins of organized patterns that can be coped with because of their inherent chaos). No loyalty or voice expectations.	Individualized with equality (ego-focused groups that are appropriately sized so as to be exploitable because of their inherent fluidity). Loyalty given only if profitable to do so.
Dominant motivation:	To be approved by authority figures so as to be recognized as a member of a hierarchy that promises the satisfaction of their physical and psychological security needs.	To achieve the recognition and acclaim of people in the group to which they belong because they are popular, committed and trusted.	To survive against the odds.	To win the highest level of material success possible, so as to be recognized and acclaimed by other materially successful people.

Dimension	Hierarchist	Enclavist	Fatalist	Individualist
Primary source of self-esteem:	Approval by authority figures.	Recognition and acclaim by those committed to a common cause.	Seeing themselves as survivors against the odds.	Recognition and acclaim by the materially successful for being one of them.
Primary metalife goal:	To be approved by authority figures.	To be acclaimed by the committed.	To have self-respect as a survivor against the odds.	To be acclaimed by materially successful people.
Epistemology:	Naturalism.	Hermeneutics.	Hermeneutics.	Naturalism.
Ontology:	Structuralism.	Structuralism.	Agency.	Agency.
Methodology:	Naturalist structuralism.	Hermeneutic structuralism.	Hermeneutic agency.	Naturalist agency.
Rationality:	Bounded and functionally analytic.	Communicative and values-based.	Nonrational, inspirational and strategic.	Instrumental, synoptical, functional and strategic.
Reality:	Objective, with the truth discernible by rational thought using scientific method.	Socially constructed by discourse.	Individually determined by what is perceived to be true.	Objective, as expressed by the revealed preferences.
Authority of knowledge:	Only if verified by rational thought using scientific method.	None axiomatically given, but it can be validated by discourse.	None, as knowledge is irrelevant.	Only if measurable and verifiable.

Appendix 2.1 (cont'd)

Dimension	Hierarchist	Enclavist	Fatalist	Individualist
Nomology:	Human behavior predictable on the basis of rational thought constrained by group norms.	Human behavior predictable on the basis of group-constructed mutual understandings.	Human behavior is unpredictable.	Human behavior predictable on the basis of rational choice.
Judgment:	Reality.	Value.	Action.	Action.
Learning style:	Anticipation.	Trial without error.	Trial and error.	Luck.
Learning speed:	Slow.	Slow.	Fast.	Fast.
Problem solving:	Problems should be highly structured and thus be made decomposable.	Problems should be moderately structured with stress placed on the evaluation dimension.	Problems should neither have a structure imposed upon them nor have their causation presumed.	Problems should be moderately structured, with stress placed on means rather than goals.
Model of consent:	Hypothetical consent.	Direct consent.	Nonconsent.	Implicit consent.
Standards of consent:	Natural (or other ideal).	Expressed preferences.	None.	Revealed preferences.
Risk taking:	Success is expected.	Failure is expected.	Failure inevitable.	Rewarded success expected.
Risk-handling style:	Rejection and absorption.	Rejection and deflection.	Acceptance and deflection.	Acceptance and absorption.

Dimension	Hierarchist	Enclavist	Fatalist	Individualist
Decision making:	Prefers high degree of certainty of problem-relevant knowledge and of agreement on ends. Correct decisions generate satisfactorily efficient and effective means, derived from cognitive effort.	Prefers to presume moderate degree of certainty of problem-relevant knowledge but anticipates intense disagreement about ends. Correct decisions require 'them' to agree with 'our' decision.	Prefers to presume the unknowability of causation, consequences and remedies. Correct decisions involve random search behavior, inspiration, and risk minimization, even lotteries.	Prefers to presume a modest degree of agreement on ends and to avoid contesting objectives and values standards by reference to 'feasible' or 'achievable' ends, or to 'universal' or 'suprarational,' thus 'unexceptionable' ends. Correct decisions create the best opportunity for improvement.
Shared values and beliefs:				
on time:	Balance between short and long term.	Long term dominates short term.	Involuntary myopia.	Short term dominates long term.

Appendix 2.1 (cont'd)

Dimension	Hierarchist	Enclavist	Fatalist	Individualist
Shared values and beliefs (cont'd):				
on nature:	Bountiful within limits but perverse, vulnerable yet tolerant.	Ephemeral, fragile and unforgiving.	Erratic and capricious.	Benign and forgiving.
on technology:	Instrumental value to the expert.	Source of unacceptable risks.	Means of exploitation.	Source of exploitable opportunities.
on the market:	Isomorphic, perverse but tolerant of public intervention.	Inhospitable, threatens equality of condition.	Capricious, inhospitable, and exploitative.	Benign and exploitable.
on economic growth:	Desirable, provided sacrifices made by the collective leads to collective gain.	Of little interest, as abundance makes the maintenance of equality problematic.	Acceptable, but individuals should not expect to benefit.	Most desirable, as more material wellbeing is produced for everyone, but mostly for them personally.
on scarcity:	Justifies allocation by direct bureaucratic means, to ensure that the collective is adequately resourced.	Justifies collective actions to change inegalitarian lifestyles.	Justifies nothing, it is a capricious burden that must be borne.	Justifies the u: marketplace tc resources.

Dimension	Hierarchist	Enclavist	Fatalist	Individualist
Shared values and beliefs (cont'd):				
on human want:	The hierarchy prescribes the wants that should be met from available resources.	Needs to bring human demands down to within nature's frugal limits.	Neither wants nor resources can be managed.	Both wants and scarce resources are manageable, as is the gap between them.
on equality:	Equality is generally threatening. Envy must be controlled.	Equality of outcome is a right. Envy must be controlled.	Equality is unachievable. Envy is pointless.	Equality of opportunity permits everybody to exploit profitable risks. Envy spurs ambition.
on human nature:	People are sinful but can be redeemed by good institutions.	People are born good but corrupted by power and evil institutions in the market and public spheres.	People are capricious (some are benevolent, but most are malevolent) and cannot be trusted or changed.	People are self-seeking, and their efforts can be channeled by appropriate incentives.
on freedom:	Concerned with constraining *negative* freedoms; sees *positive* freedoms as threatening.	Concerned with enhancing *positive* freedoms, which justifies constraining *negative* freedoms.	Concern is with maximizing *negative* freedoms; skeptical of *positive* freedoms.	Concern is with maximizing *negative* freedoms, hostile to *positive* freedoms.
on blame:	Assigned to deviants.	Assigned to outsiders or traitors within.	Assigned to fate.	Assigned to bad luck or rogue behavior.

Appendix 2.1 (cont'd)

Dimension	Hierarchist	Enclavist	Fatalist	Individualist
Shared values and beliefs (cont'd):				
on apathy:	Implies consent.	Undesirable, but justified if participation is not genuine.	Justified, as participation makes no difference.	Implies consent.
on collective action:	Willing to make sacrifices and voluntary contributions, if expected.	Willing to make sacrifices and voluntary contributions, if collectively agreed.	Willing to make sacrifices and voluntary contributions, if good fortune expected.	Willing to make sacrifices and voluntary contributions, if benefits exceed costs incurred.
Salient risk faced:	Loss of control or public trust.	People cannot agree on a course and voluntary compliance cannot be achieved.	Isolation is no longer necessary for survival because the world is knowable and predictable.	Incomplete contractual relationships and problems derived from structural imperatives.
Salient surprise:	If hierarchical experts are, repeatedly, unable to understand the nature and the causation of problems or their solution.	If 'we' cannot negotiate with 'them' to determine a mutually acceptable joint perspectives on the causation of problems or their solution.	If hierarchical experts or market operators are, repeatedly, able to understand the nature and causation of problems and their solutions.	If market operators, repeatedly, find that they are unable to attribute problem causation to nonmarket factors or to determine a market solution.

Dimension	Hierarchist	Enclavist	Fatalist	Individualist
Disillusionment thresholds for a shift in social solidarity allegiance toward:				
hierarchist:		Accept that the hierarchical experts have found solutions to problems that are compatible with their values framework.	Accept that the hierarchical experts understand, and can solve, their problems.	Accept that the hierarchical experts are going to govern the marketplace.
enclavist:	Accept that they must express their concerns about the limitations of hierarchical experts and demands that all risks be minimized.		Accept that they must express their demands for experts and market operators to be used to manage risks better.	Accept that they must express their concerns about the inability of the market to take risks consistent with their value framework.
fatalist:	Accept that their future is in the incompetent hands of those who can exercise control over them.	Accept that no solution to value-important problems can be found that is consistent with their value framework.		Accept that the marketplace is so discredited that they no longer have autonomy to determine their own standing.

Appendix 2.1 (cont'd)

Dimension	Hierarchist	Enclavist	Fatalist	Individualist
Disillusionment thresholds for a shift in social solidarity allegiance toward (cont'd):				
individualist:	Accept that they must now embark on individual risk-taking initiatives that exploit market opportunities.	Accept that the solution to value-important problems involves exploiting market opportunities.	Accept that they must embark on individual risk-taking initiatives that exploit market opportunities.	
Adjustments required to change social solidarity allegiances to:				
hierarchist:		Have a common acceptance of group belonging, but must confront their true feelings in favor of inequality and differentiation.	Have a common acceptance of the group circumscription interactions, but must confront their inability to engage personally with a hierarchy.	Must confront their true feelings in favor of engagement with hierarchical groups that are the embodiment of inequality and differentiation.

Dimension	Hierarchist	Enclavist	Fatalist	Individualist
Adjustments required to change social solidarity allegiances to (cont'd):				
enclavist:	Have a common acceptance of group belonging, but must confront their reluctance to define their interpersonal relationships independently of the authority figures.		Must confront their inability to engage personally with an egalitarian social environment and their inability to relate personally to their human environment closely enough to be able to engender a commitment to any cause.	Have a common rejection of the group circumscription of social interactions, but must confront their true feelings in favor of making the necessary values commitment.
fatalist:	Have a common acceptance of the group circumscription of social interactions, but must confront their reluctance to be excluded from paternalistic protection offered by the collective.	Must confront their true feelings in favor of no longer being committed to anyone, including themselves, or to any cause.		Have a common rejection of group belonging, but must confront their true feelings about no longer being committed to themselves.

Appendix 2.1 (cont'd)

Dimension	Hierarchist	Enclavist	Fatalist	Individualist
Adjustments required to change social solidarity allegiances to (cont'd):				
individualist:	Must confront their reluctance to define their interpersonal relationships independently of the authority figures and their fear of being excluded from paternalistic protection of the collective.	Have a common rejection of the group circumscription of social interactions, but must confront their true feelings in favor of their commitment to themselves and to self-interest.	Have a common rejection of group belonging, but must confront their inability to relate personally to their human environment closely enough to be able to identify exploitable entrepreneurial opportunities.	

3

Corporate Interest and Corporate Governance

INTRODUCTION

Corporate[1] governance, according to Monks and Minnow (1995: 1), is "the relationship among various participants in determining the direction and performance of corporations;"[2] that is, between corporate owners[3] and corporate

---

[1] A corporation is an organization, a "complex pattern of communications and relations in a group of individuals" (Simon (1957: 72; but see, contestingly, Barnard 1938, Etzioni 1961, Katz and Kahn 1966, Merton 1957, Millett 1954, Parsons 1964, Weber [1915] 1947, Williamson 1986), but not all organizations are corporations. Sternberg's (1998: 27) legalistic definition of a corporation provides a relevant starting point: "an artificial person, with assets, liabilities and purposes distinct from those of its owners...[It] has an independent legal existence, and is thus capable of enjoying perpetual life." This clearly embraces all forms of private trading corporations, whether their equity is publicly tradable or privately held, or whether conducted on a profit or non-profit basis (Turnbull 1997e: 2). It would exclude commercial joint ventures and strategic alliances (Ritcher 1994), as well as unconstituted associations or networks. It would, however, clearly extend beyond private economic entities that have their own coherence, structure, and individuality (Mathews 1996b: 116–17), to embrace *public enterprises*—"an enterprise with a corporate identity, whose capital is wholly or substantially provided by central or local government" (Powell 1987: 5)—and *social organizations*—such as universities, independent hospitals, constituted clubs, societies and associations, and even religious organizations (Thompson 1973)—that are engaged in service provision, whether funded by government grants, charitable donations, membership fees or sales revenue (see Strauss et al. 1963, Turnbull 1997e: 3). Organizations that are subject to unfettered political direction and control are the concern of societal governance.

[2] The definitional terrain surrounding corporate governance is highly contested (see, for example, Blair 1995, Demb and Neuhauser 1992, Donaldson 1990, Hilmer

stakeholders;[4] corporate owners and corporate directors;[5] corporate directors and corporate managers;[6] and corporate managers and corporate employees. These corporate governance relationships are between those who govern (or who seek to select those who govern) a corporation—the corporate governors (the corporate directors, whether selected by the corporate owners or stakeholders, and corporate managers)—and the governed—those that have the authority or power to govern (the corporate managers, corporate employees and stakeholders).

The purpose of this chapter is to use Cultural Theory's *grid-group* social-control space or *social map* to gain insights into corporate governance. Adherents to each of the four *social solidarities*—hierarchist, enclavist, fatalist and individualist—offer competing perspectives on who should have the authority to determine what is in the corporate interest; on the structures and processes of corporate governance that best identify, promote and protect them; and on what constitutes the best management practices to achieve the desired corporate governance ends. Following a contextualizing discussion of corporate governance and corporate performance, these rival perspectives are, first, identified and their implications then explored.

Korac-Kakabadse et al. (2001), drawing upon Zahra and Pearce (1989), Maassen (1999) and Kakabadse and Kakabadse (2001), have identified the fol-

---

1993, Porter 1992, Shleifer and Vishny 1996, Sternberg 1998, Tricker 1984, Turnbull 1997e), but, in its broadest sense, it is "the system by which companies are directed and controlled" (Cadbury Committee 1992: para 2.5, Hampel Committee 1998: para 1.15).

[3] *Corporate owners* are individuals or legal entities that have a legally enforceable right to exercise all-inclusive authority over a corporation because of their ownership of equity, their membership under a constitution, or their statutory powers and responsibilities.

[4] *Corporate stakeholders* are individuals, groups of individuals, or legal entities that can affect, or are effected by, the achievement of the objectives of a corporation but who are not one of its *corporate owners* (see Donald and Preston 1995; Freeman 1984; Freeman and Evans 1990; Turnbull 1994, 1997c, 1997d). They constitute interest or pressure groups because they seek to represent, defend or advance a particular sectional interest or cause (Grant 1996a: 243). They may be internal or external to a corporation. They become *corporate owners* in the event of stakeholders' participation in corporate ownership, as advocated by Blair (1995), Blasi (1988) Denham and Porter (1995), Monks (1996), and Porter (1992).

[5] *Corporate directors* are individuals who are duly elected or appointed to direct and control the corporation within the legal framework of the governing jurisdiction. It is important to recognize, as Fernandes (1986: 121) points out, that "there are very significant differences in the degree of control exercised by shareholders over the directors [of private sector and public sector enterprises], and in the relationship between the board and the shareholders in the two sectors."

[6] *Corporate managers* are "those responsible for executive action" (Turnbull 1997e: 3) or management—Fayol's ([1916] 1949) classic definition of which is the process of forecasting, planning, organizing, coordinating, controlling and commanding the work of people (see also Barnard 1938, Brech and Urwick 1945, Taylor [1911] 1947). To this might be added decision making.

lowing dimensions of corporate performance that are impinged upon by corporate governance: *financial* (profitability and operating costs); *systemic* (survival, resource growth, market position, market power and goal achievement); and *social* (responsiveness to society and ethical behavior). These also constitute a set of corporate governance failure indicators. Prima facie evidence of corporate governance failure would thus include rapidly diminishing market share or market power; chronic levels of disputation with employees, creditors, financiers and other strategic stakeholders; stock market delisting; the appointment of administrators, receivers or liquidators; the hostile acquisition intentions of another corporation; persistent breaches of statutory and regulatory corporate requirements; and persistent and sustainable accusations of unethical corporate and management conduct. Mayntz (1993) distinguishes four sets of causes of governance failure: *knowledge problems* (lack of appropriate governance knowledge, an epistemological problem), *governance capacity* (lack of appropriate governance instruments, an ontological problem), *implementation problems* (lack of appropriate organizational capacities, an ontological problem), and *motivational problems* (lack of compliance by the governed, a nomological problem) (see also Dixon and Dogan 2002b).

Corporate governance failure first became a public-interest issue with the emergence of the joint-stock company, which allowed the diversification of ownership, thereby emaciating ownership power (Berle and Means 1932; see also Fama and Jensen 1983a, Hart 1995). This divorcing of ownership from control gave rise to the prospect of corporate performance failures because of corporate governance failure. Management had an unimpeded prerogative to run joint-stock companies, with no independent supervision or disclosure requirements, as accountability was not expected. No questioning occurred about the legitimacy of the use of corporate power. Indeed, there was no meaningful owner participation in strategic decision making (see Tricker 1984: 5). Adam Smith ([1776] 1977: 167) well understood this relationship between corporate shareholders and managers:

The trade of a joint-stock company is always managed by a court of directors. This court . . . is frequently subject to a general court of proprietors. But the greater part of those proprietors seldom pretend to understand anything of the business of the company...contentedly receiving such...dividend as the directors think proper to give them. ...The directors of such companies, however, being managers rather of other people's money than their own, it cannot be well expected that they should watch over it with the same anxious vigilance with which the partners in a private company frequently watch over their own.

Exacerbating the gap between ownership and control has been the emergence of complex corporate structures[7] (Tricker 1984: 54–69; see also Mak

---

[7] Organizational theorists recognize the "complex ecological character of organizational existence...[where] outcomes are produced not by a process of decision making within a single firm but by complicated networks of interacting organizations and parts of organizations" (Cyert and March [1963] 1992: 233). Corporate structural complexity

80   Responses to Governance

1982), multinational business corporations,[8] and the greater recognition that corporate owners, governors and managers do not always share common and compatible interests (Jensen and Meckling 1976, Ross 1973, Stiglitz 1987).[9] This has created a mismatch between the corporate direction and control processes,[10] on the one hand, and corporate structure[11] on the other.

---

is a product of business corporations adopting multiple levels of subsidiaries; collaborating with other independent corporations under the auspices of *associations* (under contract law), *joint ventures* (joint stakes in a separate legal entity) or *consortia* (under contract law or through joint stakes in a separate legal entity); joining *federations of companies* (with part ownership and cross-ownership); using *agency companies* (subsidiaries acting as agents for the parent entity); or creating *strategic business units* (subsidiaries responsible for a particular business element across a number of subsidiaries). These interdependencies, which are not dependent on ownership domination, are motivated by commercial advantage (such as to coordinate activities, to share developmental or product launch costs, to extend, exploit, or share learning by transferring technology and good practice, to tender as a consortium, or to combine resources to achieve common instrumental purposes), which make it problematic to define the appropriate boundary for the exercising of corporate governance (Huxham 1996; see also Huxham 1991, Gray 1989, Hudson et al. 1999, Huxham and Macdonald, 1992, Huxham and Vangen 2000). This raises the issue of *collaborative governance* (Huxham 2000). Insights into the interorganizational interactions involved can be gleaned from the work of the behavior-of-the-firm theorists (Phillips 1960; Williamson 1965, 1975, 1985) and from the organizational sociology theorists concerned with interdependence (Aiken and Hague 1968, Yuchtman and Seashore 1967), *organizational fields* (Warren 1967) and *organizational sets* (Evan 1972).

[8] A *multinational business corporation* is "a form of capitalist enterprise in which the financial structure, managerial control, and integration of productive activity span national boundaries and are oriented to international (or global) markets" (Marshall 1998: 436; see also Barnet and Cavanagh 1994, Barnet and Muller 1974, Brown 1970, Dunning 1993, Jones 1996c, Julius 1990, Kindleberger 1970, Levi 1990, McMillan 1973, Morgan et al. 2001, Neufield 1971, Wilkins 1970). Reinicke (1998: 12) elaborates: "A global firm is not a loose aggregation of national firms, but instead is governed by a set of globally integrated strategies that rationalize the allocation of all resources across the entire market spectrum. Not only is such an organizational structure spread geographically across multiple national territories, but its geometry continues to change as companies adjust to changing economic and political conditions."

[9] This is demonstrable, for example, with respect to takeovers and mergers (Burrough and Helyar 1990, Shleifer and Summers 1988) and to the undertaking of long-term planning and investment (Congdon 1997, Davies 1996, Marsh 1990).

[10] Tannenbaum's (1962: 16) classic definition of *control* is "any process in which a person or group of persons or organization of persons determines, i.e. intentionally affects, what another person or group or organization will do." This implies that the controller has the power and the ability to modify or change behavior by means of a system of rewards and punishments. When *control* requires a standard of performance (Downs 1967: 144, Etzioni 1965: 650) then, following Turnbull (1997e: 3), it becomes *regulation*.

[11] The "management-prescribed roles" (Kahn 1974: 496) that are demarcated by an organization's structure must be aligned with its goals so that the necessary strategies of

The protection of the public interest[12] has long involved the statutory definition of the rights, responsibilities and obligations of shareholders and those that govern in their stead.[13] The statutory intent has been to prevent systematic, and even institutionalized, abuses of corporate power (see, for example, Pearce and Tombes 1998, Punch 1996) and corporate performance failure because of the lack of independent checks on management (Tricker 1984: 5, 10).

The corporate governance challenges now facing society have been summed up by Millstein and Katsh (1981: 239; see also Keasey and Wright 1993, 1997; O'Sullivan 2001; Vives 2000): "At issue ultimately is whether the nation, in responding to these concerns [about unrestrained corporate power], will essentially continue its traditional preference for pluralism...or will it, instead, accelerate the decline of pluralism either by relegating greater responsibility in all areas to government or by requiring fundamental changes in the internal governance structure of our major corporations? Or will the nation adopt some combination of the above courses of action. In some countries, the principle that ownership gives power to govern a corporation is endorsed—as in the United Kingdom and the United States; in others, it justifies the statutory engagement of stakeholders in the corporate governance process—as in Germany (Charkham 1994, Kakabadse and Kakabadse 2001). In defense of ownership sovereignty, Sternberg (1998: 20) argues that many of the criticisms of corporate governance stem from dissatisfaction with business purposes or outcomes rather than with corporate governance per se. Confusion thus abounds over the positive and normative dimensions of corporate objectives and how they should be achieved. As Robinson (1998: 7) expresses it: "ideas about what objectives firms *do* pursue and what they *should* pursue have become confused with views on the *means* of achieving corporate objectives." And Tricker (1984: 5; see also Mitroff 1983) concludes: "In recent decades the public interest domain within the corporate governance terrain has, contestedly, been extended to matters of governance from those external to the enterprise, on matters of corporate accountability, regulation and public policy."

Societies' expectations of corporate behavior are set within the prevailing set of cultural norms, which have been hardening against corporate autonomy in recent decades. This has happened in response to well-publicized incidences of business wrongdoing (see, for example, Frooman 1997, Punch 1996) and business decision making that have created uncompensated external costs borne by

---

control (Child 1972) are in place to monitor goal achievement as part of internal corporate accountability.

[12] Lasswell (1930: 264) conceptualized the *public interest* as displaced *private interests*: "the displacement of private affects upon public objects. The affects which are organized in the family are redistributed upon various social objects such as the state."

[13] This involves defining who can and cannot be directors; the appropriate way by which they are elected; their fiduciary duties with respect to shareholders, which, according to Monks and Minnow (1991: ch. 3) has been seriously eroded in the United States; their powers and responsibilities, particularly with respect to approval and accountability rules; and the situations that are deemed to constitute conflicts of interest and the appropriate methods for their resolution.

individuals, communities, governments, and future generations. Societies now, rightly or wrongly, hold business "responsible for many of the evils of the modern world" (Sternberg 1998: 19; see also Davies 1996: 5–6; Julius 1990, 1997). Nader and Green (1979; see also Nader et al. 1976) express the radical position: "[The giant corporations] are tantamount to private governments....[A giant corporation] is largely unaccountable to its constituency—shareholders, workers, consumers, local communities, taxpayers, small businesses, and future generations."

Societies have evidenced a willingness to exercise significant social control over all corporations. They are prepared to go well beyond merely seeking to control industry entry, to combat fraud, or to regulate restrictive practices by embracing social regulation in order to protect particular social groups. They have imposed upon corporations a variety of social obligations, such as occupational health, safety and welfare requirements, consumer protection, environmental protection and planning restrictions, technology assessment, and antitrust (antimonopoly) restrictions. They have also imposed expectations of social responsibilities on corporations (Child 1969, Kochan and Syrett 1991, Moir 2001, Wilson 2000), thus holding them to public account, much to Hayek's chagrin (1979: 82; see also 1978), for their support of good causes and for acting in the public interest. Some societies, notably, Germany (Charkham 1994, Kakabadse and Kakabadse 2001), have sought to achieve their corporate social objectives by the statutory imposition on corporations of corporate governance mechanisms that reflect the values of consensus, solidarity, community, and inclusiveness. Other societies, such as the United Kingdom and the United States (Charkham 1994, Kakabadse and Kakabadse 2001), have opted for the social regulation of corporations by the state.[14] What these social obligations,[15] responsibilities and control mechanisms are is a matter of public policy, and their determination involves the state in a delicate balancing act between individual autonomy (the protection of the *positive* freedom of corporate owners, governors and managers) and collective control[16] (constraining their *positive* freedom to promote the *negative* freedom of stakeholders).

---

[14] The state can be viewed as "a distinct set of political institutions whose specific concern is with the organization of domination, in the name of the common interest, within a delimited territory" (Burnham 1996: 472). Laumann and Knoke (1987:5) perceive the state as "a complex system of governmental and nongovernmental organizations that struggle for power and legitimacy in the making of public policies." Mitchell (1999: 95) considers it to be "an effect of mundane processes of spatial organizations, temporal arrangements, functional specifications, supervision and surveillance, and representation that creates the appearance of a world fundamentally divided into state and society and state and economy."

[15] For a discussion of corporate social responsibilities, see Ackerman and Bauer 1976, Bowen 1953, Carroll 1979, Heald 1970, Preston and Post 1975; but see also Chamberlain, 1973.

[16] This control can be achieved by using force, coercion, manipulation, persuasion or legitimate authority. It can involve the use of positional or legitimate power; expert power; personal, referent, or integrative power; resource, reward or exchange power; or

THE CORPORATE INTEREST: WHO SHOULD DETERMINE IT?

Corporations exist only because of the actions of people. As Gross (1964: 502) remarks: "people act together in organizations because by so doing they can satisfy interests that otherwise might not be satisfied as well or at all.... These satisfaction objectives relate to the interests of both members and nonmembers. Most organizations are both 'self-serving' and 'other-serving'." This raises a sequence of questions. Whose interests should a corporation be required to consider? Whose interests should a corporation be required to serve? Who should determine the corporate interest from among the diverse set of self-serving and other-serving interests, some of which may be mutually compatible or common interests, while others may be mutually incompatible or conflicting interests? Who should prioritize the dimensions of the corporate interest and then determine and prioritize the interest-satisfying corporate objectives that give rise to prioritized goal-oriented corporate action?

Adherents to each of the competing *social solidarities* have rival perceptions on the knowability of the corporate interest, on the appropriate role of the corporate owners, stakeholders and managers in its identification, prioritization, and satisfaction; and on corporate governance capacity—and thus on corporate governability. They would consider their balance between individual autonomy and collective control to be the only legitimate one. Thus they believe their approach to the resolution of conflicting interests to be the only acceptable one. They would, inevitably, resist the propositions advanced by adherents to competing *social solidarities* on the determination of the corporate interest. As a consequence, the extent to which the governed and the governors are in dispute over the respective roles of the corporate owners, stakeholders, directors and managers in the definition of the corporate interest is determined by the extent to which they adhere to the same *social solidarity*, and thus share a common view on how the corporate interest should be determined.

Individualist Perspective

To individualists, the corporate interest would be knowable only through preferences revealed in the marketplace,[17] whether that be the capital market (for owners' and financiers' interests), the commodity market (for customers', end users' and suppliers' interests) or the labor market (for employees' interests), as embodied in explicit or implicit contracts. Whatever common interests emerge are the product of contract negotiation. Because individualists would presume that others, like themselves, would not make voluntary contributions

---

physical, coercive or threat power (Allison 1996b, Boulder 1990, French and Raven 1959, Hales 2001).

[17] Reinicke (1998; see also Granovetter 1985) argues that this is an atomized, undersocialized and depoliticized view of human action, one involving the marketplace as a separate and differentiated sphere of modern society, unrelated to its broader historical, political and social context. Thus, he concludes: "Economic rationalism would prevail over political, social, and judicial rationality" (Reinicke 1998: 67).

or sacrifices in the 'corporate interest,' the only 'categorical interests' that a corporation needs to serve are of those with whom they have a contractual relationship, and even then, only to the extent of the contractual obligation that has been defined. Those stakeholders who are without a contractual relationship are presumed to have their interests protected and promoted by the state, as a matter of public policy, which defines and enforces whatever rights they are given in the 'public interest.'[18] These rights are thus part of the socially determined legal framework that constrains corporate action.

Individualists would argue that, since the authority to govern a corporation is derived from ownership,[19] the power to determine which interests should be embodied in the corporate objectives that guide corporate action, should rest solely with the corporate owners, as determined and implemented on their behalf by the corporate directors they elect or appoint as their trustees. They would argue that public policy objectives cannot be imposed on corporations without "violating their very reason for being" (Sternberg 1998: 25; see also 1996a). As Robinson (1998: 8) remarks: "Because corporations are owned by their shareholders, it is those shareholders they should serve not the stakeholders." Accountability for the corporation's performance, viability, sustainability and ethical conduct[20], within the dual context of the designated corporate objectives and the legal framework of the governing jurisdiction, is thus perceived as the corporate managers being held accountable by the corporate directors, who are, in turn, accountable to the corporate owners, preferably by means of reports and audits (notably financial audits, duty-of-care audits, fraud audits and governance audits[21]).

To individualists, then, the corporate interest would be knowable by law-abiding corporate directors as a set of corporate objectives that reflect the will

---

[18] This raises an important ethical dilemma, which Reeve (1996b: 434) ably articulates:

One recurrent controversy about rights is just how weighty they should be. Are rights ways of establishing important claims, but claims which are defensible or alienable? Or are rights vetoes...which cannot be put into a balance?...On the one hand, to respect property rights when the lives of thousands could be saved by overriding it looked fetishistic; on the other, to allow rights to be overruled by considerations of general utility is alleged to neglect the integrity and separateness of persons.

[19] This proposition is rooted in British nineteenth century individualism, self-help and Protestant nonconformity, supported by a mistrust of government and abhorrence of bureaucracy, by a Spencerian conviction of the survival of the fittest and by a professionalism rooted in self-interest (Smiles [1859] 1968, Macfarlane 1978, Tawney 1938).

[20] Sternberg (1998: 39) posits an "ordinary decency" ethical principle, which would no doubt appeal to individualists: corporate activities should be conducted "with honesty, fairness, the absence of physical violence and coercion, and a presumption in favor of legality" (see also Sternberg 1994; but compare Burrough and Helyar 1990, Monks and Minnow 1991, Punch 1996, Shleifer and Summers 1988).

[21] "Governance audits [are] designed specifically to determine the extent to which a company's structures and systems, procedures and policies were actually directed at achieving the constitutional corporate objectives" (Sternberg 1998: 128).

of corporate owners, constrained by the corporation's contractual obligations to its customers or end users, employees, suppliers, financiers and other non-members, and by the statutory social obligations and responsibilities coercively imposed upon it by the state.

Enclavist Perspective

To enclavists, the corporate interest would be knowable and embraces an inclusive set of categorical interests that reflect the shared values and language that create a social bond and identity for particular groups of corporate stakeholders. These categorical interests are determined through constrained, consensus-seeking group-norming and -forming values discourses. Enclavists would uphold the propositions that the only legitimate corporate objective is "balanced stakeholder benefits" (Sternberg 1998: 96) and that informed and trusted stakeholders are more likely to have the corporate interest at heart. They would also endorse the principle that corporations should conduct their affairs for the benefit of all their stakeholders,[22] to whom they should be accountable (Sternberg 1998: 94; see also Donaldson and Preston 1995, Turnbull 1994).

Enclavists, with their preoccupation with being seen to be committed to the categorical good, would presume that others, like themselves, would be willing to make voluntary contributions and sacrifices in the corporate interest if it was also in the categorical interest.

Enclavists would agree with Hirst's (1994: 152) proposition that "corporate structures can only enjoy the autonomy of 'civil society' if they in fact belong to it, if they cease to be autocratic and accountable to the majority of those who are members in fact, but at present have no rights to participate in their governance." They would argue that the authority to govern a corporation is derived from society,[23] in return for the corporation's use of its resources and access to the special privileges it provides (Dahl 1985).[24] Thus, the power to determine which of the categorical interests are embodied in the corporate objectives should rest with corporate directors who are elected or appointed by both the corporate stakeholders and corporate owners. Accountability for the corporation's performance, viability, sustainability and ethical conduct, within the dual context of the designated corporate objectives and the legal framework of the governing jurisdiction, is thus perceived as the corporate managers being held accountable by the corporate directors, who are, in turn, accountable to the cor-

---

[22] For a discussion of stakeholder conflicts in the context of globalization, see Julius 1990.

[23] Hirst (1994: 146) argues that corporations are too powerful to be regarded as private shareholder associations, they thus need to be made more accountable to those affected by them, which means that they need to be governed by the participation of their stakeholders.

[24] Hirst (1994: 145) points out that corporations enjoy very real state-granted privileges, most notably, the granting of limited liability, legal entity or personality status, and designated legal immunities to managers, without which corporate power could not survive.

porate stakeholders and owners, preferably by means of frequent meetings to discuss reports and audits (extending beyond financial audits, duty-of-care audits and fraud audits, to include governance audits, environmental impact assessments, technology impact assessments, and social impact audits).

To enclavists, then, the corporate interest would be knowable as a set of corporate objectives that embody an agreed set of stakeholder categorical objectives. Their achievement is believed to be central to corporate survival, stability and well being and in the 'public interest.'

Hierarchist Perspective

To hierarchists, the corporate interest would be knowable and grounded in a notion of the 'corporate good,' as articulated by a corporation's managerial elite. Hierarchists would endorse the proposition that the managerial elite, because of its superior knowledge, skills and experience, understands not only what is in the best interests of both the corporate owners and the corporate stakeholders, but also how best to balance those interests. Hierarchists would presume that others, like themselves, would be willing to make voluntary sacrifices and contributions to collective corporate action, if they were deemed by the managing elite to be for the 'corporate good.'

Heirarchists would argue that the authority to govern a corporation is derived from managerial ability. Thus, the power to determine which dimensions of the corporate interest should be embodied in the corporate objectives should rest with the corporate managers. They would argue that the corporate owners should select the corporate directors from among the managerial elite of the corporation itself and, perhaps, corporations related to it—members of a family of firms interconnected by corporate history, integrated operations, and interlocking shareholdings (Sternberg 1998: 80). Accountability for the corporation's performance, viability, sustainability and ethical conduct, within the dual context of the designated corporate objectives and the legal framework of the governing jurisdiction, is thus perceived as corporate managers being responsible only to themselves, as corporate directors, and thus indirectly to the corporate owners, preferably by means of financial reports tabled at infrequent meetings.

To hierarchists, then, the corporate interest would be knowable as a set of corporate objectives that reflect the corporate good, as determined by the managing elite, who have the best interests of the corporation at heart, and who are thus best able to balance the competing interests of the corporate owners, stakeholders and managers, thus ensuring continuity between the past, present and future.

Fatalist Perspective

To fatalists, the corporate interest would be unknowable because of capriciousness and uncertainty. Since the corporate interest cannot be intentionally and instrumentally promoted and protected, then it makes no difference who has the authority to give direction to a corporation. They would presume that the corporate directors and managers can and do exercise coercive power, which can never be legitimized. Their perception of corporate accountability is that neither the corporate directors nor the corporate managers can be made accountable for corporation performance, viability, sustainability or ethical conduct to its corporate owners or corporate stakeholders, both of whom are also presumed to be indifferent to people's needs and, in any event, powerless.

To fatalists, then, the corporate interest is unknowable, but a corporation is governable because its ruling powers, whoever they may be and however appointed, can and do exercise the necessary coercive power that enables them to govern as they see fit.

GOOD CORPORATE GOVERNANCE: WHAT IS IT?

Adherents to each of the competing *social solidarities* have a rival perception of the most appropriate corporate governance arrangements. These reflect what they believe to be the most appropriate balance of governance power among the corporate owners, stakeholders, directors, managers and employees, with respect to corporate direction—forecasting, planning and deciding the corporate future—and to internal regulation—organizing, coordinating, controlling and commanding of the work of people in a way that identifies, prevents and corrects deviations from an agreed standard of corporate performance. Thus, they have rival perspectives on what constitutes good corporate governance. As a consequence, the extent to which the governed and the governors are in dispute over the respective roles and responsibilities of the corporate owners, stakeholders and managers in the promoting and protecting of the corporate interest is determined by the extent to which they adhere to the same *social solidarity*, and thus share a common view on what constitutes good corporate governance.

Individualist Perspective

Individualists would see the social sphere as threatening to the corporate sphere's interests. Since only owners, who are the ultimate carriers of any corporate failure risk, have any legitimate claim to corporate authority, individualists would prefer a corporate governance mode where the corporate owners are in the ascendancy—the ownership (market or self-regulation) mode. This is characterize by Hawley and Williams (1996: 21) as "the simple finance model." Thus, law-abiding corporate directors, acting as trustees for the corporate owners, negotiate enforceable, explicit and implicit contracts with the corporate managers and ensure that the affairs of the corporation are conducted by the corporate managers in accordance with its contractual or statutory obligations to the corporate owners, directors, stakeholders and employees. Individualists would certainly question whether there is any moral basis upon which stakeholders, whom they see as being perpetually inclined to act as pedantic rent seekers, could make a claim for legitimate corporate authority. Any voluntary stakeholder engagement in the corporate governance processes would be tolerated by individualists only if it is deemed by the corporate owners to be in the 'corporate interest.'[25] The corporate owners, individualists believe, should have no unnecessary constraints placed on their *positive* freedom.

Individualists would be attracted to the ideas that "management is about running business; governance is about seeing that it is run properly" (Tricker 1984: 7) and that "[the managers] must be free to drive their companies forward but exercise that freedom within a framework of effective accountability" (Cadbury Committee[26] 1992: 3). Thus, they would prefer a corporate governance structure that gives corporate owners leverage, through their influence on the corporate directors,[27] on the direction and control of corporate affairs. Sternberg (1998: 21) argues that corporate governance is about three elements: principals, agents and outcomes.[28] This involves the corporate directors in constructing rules and incentives to ensure that corporate managers behave in a way that promotes and protects the corporate owners' expressed interests (see also Jensen and Meekling 1976).

Individualists would thus prefer strong corporate governance bodies that can dominate corporate management, particularly as management prerogatives and

---

[25] Corporate owners may well choose to diminish the threat posed by *corporate strategic stakeholders*—"those groups without whose support the organization would cease to exist" (Freeman 1984: 31; see also Turnbull 1997c, 1997d)—by engaging them in the corporate governance process or, in the context of publicly owned social organizations or state enterprises, by engaging them in the governance processes of the public agencies that constitute the *corporate owner*.

[26] Formally, the Committee on the Financial Aspects of Corporate Governance (Chair: Sir Adrian Cadbury), sponsored by the Financial Reporting Council, the London Stock Exchange and the British accounting profession.

[27] Pound (1992: 83) argues that there is emerging in the United States a "new form of governance based on politics rather than finance," which will provide more effective and less expensive shareholder oversight. Hawley and Williams (1996: 29) classify it as "the political model of governance," as described by Gundfest (1990) and Pound (1992), whereby "active investors seek to change corporate policy by developing voting support from dispersed shareholders, rather than by simply purchasing voting power or control."

[28] This raises the issue of *opportunism*, whereby agents "will operate in ways which maximize their interests rather than the firm's interests" (Parsons 1995: 328). This highlights two issues. The first is *adverse selection*, where, because of resources, information and time constraints, principals cannot make a complete scrutiny of the managers they employ as agents. Aware of these constraints, managers do not fully disclose to their prospective principals their abilities, skills, honesty or industriousness (Parsons 1995: 328; see also Hillier 1997). The second is *moral hazard*, where "given the opportunity agents...will maximize their own utility and interests rather than that specified in terms of the contract" (Parsons 1995: 328). These issues, in turn, raise the fundamental proposition of organizational economics (Barney and Ouchi 1986), based on the premises of *transaction cost* and *agency theory* (Alchian and Demsetz 1972; Stiglitz 1987; Williamson 1979, 1984), that to increase efficiency in the face of opportunism requires market pressures to come into play. Thus, by ensuring that there is systematic rivalry among the agents, transaction costs will be lowered, because the capacity to monitor and control principal-agent transactions is enhanced, thereby reducing *agency costs*. In other words, the cost of monitoring the agent, bonding the agent to the principal, and any residual losses (Fama and Jensen 1983b, Jensen and Meekling 1976).

associated organizational legitimizations are well-rewarded expert activities (Crystal 1991). This makes attractive a unitary board of corporate directors that can act as the corporate owners' trustee, steward, and watchdog (Sternberg 1998: 31).[29] Such a board should be dominated by external (nonexecutive or independent) members, whose roles and responsibilities can be proscribed to promote the interests of corporate owners, for individualists would be skeptical of the capacity of corporate directors who are also corporate managers to act in the best interests of corporate owners. They would also endorse the idea of a nonexecutive audit committee (Tricker 1984: 193–96; see also Collier 1997, Mills 1997), and even a governance committee, so as to ensure a strict adherence to corporate purpose and serve as a conduit for concerns about corporate conduct (Sternberg 1998: 128–29).

Depending on the statutory or constitutional requirements binding the corporation, individualists would prefer to have the corporate owners either choose by vote the corporate directors from among a group of people they nominate or select them as they see fit. Such voting as does have to take place should be voluntary and on a one share, one vote basis. This means that only those who see a net benefit in voting would do so, with abstainers being considered to have given their tacit consent.

The way individualists would see corporations being directed and controlled reflects the way they prefer to organize themselves. Given their preference for negotiating contractual relationships, they would be favorably disposed to a particular set of internal governance orientations, structures and processes (see, for example, Scanlon 1977), one that created an organization with particular features. It would have a primary concern with outputs and outcomes. It would have an organic or organismic structure[30] (Altman and Baruch 1998), charac-

---

[29] Sternberg (1998: 31) argues that a board's definitive responsibility is to direct the corporation toward achieving the corporate purposes set out by shareholders. Thus it must, inter alia, determine corporate policies; authorize strategic corporate decisions; appoint senior managers and auditors; nominate directors; monitor corporate and management performance; and determine executive remuneration, by linking pay and performance to the corporate mission on the basis of the "distributive justice principle" that "those who contribute most to the organization deserve most from the organization" (Sternberg 1998: 38; see also Ezzamel and Watson 1997; Main et al. 1996; Ogden and Watson 1996; Sternberg 1994, 1996a). The board must also establish and monitor internal control systems to ensure that corporate actions that are not taken directly by the board are nevertheless legal and are directed at achieving corporate objectives.

[30] Individualists, ever seeking greater personal autonomy, would, no doubt, also accept the desirability of a matrix organization structure in situations where there are highly salient organizational elements that are simultaneously necessary for goal achievement; where there are uncertainty, complexity and interdependence of tasks; and where there is a resource scarcity that demands frugality (Davis and Lorsch 1977). They would accept that its multiple command system violates Fayol's ([1916] 1949) principle of unity of command, but would argue that compliance is a product of the self-determined coercive influence of financial incentives, not organizational coercion. They would also endorse Williamson's (1975 and 1986) decentralized, multidivisional (M-form) structure in markets with product and segmentation diversity (Chandler 1962: 382–83). They would be

terized by low complexity,[31] low formalization[32] and low centralization[33] (Burns and Stalker 1961, Hague 1978), because they believe that decisions should be taken closest to the point where the need for such decisions arises, thereby maximizing individual autonomy. It would also have an autocratic decision-making process (Vroom and Yetton 1973; see also Vroom and Jago 1988), which can become consultative when necessary, and which uses instrumentally rational corporate policy analysis, premised on the self-interest motivation of all corporate policy actors, to facilitate "optimal" decision making.[34] Finally, it would have a "competition or rivalry" mode of control (Hood 1998: 56–57), which involves "systematic rivalry among individuals and work units for selection, [expenditure] votes, promotion, salaries, prestige, prizes, space, equipment, resources."[35]

Individualists would consider corporations to be governable, but only if the self-interests of corporate owners, directors, managers and employees are aligned by means of a negotiated set of implicit and explicit contracts with zero noncompliance tolerance and full restitution as the ultimate sanction. They

---

attracted to the idea that, because this organizational design constitutes a weak holonic form (Smuts 1926; see also Mathews 1996a), it is, as Simon (1962) describes, a stable intermediate form in which interaction is weak but not negligible.

[31] The lower the degree of vertical, horizontal and spatial differentiation (or complexity) in an organization, the smaller the communications distortions and the shorter the decision response time will be.

[32] The lower the degree of job standardization (or formalization) in an organization, the greater the degree of staff decision-making discretion will be.

[33] The lower the degree to which decision making is concentrated at a single point (or centralization) in an organization, the greater the degree of decision-making autonomy at the periphery will be.

[34] In terms of Thompson's (1967) decision-making strategies matrix, individualists would prefer judgmental decision-making strategies, as they are inclined to be certain about outcome preferences but uncertain in their beliefs about cause-and-effect relations.

[35] This builds upon Williamson's (1975, 1986) proposition that an organizational design that decentralizes an organization into relatively self-contained quasi-autonomous subunits—creating an multidivisional (M-form) structure—can lower transaction costs because it overcomes the problems of bounded rationality in large, uniform hierarchies and exploits opportunistic behavior by creating a system in which subunit performance can be measured and compared. Laurence and Lorsch (1967), following Selznick (1957: 8–9), point out, however, that greater structural differentiation creates a greater potential for interdepartmental conflict, as each subunit develops its own ways of handling its own particular environmental uncertainties. Thompson (1967) offers an alternative explanation for subgroups rivalry, in terms of individuals becoming too attached to competing organizational subgoals, which have been factored into corporate mission in order to build commitment to corporate purpose, thus facilitating problem solving. Subunit rivalry requires some method of organizational integration and conflict resolution, such as Selznick's (1957: 90) idea of the institutional embodiment of purpose, which uses social norms to reinforce corporate purpose. Williamson (1986) argues that if general management does have to become reengaged in the day-to-day operations of a subunit within an M-form structure, then transaction costs will increase and a corrupted M-form structure will emerge.

would, instinctively, understand and accept that a corporation's latent goal is to secure "individual freedom to contract" (Schwarz and Thompson 1990: 67) by "magnifying the competition of leaders" within a "secret weaponry" culture, so as to ensure that the leader does not lose power (Douglas 1994: 78). Indeed, as Hood observes (1998: 28), their organizational Achilles' heel is a "tendency to put individual before collective benefit."

The individualists' salient corporate governance risk, which stems from the incapacity of the naturalist-agency methodology to identify causal relationships and to take account of structural imperatives, is the principal-agent problem of how agents "could be prevented from shirking in conditions where corporate ownership and control are divided" (Hood 1998: 102, n. 3; see also Berle and Means 1932; Fama and Jensen 1983a, 1983b; Leibenstein 1976; Ross 1973) in the absence of other structuralist constraints, such as constructed patterns of obligation or loyalty.[36] Central to this are two risks that face the principals. The first is that, because of uncertainty and opportunism, they will not be able to specify, completely and comprehensively, the implicit and explicit contracts they have with their agents, in terms of the activities, outputs and outcomes they are expected to deliver in return for their remuneration (Hood 1998: 102, n. 3; see also Aggarwal and Samwick 1999, Haubrich 1994, Garen 1994, Janakiraman et al. 1992, Jensen and Murphy 1990).[37] The second is that they will not be able to enforce the executed contracts. In the absence of a comprehensive set of complete and enforceable contracts, the principals will be unable either to the cause of corporate governance problems to nonmarket factors, or to determine a market solution to those problems.

Individualists, if faced with the prospect of an ownership (market) self-regulation malfunction because law-abiding people are unable to specify completely and enforce their contracts, would, in the first instance, blame bad luck or rogue behavior by those who have not acted in accordance with the terms of their contracts or the law, or who have not developed an appropriate sense of attribute personal honor, guilt or shame in their interpersonal relationships. Their envisaged solution would be for more diligence to be applied to the drafting of principal-agent contracts and to their enforcement, because their agency ontology enables them to presume that people are motivated by personal incentives rather than collective commitments, and because their naturalist epistemology enables them to presume that they can make reliable predictions about the consequences of human behavior by observing patterns in, and corre-

---

[36] Hawlcy and Williams (1996: 65) note that, in the United States, management controls "the information that does reach the board. The result can be the board knowing too little, too late and, even if it is willing to act to confront a growing problem or crisis, it is often unable to do so."

[37] As Turnbull ([1997] 2000: 9) notes: "In an ideal world, the managers would sign a complete and comprehensive contract that specifies exactly what they could do under all states of the world and how profits would be allocated. The problem is that most future contingencies are too hard to describe and foresee, and, as a result, complete contracts are technologically unfeasible."

lations between, forms of behavior. This solution would be expected to initiate the economic calculations needed to induce the instrumental compliance necessary to correct governance failure. Then, if their prospects for material success are still threatened, they would exit (Hirschman 1970) by withdrawing from the corporation in order to minimize their material losses and to renegotiate their contractual relationships.[38]

Enclavist Perspective

Enclavists would see a blurred boundary between the corporate and the social spheres, which should be expanded if they conceal any unequal power relations in the corporate sphere.[39] They would prefer a corporate governance mode where the corporate stakeholders and owners are jointly in the ascendency—the stakeholder (interactive or codeterminant) mode (Hawley and Williams 1996: 21). Thus the corporate stakeholders work together with the corporate owners and managers, on the basis of trust, loyalty and reciprocity, to codetermine, promote and protect a set of corporate interests that embraces a comprehensive set of categorical interests. Enclavists would argue that this interactive or cooperative form of corporate governance would be both for the corporate good—by ensuring the corporation's survival, stability and wellbeing—and in the 'public interest.'

Because enclavists see corporate managers as always at risk of taking immoral and corrupt actions, they treat them with constant vigilance. They would see the need to ensure that corporations take into account the interests of a wide range of stakeholders,[40] so that they operate to the benefit of society as a

---

[38] For a discussion of governance-by-exit, see Wong 1996; see also Short and Keasey 1997.

[39] Associationalists would see *mutualism* (the doctrine that mutual dependence is necessary for social wellbeing) as the bridge connecting the social and corporate spheres, one that engenders *cooperative corporate forms*, such as corporations owned and run by their members, with profits shared among them (see Hirst 1994: 147–48; see also Donald 1942; Preston 1996, 1998) or *ownership transfer organizations* (Turnbull 1991a, 1991b).

[40] Associationalists would assert the need for *corporate democratization* (see Dahl 1985, Schuller 1985) to go beyond the socialist or syndicalist issues of *worker self-management* (workers given full democratic control over the state-owned enterprises in which they are employed), *workers' control* (workers given a significant influence over managerial decision making in capitalist enterprises in which they are employed [Kolaja 1965]), or *industrial democracy* (workers encouraged and able to participate in workplace governance [Andriessen and Coetsier 1984, Blumberg 1968, Scanlon 1948, Schuchman 1957; but see also Wall and Lischeron 1977]), involving *trade union representation, joint consultation, works councils* (Lecher et al. 1999) or *worker-directors*. They argue that when making decisions corporate directors should have a legal duty to consider and give due regard to the interests of shareholders, employers, consumers, and the community (Hirst 1994: 151; see also 1997a). They would also advocate (Hirst 1994: 151) corporate downsizing through legislation on *anticoncentration* (to prevent further corporate mergers and takeovers), *deconcentration* (to break up large corporations) and

whole,[41] thereby maintaining the confidence of investors and the ability to attract long-term capital.[42] Enclavists, of course, would presume that stakeholders want to participate actively in corporate decision making.

Good corporate governance, to enclavists, is based on three principles: that the corporate interest should be inclusive of the stakeholders' categorical interests; that all interactions should be on the basis of mutual trust; and that stakeholders should participate actively in, and give their consent to, corporate decisions. They would thus prefer to negotiate with, and accommodate, the interests of corporate stakeholders, owners and managers within the corporate governance process.[43] They would be attracted to the idea that a corporate governance structure should be inclusive, egalitarian and facilitate deliberative strategic decision making.[44]

Thus enclavists would prefer the corporate governance structure envisaged by Blair (1995: 322), one that "enhances the voice of and provides ownership-like incentives to those participants in the firm who contribute or control critical, specialized inputs (firm specific human capital) and to align the interests of these critical [Turnbull's ([1997] 2000: 4) "strategic"] stakeholders with the interests of outside, passive shareholders."

Enclavists would, without doubt, support a compound or multitier board of governors,[45] comprising at least a supervisory board, responsible for generally

---

constellations (to facilitate multicorporation partnerships in the form of associations, consortia and federations).

[41] This would be achieved by creating a *social market*—the social governance of markets (Bruyn 1991)—as in Germany, for example, where Article 14(2) of the Constitution expresses a *social market* philosophy: "Property imposes duties. Its use should also serve the public weal" (Charkham 1994: 10; see also Kakabadse and Kakabadse 2001).

[42] For a discussion of relationship investing, see Porter 1992, Monks 1994.

[43] Hill and Jones (1992) have extended agency theory to embrace stakeholder contractual relationships.

[44] Stakeholder theorists and advocates have identified, as appropriate corporate directors, member-elected nonexecutives (Baysinger and Hoskisson 1990, Institute of Directors 1982, Johnson et al. 1993, Mayer 1996, Pettigrew and McNulty 1995, Turnbull 1997c), public interest representatives (UK 1977), consumers and customers (Tricker 1984), employee representatives (European Commission 1983, Shanks and Grantham 1980, UK 1977), trade unions (Turnbull 1997e), suppliers and creditors (Tricker 1984), external financiers (Tricker 1984, Holland 1994, MacMillan et al. 1996), trade associations (Turnbull 1997e), professional associations (Turnbull 1997e), media (Turnbull 1997e), political groups (Donaldson and Preston 1995), members of the host community (Porter 1992), and even competitors (Turnbull 1997e). For a critique of stakeholder theory, see Sternberg 1996b, 1997a , 1997b.

[45] This describes the existence of two or more centers of corporate control, whether required by law, the constitution of the firm or created by external relationships (Turnbull 1997e: 4; see also Bancaire 1996, Bernstein 1980, Guthrie and Turnbull 1995, Hatherly 1994, Tricker 1980). Compound boards with two or three tiers can be found in Japan and are a statutory requirement in parts of Europe, notably, Germany, Netherlands, Belgium, France, Italy and Luxembourg (Analytica 1992, Charkham 1994, Kakabadse

overseeing the corporation, and for appointing and supervising and monitoring management; and a management board, responsible for running the corporation (Tricker 1984: 197; see also Hirst 1994; McGregor 1980; Schuchman 1957; Turnbull 1993, 1995). They would also advocate the use of ad hoc focused committees.[46]

Depending on the statutory or constitutional requirements binding the corporation, the corporate stakeholders and owners would either choose by separate vote the corporate directors from among a group of people they separately nominate, or separately select them as they see fit.[47] Such voting as is necessary would, preferably, be compulsory, because abstention must be actively discouraged at all costs, and the voting system should involve designated corporate constituencies (shareholders and stakeholder groups) electing corporate governors on the basis of one vote per shareholder[48] or per stakeholder.

The way enclavists would see corporations being directed and controlled reflects the way they prefer to organize themselves. Because enclavists prefer to organize in groups that are small enough to enable effective engagement (see, for example, Likert 1961, ch. 10), that have an ethical orientation, and that facilitate a shared opposition to the outside world, they would be favorably disposed to a particular set of internal governance orientations, structures and processes, one that created an organization with particular features. It would have a primary concern with process as much as goals and endstates (Hood 1998: 131). It would have an organic structure[49] (Altman and Baruch 1998), with low complexity, low formalization and low centralization (Burns and Stalker 1968, Hague 1977, Mintzberg 1989) so as to disperse power. They believe that cooperation should be noncoercive and achieved through empowerment so as to produce behavioral compliance (Etzioni 1961), which reflects a commitment to shared values, accepting that this may well mean roles are ambiguous and negotiable.[50] It would also have a group decision-making process (Vroom and

---

and Kakabadse 2001). Indeed, the European Commission's 5th Directive in 1972, which was concerned with corporate governance and employee participation, proposed that all large corporations within its jurisdiction should have two-tier boards (Tricker 1984: 197).

[46] Associationalists (Hirst 1994: 151) would argue that a Supervisory Board should institute a Works Council, with authority to codetermine corporate policy, below which is a comprehensive system of employee participation.

[47] Enclavists would not be very sympathetic to the idea of independent corporate directors (Turnbull 1997b) dominating the corporate governance structures.

[48] Sternberg (1998: 56–59) describes this as "shareholder democracy."

[49] Enclavists, ever seeking greater group empowerment, would no doubt also accept, in the appropriate circumstances, a matrix organization structure with a multiple command system (Davis and Lorsch 1977), because compliance is a product of moral commitment not coercion. They would also endorse Williamson's (1975 and 1986) multidivisional (M-form) structure and other forms of holonic structures (Smuts 1926; see also Mathews 1996a, Simon 1962) or holarchies (Koestler 1967), such as autonomous manufacturing cells (Mathews 1996a) and an organization that is a hierarchy of teams (Conti and Warner 1996).

[50] Enclavists would feel comfortable with clan organizations, where "the normative control exerted by a powerful corporate value system, coupled with a high level of face-

Yetton 1973; see also Vroom and Jago 1988) that presumes corporate policy is the outcome achieved by balancing the competing interests of diverse interest groups by means of intersubjective, critically reflective communications, so as to facilitate consistent, congruent and cogent decision making in the interests of corporate stakeholders, owners and managers.[51] Finally, it would have a "mutuality" mode of control with peer group or face-to-face accountability (Hood 1998: 60–64; see also 125–28), which "places heavy stress on using group process to check individuals" (Hood 1998: 51; see also Hague et al. 1975, Goodin 1992).

Enclavists consider corporations to be governable, but only if the corporate stakeholders are given the necessary power to engage in interactive corporate governance processes, so as to inculcate an agreed set of stakeholder categorical interests that they consider to be central to corporate survival, stability and wellbeing. They would, instinctively, understand and accept that an organization's latent goal is to secure "the survival of the collectivity" (Schwarz and Thompson 1990: 67) by dampening "dissidence or clarifying factions" within a "betrayal" culture, so as to identify "individual treachery" (Douglas 1994: 78). Their organizational Achilles' heel is an "unwillingness to accept higher authority to break deadlocks" (Hood 1998: 28).

Thus enclavists' salient corporate governance risk, which stems from the inherent relativism of the hermeneutic-structuralist methodology, is that the corporate stakeholders, owners and managers cannot agree on a set of 'common interests' that need to be jointly protected and promoted in the 'corporate interest.'[52] In the absence of a decision-making process that is harmonious, trustworthy and codetermining, enclavists would not be able to externalize blame for any corporate governance failure onto particular risk takers or particular secret enemies within the corporate governance process.

Enclavists, if faced with the prospect that people cannot construct mutual understandings and acceptable joint perspectives that evoke moral commitment to the identification and correction of governance failures, would, in the first instance, to voice[53] (Hirschman 1970) blame, accusing the risk takers and secret

---

to-face manager-subordinate interaction and centralized control over performance outputs and personnel inputs, permits a fluid, ad hoc division of labour and decentralized decision-making" (Hales 2001: 181), provided it has a set of corporate values that are compatible with the 'categorical interests.'

[51] In terms of Thompson's (1967) decision-making strategies matrix, enclavists would prefer compromise decision-making strategies, as they are inclined to be uncertain about competing outcome preferences, but certain in their beliefs about cause-and-effect relations.

[52] As a consequence of this, a corporation "oscillates between periods of stability interspersed by sudden abrupt changes" (Altman and Baruch 1998: 782)—akin to Eldredge's punctuated equilibria (see also Gould 1989), Hannan and Freeman's (1989) *organizational ecology* or Crozier's (1964) *bureaucratic change process.*

[53] "To resort to voice, rather than exit, is for the…member to make an attempt at changing the practice, policies, and outputs of…the organization to which one belongs" (Hirschman 1970: 30).

enemies within the corporate governance process who do not share their commitment to interactive governance success for accepting too many risks that were too high. They would, no doubt, threaten to leave the corporate governance process if confronted with a value conflict over how best to correct a corporate governance failure. Their envisaged solution would be, first, to demand the removal of the risk takers and secret enemies from within the corporation. Then they would seek to empower more and different people to engage fully in corporate interactive governance processes. This is solution is based on two presumptions. First, their structuralist ontology enables them to presume that people are motivated by moral commitments to collectively agreed processes and outcomes. Second, their hermeneutic epistemology enables them to presume that people willingly engage in reasoning that is intersubjective and values-based, involving critically reflective communications using processes that enable them to make and question arguments and so determine the validity of normative judgements. This solution would involve developing strategies that would not only correct governance failure, but also evoke a moral commitment to interactive governance success.

Hierarchist Perspective

Hierarchists would see the corporate sphere as being clearly demarcated from the social sphere. To them, the corporate sphere is very much the domain of paternalistic managing elites.[54] They would prefer a corporate governance mode where the corporate managers are in the ascendency—the stewardship (hierarchy) mode (Hawley and Williams' 1996: 21). Thus their privileged positions give them a prospective responsibility to take an inclusive perspective of the corporate interest, and ipso facto its stakeholder categorical interests, when determining the corporate good. Because hierarchists are inclined to presume that managing elites are benign and benevolent, they would adhere to the proposition that "successful management will naturally wish to do well for the employees, their consumers, their suppliers and other stakeholders" (Robinson 1998: 8).

Good corporate governance, to hierarchists, is grounded in the principle that the corporate good must be defined, promoted and protected by the managing elite.[55] They would be sympathetic to Donaldson and Davis' (1994) proposition

---

[54] In private sector corporations, the managing elites are located within either the corporation or its affiliated corporations. In the public sector, however, the managing elites may also be found in supervisory ministries and other public agencies that constitute the *corporate owner*. In the case of state enterprises, for example, these external managing elites are inclined to ensure that "the powers and authority of the boards are inadequately defined. As a result, boards often find themselves helpless, sandwiched between the political power of the state [the societal governing elite] and the managerial power of the enterprises' professionals [the corporate managing elite]" (Fernandes 1986: 121).

[55] Hierarchists would instinctively find entrancing the French view that "giving the président directeur-général almost absolute power in a French company is in accordance

that managers, motivated by achievement, responsibility (prospective if not always retrospective) and power needs, are good stewards of the corporation, working diligently to achieve sustainable corporate profit and adequate shareholder returns.[56] This would leave corporate strategic management in the hands of the managing elite.

Hierarchists would thus prefer weak corporate governance bodies that can be dominated by the managing elite[57] and that secure commitment to agreed ends rather than give direction or establish controls. They would prefer large and hierarchical unitary boards, comprised, predominantly, of internal corporate managers and those managing the corporate members of a family of firms connected by a shared history, complementary operations, and interlocking shareholdings (Sternberg 1998: 80), which Kester (1992) describes as contractual governance. These unitary boards would have a self-determined set of roles and responsibilities, circumscribed only by any legal requirements deemed to be in the 'public interest.'

Depending on the statutory or constitutional requirements binding the corporation, the corporate owners would either choose by vote or select the corporate directors, but only from among a group of people nominated by the managing elites on the basis of the knowledge, skills, experience, and attributes they would bring to the corporate governance process. Such voting as is necessary should take place, preferably, on a voluntary one voting-share, one vote, basis, as apathy implies consent.[58]

---

with the French tradition of strong centralized leadership which goes back through de Gaulle and Napoleon to Louis XIV" (Charkham 1994: 119).

[56] As Hawley and Williams (1996: 29) conclude: "The logical extension [of the stewardship model] is either toward an executive-dominated board or toward no board at all." Hierarchists would no doubt be impressed with the Japanese practice whereby the large corporations are controlled by a management committee (*jomukai*) comprised of the president and the senior directors, all of whom have worked their way up through the ranks (Charkham 1994: 85). They would also feel comfortable with the general practice in the United States, as characterized by Herzel and Shepro (1990: 34): "The CEO [Chief Executive Officer] would probably be the chairman of the [board] meeting and completely in charge. Generally, he controls both the agenda and the flow of information to the directors. He dominates the meeting and the board plays quite a secondary role." They would concur with Mace's (1971: 5) verdict that Directors are merely "ornaments on a corporate Christmas tree."

[57] Hierarchists would expect managing elites to use their influence, through political processes, to ensure that the political, legal and regulatory environments within which their corporations operate are friendly to management (for a discussion of this issue in the United States context see Monks 1996, Monks and Minnow 1991).

[58] Hierarchists would be impressed with Japanese practice whereby shareholders, who are not expected to challenge board appointments, show their approval of the managerial elite's selection of new board members at a perfunctory and ceremonial annual general meeting by sustained applause (Tricker 1994: 47, 79, 81, 84). They would also be impressed with corporate election processes in the United States, which have been described by Epstein (1986: 13) as "procedurally more akin to the elections held by the Communist Party of North Korea than those held in Western Democracies." They would

The way hierarchists would see corporations being directed and controlled reflects the way they prefer to organize themselves. Given their organizing inclination toward large groups that reward loyalty and respect formal status distinctions, they would be favorably disposed to a particular set of internal governance orientations, structures and processes that create an organization with particular features. It would have a primary concern with inputs and getting the process right (Cutting and Kouzmin 2001). It would have a mechanistic, or 'machine,' structure[59] (Altman and Baruch 1998), with high complexity, formalization and centralization (Burns and Stalker 1961, Mintzberg 1989).[60] It would also have an autocratic decision-making process (Vroom and Yetton 1973; see also Vroom and Jago 1988), which can become consultative when necessary, that presumes corporate policy is the product of institutional activity by the managing elite intended to promote and protect the corporate good, using functional-analytic policy analysis to generate a set of objective facts that would facilitate satisficing decision making by rule-based decision makers content with incremental policy changes.[61] Finally, it would have an "oversight" mode of control, with regulatory compliance depending on the ease of violation detection, the probability of sanctions being imposed on violators, and the magnitude of the imposed sanctions (see Young 1992: 176), and with hierarchical

---

be disdainful of critics who bemoan the private shareholder's role in the governance of the company as little beyond being sent proxy forms for the board's nominees, or perhaps attending a routine annual general meeting of shareholders (Hirst 1994: 145; see also Lorsch and McIver 1989). Hawley and Williams (1996: 56–60) identify a range of constraints imposed on shareholders that arise from security or shareholding laws, agenda setting by management at annual general meetings, proxy procedures, voting arrangements, and corporate bylaws.

[59] Hierarchists would value the sense of purposive order and belonging engendered in a J organization, the archetypal Japanese work organization. which "entails a 'despecialized' division of labour coupled with a rationalised and formalized physical work process, held together by a bureaucratic employment relationship, a consultative planning process, centralized performance and recruitment controls, extensive face-to-face supervision and, crucially, the normative power of a strong corporate culture" (Hales 2001: 171).

[60] Pugh and Hickson (1976) drew upon these structural dimensions to define an organization's *structuring of activities* and *concentration of authority*. They then differentiated between *workflow bureaucracies* (those that are highly structured but do not have a high concentration of authority), *personnel bureaucracies* (those that are not very structured but have a high concentration of authority) and *full bureaucracies* (those that are highly structured and have a high concentration of authority). Parsons (1951) considered that in all bureaucratic organizations, roles should be seen as universalistic, specific, effectively neutral and collectively oriented. Jones (1991), however, argues that differentiated structures may become segmented into tightly closed systems serving self-serving vested interests. In this context, Shareef (1994: 490) highlights the importance of subsystem congruence, including values congruence.

[61] In terms of Thompson's (1967) decision-making strategies matrix, hierarchists would prefer computational decision-making strategies, because they are inclined to be certain about both outcome preferences and their beliefs about cause-and-effect relations.

accountability (Hood 1998: 51–55), which implies "a ladder of authority, conscious oversight and inspection, formal power to approve or elect, to pronounce on disputes and complaints, to forbid, command, permit, and punish" (Hood 1998: 51; see also Fayol [1916] 1949, Rose-Ackerman 1978).[62]

Hierarchists consider corporations to be governable, but only if the managing elite are given the necessary power to design and implement a system of hierarchical governance. They would, instinctively, understand and accept that an organization's latent goal is to secure its "internal structure of authority" (Schwarz and Thompson 1990: 67), by supporting group controls over the individual within a punitive culture, so as to ensure that the group does not lose commitment (Douglas 1994: 78). Their organizational Achilles' heel, according to Hood (1998: 28, also 73–97) is a "misplaced trust in authority and expertise coupled with high mobilization capacity."

The hierarchists' salient corporate governance risk, which stems from the explanatory weaknesses of the naturalist-structuralist methodology, is the managerial elite's loss of control or trust, because they were repeatedly unable to understand either the nature and causation of corporate governance problems or why their solutions are unable to secure compliance by free individuals, because they presume a structuralist ontology. In the absence of managerial trust and control, hierarchists would not be able to apportion blame for any corporate governance failure to the deviants who failed to comply with corporate rules and regulations.

Hierarchists, if faced with the prospect that the corporate managing elite is unable to correct hierarchical governance failures, would, in the first instance, express loyalty (Hirschman 1970) to them, in the hope that solutions would eventually emerge, and would blame noncompliant deviants. Their acts of loyalty would probably include suppressing any information that is critical of the corporate management elite's governance performance; and punishing those within the global governance mechanisms who threaten to make disclosures critical of their interpretation of the cause of, and solutions to, hierarchical governance failures. Their envisaged solution would be to strengthen hierarchical controls. This solution is a product of two presumptions. One is that compliance follows a cognitive commitment (Etzioni 1961) made after a rational calculation in the context of prescribed rules and regulations, supported, perhaps, by a deontological moral code, both of which are sanctioned by their structuralist ontology. The other presumption is that people can identify social reality through the observation of patterns in, and correlations between, forms of behavior, which reflect and represent structuralist constraints on their behavior. This is sanctioned by their naturalist epistemology. Such a strengthening of controls could involve setting aside or modifying rules and regulations, using publicity and persuasion to encourage compliance, strengthening disincentives,

---

[62] This demands adherence to Fayol's ([1916] 1949) principle of unity of command, because compliance is a product of the coercive influence of the needs-satisfying capacity of hierarchical organization, which would make unacceptable a matrix organization structure because has a multiple command system (Davis and Lorsch 1977).

Fatalist Perspective

Fatalists would not discriminate between the corporate and the social spheres, both of which are perceived as capricious, fearful and untrustworthy realms. While they would inevitably be alienated from the corporate directors and managers, they would also be deferential to them. They would expect the powers that be to exercise the necessary coercive power required to govern a corporation as they see fit. This means that corporations could well be benign in intent, the consequences of which are unknowable, but, inevitably, they are malevolent in action, the outcome of which is experienced.

Good corporate governance, to fatalists, is grounded in one simple principle: that it should not expect people's constructive engagement. Thus, fatalists would be attracted to the idea of a corporate governance mechanism that minimizes the potential for intentional and coercive corporate action by constraining the power of those powerful, self-seeking corporate directors and managers, who continually attempt to initiate exploitative corporate action. They would thus feel least alienated if a corporation had a unitary board of corporate directors, whose roles and responsibilities are circumscribed by a set of legal requirements that minimizes their exploitative and coercive inclinations and capacities.

To a fatalist, how corporate directors are selected or elected is irrelevant and unimportant, as long as they are not involved with the process. Such voting as is necessary should, then, be voluntary, as apathy is a justifiable act. This is because fatalists consider that it really makes no difference who the corporate directors are or how they are elected.

Fatalists would expect, and thus feel least indisposed to, a set of internal governance orientations, structures and processes that gave rise to "low-cooperation, rule-bound approaches to organization" (Hood 1998: 9), one that creates an organization with particular features. It would have a primary concern with inputs and process, but can accommodate ambiguous, mutually reinforcing perceptions of its intent, understanding, history and organization (March and Olsen 1976). It would have a mechanistic structure, with high complexity, formalization and centralization, and with a hierarchy based on well established criteria—probably seniority but certainly not merit (Altman and Baruch 1998, Hoppe 2000).[63] It would also have an autocratic decision-making process (Vroom and Yetton 1973; see also Vroom and Jago 1988), which is dominated by unknowing and untrustworthy vested interests. These interests respect neither the truthfulness of facts nor the sanctity of abstract values, and they realis-

---

[63] Fatalists would find the multiple command system of a matrix organization (Davis and Lorsch 1977) alienating because it would give two unknowing and untrustworthy superiors control over their working life, and they would expect to be the victims of the inevitable personal and organizational conflicts that would occur between them.

tically accept that corporate policy is, because of the limits of human cognition, the product of garbage-can-like decision processes (March and Olsen 1976), characterized by Cohen et al. (1972: 2) as "a collection of choices looking for problems, issues and feelings looking for decision situations in which they may be aired, solutions looking for issues to which they may be answers, and decision makers looking for work."[64] Finally, it would have a "contrived randomness" mode of control with hierarchical accountability (Hood 1998: 64–68; see also Rose-Ackerman 1978), which involves "'dual key' operations (that is, several people needed to commit funds or other resources, or separation of payments and authorization) with an unpredictable pattern of posting decision makers or supervisors around the organization's empire" as well as "random internal audits" (Hood 1998: 65).

Fatalists consider corporations to be governable, but only if the corporate powers that be are able to exercise the required coercive power to govern as they see fit. Fatalists would, instinctively, understand and accept that an organization's latent goal, like their own, is survival, which requires a governance capacity to cope with an inevitably uncertain internal and external environment. This is done by never imposing a set of principles by which to select or develop a coherent set of goals (Schwarz and Thompson 1990: 67), so as to avoid the worst that fate can deliver. The fatalists' organizational Achilles' heel is an "unwillingness to plan ahead or to take drastic measures in extreme circumstances" (Hood 1998: 28).

The fatalists' salient corporate governance risk is that their self-chosen isolation has been in vain. This stems from their presumption that corporate engagement is pointless, as no one is able to establish that the social world is knowable, which means that the corporate interest cannot be intentionally and instrumentally promoted and protected. This is premised on the inherent relativism of the hermeneutic-agency methodology and its inability to identify causal relationships and structural imperatives.

Fatalists, if faced with the prospect that the corporate interest can be intentionally and instrumentally promoted and protected, would, in the first instance, deny that such a proposition can be proven, and then would blame fate for the fact that their self-chosen isolation has been in vain. Their envisaged solution would be to leave well enough alone. This follows from their hermeneutic epistemology, which requires them to presume that people can only contestably know the subjective social world as what they believe it to be, and their agency ontology, which permits the presumption that people's actions are constrained by their subjective perceptions of social reality. This solution would involve resisting vigorously any fate-tempting corporate governance innovation, which would only make matters worse. Then, if their survival interests are threatened they would exit (Hirschman 1970) by withdrawing from the corporate governance processes.

---

[64] In terms of Thompson's (1967) decision-making strategies matrix, fatalists would prefer inspirational decision making strategies, as they are inclined to be uncertain about both outcome preferences and their beliefs about cause-and-effect relations.

GOOD CORPORATE MANAGEMENT: WHAT IS IT?

"Beyond the definition of mission and roles lies the task of building purpose into the social structure of the enterprise, or of transforming a neutral body of men [*sic*], into a committed polity"; this is the challenge Selznick (1957: 90) issues to corporate directors and managers. Building such a corporate commitment is the purpose of management, which Hershey and Blanchard (1993: 5) define as "the process of working with and through individuals and groups and other resources to accomplish organizational goals." What constitutes good management processes and practices in any corporation reflects the past cumulative judgements of the corporate directors and managers on human nature and the motivations of those they manage. Cultural Theory postulates that each of the four *social solidarities* has its perception of what constitutes good management.

Adherents to a particular *social solidarity* consider only their good management propositions to be authoritative. They would, inevitably, resist the good management propositions advanced by adherents to competing *social solidarities*. As a consequence, the extent to which the employees resist governance processes and practices—because the management processes are based on what employees deem to be inappropriate human nature, motivational and sociocognitive assumptions—is determined by the extent to which both sides adhere to the same *social solidarity,* and thus share a common view on what constitutes good management.

Individualist Perspective

To individualists, good corporate management is *managing for results*, with a focus on performance. Thus, managers improve results by relying on a decentralized authority distribution, so as to expand the ways in which work is conducted, with individuals expected to use their devolved authority to achieve management-established targets and with control being exercised ex post facto (Feldman and Khademain 2000: 150).

Human behavior is predictable, to individualists, on the basis of self-interest. Thus, people are presumed to be instrumental, applying functional-strategic rationality to make purposive and predatory decisions on the basis of their own self-interest. They are presumed to be egoistic and hedonistic, with their self-esteem derived from being, and being seen to be, materially successful. Individualists thus consider that corporate commitment can only occur if it is profitable to them[65] (Schwarz and Thompson 1990: 66). With this set of hu-

---

[65] Individualists, with their *homo economicus* or *rational economic man* perspectives (Schein 1980), would be sympathetic to Herzberg's (1966) Adam concept of human nature, and would thus presume that people are concerned predominantly with satisfying their safety, security and interpersonal relations needs. They would also be attracted to McGregor's (1960; see also 1967) Theory X human nature assumptions: that people are essentially indolent, unambitious, self-centered; are indifferent to organizational needs and prefer to be directed so as to avoid responsibility; and are gullible. Therefore, they

Corporate Interest and Corporate Governance 103

man nature assumptions, individualists would be favorably disposed to a particular set of organizational and management arrangements.

An organization would be pictured (Morgan 1986) by individualists as a 'living organism'[66] or in a state of flux and transformation,[67] and would preferably have an entrepreneurial orientation (Mintzberg 1989). Thus, it would be willing to operate at the edge of its competence. It does so by dealing with what it does not yet know using an integrative approach to problem solving that challenges established practices by going beyond received wisdom (Kanter 1984, 1989). It would have a strategic apex with little or no technostructure, but a significant degree of horizontal and/or spatial subunit differentiation. It would have an organizational culture[68] that is focused not only on tasks (Altman and

---

would also believe Barnard's (1938: 159) proposition that "incentives represent the final residue of all conflicting forces in organization" and that people are rational agents who respond to inputs (such as instructions) in systematic ways and can best be motivated by financial incentives (see also Bushardt et al. 1986, Clark and Wilson 1961, de Grazia 1960, Fayol [1916] 1949, Gellerman 1968, Taylor [1911] 1947, Whyte 1955). They would anticipate that employees will be dissatisfied at work in terms of Herzberg et al.'s (1959; see also Herzberg 1966) job hygiene work environment factors, most notably money, status and security. Their sense of competition would make individualists particularly sensitive to remuneration equitability in terms of the distributive justice outcomes achieved (Adams 1965, Greenberg 1987). The underlying presumptions of motivation based on financial incentives are: (1) that individuals value financial rewards as a means of satisfying their needs, the most important of which are Maslow's (1970) physiological, safety (security) and esteem needs, and Riesman's (1950) and Packard's (1959) prestige needs (see also Furnham 1984, Porter and Lawler 1968), and perceive that these rewards justify the effort; (2) that organizational performance can be measurably attributed to an individual's work contribution; (3) that increased individual performance does not become a new minimum standard (Handy 1976: 25; see also Vroom 1964). The *psychological contracts*—unwritten sets of expectations (Schein 1978)—between the governors, who would be presumed to prefer exercising resource, reward, economic or exchange power (Boulder 1990, French and Raven 1959, Hales 2001), and the governed, who would be presumed to be calculative. The governors would specify quite explicitly the financial rewards that would follow the rendering of services. The governed would be expected to have work commitment, in Morrow's (1983) terms, based on their careers, which would achieve Etzioni's (1961) *remunerative-calculative* organizational engagement.

[66] Morgan's (1986) *living organism* metaphor characterizes an organization as being preoccupied with adaptiveness rather than orderliness, and thus an open and flexible system that gives full scope to human capacities.

[67] Morgan's (1986) *flux and transformation* metaphor characterizes an organization as being in a constant state of change.

[68] "Like the culture of a tribe, a corporate culture is an amalgam of the heroes and villains, of the commandments, of the crimes and punishments, of all the oral mythology that permeates the tribe" (Foy 1980). Schein (1985) identifies three organizational culture dimensions: basic assumptions—those learned, unconsciously held responses that determine group perceptions, which may generate less-than-satisfactory crisis agreements (Taras 1991); values and beliefs; and visible artifacts, such as dress codes and

Baruch 1998), whereby management is regarded as solving a series of task-related problems involving the adjustment, redefinition and renegotiation of individual tasks (Handy 1979), but also on supporting quid pro quo exchanges between individuals (Douglas 1994: 176).[69] This organizational culture would have, in terms of Hofstede's (1988, 1991) cultural dimensions, low power distance[70] and uncertainty avoidance,[71] but high individualism[72] and masculinity.[73]

The preferred leadership style would be that of a "developer" (Altman and Baruch 1998: 780), within a consultative management system (Likert 1961, 1967). This leadership style (Nichols 1986) is characterized by Hershey and Blanchard's (1969, 1993) low relationship[74] and low task[75] behavior pattern, which facilitates individual autonomy by appropriately delegating decision making and implementation responsibility.[76]

---

office layout (Domahidy and Gilsionan 1992). For a review of the controversy surrounding organizational culture, see Legge 1994 and Anthony 1994.

[69] In terms of Burns' (1966; see also Burns and Stalker 1961) three social systems that make up an organization—the *formal authority* system, which is the most overt; the *cooperative career* system of competitive people with aspirations seeking advancement, which influences the way they react to formal decisions in terms of their career structure; and the *political* system, which influences the way politically competitive people react to formal decisions in terms of the power structure—individualists would operate through the *formal authority* and *cooperative career* systems to promote their own self-interest, preferring, as far as possible, to free ride on other self-interested people who choose to use the *political* system to achieve their ends.

[70] Hofstede's *power-distance* dimension is the distance or personal gap that is felt to exist between subordinate and superior.

[71] Hofstede's *uncertainty-avoidance* dimension is the degree of comfort felt when coping with uncertainty.

[72] Hofstede's *individualism* dimension is the degree to which *individualism* (which emphasizes the right of an individual to a private life and opinion and to take personal initiatives and seek achievement if desired) dominates *collectivism* (which emphasizes the protection of the individual by group membership in return for group loyalty).

[73] Hofstede's *masculine* dimension is the degree to which the *masculine* values of performance, money, material standards, speed and size dominate the *feminine* values of quality of life, the importance of people and environment, service per se motivates, and the proposition that small is beautiful.

[74] Relationship behavior is the extent to which leaders are likely to maintain personal relationships between themselves and their followers by opening up communication channels, providing socioemotional support, giving 'psychological strokes,' and engaging in other facilitating behaviors (Hershey and Blanchard 1993: 129).

[75] Task behavior is the extent to which leaders are likely to organize and define the roles of their followers—to explain what activities each is expected to do, and when, where, and how these tasks are to be accomplished. It is characterized by an endeavor to establish well-defined organizational patterns, communication channels and ways of accomplishing jobs (Hershey and Blanchard 1993: 129).

[76] This broadly corresponds with Stogdill and Coons' (1957) *low consideration* (relationship behaviors) and *low initiating structures* (task behaviors) leadership style, and with Blake and Mouton's (1982, 1984) low concern-for-production and low concern-for-people, or *impoverished,* leadership style, because it provides little structural or so-

The preferred organizational response to change in the external environment would be that of a "prospector" (Altman and Baruch 1998: 780), forever seeking out and exploiting new opportunities, even at the risk of over-extension (Miles and Snow 1978). The external environment would be perceived and characterized as "disturbed reactive" (Thompson and Taylor 1986: 12) in terms of its rate of change and the predictability of its direction (Emery and Trist 1965).

The preferred management process would involve creating incentives for the rewarding of desirable behaviors and disincentives for the punishment of undesirable behaviors,[77] with the expected induced response being instrumental compliance (Etzioni 1961) with the corporate rules and procedures, based on an economic calculation of the compliance costs and benefits. In the face of corporate decline, individualists would blame rogue behavior or bad luck and expect people to exit (Hirschman 1970) by withdrawing from the corporation in order to minimize their material losses and renegotiate their contracts.

Enclavist Perspective

To enclavists, good management is *managing for inclusion*, with a focus on building capacity to achieve results. Thus, managers encourage employees, as well as members of the general public and other relevant organizations, to work together toward results over which they may have little direct influence. They do this by decentralizing authority, and emphasizing empowerment, teamwork, and continuous improvement to increase participation, with management control determined by how they implement participation (Feldman and Khademain 2000: 150).

Human behavior is predictable, to enclavists, on the basis of group-constructed understandings. Thus, people are presumed to be cooperative by nature; ever willing and able to construct the mutual understandings that form the basis for reasoning.[78] They are thus presumed to be able and willing to en-

---

cioemotional support when needed by group members. In terms of Tannenbaum and Schmidt's (1957) leadership behavior continuum, this leadership style involves managers defining limits and followers making decisions.

[77] The appropriate control mechanism would be *self-control* (under the self-determined coercive influence of financial incentives) involving the modifying, repressing or inhibiting of behavior to conform with a set of internalized rules and norms of behavior relating the *processes* (methods of work), *outputs* (standards) and internalized values to the ethical conduct of those carrying out the work itself (Hales 2001: 47).

[78] Postmodern organizational theorists would empathize with the underpinning propositions of "communal negotiation, the importance of social processes in the observational enterprise, the sociopractical functions of language, and the significance of pluralistic cultural investments in the conception of the true and the good" (Gergen and Thatchenkery 1998: 26). In this context, Morgan (1983: 12–13) perceived research as "a process of interaction...designed for the realization of potentialities"; Argyris and Schön (1985) and Schön (1983) connect research and social action; Cooperrider and Srivastva (1987) speak of *appreciative inquiry*; Reason and Rowan (1981) advocate the use of *dialogic methods* (see also Bakhtin 1981); and Gergen (1994) speaks of *generative theo-*

gage in communicative-value rationality, involving intersubjective, critically reflective communications, in order to gain understanding in a group context. This means that because discourse occurs in an open environment characterized by broadly diffused transformations (Bakhtin 1981), patterns of human activity are ever dynamic, at times incrementally, sometimes disjointedly (Gergen and Thatchenkey 1998: 28).

Enclavists presume that people need to belong to a group in which they are popular, liked and trusted. Their self-esteem is presumed to be derived from being recognized and acclaimed for being committed to a common cause. Thus, to enclavists, their corporate commitment is to those with whom they share common values and a common vision.[79] With this set of human nature assump-

---

rizing that challenges conventional organizational wisdom and creates new organizational conceptualizations. For a discussion of postmodern organization theories, see, for example, Berquist 1993, Boje et al. 1996, Chia 1995, Clegg 1990, and Hassard, 1994.

[79] Enclavists, with their *social man* perspectives (Schein 1980), would be sympathetic to Herzberg's (1966) presumptions of the Abraham concept of human nature, and would thus presume that people are concerned predominantly with satisfying human needs of understanding, achievement, and psychological growth and development. They would also be attracted to McGregor's (1960; see also 1967) Theory Y human nature assumptions, which are that people find work as natural as rest and recreation, can assume responsibility, are not resistant to organizational needs if they feel committed, can be creative in solving organizational problems, and are willing to direct their behavior toward organizational goals. Enclavists would believe that employees may very well be dissatisfied with some of Herzberg et al.'s (1959; see also Herzberg 1966) job hygiene work environment factors, notably working conditions, money, status and security. Enclavists' sense of fairness would make them particularly sensitive to remuneration equitability issues, both with respect to the distributional justice outcomes achieved and, perhaps more importantly, to the procedural justice achieved by the methods used to determine remuneration (Adams 1965, Greenberg 1987). They would believe that people can best be motivated by setting goals (Locke 1968, Locke and Latham 1990) to which they can make a commitment. There are two underlying presumptions of motivations that focus on goal setting (see, for example, House and Mitchell's (1974) path-goal theory). First, there is a presumption of congruence between individual and organizational goals, which enables an organization to meet individuals' needs. The most important of these needs are Maslow's (1970) social (affiliation or acceptance), esteem and self-actualization (distinctive psychological potential) needs; Ardrey's (1967) identity, security and stimulation needs; Alderfer's (1972) existence, relatedness and growth needs; McCelland's (1961, 1967; see also McCelland et al. 1953) achievement, power and affiliation needs, and Herzberg et al.'s (1959; see also Herzberg 1966) achievement, recognition, responsibility and advancement needs. Second, individuals are presumed to want to share responsibility for goal setting and achievement decisions. The *psychological contracts* between the governors, who would be presumed to prefer to exercise personal, referent, normative and integrative power (Boulder 1990, French and Raven 1959, Hales 2001), and the governed, who would be presumed to be cooperative, would act on the premise that people tend to identify with organizational goals, which they pursue creatively in return for just rewards, and thus they should be given more voice in their selection and more discretion in the choice of goal-achievement strategies (Handy 1976: 41). The governed would be expected, in Morrow's (1983) terms, to have a work commit-

tions, enclavists would be favorably disposed to a particular set of organizational and management arrangements.

An organization would be pictured (Morgan 1986) by enclavists as a political system,[80] or a configuration of cultures,[81] and would preferably have a missionary orientation, with a rich array of distinctive shared values and beliefs (Mintzberg 1989).[82] It would concentrate on the "[inter]personal relations of bonding insiders together against outsiders"[83] (Douglas 1994: 176). Its organizational culture would be centered existentially on the person, such that the organization would be perceived to exist in order to help people achieve their personal goals (Altman and Baruch 1998, 780; see also Handy 1979).[84] This organizational culture would have, in terms of Hofstede's (1980, 1991) cultural dimensions, low power-distance, individualism, and masculinity, but a high uncertainty avoidance.

The leadership style would preferably be that of a "coach" (Altman and Baruch 1998: 780, Ellis 1991), within a participative-group type of management system (Likert 1961, 1967). This leadership style (Nichols (1986) is characterized by Hershey and Blanchard's (1969, 1993) high relationship and low

---

ment based on the value they place on work as an end in itself, on their absorption and involvement in their job, and on their organization and sectional interest loyalties, which would achieve Etzioni's (1961) *normative-moral* organizational engagement.

[80] Morgan's (1986) *political system* metaphor characterizes an organization as having many stakeholders with potentially conflicting interests that need to be negotiated.

[81] Morgan's (1986) *cultures* metaphor characterizes an organization as having a fragmented organizational culture, with people in each subculture sharing common values, expressed through language, symbols and ceremonies, that enable them to interpret situations and events in similar ways.

[82] Enclavists would also be attracted to Mintzberg's (1989) *adhocracy* or *innovative* organization, with its distinctive characteristics of organic structure, decentralization and mutual adjustments by direct cooperation; and they would have empathy with his *political organization*, with its lack of a coordination mechanism and its propensity for conflict.

[83] In terms of Burns' (1966; see also Burns and Stalker 1961) three social systems that make up an organization, enclavists would undermine any opposition they face from the *formal authority* or *cooperative career* systems by operating through the *political* system in order to inculcate their particular shared common values and common vision throughout a corporation.

[84] Peters and Waterman (1982) argue that communicating a values-driven performance philosophy is an important ingredient of corporate excellence, which can be achieved by means of *management by wandering around* (see also Peters 1988, 1994a, 1994b).

task behavior pattern,[85] which shares ideas and facilitates decision making, thereby empowering individuals.[86]

The preferred organizational response to change in the external environment would be that of a "defender" (Altman and Baruch 1998: 780), seeking to ensure stability by doing what the organization knows how to do well (Miles and Snow 1978). The external environment would be perceived and characterized as "placid clustered" (Thompson and Taylor 1986: 12; see also Emery and Trist 1965).

The preferred management process would involve inspiring a sense of performance consciousness in the form of a mutually agreed set of high expectations that are compatible with both categorical and corporate interests. Communicating a values-driven performance philosophy would do this by stimulating and facilitating the necessary behavior change by empowering staff to become creative risk takers and innovators.[87] The expected response would be compliance because of a moral commitment (Etzioni 1961). In the face of corporate decline, the enclavists' first and natural response would be to exercise voice (Hirschman 1970), in order to support their faction's strategies for reversing the decline. By so doing, they would be recognized as trustworthy, dependable, factional insiders. Acts of voice would include blaming those in positions of authority for taking too many risks, accusing them of having an inappropriate set of values, and threatening to exit (Hirschman 1970) or withdraw from any engagement with the corporation, should a value conflict emerge on how to reverse the decline.

Heirarchist Perspective

To hierarchists, good corporate management is *managing for process*, with a focus on employee compliance. Thus, policies with minimal discretion given to employees are implemented, as administrative *processes* are strictly controlled by rules and regulations that define who should complete a task, and how and when it should be done, with control exercised ex ante (Feldman and Khademain 2000: 150).

Human behavior is predictable, as far as hierarchists are concerned, on the basis of rational thought constrained by hierarchically determined values and

---

[85] This broadly corresponds with Stogdill and Coons' (1957*)* *high consideration* (relationship behaviors) and *low initiating structures* (task behaviors) leadership style, and with Blake and Mouton's (1982, 1984) low concern-for-production and high concern-for-people, or *country club*, leadership style, under which production is incidental to the lack of conflict and good fellowship.

[86] In terms of Tannenbaum and Schmidt's (1957) leadership behavior continuum, this leadership style involves managers permitting followers to function within the limits they define.

[87] The appropriate control mechanism would be *mutual control*, involving the mutual enforcement of group behavior norms relating to *inputs* (as standards of recruitment to the group), *processes* (as work methods), *outputs* (as performance standards), and *values* (as ethical standards) (Hales 2001: 47).

beliefs. To hierarchists, corporate commitment is to the correct procedures and to the managing elite, because people value the personal physical and psychological safety and security that result from the order, clarity and authority provided by well-defined organizations and systems, and because their self-esteem is derived from gaining approval from authority figures.[88] With this set of human nature assumptions, individualists would be favorably disposed to a particular set of organizational and management arrangements.

An organization would be pictured (Morgan 1986) by hierarchists as a machine[89] or a brain,[90] and would preferably have a bureaucratic orientation (Weber [1915] 1947). It would have a centralized technostructure, standardized work processes, specialized work tasks, order and discipline, and a unity of direction (through a scalar chain) and control. Individuals' interests would be subordinated to the corporate interest, and thus there would be an insistence on hierarchical obedience and organizational loyalty (Burns 1966, Burns and

---

[88] Hierarchists, with their *homo hierarchus* perspectives (Dumont 1970), would be sympathetic to Herzberg's (1966) presumptions of the Adam concept of human nature, and to McGregor's (1960; see also 1967) Theory X human nature assumptions. They would believe that employees could very well be dissatisfied with some of Herzberg et al.'s (1959; see also Herzberg 1966) work environment factors, notably working conditions, money, status and security. Hierarchists' respect for rules and regulations would make them particularly sensitive to the procedural justice achieved by the methods used to determine remuneration (Adams 1965, Greenberg 1987). They would believe that people can best be motivated by the organizational satisfaction of their needs. The needs emphasized would be Maslow's (1970), physiological, safety (security), social (affiliation) and esteem needs; Ardrey's (1967) identity, security and stimulation needs; Adler's 1938) power needs; White's (1959) competence needs; and McCelland's (1961 and 1967; see also McCelland et al. 1953) achievement, power and affiliation needs. The underlying presumptions of motivation based on needs-satisfaction are that the individual has a set of valued personal needs that are knowable by the governors and can be satisfied through work. Hierarchists would presume that employees are largely concerned with Herzberg et al.'s (1959; see also Herzberg 1966) job hygiene work environment factors, especially policies and administration, supervision, working conditions and interpersonal relations. The *psychological contracts* between the hierarchist governors, who would be presumed to prefer legitimate, expert and knowledge power (Boulder 1990, French and Raven 1959, Hales 2000), and the governed, who would be presumed to be predominantly calculative, would make quite explicit the rights and obligations of the corporation in terms of the needs that would be met in return for services rendered (Handy 1976: 41). The governed would be expected to have a work commitment, in Morrow's (1983) terms, based on the value they place on their organization loyalty, which would achieve a weak form of Etzioni's (1961) *remunerative-calculative* organizational engagement.

[89] Morgan's (1986) *machine* metaphor characterizes an organization as being benevolent with an orderly set of arrangements about who does what and who controls whom.

[90] Morgan's (1986) *brain* metaphor characterizes an organizations as having intelligent people spread throughout it, which means that it is able to correct errors, deal with uncertainty, and accept self-criticism.

Stalker 1961, Fayol [1916] 1949, Radner 1992, Taylor [1911] 1947).[91] There would be "top-down bonding of individuals" (Douglas 1994: 176), through the fostering of an appropriate esprit de corps. Its organizational culture would emphasize role (Altman and Baruch 1998), and thus support compliance and permit little questioning of the rules and orders of what to do once they have been given by a legitimate authority[92] (Bardach and Kagan 1982, Cutting and Kouzmin 2001, but see also Brennan and Buchanan 1985). This would support a club culture, whereby strong leaders have power and use it (Handy 1979). It would have, in terms of Hofstede's (1980, 1991) cultural dimensions, high power-distance, masculinity and uncertainty avoidance, but low individualism.

The preferred leadership style would be that of a "parent" (Altman and Baruch 1998: 780), within a benevolent-authoritarian type of management system (Likert 1961, 1967). This leadership style (Nichols (1986) is characterized by Hershey and Blanchard's (1969, 1993) high relationship and high task behavior pattern,[93] which involves explaining decisions, providing opportunities for clarification, and monitoring performance, thereby ensuring leadership control.[94]

The preferred organizational response to change in the external environment would be that of an "analyzer" (Altman and Baruch 1998: 780), seeking to bal-

---

[91] Hierarchists would also feel secure in Mintzberg's (1989) *diversified organization*, with its limited vertical decentralization that permits a degree of subunit autonomy (self-sufficiency) within a centralized control framework; or his *professional organization*, with its standardization of skills and working autonomy underwritten by the authority of expertise.

[92] In terms of Burns' (1966; see also Burns and Stalker 1961) three social systems that make up an organization, hierarchists would overtly acknowledge the supremacy of the *formal authority* system but would operate covertly through the *cooperative career* and *political* systems to reinforce and enhance their own standing in the organization (by, for example, seeking to address a particular change, innovation and uncertainty). They would do so even if this resulted in what Burns describes as an ambiguous figure system (an unofficial pairing of the chief executive with people at different positions in the management structure), a mechanistic jungle (the creation of new administrative subunits so that the formal authority system can regain control) or a committee system (the creation of committees to address issues that might threaten the power of the formal authority system).

[93] This broadly corresponds with Stogdill and Coons' (1957) *high consideration* (relationship behaviors) and *high initiating structures* (task behaviors) leadership style, and with Blake and Mouton's (1982, 1984) *high concern-for-production* and *high concern-for-people*, or *team*, leadership style.

[94] Whitehead (1936: 72–73) caught the essence of this style of leadership:

The leader shares with his group a profound loyalty to the technical procedures....[He] is trusted as one who has unusual skill in these technical procedures...[and] being a man [sic] of intelligence, obtains an unusual insight into the causal relations involved in his procedures...[he] continues in his traditional procedures,...because he sees the 'reasons why.'....Sooner or later in his semi-irrational reveries and reflections, [he] stumbles on a technical improvement. He adopts this without misgivings because the group has accorded him the right to make decisions in technical matters. The group follow their leader and adopt the improved process without question.

ance risk and outcomes as a follower rather than an initiator of change (Miles and Snow 1978). The external environment would be perceived and characterized as "turbulent" (Thompson and Taylor 1986: 12; see also Emery and Trist 1965).

The preferred management process would involve the use of a hierarchical command-and-control process to permit the managing elite to determine and police what are acceptable (desirable) or unacceptable (undesirable) behaviors in terms of the desired corporate governance outcomes. The hierarchists' expected response to such management processes would be compliance because of a cognitive commitment (Etzioni 1961), derived from rational calculation in the context of structural processes, perhaps in the form of prescribed rules and regulations, supported, perhaps, by a deontological moral code.[95] In the face of corporate decline, the hierarchists' first and natural response would be loyalty, (Hirschman 1970) with the expectation that the decline can be reversed by the managing elite. Acts of loyalty could include suppressing information critical of the managing elite's performance and threatening and punishing those nonconforming individuals who have made, or may make, disclosures critical of the managing elite's interpretation of the causes of, or the solutions to, corporate decline.

Fatalist Perspective

To fatalists, good corporate management is *managing for survival*, with a focus on plausibility: organizational goals can only evolve from action, because they cannot be predetermined; learning can only be by trial and error, because technology is unclear; who is involved in what is ever changing, because participation is fluid.[96] Management control is thus achievable through practices that embrace contrived randomness.

Human behavior is, to fatalists, unpredictable, because agency is constrained by subjective perceptions of social reality. What an individual believes to be real is, in fact, reality. Thus people are presumed to engage in nonrational, inspirational-strategic reasoning because validity, truth, and efficiency are irrelevant. Plausibility is presumed to be the basis for reasoning, which involves a Weickian-like sense-making process (Weick 1995). Because fatalists are perceived to have a dominant commitment to their own survival, they have no in-

---

[95] The appropriate control mechanism would be *external control* (given the weaker coercive influence of needs-satisfying motivators) involving both formal and impersonal rules relating to *inputs* (about recruitment, qualifications and experience), *processes* (as technical methods and procedures) and *outputs* (as performance measures and standards); and informally transmitted values (as organizational ethos or philosophy) achieved by direct management supervision in the form of personal monitoring and work surveillance (Hales 2001: 47–48).

[96] This characterizes March's (1988, 1994) *organized anarchy* (see also Cyert and March [1963] 1992; March and Olsen 1976, 1989).

stitutional commitment.[97] With this set of human nature assumptions, fatalists, who expect to be alienated, would be most reconciled to a particular set of organizational and management arrangements.

An organization would be pictured (Morgan 1986) by fatalists as a psychic prison[98] or an instrument of domination,[99] and would have a bureaucratic orientation (Altman and Baruch 1998), with an obsession for control (Mintzberg 1989). Conflicts would never be resolved, uncertainties would always be avoided, and solutions would inevitably be shortsighted and simplistic. Thus, the organization would establish, by trial and error, what it can do, and would adapt its goals accordingly. Fatalists would expect an organization to have a culture that emphasizes power, one that reinforces the authority of a superior over subordinates. Therefore they would support a club culture under which strong leaders would be permitted, if not expected, to exercise power (Handy 1979).[100] It would have, in terms of Hofstede's (1980, 1991) cultural dimensions, high power-distance, masculinity and uncertainty avoidance, and a low individualism.

---

[97] Fatalists, with their self-chosen isolationist perceptions, would be sympathetic to Herzberg's (1966) presumptions of the Adam concept of human nature, and to McGregor's (1960; see also 1967) Theory X human nature assumptions. They would certainly believe that alienated employees would be generally dissatisfied with Herzberg's et al.'s (1959; see also Herzberg 1966) job hygiene work environment factors, particularly policies and administration, supervision, and working conditions. The fatalists' cynicism and distrust would make them particularly sensitive to the issues of equity of remuneration, both in terms of the distributional justice outcomes achieved and the procedural justice achieved by the methods used to determine remuneration (Adams 1965, Greenberg 1987). Thus, compliance occurs only because of fear of punishment that would diminish their capacity to meet their physiological and safety (security) needs (Maslow 1970). The underlying presumptions are (1) that individuals comply because they are sufficiently fearful of punishment for noncompliance; and (2) that those threatening punishment have the power to punish. The *psychological contract* between the governors, who fatalists expect to exercise coercive, physical or threat power (Boulder 1990, French and Raven 1959, Hales 2001), and the governed, who would be presumed to require coercion to comply, would quite explicitly articulate the rules to be followed and the punishments for noncompliance (Handy 1976: 40). The governed would be presumed to have no work commitment, which would result in Etzioni's (1961) *coercive-alienative* organizational engagement.

[98] Morgan's (1986) *psychic prison* metaphor characterizes an organization as one in which people become trapped in a particular organizational mind set that dominates their thinking in a way that does not allow them to see organizational reality clearly from any other perspective.

[99] Morgan's (1986) *instrument of domination* metaphor characterizes an organization as one that is willing to glorify the managing elite at the expense of sacrificing people, by crippling them through work accidents, disease and stress, by discarding them after years of service, or by polluting their environment.

[100] In terms of Burns' (1966; see also Burns and Stalker 1961) three social systems that make up an organization, fatalists would acknowledge the power of the *formal authority* system, deny the relevance to them of the *cooperative career* system, and accept their impotence in the *political* system.

The leadership style fatalists would expect would be that of a "driver" (Altman and Baruch 1998: 780) within an exploitative-authoritarian type of management system (Likert 1961, 1967). This leadership style (Nichols 1986) is characterized by Hershey and Blanchard's (1969, 1993) low relationship and high task behavior pattern,[101] which involves providing specific instructions and closely supervising work performance, thereby ensuring dominant leadership.[102]

The preferred organizational response to change in the external environment would be that of a "reactor" (Altman and Baruch 1998: 780), characterized by hesitancy born of the uncertainty and confusion that inevitably follows (Miles and Snow 1978). The external environment would be perceived and characterized as "placid randomized" (Thompson and Taylor 1986: 12; see also Emery and Trist 1965).

The expected management processes would involve hierarchical command-and-control.[103] The expected response induced by such management processes would be an alienative compliance (Etzioni 1961), born of the fear of force, threat and menace.[104] In the face of organizational decline, fatalists would neither express loyalty, as the powers are viewed as untrustworthy, nor would they use voice, as this would require them to take a position that would make them less isolated. They would exit (Hirschman 1970) by withdrawing from the corporation only as a last resort, if their survival interests are threatened.

CORPORATE GOVERNANCE ANTAGONISMS

Because adherents to any particular *social solidarity* would resist the flawed approaches to corporate governance and management advanced by adherents to any competing *social solidarities*, trench warfare is inevitable.

Individualists, if trapped in, or subject to, a failing corporate governance mode posited by adherents to another *social solidarity*, would, in the 'corporate interest,' seeing themselves as commonsense saviors of their own self-interest, take the necessary steps to limit the power of corporate managers, employees and strategic stakeholders by imposing on them enforceable, explicit, performance-reward contracts with a zero noncompliance tolerance and full restitution as the ultimate sanction.

Enclavists in such a situation would, in the corporate interest, seeing themselves as passionate saviors of the categorical interests to which they are com-

---

[101] This broadly corresponds with Stogdill and Coons' (1957) *low consideration* (relationship behaviors) and *high initiating structures* (task behaviors) leadership style, and with Blake and Mouton's (1982, 1984) *high concern-for-production* and *low concern-for-people* or *task* leadership style.

[102] In terms of Tannenbaum and Schmidt's (1957) leadership behavior continuum, this leadership style involves leaders making decisions and announcing them.

[103] Fatalists would, no doubt, concur with Braverman's (1974) perception of the capitalist firm as intent on disempowering and deskilling workers so as to remove their capacity to obstruct or resist the achievement of maximum profits.

[104] The appropriate control mechanism would be *external control* (Hales 2001: 47), particularly by means of random direct supervision.

Enclavists in such a situation would, in the corporate interest, seeing themselves as passionate saviors of the categorical interests to which they are committed, demand that all stakeholders be permitted to engage fully in corporate governance processes, so as to build a congruence between the categorical interests of the stakeholders and the interests of the corporate owners and managers, and to design organizational structures and processes that would achieve a values-driven compliance.

Hierarchists in the same circumstances would, in the 'corporate interest,' seeing themselves as the rational saviors of the corporate good as articulated by the managing elite, seek to impose formal corporate governance structures and command-and-control processes, administered with a zero noncompliance tolerance and substantial sanctions.

Fatalists in the same situation would, seeing themselves as victims of the corporate powers that be, feel vindicated, because they correctly anticipated the so-called corporate experts getting it wrong, and so would become prophets of doom.

CONCLUSION

The corporate governors' ability to conduct the affairs of their corporation as they see fit is a function of the limitations they place upon themselves. These limitations emerge because of the corporate governance and management propositions they hold to be true (Dixon and Dogan 2002b, 2002d). This limits their ability to manipulate or constrain the behavior of those they seek to affect, who may be located within the corporation or in its external environment. The extent to which this occurs depends on the extent to which their actions violate or reinforce the corporate governance and management truths of those whose behavior they are seeking to affect. Adherents to each of the four *social solidarities* have a distinctive but flawed perspective on whether the corporate interest is knowable; on what the roles of the corporate owners, stakeholders and managers should be in identifying and prioritizing the corporate interest; on the appropriate governance structures and processes; and on the management processes and practices that best achieve the corporate objectives. They thus have distinctive perspectives on what constitutes good corporate governance and management.

Individualists would assert that only the corporate owners have corporate governance authority, so they should determine what is in the 'corporate interest,' as both the corporate stakeholders and managers have their categorical interests protected by law or contracts. This means that good corporate governance and management must reinforce their control, by means of a set of negotiated contractual relationships that are expected to solicit instrumental compliance.

Enclavists would argue that the corporate stakeholders and owners should codetermine what is in the 'corporate interest,' thereby ensuring that there is a synergy between the stakeholders' categorical and the corporate interests, which is of central importance not only to the corporation's performance, viability and sustainability, but also to the protection of the 'public interest.' Thus good corporate governance and management must be inclusive, empowering and focused on enhancing the set of categorical interests that constitute the corporate interest. This is expected to achieve behavioral compliance by building a moral commitment to a common cause.

Hierarchists would consider it obvious that the managing elite is best placed to determine what is in the corporate good. They alone should balance the competing categorical interests to determine corporate objectives. Thus, good corporate governance and management involve formal corporate governance structures and command-and-control management processes that are expected to solicit behavioral compliance because of a cognitive commitment to the managing elite.

Fatalists would consider the corporate interest to be unknowable and thus believe that it cannot be intentionally and instrumentally promoted and protected. Consequently, who determines the corporate objectives, and on what basis, is unimportant, for whoever has the power to do so will be self-serving and inevitably eager to initiate exploitative corporate action. Fatalists accept that corporate governance may sometimes be benign in intent but believe that inevitably it is malevolent in action. They would, however, consider that corporate governance and management should involve organizational goals evolving from action, learning by trial and error, and fluid participation, because they expect the 'corporate experts' to get it all wrong. They thus expect to be alienated from the corporate powers that be, and their organizational engagement can only be on the basis of alienative compliance.

Adherents to each *social solidarity* thus accept that a corporation is governable, but only if their distinctive approach to governing is adopted. Adherents to one *social solidarity* consider their balance of corporate interests to be the only legitimate one. Thus they consider their approach to corporate governance and management to be the only acceptable one. They would, inevitably, resist the propositions of other competing *social solidarities* regarding the identification, prioritization, promotion and protection of the corporate interest. As a consequence, the extent to which the processes of those who seek to govern the corporation are resisted by those whose behavior they are seeking to affect is determined by the extent to which they adhere to the same *social solidarity*. If they do, they would share a common view not only on what the corporate interest is, but also on the best enabling environment that would ensure its proper identification, prioritization, promotion and protection—what constitute the most appropriate corporate governance roles and responsibilities of the corporate owners, stakeholders, directors and managers; the most appropriate governance and management structures; and the most appropriate management processes and practices. If they do not, the result will be corporate governance disillusionment, even despair, among the governed, which may lead to their withdrawal from, or rebellion against, the corporate governors' processes. This theme is developed in detail in Chapters 6 and 7.

Appendix 3.1
The Competing Social Solidarities on the Corporate Interest and Corporate Governance

Dimension	Hierarchist	Enclavist	Fatalist	Individualist
Reality:	Objective, with the truth discernible by rational thought using scientific method.	Socially constructed by discourse.	Individually determined by what is perceived to be true.	Objective, as expressed by the revealed preferences.
Nomology:	Human behavior predictable on the basis of rational thought constrained by group norms.	Human behavior predictable on the basis of group-constructed mutual understandings.	Human behavior is unpredictable.	Human behavior predictable on the basis of rational choice.
Dominant motivation:	To be approved by authority figures so as to be recognized as a member of a hierarchy that promises the satisfaction of their physical and psychological security needs.	To achieve the recognition and acclaim of people in the group to which they belong because they are popular, committed and trusted.	To survive against the odds.	To win the highest level of material success possible, so as to be recognized and acclaimed by other materially successful people.

Dimension	Hierarchist	Enclavist	Fatalist	Individualist
Primary source of self-esteem:	Approval by authority figures.	Recognition and acclaim by those committed to a common cause.	Seeing themselves as survivors against the odds.	Recognition and acclaim by the materially successful for being one of them.
Primary metalife goal:	To be approved by authority figures.	To be acclaimed by the committed.	To have self-respect as a survivor against the odds.	To be acclaimed by materially successful people.
Methodology:	Naturalist structuralism.	Hermeneutic structuralism.	Hermeneutic agency.	Naturalist agency.
Predisposition toward:				
governance mode:	Stewardship (hierarchical) mode.	Stakeholder (interactive) mode.	No preference as none can make any difference.	Ownership (market) mode.
owners:	The managing elite knows what is in their best interests.	Interests are presumed to conflict with corporate stakeholders' interests.	Untrustworthy and indifferent to people's needs, but presumed to be powerless.	Ownership bestows the sole right to govern a corporation.

Appendix 3.1 (Cont'd)

Dimension	Hierarchist	Enclavist	Fatalist	Individualist
directors:	Trustees elected or appointed by the corporate owners from among the managing elite as their trustees.	Trustees elected or appointed by the corporate owners and stakeholders to ensure that the corporation produces balanced stakeholder benefits.	Their power to govern, however acquired, can never be legitimated. Seen as powerful, unaccountable, untrustworthy and indifferent to people's needs.	Trustees elected or appointed by corporate owners to protect and promote the corporate owners' interests.
stakeholders:	The managing elite knows what is in their best interests.	Society bestows upon them the moral right to cogovern a corporation, because of its use of society's resources and the special privileges it gains from society.	Untrustworthy and indifferent to people's needs, but presumed to be powerless.	Inclined to be pedantic rent seekers, who threaten the power of the corporate owners. The only rights they have are those conferred by law or contractual agreements.
managers:	Managerial ability bestows upon them the sole right to govern a corporation.	Always at risk of taking immoral and corrupt actions, thus must be treated with vigilance.	Untrustworthy and indifferent to people's needs, but presumed to be powerful and unaccountable.	Place self-interest above the corporate interest.

Dimension	Hierarchist	Enclavist	Fatalist	Individualist
Predisposition toward (cont'd):				
employees:	Serfs.	Committed.	Alienated.	Mercenaries.
Corporate interest:	Knowable as a set of corporate objectives grounded in a notion of the corporate good, as articulated by a corporation's managerial elite.	Knowable as a set of corporate objectives embodying an agreed set of stakeholder categorical interests that is both for the corporate good and in the public interest.	Not knowable because of capriciousness and uncertainty.	Knowable as a set of corporate objectives that reflects the will of the corporate owners.
Corporate mission:	Balance benefits to corporate managers, owners, stakeholders and employees.	Balance corporate stakeholder benefits.	Survival.	Maximize value to corporate owners.
Accountability:	Corporate managers are responsible to themselves, as the corporate directors, and thus indirectly to the corporate owners.	Corporate managers are accountable to the corporate directors, who are jointly accountable to the corporate stakeholders and owners.	Neither the corporate managers nor the corporate directors can be made accountable to anyone.	Corporate managers are accountable to the corporate directors, who are accountable to the corporate owners.

Appendix 3.1 (Cont'd)

Dimension	Hierarchist	Enclavist	Fatalist	Individualist
Governability:	Corporations governable, but only if the managing elite are given the necessary power to do as they see fit.	Corporations governable, but only if the corporate stakeholders are given the necessary power to address categorical interests.	Corporations governable, but only if the corporate powers that be exercise the necessary coercive power to govern as they see fit.	Corporations governable, but only if the self-interests of corporate owners, directors, managers, and employees are contractually aligned.
Governance challenge:	To establish corporate governance mechanisms that the managing elite can dominate.	To establish corporate governance mechanisms that facilitate the codetermining, protecting and promoting the corporate interest.	To establish corporate governance mechanisms that do not expect or require people's constructive engagement.	To establish corporate governance mechanisms that can dominate corporate management, employees and stakeholders.
Salient threat:	The inability of the corporate managing elite to understand the nature, causation and solution to corporate governance problems.	The inability of corporate stakeholders, owners and managers to engage in harmonious collective decision making that identifies, promotes and protects the codetermined corporate interest.	The ability of anyone to establish that the corporate interest can be intentionally and instrumentally promoted and protected, so revealing that their self-chosen isolation has been in vain.	The inability of principals to specify completely their contracts with their agents and to enforce them with a zero non-compliance tolerance and full restitution as the sanction.

Dimension	Hierarchist	Enclavist	Fatalist	Individualist
Governance salient focus:	Inputs and process.	Process as much as outcomes.	Inputs and process.	Outputs and outcome.
Governance structure:	Large and hierarchical unitary board of directors dominated by the managing elite drawn from within the corporation or from related corporations.	Compound board of directors, made up of a supervisory board (comprising the corporate directors) and a management board (comprising the corporate managers).	Unitary board of directors whose roles and responsibilities are tightly circumscribed by legal requirements that minimize exploitative and coercive corporate behavior.	Unitary board of directors dominated by external members, with non-executive audit and governance committees.
Election of directors:	Voluntary elections on a one share, one vote, basis, with all candidates nominated by the managing elite.	Compulsory election on the basis of one vote per shareholder or stakeholder in designated corporate constituencies, with all candidates nominated by the corporate stakeholders or owners.	Voluntary elections, but basis makes no difference.	Voluntary elections on a one share, one vote, basis, with all candidates nominated by the corporate owners.
Organizational structure:	Mechanistic (perhaps a J organization).	Organic (perhaps a matrix, M-form or another holonic form).	Mechanistic.	Organic (perhaps a matrix, M-form or another holonic form).

Appendix 3.1 (Cont'd)

Dimension	Hierarchist	Enclavist	Fatalist	Individualist
Decision-making process:	Autocratic (perhaps a degree of consultation) decision-making process, involving institutional activity by the managing elite, using functional-analytic policy analysis to generate a set of objective facts that would facilitate satisficing decision making.	Group decision-making process that balances competing categorical interests by engaging in communicative-rational policy analysis to facilitate consistent, congruent and cogent decision making.	Autocratic decision-making process that is expected to be dominated by unknowing and untrustworthy vested interests, and that involves garbage-can-like decision processes.	Autocratic (perhaps a degree of consultation) decision-making process that uses instrumentally rational corporate policy analysis premised on self-interest motivation, and judgmental decision-making strategies to facilitate optimal decision making.
Organizational control:	Command-and-control, with hierarchical accountability.	Mutuality, with group and hierarchical accountability.	Contrived randomness, with hierarchical accountability.	Competition or rivalry, with hierarchical accountability.
Organizational picture:	A machine or a brain.	A political system, or a configuration of cultures.	A psychic prison or an instrument of domination.	A living organism or in a state of flux and transformation.

Dimension	Hierarchist	Enclavist	Fatalist	Individualist
Organizational orientation:	Bureaucratic (as well as diversified or professional).	Missionary (as well as adhocracy or political).	Bureaucratic (as well as organized anarchy).	Entrepreneurial.
External response:	Analyzer in a turbulent environment.	Defender of a placid-clustered environment.	Reactor in a placid randomized environment.	Prospector in a disturbed reactive environment.
Organizational culture:	Role.	Person.	Power.	Task.
power-distance:	High.	Low.	High.	Low.
uncertainty-avoidance:	High.	High.	High.	Low.
individualism:	Low.	Low.	Low.	High.
masculinity:	High.	Low.	High.	High.
Human nature:	Adam and Theory X.	Abraham and Theory Y.	Adam and Theory X.	Adam and Theory X.
Human behavior:	Predictable on basis of rational thought constrained by group norms.	Predictable on basis of group-constructed mutual understandings.	Unpredictable.	Predictable on basis of rational self-interest.

Appendix 3.1 (Cont'd)

Dimension	Hierarchist	Enclavist	Fatalist	Individualist
Human need priorities:	Physiological, security, safety, identity, affiliation, social, stimulation, competence, achievement, responsibility, advancement power and esteem.	Security, existence, identity, stimulation, growth, relatedness, affiliation, social, achievement, power, esteem and self-actualization	Physiological and safety.	Physiological, safety, esteem and prestige.
Motivator:	Needs satisfaction.	Goal setting.	Fear of punishment.	Financial incentives.
Work commitment:	Organization loyalty.	Value placed on work as an end in itself.	None.	Career.
Psychological contract:	Based on legitimate, expert, knowledge and exchange power.	Based on referent, normative and love power.	Based on coercive, physical and threat power.	Based on reward, exchange and economic power.
Organizational engagement:	Remunerative-calculative (weak form).	Normative-moral.	Coercive-alienative.	Remunerative-calculative (strong form).
Compliance:	Follows a cognitive commitment.	Follows a moral commitment.	Alienative compliance.	Instrumental compliance.

Dimension	Hierarchist	Enclavist	Fatalist	Individualist
Behavior control:	External control (direct supervision) mechanisms.	Mutual control (by members of the work group, occupation or profession) mechanisms.	External control (random direct supervision) mechanisms.	Self-control (under the coercive influence of financial incentives) mechanisms.
Leadership style:	Parent (team).	Coach (country club).	Driver (task).	Developer (impoverished).
Manager's salient functions:	To explain decisions and provide opportunities for clarification, and monitor performance.	To communicate a values-driven performance philosophy that stimulates and facilitates the desired behavior change.	To administer coercive hierarchical command and control processes.	To solve task-related problems, and to support quid pro quo exchanges between individuals.
Corporate social systems:	Operates overtly through the formal authority system but covertly through the cooperative career and political systems.	Operates through the political system to undermine any opposition derived from the formal authority or cooperative career system.	None, but acknowledges power of the formal authority system, denies the relevance to them of the cooperative career system, and accepts their impotence in the political system.	Operates through the formal authority and cooperative career systems, free rides on those using the political system whenever possible.

Appendix 3.1 (Cont'd)

Dimension	Hierarchist	Enclavist	Fatalist	Individualist
Response to the failure of their preferred corporate governance mode:	Express loyalty toward the managing elite, then blame deviants.	Voice blame by accusing the risk takers and the secret enemies within, and then demand more people be empowered to engage fully in an inclusive corporate governance process.	Blame fate, then exit by withdrawing from the corporate governance processes if organization decline threatens survival.	Blame bad luck or rogue managers, employees and strategic stakeholders. If organization decline threatens their material success they would threaten to exit by withdrawing from the corporation.
Response if trapped in, or subject to, a failing corporate governance mode posited by another *social solidarity*:	Would see themselves as the rational saviors of the corporate good, and would seek to impose formal corporate governance structures and command-and-control processes.	Would see themselves as passionate saviors of their categorical interests, and would demand that all stakeholders be permitted to engage fully in the corporate governance process.	Would see themselves as vindicated victims of the corporate powers that be, and would become prophets of doom.	Would see themselves as common-sense saviors of their own self-interest and would take the necessary steps to limit the power of corporate managers, employees and strategic stakeholders by imposing on them enforceable, explicit, performance-reward contracts.

4

Public Interest and Societal Governance

INTRODUCTION

The concept of governance has been routinely used in the sociopolitical realm for several centuries, generally in Mayntz's (1993: 11) sense of "a mode of social co-ordination or order."[1] In recent decades, however, it has achieved a new level of prominence for two fundamentally interrelated reasons (Alcentara 1998; Kooiman 1999; Majone 1997; Pierre and Peters 2000; Rhodes 1996, 1997; Stoker 1997; Weller et al. 1997). First, there has been a growing awareness that national governments are not the only crucial actors in addressing major societal issues (Miller and Rose 1990, Sternberger 1999). Second, it has become widely accepted that patterns of state-society interaction can no longer be considered static and unilateral.

The purpose of this chapter is to use Cultural Theory's *grid-group* social-control space or *social map* to gain insights into societal governance. Adherents

---

[1] Young (1994: ix) usefully distinguishes between *governance systems* ("social institutions or sets of rules guiding the behavior of those engaged in identifiable social practices") and *government systems* ("organizations or material entities established to administer provisions of governance systems"). Kooiman (1999: 70) defines societal (or sociopolitical) governance as: "all those interactive arrangements in which public as well as private actors participate aimed at solving societal problems, or creating societal opportunities, and attending to the institutions within which these governing activities take place." The United Nations Development Program (UNDP 1997: 2) defines it more narrowly as: "the exercise of political, economic and administrative authority of a country's affairs at all levels. Governance comprises the complex mechanisms, processes and institutions through which citizens and groups articulate their interests, mediate their differences and exercise their legal rights and obligations....Governance includes the state, but transcends it by taking in the private sector and civil society." Burns (1999) describes this as organic governance.

to each of the four *social solidarities*—hierarchist, enclavist, fatalist and individualist—offer competing perspectives on what constitutes the public interest[2] and whether it is knowable to the societal collective; on the structures and processes of civil government that best identify the public interest and oversee its promotion and protection; and on the societal governance modes and regulatory instruments that can best promote and protect the public interest. Following a contextualizing discussion of the changing nature of state-society interactions, these rival perspectives are, first, identified and their implications then explored.

Societies in all countries can be characterized by their increasing diversity, dynamics and complexity of their socioeconomic, political, cultural and natural environments (Kooiman 1999; see also Crowley 1994, Pierre and Peters 2000), which have changed greatly from those which existed even 25 years ago. Advanced liberal democracies, in particular, are experiencing dynamic processes of economic and social differentiation, which have made them "institutionally rich" (Streeck 1991: 27; but see Olsen 1982). This has changed the role of governments, particularly as they seek to address the perceived incapacity of hierarchical governing structures, processes and instruments to respond to the governance challenges of this new world, which Moran (2000: 11) identifies as "distrust, fear of risks, consumerism, legalism and democracy" (see also Beck 1992, Giddens 1990). The response has been a gradual transition away from hierarchical governance modes[3] toward new patterns of state-society interactions, or forms of sociopolitical governance. Two such societal governance modes have been identified: network (interactive) governance[4] and market self-regulation

---

[2] The concept of the *public interest* draws upon three traditions of political thought: *utilitarianism* (the proposition that the wellbeing of society should be the overriding goal of public policy, thus social action is right if it maximizes social wellbeing by, in Benthamite terms, achieving the greatest happiness for the greatest number of people [Bentham [1789] 1970, Mill [1865] 1968, Scarre 1996]), *civic republicanism* (the proposition that the different interests that exist in civil society should be subordinated to the interests of all those in that society); and the *general will* (the outcome when citizens make political decisions for the good of society as a whole rather than for the good of a particular group, [Rousseau [1762] 1973; see also Levine 1993, Slevin 1996b]). It has two distinct formulations: (1) the common interests of people as members of the public (Gross 1964: 522; see also Ley and Perry 1959); and (2) the aggregation of the private interests of those affected or likely to be affected by a public policy or collective action (Apperley 1996b). It overlaps the concepts of the *common* or *collective good* (the good that is commonly or collectively shared by a group of persons that cannot be disaggregated [Reeve 1996b]). It stands in contradistinction to *private interests*. Lasswell (1930: 264) conceptualized the *public interest* as displaced *private interests*: "the displacement of private affects upon public objects. The affects which are organized in the family are redistributed upon various social objects such as the state."

[3] *Hierarchical governance* is where individuals or groups of individuals (organizations) are subject to a set of enforceable rights and obligations designed and implemented by politicoadministrative institutions with a territorial mandate.

[4] *Network, interactive or cogovernance* (Kooiman 2001; see also Kooiman and van Vliet 1995) is a situation in which individuals or groups of individuals voluntarily cede some autonomy to a voluntary network to which they belong, in return for agreed com-

governance[5] (Kooiman 1993, 1999).[6] Each of these three governance modes has a separate logic of collective action and of social order (Streek and Schmitter

---

mon rights and acceptable common obligations. By so belonging, they share, with other network members, its commitment to a common set of governance values and a presumption that network interactions are on the basis of loyalty, trust (see Ring and Smith 1997, Vangen and Huxham 1998) and reciprocity (see Alcentara 1998; Colebatch and Lamour 1993; Jessop 1997; Peters 1998; Rhodes 1996, 1997; Thompson et al. 1991). A network may be defined as "a relatively stable set of mainly public and private corporate actors. The linkages between the actors serve as channels for communication and for the exchange of information, expertise, trust and other policy resources. The boundary of a network is not, in the first place, determined by formal institutions but results from a process of mutual recognition dependent on functional relevance and structural embeddedness" (Kenis and Schneider 1991: 41–42). Streeck and Schmitter (1991: 228) talk of *interest governance* (see also Cawson 1985, 1986; Hollingsworth and Lindberg 1985; Jessop 1990; Middlemas 1979; Schmitter 1974; Schmitter and Lehmbruch 1979), also called *democratic corporatist governance* (Börzel 1997, Elder et al. 1982, Fitzmaurice 1991, Hancock 1989, Hancock and Schiller 1991, Jessop 1979, Kickert et al. 1997, Kooiman 1993, Kooiman and Van Vliet 1993, Mayntz 1993, Merrien 1998, Messner 1997). Laumann and Knoke (1987) identify the following forms of networks: *state directed, concertation, pressure pluralist, clientela pluralism, parantela pluralism, industry-dominant pressure pluralism.*
"The metaphor of a network...seeks to focus on the pattern of formal and informal contacts and relationships which shape policy agendas and decision-making....Network analysis is based on the idea that a policy is framed within the context of relationships and dependencies" (Parsons 1995: 185; see also Atkinson and Coleman 1989; Carlsson 2000; Cook and Skogan 1991; Hay 1998; Heclo 1978; Jordan 1990; Jordan and Schubert 1992; Kenis and Schneider 1991; Kickert 1993b; Kingdon 1984; Klijn and Koppenjan 2000; Marin and Mayntz 1991; Marsh 1998; Mayntz 1993; Messner 1997; Peters 1996, 1998; Rhodes 1988, 1990, 1996, 1997; Richardson 1982; Richardson and Jordan 1979; M. J. Smith 1993; Thomson et al. 1991; van Waarden 1992; Wilkes and Wright 1988; as well as Dahl 1961, 1971, 1982; Dahl and Lindblom 1976; but see Blom-Hansen 1998; Börzel 1997, 1998; Brans 1997; De Bruijn and Ringeling 1997; Salancik 1995).

[5] *Market self-regulation* is the self-regulating market form of society (Polanyi 1957) in which buyers and sellers negotiate enforceable contracts, with a zero noncompliance tolerance and full restitution as the ultimate sanction. They conduct their affairs in accordance with their contractual obligations within the rules of the law of property, tort and contract. Kooiman and van Vliet (2001: 360) see this as subsumed under the broader rubric of self-governance: "the capacity of social entities to provide the necessary means to develop and maintain their identity, by and large, by themselves—and thus show a relatively high degree of social-political autonomy." They distinguish a *systems-* (structure-)*oriented* perspective on self-governance—*an autopoietic system*, which, drawing upon the biological metaphor of a closed living system that is self-referencing, self-organizing and self-steering, governs itself through a labyrinth of interaction processes involving the constituent members that make up its identity (see, for example, In't Veld et al. 1991, Kickert 1993a; see also Brans and Rossbach 1997, Dunsire 1996, Teubner 1993; but see Ostrom et al. 1992)—from an *actor-* (agency-)*oriented* perspective—*an actor constellation system*, which draws upon internal or Eigen dynamics, where positive and negative feedback are central, to argue that a social system governs itself by means of a process of mutual stimulation between identifiable actors who are searching for mutu-

1991). As Hay (1998: 39) sensibly argues, however, they do not exist independently of each other. This has led to much debate about the meaning and purpose of government and its public agencies and about how they can, and should, be judged and held accountable for their actions and performance.

It has been argued that one consequence of the new sociopolitical environment has been the creation of a state too big for small problems, yet too small for big problems (Kazancigil 1998). Given the increased plurality of agents of government and of civil society (Kaviraj and Khilnani 2001) participating in the policy process and the growing complexity of issues to be decided upon (Messner 1997), it is perhaps not surprising that some contributors to this debate question whether modern societies are, in fact, governable[7]—the crisis of governability or the legitimation crisis (Crozier et al. 1975, Dror 1994, Foucault 1991, Mayntz 1993, Offe 1984, Willke 1990)—the "exhaustion of the traditional forms of state intervention" (Merrien 1998: 57); while others contemplate the desirable alternatives, calling upon the *minimal state* (Nozick 1974), the *enabling state* (Gilbert and Gilbert 1989), the *active society* (Etzioni 1968) or the *network society* (Messner 1997).

---

ally reinforcing or curbing behavior patterns (see also Kooiman 2000 and Kooiman and Associates 1997). Hayek (1991) talks of spontaneous, or grown, order, which stands in contradistinction to organized, or made, order.

[6] The alternative triad of terms are: self-governing, hierarchical governing and co-governing (or interactive governing) (Kooiman 1997); markets, solidarity and politics (Mayntz 1993); markets, clans and bureaucracies (Ouchi 1980); price, trust and authority (Bradach and Eccles 1991); and market, community and state (Streek and Schmitter 1991: 228) speculatively adding a fourth governance mode—associations—in recognition of the "specific contribution of associations and organized concertations to social order" (see also Hollingworth and Lindberg 1985).

[7] The discourse on governability of *advanced liberal democracies* must be separated from the corresponding discourse for *failed states*. That *advanced liberal democracies* have become ungovernable, so it is argued, is because while the range of intractable problems, especially economic problems, that government is expected, perhaps unrealistically, to deal with has increased, its capacity to solve them has diminished (see, for example, Messner 1997: 121, 147). In part, this is because government's failure to ensure life quality and prosperity has undermined its legitimacy, which, in turn, has increased resistance to its authority. That *failed states* are is because of the breakdown in the ability of government to govern at all. Thurer (1999: 731–32) argues that *failed states* have three common characteristics. First, they are essentially associated with internal and endogenous problems, even though these may incidentally have cross-border impacts. Their failure, then, is a product of the implosion, rather than explosion, of the structures of state power and authority causing the disintegration and destruction, rather than dismemberment, of the state. Second, they experience a total or near total breakdown of structures guaranteeing law and order, not merely the fragmentation of state authority seen in civil wars, where clearly identified military or paramilitary rebels fight either to strengthen their own position within the state or to break away from it. Third, they lack the institutions capable, on the one hand, of representing the state at the international level and, on the other, of being influenced by the outside world. Either no institution exists that has the authority to negotiate, represent and enforce or, if one does, it is wholly unreliable, typically acting as "statesman by day and bandit by night."

The governed in a society can no longer be readily directed or controlled by the use of direct command or coercive power by the societal (or national) governing (political and administrative) elites.[8] The role of the state, particularly its direct provision role, is being increasingly strategically constrained, as governments and their host societies acknowledge the perceived ineffectiveness of command-type public policy instruments (Hult and Walcott 1990, Kooiman 1993, Weimer and Vining 1992)—governance failure (Bovens and t'Hart 1996, Bovens et al. 2001, Gray 1998, Sieber 1981)—in the context of fiscal policy constraints and the constraints engendered by globalization forces in the form of emerging ecological, economic, financial and technological interdependencies (Hulsink 1996, Messner 1997, Zecchini 1996).

The growing and contested trend away from direct public services provision by command toward provision by alternative service delivery modes in a decentralized politicoadministrative environment has resulted in a trend within the polity toward *governing without government*[9] (Rhodes 1997: 46; see also Peters 1997, Peters and Savoie 1998, Rhodes 1996).[10] In this new governance environment, the protection of the public interest involves a careful and constant balancing act, one that balances the governance needs (or opportunities) against governance capacities (Kooiman et al. 1999: 2–3).

The state's governance role has become more complex (Rose 1996) in the face of a diverse array of modes of service provision. On a command-market spectrum these would range from *central* (national) public provision, to *devolved* (local and regional) public provision, through *managerialized* (corporatized and commercialized) public provision, *supranational* (external to the nation-state) public provision, *communal* (nongovernmental, nonprofit) provision, to *market* (privatized for profit) provision. This spectrum is complicated by the emergence of multiorganizational partnerships involving agencies at the same or different points along this spectrum (Lowndes and Skelcher 1998). Each of these public services provision modes constitutes a distinctive delivery regime that influences the nature of its relationship with the state in an environment in

---

[8] The societal governing elites comprises those individuals who are engaged in directing (the *political elite*) or administering (the *administrative elite*) national territorial political units, because they have been elected or appointed to do so, because they have the hereditary right to do so, or because they have taken for themselves the power to do so.

[9] Rosenau (1992a: 3) observes that governance without government is "a system of rule that is as dependent on intersubjective meaning as on formally sanctioned constitutions and charters...a system of rule that works only if it is accepted by the majority (or, at least, by the most powerful of those it affects)." See also Kothari 1987.

[10] In western societies, the basis of governance relations has shifted from one of *trust* (evidenced by the diminution of institutional regulations, and an emphasis on shared values and informal relationships and networks) to one of *confidence* (evidenced by a higher incidence of contractual relationships and formal regulations). Power (1997) convincingly demonstrates that the dismantling of command in the United Kingdom has produced an audit explosion resulting in the expansion of state surveillance and direction (see also Humphrey et al. 1993).

which there may be incongruent, even incompatible, public and private (more broadly, nonpublic) motivations (Jessop 1997). This makes it more difficult for them to perform their governing role effectively, efficiently and legitimately (Kooiman and Van Vliet 1995; see also Bovens et al. 2001). Thus creating for them a set of new governance challenges.

Determining what the public interest is (Brown 1994, Dahl 1982, Elster 1991a, Plant 1991, Sandel 1982, Walzer 1983, Ward 1983, Wolff 1973), and how it differs from private interests, involves a delicate balancing act: on one side is self-interest or individual autonomy (promoting *positive* freedom),[11] on the other side is the public interest or societal control (constraining *positive* freedom to promote *negative* freedom). To determine this individual autonomy-social control balance, political institutions engage in aggregative and integrative processes to derive the 'will' of the people.[12] An aggregative process derives this through political campaigns and political bargaining. An integrative process involves deliberation between societal governors and those they seek to govern. What, then, is in the 'public interest' is a matter of politics; how it is promoted and protected is a matter of societal governance (Kooiman 1993, 1999; Loughlan and Scott 1997; Peters 1996, 1998; Peters and Savoie 1998; Rhodes 1997; Wilks, 1996). There has, however, long been debate about whether any governance mechanism can even be, let alone remain, focused on the public interest (Edelman 1964, Lowi 1969; Peltzman 1976; Schubert 1960), and about the causes of governance failure (Donohue 1989, Gormley 1994, Kettle 1993). Mayntz (1993) distinguishes four sets of causes of governance failure: *knowledge problems* (lack of appropriate governance knowledge, an epistemological problem), *governance capacity* (lack of appropriate governance instruments, an ontological problem), *implementation problems* (lack of appropriate organizational capacities, an ontological problem), and *motivational problems* (lack of compliance by the governed, a nomological problem) (see also Dixon and Dogan 2002a).

THE PUBLIC INTEREST: WHO SHOULD DETERMINE IT?

Public interest, as displaced private interests (Lasswell 1930, 1948), is premised on the proposition that the private sphere can do 'harm' to others, so justifying the public sphere's intervention to 'correct' the 'adverse' consequences of such private actions (Mill [1863] 1968).[13] Adherents to each of the

---

[11] To which end the state can use force, coercion, manipulation, persuasion or its legitimate authority (see Allison 1996b), which can involve the use of position or legitimate power; expert or knowledge power; personal,; referent, normative or integrative power; resource, reward, economic or exchange power; or physical, coercive or threat power (Boulder 1990, French and Raven 1959, Hales 2001).

[12] Cultural Theorists suggest that the 'will' of the people is the product of a perpetual process of reforming patterns of collective preferences driven by the competing *social solidarities* (see, for example, Douglas et al. 1998: 324–25).

[13] The Millsian view of the state-citizen relationship is explored within a Cultural Theory framework in Wildavsky and Lockhart 1993. For a Cultural Theory perspective

competing *social solidarities* have rival perspectives on the knowability of the public interest and on the state's governance capacity.[14] They each accept that society is governable, but only if their preferred mode of societal governing is adopted. They each consider their balance between individual autonomy and collective control to be the only legitimate one. Thus, they each consider their approach to the identification of the public interest is the only acceptable one. Thus, they each consider their approach to the determination of the public interest to be the only acceptable one. They would, inevitably, resist the public interest propositions advanced by adherents to another competing *social solidarity*. As a consequence, the extent to which the governed and the governors are in dispute over the defining of the public interest is determined by the extent to which the societal governors and those they seek to govern adhere to the same *social solidarity* and thus share a common view on what constitutes the public interest.

Hierarchist Perspective

The public interest, to hierarchists, is knowable and grounded in the notion of societal common good, as articulated by a society's governing elite.[15]

Hierarchists would presume that people, whether individually or in groups, would be willing to make any expected sacrifices for the collective, or voluntary contributions to collective action, if they were deemed by the societal governing elites to be for society's common good. Hierarchists would do so because of their preoccupation with retaining the protection of a hierarchical social order that is based on positional authority.

To hierarchists, then, the public interest is knowable and can be promoted and protected—and, thus, society is governable—but only if there is continuity between the past, present and future, which can only be preserved by the societal governing elites, who have the society's common good at heart and who thus can best articulate public interest propositions to be promoted and protected by them.

---

on externalities, see Wildavsky et al. 1998; on public goods, see Wildavsky and Malkin 1991; and on collective action, see Douglas 1989.

[14] This is the state's capacity to acquire adequate and reliable knowledge of the 'adverse' consequences of the private sphere's actions in a timely enough manner to be able to 'correct' them—to resolve the conflicting public and private sphere claims—while maintaining an 'acceptable' balance between individual autonomy and societal control. For a discussion of knowledge utilization in policy making, see Wittrock 1982.

[15] Hierarchists draw support from Schumpeter (1976: 291), who argues that leaders of society need to be drawn from "a social stratum, itself a product of severely selective processes, that takes to politics as a matter of course...[Leaders are thus people who] have successfully passed the test in other fields—served, as it were, an apprenticeship in private affairs."

Enclavist Perspective

The public interest, to enclavists, is knowable and embraces an inclusive set of categorical interests (or categorical goods)[16] (Streeck and Schmitter 1991: 236), which reflects the shared values and language that create a social bond and identity for a particular group of people—a community of interests or an interest group[17]—as determined through constrained, consensus-seeking group-norming and -forming values discourses.[18]

Enclavists, with their preoccupation with being seen to be committed to the categorical good, would presume that people, whether individually or in groups, would be willing to make any voluntary sacrifices for the collective, or any voluntary contributions to collective action, provided they were mutual agreed to be in the public interest.

---

[16] Streeck and Schmitter (1991: 236) argue it is in the interest of organized groups to seek, for their own self-interest, a *categorical good* that is identical, or at least partially compatible, with a *collective good*. This depends on two factors: the way in which group interests are organized, and the complex bargaining process that takes place between organized groups and the state. Etzioni (1993: 217) argues that a community is made up of special interest groups that are either "out to gain all they can, with little concern for the shared needs of the community" (see also Milner 1991, Olsen 1965) or they "vie with one another yet voluntarily limit themselves when they impinge on the common interests."

[17] *Interest* (pressure or lobby) *groups* are groups of people or organizations joining together to represent, defend or advance a particular interest that may be categorized as *sectional* (representing a particular defined interest, such as trade unions and shareholder associations), *protective* (defending a particular defined interest) or *promotional* (advancing a particular cause, such as environmentalism); and as *insiders* (those regularly involved in the relevant policy formulation process) or *outsiders* (those that seek to influence policy development but are excluded from the relevant policy formulation process) (Grant 1996b). They also include *nongovernmental organizations* (NGOs) (whether local, national, or global): "Some are issue- or task-oriented; others are driven by religious or political ideology. Some have a broad public-interest perspective; others have a narrow private-interest focus. They range from small, poorly funded, grassroots entities to large, well-supported, professionally staffed bodies. Some operate individually; others have formed networks to share information and tasks and to enhance their impact" (The Commission on Global Governance 1995: 254; see also Buechler 1999, Clayton 1993, Inglehart 1990, Lewis 1999, Waterman 1998); *social movements* (embracing political parties and campaigning organizations, as well as individuals organized around ideas that create new forms of social and political identity, see Grant 1996b). These may be classified as *transformative* (oriented toward achieving total social transformation, such as Christian and Islamic fundamentalists, millenarian movements), *reformative* (oriented toward achieving partial or targeted social reform, such as religious moral crusades), *redemptive* (oriented toward achieving total change in a person, such as sectarian organizations and movements) or *alternative* (oriented toward achieving partial change in an individual, such as antismoking or antialcohol organizations) (Aberle 1966).

[18] As Kymlicka (1990: 206) expresses it, a community's "way of life forms the basis for a public ranking of conceptions of the good, and the weight given to an individual's preferences depends on how much she [*sic*] conforms or contributes to this common good."

To enclavists, then, the public interest is knowable and can be promoted and protected—and, thus, society is governable—but only if it is assumed that society's survival, stability and wellbeing depend on sophisticated and subtle interpersonal interactions taking place between interest groups and the societal governing elites on the basis of a sense of mutual trust and a shared commitment to a set of agreed categorical interests that become public interest propositions to be promoted and protected by the state.

Fatalist Perspective

The public interest, to fatalists, is not knowable because of capriciousness and uncertainty. As Thompson et al. (1999b: 13–14) put it, to fatalists the issue always is: "Why bother! Every penny that is spent to do something about something about which nothing can be done is a penny wasted, and it is important that resources not be poured into that bottomless pit. If the cat is out of the bag...it cannot be put back."

Fatalists, with their preoccupation with survival, would presume that people, whether individually or in groups, would not make either voluntary sacrifices for the collective or voluntary contributions to collective action in the so-called public interest unless it were in their interests to do so, for their own survival.

To fatalists, then, the public interest is unknowable and cannot be intentionally and instrumentally promoted and protected. Nevertheless, society is still governable, but only if the societal governing elites can, and do, exercise the coercive power that enables them to govern as they see fit, although that can never be legitimized.

Individualist Perspective

The public interest, to individualists, is knowable only as people's revealed preferences in the marketplace.[19] It is thus the summation of all private interests.

Individualists, with their preoccupation with their own material success, would presume that people, whether individually or in groups, would make neither voluntary sacrifices for the collective nor voluntary contributions to collective action in the so-called public interest unless it was in their self-interest to do so.

To individualists, then, the public interest would be knowable and can be promoted and protected—and, thus, society is governable—but only when the societal governing elites' role is limited to ensuring society's safety and secu-

---

[19] Individualists would most willingly follow in the footsteps of Adam Smith ([1776] 1977) and link individual self-interest with the good of society. They would thank Arrow (1954) for demonstrating the impossibility of determining a collective preference ranking of a set of options. They would solemnly agree with Riker's (1982: 238) pronouncement that government does not and cannot know the 'will' of the people.

rity, and to determining the legal framework that defines and enforces property rights,[20] thus enabling the satisfaction of revealed market preferences.

GOOD SOCIETAL GOVERNING STRUCTURES AND PROCESSES: WHAT ARE THEY?

The polity—the politicoadministrative and judicial structures and processes that identify, promote and protect the public interest—that exist in a society reflects the influence of the *social solidarities* as they were counterbalanced in the past, because they reflect that society's cumulative judgments over time on the appropriate balance between individual autonomy and societal control. The polity as it is accepted reflects the influences of *social solidarities* as they now exist. Cultural Theory postulates that the legitimacy of a particular polity depends on what people accept as the appropriate limitations that their society should place on their autonomy, whether as individuals or as group members, which, in turn, depends on which of the four *social solidarities* they adhere to.

Adherents to each of the *social solidarities* consider only their preferred polity to be legitimate and authoritative. They would, inevitably, resist those advanced by adherents of competing *social solidarities*. As a consequence, the extent to which the governed resist the processes of civil government is determined by the extent to which they adhere to the same *social solidarity*, and thus share a common view on the appropriate autonomy-control balance that legitimizes the polity.

Hierarchist Perspective

Hierarchists see the public sphere as being clearly demarcated from the private sphere (Thompson et al. 1999b: 7). The public sphere would be seen as the domain of the societal governing elites. They would be perceived as having the right to rule.[21] They would, however, be expected to accept responsibility for those who give them loyalty and obedience. So, government would be perceived as being benign in intent and benevolent in outcome (see also Schwarz and Thompson 1990: 67).

Hierarchists would adhere to Weber's ([1915] 1947) principle of rational-legal authority. They believe that authority rests on the legality of normative rules and the right of those elevated to authority to give commands. They would

---

[20] For individualists, the right to private property (Becker 1977) is premised on the proposition that allowing people to own property is the most efficient way of running society. They would readily accept the proposition that owning property is necessary for personal development. They would, however, not only feel insecure and ambivalent about possession being the foundation of property ownership, but also heartily dismissive of the idea that ownership should rest with those whose labor is used to create property.

[21] This proposition underpins a variety of authoritarian political perspectives, most notably, as polar points, *monarchism* (where the right to rule is hereditary) and *despotism* (where the right of autocratic rule is achieved by tyranny), each demanding, to varying degrees, obedience from the governed, taken to the extreme in totalitarian one-party states, military dictatorships and states where military values permeate civil society.

thus give allegiance, and be deferential, to those who govern them (Thompson et al. 1990). They would also be willing to participate, as expected, in the hierarchical governance process, because the collective acceptance of this logical hierarchical order, and its delegated authority structure, facilitates orderly and efficient processes (Cutting and Kouzmin 2000). They would thus readily accept Somit and Peterson's (1995, 1997) biopolitical argument that homo sapiens has an inherent preference for hierarchically structured sociopolitical systems, with a strong tendency toward obedience, dominance and subordination.

Hierarchists would have a preference for a bureaucratic provision of public services, whereby the function of the societal administrative elite is to pursue the common good, as defined by the societal political elite. They would hold the view that supremacy of the collective over the individual must be reinforced by the public sphere engaging in some form of central or indicative planning of the market sphere.

Hierarchists would be attracted to a political metanarrative that legitimates the hierarchical bonding of individuals, reinforces the supremacy of the collective over the individual in all spheres of life, and preserves authority structures (Wildavsky and Chai 1994). They would be attracted to the idea of Plato's guardian-style polity[22] (Hendriks and Zouridis 1999: 125, Ney and Molenaers 1999), one that enables government to be elitist, stable and strong, where loyalty and compliance are expected and technical rationality[23] rewarded. Such a polity would preferably have a unitary political structure[24] with an unwritten constitution and a unicameral legislature, which permits the unfettered executive dominance of both a unicameral legislature and the judiciary.

When, however, confronted with a democracy, hierarchists would prefer an electoral system with three features. The first is limited suffrage, based on the demarcation of status by factors such as age, educational attainment, or professional rank. The second is voluntary voting, for even though apathy (abstention) reflects poorly on the citizenry's civic consciousness, it is taken to imply consent. The third is a first-past-the-post voting system with single-member constituencies, so as to ensure political stability.

Hierarchists would prefer a judicial system that seeks three goals. The first is to uphold, most rigorously, law and order and the protection of property rights in accordance with the societal governing elites' conception of the common

---

[22] The *guardian-style* approach to government goes back to Plato's *The Republic*, where he argued that rulership should be entrusted to that minority of people who, by reason of their superior insight and virtue, are particularly qualified to govern (Hendriks and Zouridis 1999: 125). It recalls the Hegelian ideas of the state as a *spiritual entity* or, as Hennis pleads (cited in Messner 1997: 80), a state with "power to create unity," and able to act as "protector, guardian, promoter of morality...guarantor of moral standards."

[23] For a discussion of culture, technical rationality and organizational culture, see Adams and Ingersoll 1990.

[24] Alternatively, if regional identities dominate a society, then hierarchists would prefer a confederation, which is constitutionally less constraining on the periphery, thus enabling the societal governing elites in the constituent regions to retain their decision-making autonomy.

good. The second is to limit the power of the judiciary over the other branches of government by prohibiting the judicial review of administrative discretion; by restricting freedom of access to any public information because, in their view, it must remain secret in the national interest; and by inhibiting judicial policy making that impacts on the public sphere. The third is to ensure that the state has power over the private sector, by means of strictly enforced statutory market regulations and by having a statutory right of access to information in the market sphere, so that market abuses and misdemeanors can be monitored and duly punished.

The preferred polity for hierarchists would have a public policy process that presumes that policy is the product of a decision-making system (as described in Dye 1972). This would involve institutional activity by the societal governing elites[25] (Lasswell 1958) that promotes and protects the common good (Weber [1915] 1947; see also Gerth and Mills 1991), using functional-analytic policy analysis[26] that would give rise to a set of objective facts that would facilitate satisficing decision making (Simon 1960. 1978; Lasswell 1958), by rule-based decision makers (Jensen 1999), that would produce incremental policy changes (Lindblom 1959).

Enclavist Perspective

Enclavists see the public sphere as having blurred boundaries with the private sphere (Thompson et al. 1999b: 7), which should be expanded if they conceal any unequal power relations in the private sphere. Enclavists would have a preference for the public and private spheres to work together to promote, in the public interest, their categorical interests, which reflect their shared values, as determined through constrained, consensus-seeking values discourses. Only in this way can the collective's survival, stability and wellbeing be attained. Because enclavists see the public sphere, like the private sphere, as always being at risk of being amoral, if not immoral, and corrupt, it has to be treated with constant vigilance. This would require the people to participate actively in, and give their consent to, collective decisions. Then, and only then, would the public sphere become benign and paternalistic, and thus a means of securing the good life for everyone. Government would thus be perceived by enclavists to be in-

---

[25] For a discussion of the elitist theories of the state, see Dunleavy and O'Leary 1987: 136–202. For other elite variants, see Keynes 1926 (*intellectual elite*), Young 1958 (*technocratic elite*), and Illich 1975 (*professional elites*).

[26] To hierarchists, this form of analysis involves abstract thinking, using naturalist research methods, to understand the nature and consequences of highly structured problems. This is done by drawing upon formal internal and external information sources (see Parsons 1995: 385), such as departmental research and inquiry, internal think-tank reports, internal expert reports, commissions and committees of inquiry, judicial reviews, reports from the legislature, commissioned research, and formal consultation, which permits the identification of a constrained set of solutions, given a set of hierarchically determined objectives (values and beliefs).

trusive in intent but could be made benevolent in outcome (see also Schwarz and Thompson 1990: 67.

Enclavists would adhere to Weber's ([1915] 1947) principle of charismatic authority.[27] They believe that authority rests on the acceptance of the normative patterns of social order ordained by the individual who is the focus of devotion because of his or her specific and exceptional sanctity, heroism or exemplary character. They would thus, almost inevitably, be in dissent with those who govern them, but, nevertheless, they would willingly engage in governance processes (Thompson et al. 1990) in order to ensure that their values and beliefs, if not made the basis of collective action, are at least heard. Indeed, if expressions of collective will about the common good can be captured and articulated as a categorical good then group members can embrace them in the belief that they are for their personal good (Cutting and Kouzmin (2000a). Enclavists would have a preference for partnership provision of public services, whereby the relevant community of interests would come together in pursuit of an agreed set of categorical interests.

Enclavists would be attracted to a political metanarrative that bonds group members together against outsiders, reinforces the collective's responsibility to promote their perceptions of equality, the dignity[28] and rights[29] of the individual, a sense of fellowship and community,[30] and *negative* freedom (Wildavsky and Chai 1994).

When confronted with democracy, they would be attracted to the Aristotelian idea of a deliberative democracy[31] (Ney and Molenaers 1999; see also

---

[27] Weber ([1915] 1947: 157; see also 1968) defines charisma as "a certain quality of an individual personality by virtue of which he [*sic*] is set apart from ordinary men and treated as endowed with supernatural, superhuman, or at least specifically exceptional powers or qualities. These are such as are not accessible to the ordinary person, but are regarded as of divine origin or as exemplary, and on the basis of them the individual concerned is treated as leader."

[28] The proposition that all people should be treated with due respect as the foundation of all other moral duties and obligations (Downie and Telfer 1969).

[29] A distinction can be drawn between *rights* as *justified practices* (that is, rights as justified ways of acting, or of being treated) and *rights* as *justified claims* (that is, rights as justified claims or principles with respect to particular practices, whether they exist or not). Both of these types of rights are justified and enforced because they are socially established (Held 1984).

[30] Enclavists would have empathy with the communitarian perspective of a social order in which people are bound by common values that foster close communal bonds on the premise of the interaction between social context and individuals' self-conception (Reeve 1996c: 91; see also Dixon et al. 2002).

[31] *Deliberative democracy* overlaps with the concepts of *participatory democracy* (with its emphasis on deliberation, inclusiveness and egalitarianism [Hendriks and Zouridis 1999: 126, Sanderson 1999]); *government by discussion* (Barker 1945: 32–48); *civic republicanism* (with its concern for mobilizing public commitment [Barber 1984, Arendt 1958]), *consensual democracy* (Elder et al. 1982, Lipjhart 1984, Mansbridge 1983, Philips 1995); *discursive democracy* (with its primary concern for deliberative processes within public communication in a decentered and self-critical society [Haber-

Cohen 1989, Fiskin 1991), a polity that enables citizens to participate in deliberative power because government emphasizes "the importance to effective democracy of fair and open community deliberation about the merits of competing political argument" (Uhr 1998: 4).

Enclavists, who would readily endorse the principle of subsidiarity,[32] would prefer a devolved, multitier political structure, where the upper levels (national or regional) delegate some of the power to govern to lower levels (regional or local), so as to minimize the distance between the governed and the societal governing elites. In order to disperse political power, it would have a bicameral legislature, the executive would be subservient to the legislature, and the judiciary would be independent of both. It would also have a written set of enforceable human rights as inalienable moral entitlements.

Enclavists, as egalitarians who consider that apathy (abstention) must be actively discouraged at all costs, would prefer an electoral system with proportional representation, multiple-member constituencies, universal suffrage and, very definitely, compulsory voting.

Enclavists would prefer a judicial system that seeks three goals. The first would be to enforce, most vigorously, all human rights, law and order, and property rights that are in accordance with their socially constructed interpretation of fundamental societal values. The second would be to undertake judicial reviews of administrative discretion and judicial policy-making to fill any policy vacuum. The third would be to enforce statutory freedom of access to most information in the public and market spheres, so that abuses, misdemeanors, inefficiencies and inequities can be monitored and exposed to public scrutiny.

The polity preferred by enclavists would have a public policy process that presumes policy is the outcome achieved by balancing the competing interests

---

mas 1996a, 1996b; Young 1990, 1995]), *differentiated universalism* (with its emphasis on the differentiated notion of rights reflecting the multiple group differentiation that necessitates linkages to realize differential objectives [Lister 1995, 1997, 1998; Yeatman 1993; Young 1989, 1990]), and *associative or associational democracy* (resurrected by Dahl (1971) as the concept of *polyarchy* to capture the idea that *representative democracy* should involve a substantial degree of interest group influences on government [Cohen and Rogers 1992, Hirst 1994, Matthews 1989]). Etzioni (1968, 1993, 1995) argues that public policies should always seek to promote an *active society* in which people would be more engaged with their community and in which "political action and intellectual reflection would have a higher, more public status" (1968: 635; see also Cross 2001), achieved by raising individual and societal consciousness. An *active society* is "capable of knowing and transforming itself" (Etzioni: 1968: 365). This process leads toward a *cooperative state* (Messner 1997), a *communitarian state* (Kymlicka 1990) in which individuals are encouraged to conform to the common good and discouraged from pursuing their own interests, or a *radical* (alternatively a *grassroots* or *direct*) democracy (Castells 1983, Lowe 1986).

[32] This is the location of authority at the lowest possible level of a hierarchy (Wincott 1996: 482).

of diverse interest groups (as described in Dye 1972).[33] It would thus engage with the people, using communicative-value policy analysis,[34] so as to facilitate "consistent, congruent and cogent" collective decision making (Fischer and Forester 1993: 5–7; see also Dryzek 1987, Hoppe 1993, Jensen 1999, Majone 1989, Ney and Thompson 1999, Paris and Reynolds 1983).

Fatalist Perspective

Fatalists would not discriminate between the private and the public spheres (Thompson et al. 1999b: 7), both of which they see as being unknowable, capricious and fearful realms. Neither can be trusted.[35] Both are indifferent to people's needs. Thus, any engagement with the public sphere is pointless, as little benefit can be expected from any collective action. Government might, perhaps, be sometimes benign in intent, the consequences of which are unknowable, but it is inevitably malevolent in action, the consequences of which are experienced.

Since the public interest cannot be intentionally and instrumentally promoted and protected, then it makes no difference who has the authority to exercise the coercive power of the state. They would expect the powers that be to exercise the necessary power to govern society as they see fit. Such use of state power, however, can never be legitimized. They would thus expect to be coercively alienated from, but nevertheless, deferential to, those who govern them (Thompson et al. 1990). Thus they would be unwilling to engage in any way with the governance process. Fatalists are willing to compromise their personal agendas to accommodate the current political reality.[36] They would thus be at-

---

[33] For a discussion of the pluralist and neopluralist theories of the state, see Dunleavy and O'Leary 1987: 13–71, 271–315. Network theory gives some insights into the processes involved:

[The policy process] can ...be seen as a collection of games between actors. In these games, each of the various actors has its own perceptions of the nature of the problem, the desired solution and of the other actors in the network. On the basis of these perceptions, actors select strategies. The outcomes of the game are a consequence of the interaction of strategies of different players in the game. These strategies are however influenced by the perceptions of the actors, the power and resource divisions in the network and the rules of the network. (Klijn and Koppenjan 2000: 140)

[34] To enclavists, this form of analysis draws on hermeneutic research methods. It emphasizes: the claims and rhetoric of analysis; the agenda-setting power of policy argument; the possible construction of problems in different languages, discourses and frames; the desirable role of practitioner in problem construction; and that political power shifts reflect shifts in policy elites and in policy language (Edelman 1988). It also seeks to ensure that desirable policy options are not excluded from consideration. Examples of this analytical approach include Etzioni's (1968) the *mixed scanning* model, Dror's (1968, 1976) *the optimal rational decision-making* model, and Gershuny's (1976) *iterative mixed scanning* model.

[35] Insights into this distrust of public institutions can be gleaned from Sztompka's (1996: 38, 52) discussion of the *syndrome of distrust* (see also Rose 1994).

[36] This is consistent with Wildavsky's (1984) view that fatalists are politically mute, or, in Douglas and Ney's (1998: 123) terms, "cut off from political maneuvering and influence." Even the politically mute and cut off must recognize authority, even if only

tracted to a political metanarrative that reinforces both their existentialist preoccupation with the human condition, the limitations of reason, and the irreducibilty of their experience; and their belief that the collective is distant, capricious and unresponsive to their needs. Thus fatalists believe their needs are of no relevance to anyone except themselves, thus how public services are delivered is of no importance.

Fatalists would be least alienated by a polity in which government is minimally coercive and intrusive.[37] It thus would have a centralized political structure with a weak regional or local administrative structure, so as to maximize the distance between the governed and the societal governing elites. It would have a unicameral legislature, one that would minimize their engagement with the polity, to which the executive would be subservient, and an independent judiciary, in the naïve hope that coercion might just be constrained.[38] It would also have an unwritten constitution, so as to ensure that there are few social obligations that might threaten their isolation.

Fatalists, who value political stability and consider apathy (abstention) justifiable, would have a preference for an electoral system that has first-past-the-post voluntary voting in single-member constituencies, with limited suffrage.

Fatalists would prefer to have a judicial system that is willing to limit their exploitation by the state and the marketplace, by enforcing law and order, protecting property rights, undertaking judicial reviews of administrative discretion, enforcing statutory market regulations, and making judicial policies.

The public policy process expected by fatalists would be one that is dominated by unknowing and untrustworthy vested interests, which respect neither the truthfulness of facts nor the sanctity of abstract values, and which realisti-

---

by their defaulting passive behavior, otherwise they would become *hermits* and stand outside any social coupling and would be disdainful of the ways a society seeks to grip its members (see also Thompson et al. 1990, 1999b).

[37] Fatalists might well feel attracted to the anarchist proposition that a society without the state is desirable but they would certainly doubt its feasibility. Their agency ontological inclinations may well make them broadly amenable to the notion that people have no general obligation to obey the commands of the state, and might instill in them a vague sense of hope that the state could be abolished. Their hermeneutic-agency methodological disposition, however, would make them skeptical that there could ever be a transition from state to anarchy and that some kind of stateless society that delivers social order could ever be achieved. This is regardless of whether such a stateless society is based on natural laws and perfectionist ethics (Hurka 1993) in the classical or socialist tradition; on natural rights and egoism in the individualist tradition; or on permanent and irreducible pluralism in the postmodernist tradition (Miller 1984).

[38] Fatalists would feel empathy for the view expressed by Diodorus, an Athenian, during the Mytilenian Debate of 427 BC, that the impulses of men will lead them to act dangerously for as long as their ambitions are fed by pride and insolence, their poverty requires them to act boldly, and their life is dominated by endless passion, for the forces of law cannot restrain human nature from pursuing its course: "Cities and individuals alike, all are by nature disposed to do wrong, and there is no law that will prevent it" (cited in Thucydides [401 BC] 1972: 3.45).

cally accept that public policy is, because of the limits of human cognition, the product of garbage can-like decision processes (March and Olsen 1976).

Individualist Perspective

Because individualists see the public sphere as a threat to the private sphere, they believe that it should be made smaller wherever and whenever possible (Thompson et al. 1999b: 7). They also believe that the public sphere should take no intentionally instrumental actions for enhancing people's wellbeing, as it cannot know their preferences. Because the societal governing elites are inherently coercive, intrusive and constantly at risk of being inefficient, individualists believe that they must be treated with constant vigilance. This requires government to be held strictly accountable for its inputs and outcomes by means of effective public scrutiny, so as to ensure not only that any private costs incurred are both minimized and compensated by the collective, but also that the market provision of public services is maximized. Government would thus be seen to be intrusive in intent and malevolent in outcome (see also Schwarz and Thompson 1990: 67).

Individualists would question whether there is any basis upon which government can claim legitimate authority, as it perpetually acts as a pedantic rent seeker (see, for example, Tilly 1990). They would prefer strong societies and weak states (Migdal 1988). They would tolerate government only to the extent that it ensures society's security and safety, acts as a Rawlsian agency of justice (Rawls 1971), and provides a judicial-legal framework that defines and enforces property rights,[39] which are the subject of exchange between individuals, so permitting private ends to be peacefully pursued (Hobbes [1651] 1968, Oakeshott 1975; see also Bernholz 1993).[40] They would thus be willing to give allegiance to those who govern them and to engage with the governance process (Thompson et al. 1990), but only so as to ensure that the balance between autonomy and control always favors the individual over the collective.

Accordingly, individualists would be attracted to a political metanarrative that advocates the individual's moral supremacy over a collective (Wildavsky and Chai 1994). In the belief that the collective's intrinsic coerciveness and intrusiveness inevitably result in the imposition of unnecessary constraints on *positive* freedom and individual responsibility, which generate perverse incentives and constrain market behavior, individualists would posit that the collective has an obligation to create opportunities for entrepreneurial exploitation.

---

[39] They would certainly see as fundamental their right to use as they see fit their private property for their own benefit. Indeed, they would undoubtedly agree with Epstein's (1985) libertarian proposition that any government action that constrains private property rights, in order to protect the public interest, and imposes any sort of cost (including the opportunity cost of profits forgone), constitutes government 'takings'—'regulatory takings' (Fischel 1995)—and should be justly compensated by the state.

[40] The Hobbesian view of the state-citizen relationship is explored within a Cultural Theory framework in Wildavsky and Enzell 1998.

When confronted with democracy, individualists would be attracted to the Lockean idea of a protective democracy,[41] in which government is weak, unobtrusive and small (Hendriks and Zouridis 1999: 126, Ney and Molenaers 1999).[42] Thus, their preferred polity would have a written constitution that guarantees *positive* freedoms; that empowers local government within a decentralized, multitier political structure; that has a bicameral legislature; and that ensures a strict separation of the powers of executive, legislative and judicial branches of government. Their intent would be to create a complex web of checks and balances that constrains the power of government.

Individualists, because it is in their self-interest to have political stability, would prefer an electoral system that has first-past-the-post voluntary voting in single-member constituencies, with universal suffrage. This would ensure that they cannot be excluded from voting if they see a net benefit in so doing, but they can abstain, implying their tacit consent, if they see only a net cost in doing so.

The preferred polity of individualists would have a judicial system that seeks four goals. The first is to enforce, most rigorously, property rights and maintain law and order, so as to maintain confidence and stability in the marketplace. The second is to undertake judicial reviews of administrative discretion and enforce freedom of access to most information in the public sphere, so that its inefficiencies can be identified and culled for possible commercial exploitation. The third is to limit the power of the judiciary over the private sphere, by inhibiting judicial policy making that impacts on the private sphere, by inhibiting the judicial review of management discretion, and by restricting freedom of access to any corporate information, which, in their view, must remain secret because of its commercial sensitivity.

The polity preferred by individualists would also have a public policy process that presumes that policy is the product of synoptic, instrumentally rational policy analysis[43] premised on the self-interest motivation of all policy actors, so as to facilitate optimal decision making (Quade 1976; see also Stokey and Zeckhauser 1978, Weimer and Vining 1992; but compare Elster 1991b).

---

[41] *Protective government* draws upon Locke's raison d'être for government: "the protection of individual rights, life, liberty and estate" (cited in Held 1987: 6; see also Ellis 1992, Nozick 1974).

[42] For a discussion of the New Right theories of the state, see Dunleavy and O'Leary 1987: 72–135.

[43] To individualists, this form of analysis draws upon naturalist research methods to clarify problems by decomposition, to determine objectives, and to identify, design and screen a synoptic array of options. This involves forecasting of future environment and implementation contexts, modeling to determine impacts, and evaluation to compare and rank options in terms of their cost-efficiency and cost-effectiveness, so as to permit a rational policy choice (Quade 1976; see also Stokey and Zeckhauser 1978, Weimer and Vining 1992). It would utilize external and informal sources, such as consultation reports, and informal information and advice (Parsons 1995: 385).

GOOD SOCIETAL GOVERNANCE: WHAT IS IT?

A society can choose to protect and promote the public interest by empowering one or more state territorial units to impose rights and obligations upon the governed; by permitting or facilitating a voluntary network to be co-governing,[44] whether or not it has the state's endorsement or involvement;[45] or by permitting law-abiding buyers and sellers in the marketplace to be self-regulating.

The public interest can be promoted and protected by the use of a quartet of policy instruments (Lowi 1964, 1972; see also Spitzer 1987; but compare Heclo 1972, May 1986, Sabatier 1991): *distribution policies*, which involve the distribution of new resources and have an accommodating, obliging and noncombative pattern of politics; *constituency policies*, which establish or reconfigure institutional arrangements and have a collusive, accommodating and elitist pattern of politics; *redistributive policies*, which change the distribution of existing resources and have a combative pattern of politics; and *regulatory policies* which control activities and have a pattern of politics that emphasizes interaction with pluralistic interest groups (see also Bernstein 1955, Jessop 2001, Mitnick 1980, Peltzman 1976).

The regulatory instruments that can be used to protect and promote the public interest can be classified as (Gunningham and Grabosky 1998; Gunningham and Sinclaire 1999; Majone 1994; Wilks 1996; Wright 1992, 1994): *command-and-control*[46] (such as mandatory design standards, process standards[47] and

---

[44] This is on the premise that a cogovernance network is willing to take on some of the regulatory responsibilities conventionally performed by the state and execute those responsibilities in an ethical and professional manner.

[45] Interest group mediation by means of a pattern of government-business-labor interaction involving the formal incorporation of interest groups into the public policy process has come to be known as *neocorporatism* (see Panitch 1977, 1980). Schmitter (1974: 934–36; see also Streeck and Schmitter 1991: 235) defines this as a system of interest group representation, whereby the constituent interest groups are organized into a limited number of compulsory, noncompetitive, hierarchically ordered socioeconomic bodies that are created, recognized or licensed by the state and granted a monopoly to represent their special interests in the policy process, in exchange for which they accept state controls on their leadership selection and the articulation of their demands. Grant (1985: 4) adds that a neocorporatist arrangement involves an "obligation on the part of interest organizations to secure the compliance of their members." Streeck and Schmitter (1991: 235) talk of state-assisted "private interest governments with devolved public responsibilities" (see also Hancock et al. 1991, Jessop 1990, Middlemas 1979, Milward and Francisco 1983, Schmitter and Lehmbruch 1979, Shonfield 1965).

[46] This includes, in addition to expert-determined regulations, regulations that have been negotiated with the regulated. Harter (1982) has proposed a negotiated rule-making process, whereby representatives of competing interests negotiate directly with a regulatory agency. Because participants in the rule-making process agree not to challenge in the courts the regulations agreed upon, the agency is inclined to be as inclusive as possible (but see also Coglianese 1997, Funk 1997).

[47] This includes systems of *enforced self-regulation*, whereby a regulatory agency seeks to align its regulatory standards and objectives with a regulated corporation's inte-

service-delivery or performance standards); *information* (such as voluntary codes of conduct or practice, public education programs, corporate performance reporting, community right to know, or service certification); and *economic* (such as broad-based economic instruments and supply-side incentives, particularly subsidies, tax incentives and disincentives or imposition of civil legal liability).

Adherents to each of the four *social solidarities* have a distinctive perspective on what constitutes the best configuration of governance modes, public policies, and regulatory instruments to protect and promote the public interest, which they would consider to be the only legitimate and authoritative one. They would, inevitably, resist those advanced by adherents to competing *social solidarities*. As a consequence, the extent to which the governed resist their governors' processes is determined by the extent to which they adhere to the same *social solidarity*, and thus share a common view on the appropriate autonomy-control balance that legitimizes the governors' processes.

Hierarchist Perspective

To hierarchists, good societal governance is based on the protection and promotion of the public interest by the state imposing rights and obligations upon the governed. It is grounded in three principles. The first is that there must be continuity between the past, present and future, which only the state can preserve. The second is that as the public interest can only be defined by the societal political elite. It must be protected and promoted by its subservient societal administrative elite, who, themselves, must acknowledge that privilege entails responsibility, and who must be empowered, as necessary, to guide and control individual behavior, to determine which human needs the collective should meet, and to decide who should have access to the collective's natural resources and on what basis.

Hierarchists would be predisposed to policy instruments that enhance the collective's superiority over the individual. Distributive policies would thus have a strong appeal, as they enable the societal governing elites to reinforce institutionalized inequalities when making allocative decisions. Regulatory policies would, again, have a strong appeal, as they empower the societal governing elites to influence, even enforce by sanction, desired individual, interpersonal, group or corporate behavior. Constituent policies would also have an appeal, as they give them influence, at least, over individual, interpersonal and

---

grated set of corporate risk management policies and practices by focusing on the technical features of its internal control processes that analyze, assess, control, communicate and monitor risks. The intention is to assist regulated corporations not only to develop an effective set of risk management and governance strategies, but also to build a commitment to regulatory compliance—a compliance culture—that will permit the achievement of regulatory objectives through the alignment of corporate risk management practices and hierarchical regulatory regimes (Ayres and Braithwaite 1992, Hutter 1997, Power 2000).

group behavior. In contrast, redistributive policies would have little appeal, as their outcomes could well threaten institutionalized inequalities.

The regulatory mode preferred by hierarchists would be hierarchical, whereby regulations are designed, authorized and implemented by the societal governing elites. They would only be predisposed to regulatory command-and-control instruments. These are explicit controls (Douglas and Wildavsky 1982: 180) that permit the regulators to determine, and implement with sanctions, what are acceptable (desirable) or unacceptable (undesirable) behaviors in terms of the desired governance outcomes, whether within the public or market spheres. Regulatory compliance, then, depends on the ease of violation detection, the probability of sanctions being imposed on violators, and the magnitude of the imposed sanctions (see Young 1992: 176). In contrast, information and economic instruments would have only limited appeal because, despite the fact that in the hands of the hierarchical regulators, they can be used to influence behavior, their effectiveness depends, in the absence of sanctions, on people, whether as individuals or as members of groups, voluntarily changing their behavior in the way needed to achieve the desired regulatory outcomes.

When confronted with any regulatory instrument, hierarchists would, axiomatically, comply because of their cognitive commitment, which is derived from their rational calculation made in the context of structural processes, such as prescribed rules and procedures, perhaps reinforced by a deontological moral code that builds commitment to the societal governing elites, whose power they consider to be legitimate because of their superior position or knowledge and skills; and they would expect others to do so as well.

The hierarchists' salient societal governance risk, which stems from the explanatory weaknesses of the naturalist-structuralist methodology, is the societal governing elites' loss of control or public trust, because they are repeatedly unable to understand either the nature and causation of societal governance problems, because of their adherence to naturalist epistemology, or why their solutions, which presume structuralist ontology, are unable to secure compliance by free individuals. In the absence of such trust and control, hierarchists would not be able to apportion blame for any societal governance failure to the deviants who failed to comply with society's rules and regulations.

Hierarchists, if faced with the prospect that the societal governing elites are unable to correct governance failures, would, in the first instance, express loyalty (Hirschman 1970) to them, in the hope that they will eventually find the required solutions, and blame noncompliant deviants. Their acts of loyalty would probably include suppressing any information that is critical of the societal governing elites' governance performance; and punishing those within the societal governance structures who threaten to make disclosures critical of their interpretation of the cause of, and solutions to, hierarchical governance failure. Their envisaged solution would be to strengthen hierarchical controls. There are two reason for this. First, their structuralist ontology predisposes them to presume that compliance only follows the making of a cognitive commitment (Etzioni 1961) based on rational calculation in the context of rules and regulations, as prescribed by a legitimate authority, and supported, perhaps, by a deontological moral code. Second, their naturalist epistemology cultivates the presumption that they can identify social reality through the observation of patterns in, and correlations between, forms of social behavior, which reflect and represent structuralist constraints on behavior. This solution could include setting aside or modifying rules and regulations; using publicity and persuasion to encourage compliance; strengthening disincentives; making noncompliance physically more inconvenient, difficult or impossible; and pursuing and punishing rule violators and deviant behavior with heavier sanctions.

Enclavist Perspective

To enclavists, good societal governance is based on codetermining, protecting and promoting the public interest,[48] and is grounded in four principles. The first is that the public interest must encompass categorical interests—the will of a group of people with shared values and a common language that creates a social bond and a sense of identity—that are the outcome of a constrained, consensus-seeking values discourse.[49] The second is that within those networks, all interpersonal interactions[50] must be based on mutual trust about the interpretation of unwritten or ill-specified rules and codes of proper behavior. The third is that government could take on a role in networks that ranges from passive—merely being "an actor among actors" (Klijn and Koppenjan 2000: 151)—to proactive (Klijn and Koppenjan 2000: 153–54), thereby making itself better able to ensure that the network's categorical interests are more in line with its perceptions of the public interest. This can be achieved by becoming the network's nonpartisan process manager, thus gaining the ability to influence the network's interactional processes,[51] or, alternatively, by becoming a network builder, thus gaining the ability to influence the network's values and categorical interests as well as its interactional processes. The fourth is that those who accept responsibility for protecting the public interest, so defined, must be treated with constant vigilance, which involves all cogovernance network members participating actively in, and giving their consent to, collective decisions. Thus, networks have to be managed, in terms of their constitutions and processes (Kickert et al. 1997,

---

[48] For a discussion of the governance capacity implications of cogovernance networks, see Kazancigil 1998, Messner 1997; see also Garvin 1983.

[49] For a discussion of the normative objections to cogovernance networks in terms of the state's role in the protection of the public interest and the pursuit of the common good, see De Bruijn and Ringeling 1997, Marin and Mayntz 1991, Rhodes 1996, Ripley and Franklin 1987.

[50] Hollingsworth et al. (1994: 6) observe that network-governed "transactions are conducted on the basis of mutual trust and confidence sustained by stable, preferential, particularistic, mutually obliged, and legally nonenforceable relationships. They may be kept together either by value consensus or resource dependency [see Pfeffer and Salancik 1978]—that is, through culture and community—or through dominant units imposing dependence on others."

[51] For a discussion of the underpinning interorganizational theory, see Aldrich 1979, Aldrich and Whetten 1981, Benson 1982, Cook 1977, Levin and White 1961, Negandhi 1975.

Klijn et al. 1995), with network managers being mediators and stimulators rather than central actors (Forester 1989).

Enclavists would be predisposed to policy instruments that acceptably promote their categorical interests. Redistributive policies would have a strong appeal, as they would require engagement in a values-laden discourse to determine who should win or lose, by how much, how and when; and would facilitate the removal of 'illegitimate' distinctions between people. In contrast, distributive policies would have little appeal, as they reinforce existing inequalities. Constituency policies would appeal only if they do not impose controls over individual, interpersonal, group and corporate behavior, while regulatory policies would appeal only if they stimulate and facilitate voluntary behavior change.

The regulatory mode preferred by enclavists would be a voluntary network regulation, whereby regulations are designed, authorized and implemented by cogoverning networks. Enclavists would only be favorably predisposed toward regulatory information instruments, which stimulate and facilitate voluntary, values-driven, goodness-of-heart changes (Douglas 1982a) that suggest a commitment to the desired governance outcomes, whether in the public or market spheres. Economic and command-and-control instruments would have little or no appeal. The former has only limited appeal because the financial incentives and disincentives involved may create not only differentiations within the cogovernance network membership, but also a decision environment in which voluntary changes may be construed as attributable to self-interest rather than a commitment to mutually agreed governance outcomes. Command-and-control instruments' lack of appeal is because, axiomatically, no rules that dictate how cogovernance network members must behave can be rigidly enforced by sanctions, simply because all are free to leave the network at any time.

When confronted with any regulatory instrument, enclavists would only comply, voluntarily, if by so doing they did not compromise their moral commitment (Etzioni 1961) to those with whom they share common values and a commitment to the categorical interest, which means that they would find ways of minimizing, if not avoiding, any changes that did not promote their categorical interests; and they would expect others to do so as well.

The enclavists' salient societal governance risk, which stems from the inherent relativism of the hermeneutic-structuralist methodology, is that interest groups cannot agree among themselves and with the societal governing elites on the set of common interests that need to be jointly protected and promoted in the 'public interest.' In the absence of voluntary cogovernance networks decision-making processes that are harmonious, trustworthy and codetermining, enclavists would not be able to externalize blame for any societal governance failure onto particular risk takers or particular secret enemies within the cogovernance process.

Enclavists, if faced with the prospect that people cannot construct mutual understandings and acceptable joint perspectives that evoke moral commitment to the identification and correction of governance failures, would, in the first instance, voice (Hirschman 1970) blame, accusing the risk takers and the secret enemies within voluntary cogovernance networks who, they believe, do not share their commitment to interactive governance success. They would, no doubt, threaten to leave the interactive governance process if confronted with a value conflict over how best to correct governance failure. Their envisaged solution would be to demand the removal of the risk takers and secret enemies within and the empowerment of more and different people to engage fully in voluntary cogovernance networks. They would do this because their structuralist ontology convinces them that people are best bound by a moral commitment to collectively agreed processes and outcomes, and their hermeneutic epistemology predisposes them to believe that people are willing and able to engage in reasoning that is intersubjective and values-based, involving critically reflective communications using processes that enable them to make and question arguments and so determine the validity of normative judgments. This solution would involve developing strategies that would not only correct governance failure, but also evoke a moral commitment to interactive governance success.

Fatalist Perspective

To fatalists, the least alienating form of societal governance would be one based on the simple principle that it should not require people's constructive engagement. Thus, fatalists would be attracted to the idea of societal governance processes that minimize the potential for intentional and coercive collective action by constraining the power of those powerful, self-seeking societal governing elites, which are always attempting to initiate exploitative collective action.

Fatalists would be predisposed to policy instruments that enhance their survival interests. Distributive policies would have a strong appeal because they, at least, have a chance of being included as beneficiaries. Constituency policies would appeal only if they did not impose controls that permit or facilitate their abuse and exploitation, whether by the public or market spheres. On the other hand, regulatory policies would appeal only if they offered some protection against abuse and exploitation, whether by the public or market spheres, although fatalists would expect the societal governing elites to get it all wrong. In contrast, redistributive policies would not appeal, as the untrustworthy and unknowing powers that be, when determining who should win and lose, by how much, how and when, would inevitably cast them among the losers.

Fatalists would not be predisposed to any regulatory mode or any form of regulatory instrument. Hierarchical command-and-control instruments would have no appeal, unless they offered some protection against their abuse and exploitation, whether in the public or market spheres. Economic instruments, however administered, would have appeal, but only if they provided the opportunity for them to be rewarded, should it be in their survival interest to comply with the regulations. Information instruments, however administered, would have no appeal because the so-called experts would probably have got it wrong and, in any event, they would probably be ignored by those who are marginalizing, abusing and exploiting them, whether in the public or market spheres.

When confronted with any regulatory instrument, fatalists would respond with alienative compliance (Etzioni 1961), born of fear of force, threat and menace, in the belief that the coercive, manipulative, persuasive power being exercised is not legitimate. This means that they would find ways of minimizing, if not avoiding, any changes that did not promote their survival interests; and they would expect others to do so as well.

The fatalists' salient societal governance risk is that their self-chosen isolation has been in vain. This stems from their presumption that the social world is unknowable and, thus, the public interest cannot be intentionally and instrumentally promoted and protected. This is premised on the inherent relativism of the hermeneutic-agency methodology and its inability to identify causal relationships and structural imperatives.

Fatalists, if faced with the prospect that the public interest can be intentionally and instrumentally promoted and protected, would, in the first instance, deny that such a proposition can be proven, and then blame fate because their self-chosen isolation has been in vain. Their envisaged solution would be to leave well enough alone, because their hermeneutic epistemology predisposes them to the proposition that people can only contestably know the subjective social world as what they believe it to be, and because their agency ontology convinces them that people's actions are constrained by their subjective perceptions of social reality. This solution would involve resisting vigorously any fate-tempting societal governance innovation, which would only make matters worse. Then, if their survival interests were threatened, they would exit (Hirschman 1970) by disengaging from societal governance processes.

Individualist Perspective

To individualists good societal governance is based on a market-determined public interest, protected and promoted by self-regulation (Bentham [1789] 1970, Friedman 1970, Hayek 1960, Smith [1776] 1977) and grounded in three principles. The first is that the public interest is the 'will' of the market—the aggregation of individuals' preferences as revealed in the marketplace. The second is that law-abiding buyers and sellers, with a sense of personal responsibility that is a matter of honor,[52] shame and guilt,[53] must be free to negotiate enforceable contracts and to conduct their affairs in accordance with their contractual obligations, within the rules of the law of property, tort and contract. The third is that those who take it upon themselves, misguidedly, to define, promote and protect the public interest must be seen not only as inherently coercive and intrusive, but also as constantly at risk of being inefficient. This means that they must be treated with constant vigilance, which requires them to be held strictly accountable for the outcomes of their actions (see, for example, Kaufman 1976, Weimer and Vining 1992).

---

[52] For a discussion of the concept of honor, see Pitt-Rivers 1968.
[53] For a discussion of the distinction between shame and guilt as mechanisms of social control, see Rawls 1971: sec. 65.

Individualists would be predisposed only to policy instruments that promote their self-interest.[54] Distributive policies would appeal, particularly for public goods, but otherwise only if they do not create more competition in the marketplace or if they create exploitable business opportunities. Constituency policies would appeal only if they do not constrain *positive* freedom or limit business opportunities. Regulatory policies would appeal only if they help to maintain people's confidence in the marketplace, by defining and enforcing socially acceptable market behaviors. In contrast, redistributive policies would have no appeal, as they not only stifle risk-taking initiatives and suppress the ambition of those who win from any redistribution, but also demotivate those who lose by reducing their risk-taking rewards.

The regulatory mode preferred by individualists is market self-regulation, achieved by means of enforcable contracts embodying a zero tolerance of noncompliance and full restitution as the ultimate sanction. Individualists would thus not be predisposed to accept any imposed regulatory instruments. Economic instruments, however, would be least objectionable, because they are, at least, "indirect controls" (Douglas and Wildavsky 1982: 180). They operate through the creation of incentives that reward desired behavior and disincentives that punish undesirable behavior, but they must be designed by those who understand how the market works, what the market response is likely to be, and thus, what the market consequences are likely to be. Command-and-control instruments would have appeal only if they maintain public confidence and are designed by those who understand what the market consequences are likely to be. Information instruments would appeal only if they closed down opportunities for competitors or created new opportunities for market exploitation.

When confronted with any regulatory instrument, individualists would respond with instrumental compliance (Etzioni 1961), based on economic calculations of compliance costs and benefits. This means that they would find ways of minimizing, if not avoiding, any changes that involve a net compliance cost; and they would expect others to do so as well.

The individualists' salient societal governance risk is the principal-agent problem of not being able to specify, completely and comprehensively, the implicit and explicit contracts they have with their agents because of uncertainty and opportunism, and of not being able to enforce the executed contracts with a zero noncompliance tolerance and full restitution as the sanction. This risk stems from the incapacity of the naturalist-agency methodology to identify causal relationships, a product of naturalist epistemology, and structural imperatives, a product of agency ontology. In the face of these governance prob-

---

[54] Murray (1971: 84–85) talks of the "economica res publica, those economic matters which are public, external to the individual private capitals," namely, guaranteeing property and contract, standardized currency, weights, and measures; ensuring the availability of labor, land, finance, technology, and infrastructure; orchestrating macroeconomic policy; regulating work, consumption, and external diseconomies (such as pollution); and providing ideological, educational, and communications conditions supportive of production and trade.

lems, they would be unable either to attribute the cause of market self-governance failure to nonmarket factors or to determine a market solution to societal governance failure.

Individualists, if faced with the prospect of a market self-regulation malfunction because law-abiding buyers and sellers are unable to specify completely, and enforce, their contracts, would, in the first instance, blame bad luck or rogue buyers and sellers who have not acted in accordance with the terms of their contracts or the law, or who have not developed an appropriate sense of personal honor or shame in their interpersonal relationships. Their envisaged solution would be to strengthen market self-regulation by a more stringent drafting and enforcement of contracts that have full restitution as the sanction. This solution follows from their agency ontology, which enables them to presume that people are motivated by personal incentives; and from their naturalist epistemology, which makes acceptable the presumption that they can make reliable predictions about the consequences of human behavior by observing patterns in, and correlations between, forms of social behavior. This solution would be expected to initiate the economic calculations needed to induce the instrumental compliance necessary to correct the governance failure. If their prospects for material success were threatened they would exit (Hirschman 1970) by withdrawing from the marketplace in order to renegotiate their relationships.

SOCIETAL GOVERNANCE ANTAGONISMS

Because adherents to one *social solidarity* would resist the flawed approaches to societal governance advanced by adherents to any competing *social solidarities*, trench warfare is inevitable.

Hierarchists if trapped in, or subject to, a failing societal governance mode posited by adherents to another *social solidarity*, would, in the 'public interest,' and seeing themselves as the rational saviors of the common good as articulated by the societal political elite, seek to impose hierarchical governance structures and processes. These would be enforceable command-and-control regulations administered with a zero noncompliance tolerance and substantial sanctions.

Enclavists in such a situation would, in the 'public interest,' and seeing themselves as passionate saviors of the categorical good to which they are committed, demand that people be permitted to establish, and engage fully in, voluntary cogovernance network mechanisms. These would be designed to balance the interests of diverse groups and administer regulatory regimes that permit discretion, have a low noncompliance tolerance, and have a capacity both to reward and to punish.

Fatalists in the same situation, on seeing themselves as victims of the societal powers that be, would feel vindicated. They have correctly anticipated the so-called societal experts getting it wrong. Their inclination would be to become prophets of doom.

Individualists in the same circumstances would, in the 'public interest,' and seeing themselves as the commonsense saviors of their own self-interest, take steps to establish what Polanyi (1957) called the self-regulating market form of society. They would seek to limit the power of the state, the role of which would be restricted to ensuring the safety and security of people, financial, physical and natural resources, and commodities; and to determining the legal framework that defines and enforces property rights.

CONCLUSION

The extent to which societal governors are able to establish and/or reinforce the societal governance mechanisms that enable them to govern society as they see fit, depends on the governance limitations they place upon themselves because of their adherence to a particular set of the societal governance truths (Dixon and Dogan 2002a). Their ability to manipulate or constrain the behavior of those they seek to govern depends on the extent to which their actions violate or reinforce the societal governance truths of those whose behavior they are seeking to affect. Adherents to each of the four *social solidarities* have a distinctive, but flawed, perspective on what constitutes good societal governance.

To hierarchists, the public interest—the common good as articulated by the societal political elite—would be knowable, and can be promoted and protected. Society is thus governable, but only by empowering the societal governing elites. Only they can preserve the continuity between the past, present and future. Government is thus perceived to be benign and benevolent. The idea of a polity that enables government to be elitist, stable and strong would be attractive. Good societal governance is, thus, based on strong distributive and constituent policies and hierarchically administered command-and-control regulatory instruments. This is all for the purpose of soliciting behavioral compliance because of a cognitive commitment to the societal governing elites, reinforced, where possible, by deontological moral codes.

To enclavists the public interest—inclusive of the categorical good to which they are committed—is also knowable, and can be promoted and protected. Society is thus governable, but only when people voluntarily engage in sophisticated and subtle cogovernance interactions that take place on the basis of a sense of mutual trust and shared commitment to a set of public interest propositions that embrace an agreed set of categorical interests. Government is thus perceived to be intrusive, but benevolent. The idea of a polity that enables government to be deliberative, inclusive and egalitarian would be attractive. Good societal governance is, thus, based on strong redistributive policies and cogovernance networks administering information-based regulatory instruments. This is all for the purpose of empowering people and enhancing the categorical good to which they are committed, which is expected to achieve genuine behavioral compliance by building a moral commitment to a common cause.

To fatalists, the public interest is unknowable, and cannot be intentionally promoted and protected. They would resignedly accept whatever the societal powers that be decide is best. Society is thus governable, but only if the powers that be are willing and able to exercise the required coercive power necessary to govern as they see fit. Government may well be benign in intent, at least some of the time, but is inevitably malevolent in action. The idea of a polity that requires government, interest groups and business to be less coercive and less intrusive would be attractive, but they expect to be alienated from the societal powers that be, so their engagement with them can only be on the basis of alienative compliance. Good societal governance is, thus, based on distributive policies and economic regulatory instruments that advance their survival interests, but they expect the societal experts to get it all wrong.

To individualists, the public interest—the summation of all private interests in a society—is also knowable, and can be promoted and protected. This is only possible, however, if the state's role is restricted to ensuring the people's safety and security, and to establishing a judicial-legal framework that defines and enforces the property rights that permit private ends to be peacefully pursued. Society is thus governable, but only when buyers and sellers, with a sense of personal responsibility, are free to negotiate enforceable contracts and to conduct their affairs in accordance with their contractual obligations, within the rules of the law of property, tort and contract. Government is thus perceived to be both intrusive and malevolent. The idea of a polity that requires government to be weak, unobtrusive and small would be attractive. Good societal governance is, thus, self-regulating markets. The best of the misguided governance policies and regulatory instruments are those that most enhance their self-interest. Such policies would include distributive policies, provided they create exploitable business opportunities, and regulatory policies, provided they are focused on maintaining people's confidence in the marketplace, preferably by means of economic instruments that reward desired behavior and punish undesirable behavior. Both types of government interventions, however, would have to be designed by those who understand how the market works, what the market response is likely to be, and, thus, what the market consequences are likely to be. This, in turn, would be expected to solicit instrumental compliance from the governed.

Adherents to each *social solidarity* thus accept that society is governable, but only if their preferred mode of governing is adopted. Adherents to one *social solidarity* consider their balance between individual autonomy and societal control to be the only legitimate one. Thus, they consider their approach to the resolution of conflicting public and private sphere claims to be the only acceptable one. They would, inevitably, resist the public interest conceptualization, promotion and protection propositions advanced by adherents to competing *social solidarities*. As a consequence, the extent to which the governed resist the societal governors' processes is determined by the extent to which they adhere to the same *social solidarity*. If they do, they would share a common view not only on what the public interest is, but also on the best enabling environment that will ensure its proper identification, promotion and protection. This, in turn, would determine what constitutes the most appropriate governance role for the state, the most appropriate multilevel politicoadministrative and judicial structures and processes, and the most appropriate public interest promotion policies, governance modes and regulatory instruments. If they do not, the result will be societal governance disillusionment, even despair, among the governed, which may lead to their withdrawal from, or rebellion against, the societal governors' processes. This theme is developed in detail in Chapters 6 and 7.

Appendix 4.1
The Competing Social Solidarities on the Public Interest and Societal Governance

Dimension	Hierarchist	Enclavist	Fatalist	Individualist
Public sphere:	The domain of the societal political and administrative elites, which should be extended wherever and whenever possible.	A realm with boundaries that should be expanded if they conceal unequal power relations. Must be treated with constant vigilance if it is to be made benevolent.	A capricious and fearful realm that is untrustworthy and indifferent to individual needs. Engagement is pointless and should be avoided at all costs.	A realm that should be made smaller wherever and whenever possible and must be treated with constant vigilance.
Source of:				
legitimate authority:	Rational-legal authority.	Charismatic authority.	None acknowledged.	None acknowledged.
power:	Legitimate, expert, knowledge or exchange.	Referent, normative or integrative.	Coercive, physical or threat.	Reward, resources or economic.
Governance mode:	Hierarchy.	Networks.	No preference, as none can make any difference.	Market.

Appendix 4.1 (cont'd)

Dimension	Hierarchist	Enclavist	Fatalist	Individualist
Governing mode:	Expert-led command mode.	Participatory-consensus mode.	No preference, as none can make any difference.	Market mode.
Government:	Benign in intent, benevolent in outcome.	Intrusive in intent, benevolent (perhaps) in outcome.	Benign (perhaps) in intent, malevolent in outcome.	Intrusive in intent, malevolent in outcome.
Political constitution:	Unitary political structure with a strong center and unfettered executive dominance.	Any devolved political structure that permits and facilitates deliberative decision making.	Unitary political structure with weak decentralized administration and subservience of the executive to the legislature and judiciary.	A decentralized political structure with a strong local government and a strict separation of powers.
Electoral system:	Voluntary first-past-the-post voting in single-member constituencies, with limited suffrage.	Compulsory proportional representation voting in multiple-member constituencies, with universal suffrage.	Voluntary first-past-the-post voting in single-member constituencies, with limited suffrage.	Voluntary first-past-the-post voting in single-member constituencies, with universal suffrage.

Dimension	Hierarchist	Enclavist	Fatalist	Individualist
Legal system:	Requires the upholding of law and order (most rigorously) and property rights.	Requires the upholding of human rights (most rigorously) and law and order.	Requires the upholding of law and order (most rigorously) and property rights.	Requires the upholding of property rights (most rigorously) and law and order.
The public interest:	Knowable and grounded in the notion of the common good, as articulated by the societal governing elites.	Knowable and grounded in the notion of the categorical good, as determined through consensus-seeking values discourses.	Not knowable.	Knowable only through individuals' preferences as expressed or revealed in the marketplace.
Governance challenge:	To establish societal governance mechanism that the societal political and administrative elites can dominate.	To establish societal governance mechanism that facilitate codetermining, protecting and promoting the public interest.	To establish societal governance mechanisms that do not expect or require people's constructive engagement.	To establish societal governance mechanism that will leave the market free to govern itself.

Appendix 4.1 (cont'd)

Dimension	Hierarchist	Enclavist	Fatalist	Individualist
Governance salient threat:	The inability of the societal political and administrative elites to identify, protect and promote the public interest.	The inability of interest groups and the societal governing elites to engage in harmonious cogovernance to identify, protect and promote the public interest.	The ability of anyone intentionally and instrumentally to promote and protect the public interest, so revealing that their self-chosen isolation has been in vain.	The inability of those operating in the marketplace to understand the nature and causation of, and solution to, systemic failures in the marketplace.
Societal governability:	Society is governable, but only if there is continuity protected by the societal political and administrative elites, who can articulate the common good to be promoted and protected by the state in the public interest.	Society is governable, but only if interest groups and the societal governing elites codetermine the categorical interests to be promoted and protected by the state in the public interest.	Society is governable, but only if the powers that be exercise the required coercive power to govern as they see fit.	Society is governable, but only if the market is left to govern itself, with the state's role limited to determining the legal framework that defines and enforces property rights, to ensuring the safety and security of people, financial, physical and natural resources, and commodities, and to creating exploitable market opportunities.

Dimension	Hierarchist	Enclavist	Fatalist	Individualist
Policy process:	Dominated by the executive branch.	Dominated by a plurality of interest groups.	Dominated by untrustworthy vested interests.	Dominated by self-interested parties.
Policy analytic mode:	Functional-analytic analysis that facilitates satisficing decision making.	Communicative-value rational analysis that facilitates consistent, congruent and cogent decision making.	Nonrational analysis that facilitates timely, sensible and credible decision making.	Rational analysis that is instrumental and synoptic, so as to facilitate optimal decision making.
Policy decision-making model:	A process that uses the principles of bounded rationality to make incremental policy changes.	A process that seeks to balance the interests of diverse groups.	A garbage can-like decision-making process.	A process that seeks to achieve policy goals efficiently using instrumental rationality.
Sources of policy-related information:	Internal and external-formal sources.	Internal-informal sources.	No preferences, none reliable.	External-informal sources.
Policy delivery mix:	Emphasis on public (bureaucratic) provision.	Emphasis on partnership (joint) provision.	No preference, as all are indifferent to needs.	Emphasis on market provision.

Appendix 4.1 (cont'd)

Dimension	Hierarchist	Enclavist	Fatalist	Individualist
Policy arenas:				
distribution:	Strong appeal.	Modest appeal.	Strong appeal.	Only for public goods, or to create new markets.
redistribution:	No appeal.	Strong appeal.	No appeal.	No appeal.
constituency:	Strong appeal.	Appeals, but only if no controls imposed.	Appeals, but only if no controls imposed.	Appeals, if *negative* freedoms not constrained.
regulatory:	Strong appeal.	Appeals, if behavior change encouraged.	Appeals, if protection against abuse offered.	Strong appeal, if market confidence enhanced.
Regulatory mode:	Hierarchical regulation.	Cogovernance network regulation.	No preferences, as none can be trusted.	Market self-regulation.
Regulatory instruments:				
command-and-control:	Appeals.	No appeal, as sanctions unimplementable.	Appeals, although the societal administrative elite would probably get it wrong.	Appeals if market confidence promoted, but only if they reflect an understanding of the market.

162

Dimension	Hierarchist	Enclavist	Fatalist	Individualist
Regulatory instruments (cont'd):				
information:	Appeals.	Appeals.	No appeal.	Appeals, particularly if they reduce market opportunities for competitors.
economic:	Appeals.	Limited appeal, and would have to be negotiated.	Appeals, although the societal administrative elite would probably get it wrong.	Appeals, because they provide incentives, but only if they reflect an understanding of the market.
Regulatory enforcement levels and modes:	Through formal regulatory regimes with a zero tolerance of noncompliance and substantial sanctions.	Through regulatory regimes that permit discretion, a low noncompliance tolerance and a capacity to reward and punish	Through regulatory regimes with a high tolerance of noncompliance and constrained sanctions.	Through enforceable contracts with a zero noncompliance tolerance and full restitution as the ultimate sanction.

Appendix 4.1 (cont'd)

Dimension	Hierarchist	Enclavist	Fatalist	Individualist
Compliance:	Follows a cognitive commitment.	Follows a moral commitment.	Alienative compliance.	Instrumental compliance.
Response to regulatory imposition:				
command-and-control:	Would do what is deemed to be in best interests of the collective.	Would seek to find ways of minimizing any changes that are inconsistent with their categorical interests.	Would seek to find ways of avoiding or minimizing any change that threatens their survival.	Would seek to find ways of avoiding or minimizing any change that imposes net compliance costs.
information:	Would do what is deemed to be in best interests of the collective.	Would ignore any information that is inconsistent with their categorical interests.	Would ignore any information because it is untrustworthy.	Would ignore any information unless it creates a market opportunity.
economic:	Would do what is deemed to be in best interests of the collective.	Would seek to find ways of minimizing any changes that are inconsistent with their 'categorical interests.'	Would seek to find ways of avoiding or minimizing any change that threatens their survival.	Would seek to find ways of avoiding or minimizing any change that adversely imposes net compliance costs.

Dimension	Hierarchist	Enclavist	Fatalist	Individualist
Response to the failure of their preferred societal governance mode:	Express loyalty toward the societal political and administrative elites and then blame deviants.	Voice blame, accusing the risk takers and the secret enemies within, then demand their expulsion, and empowerment of more people to engage fully in voluntary cogovernance mechanisms.	No response, as they have no preference.	Blame bad luck or rogue buyers and sellers in the marketplace, then, if prospects for material success are diminished, exit by disengaging from the marketplace in order to minimize their material losses and to renegotiate contractual relationships.
Response if trapped in, or subject to, a failing societal governance mode posited by another *social solidarity*:	Would see themselves as the rational saviors of the common good and would impose formal hierarchical governance structures and processes.	Would see themselves as passionate saviors of their categorical interests, and would demand that people be permitted to establish, and engage fully with, voluntary cogovernance networks.	Would see themselves as the vindicated victims of the societal powers that be, and would become prophets of doom.	Would see themselves as the commonsense saviors of their own self-interest, taking the necessary steps to ensure that the market becomes self-regulating, limiting the power and the role of the state to securing and facilitating market transactions.

5

Global Interest and Global Governance

> It is not beyond the powers of political volition to tip the scales toward a more secure peace, greater economic wellbeing, social justice and environmental sustainability. But no country can achieve these global public goods on its own, and neither can the global market place. Thus our efforts must now focus on the missing term of the equation: global public goods.
>
> Kofi Annan,
> Secretary General,
> United Nations,
> March 1, 1999.

INTRODUCTION

The authority of the nation-state has been increasingly threatened by the challenges emanating from globalization, particularly by the threats posed by international terrorism (Alexander 1976, Howard 1992, Jamieson 1995, Kressell 2001), as evidenced by the dramatic events of September 11, 2001, in New York. Further evidence is shown by the associated phenomena that have swept across the globe during the latter decades of the twentieth century, manifest in the international trade in drugs, and the turbulence in rogue, failed, ethnically divided and poverty-stricken countries. These challenges have not only dramatically altered the global landscape, but also, consequently, have become a dominant influence on domestic politics and international relations in and among nation-states. Much of the discussion of these globalization forces has been framed in economic and technological terms, with debate often being centered on who are, or should be, globalization's winners and losers. This hides, however, what is perhaps the most significant, and potentially enduring, development: the creation of new forms and patterns of relations and interdependencies between the state and nonstate policy actors in international arenas. The nation-state's monopoly over global governance has been increasingly challenged by

ence of nonstate policy actors, whether for-profit or not-for-profit in orientation (Archibugi and Held 1995, Rosenau and Czempiel 1992).

The purpose of this chapter is to use Cultural Theory's *grid-group* social-control space, or *social map*, to gain insights into global governance—the patterns that sustain global order.[1] Adherents to each of the four *social solidarities*—hierarchist, enclavist, fatalist and individualist—offer competing perspectives on whether the global interest[2] is knowable; on global governance mechanisms[3]—the rule-oriented international governmental organizations[4] and international regimes[5]—that can best identify, promote and protect the global inter-

---

[1] For a more general discussion of Cultural Theory and international relations, see Verweij 1995.

[2] The global interest is the common interdependent interests of many global publics with respect to activities that cross national boundaries. Stern (1995) provides a list of five international public 'goods' that he considers constitute the global interest: (1) international economic stability, (2) international security (political stability), (3) the international environment, (4) international humanitarian assistance, and (5) knowledge. For a discussion of ethics in international relations, see Frost 1996, Hutchings 1999, and Nardin 1983.

[3] Rosenau (1992a: 15) conceptualizes global governance as "those institutions and regimes that the diverse actors in the [global] system fashion...as a means of pursuing their ideational and behavioral inclinations through which global politics moves through time"—global governance without government (Rosenau and Czempel 1992). Keohane (1989: 3) defines them as "persistent and connected sets of rules (formal and informal) that prescribe behavioral roles, constrain activity, and shape expectations." The formal dimension can be articulated as "the whole construction of international relations in a system of states" (Buzan 1996b: 248), such as the European Union, or as "broad framework arrangements governing the activities of all (or almost all) the members of international society over a wide range of specific issues" (Young 1989: 13). Rosenau (1992a: 9) argues that governance in a purposive global order is not confined to a single sphere of activity, for it refers to the arrangements that prevail between international regimes, as well as to the principles, norms, rules, and procedures used to accommodate competing interests in the settling of disputes arising between international regimes. He (Rosenau 1992a: 13–14) also considers that extant global governance mechanisms are not causally linked to form a coherent pattern of governance, for they constitute an organic whole only in the sense that all those involved depend upon the same global pool of resources and all must cope with the same environmental conditions.

[4] *International governmental organizations*, also referred to as *multilateral organizations* and *world organizations*, can be classified by their membership potential (regional-to-universal) and their scope of purpose (specific-to-general purpose or issue-areas) (Jacobson 1984: 11–13; see also Diehl 1989, Feld et al. 1988, Jacobson 1984, Kratochwil and Ruggie 1986, Taylor 2001).

[5] *International regimes* are defined, diversely (see Strange [1982] 1997). Krasner (1983: 2) sees them as those "sets of implicit or explicit principles ["beliefs of fact, causation and rectitude"], norms ["standards of behavior...in terms of rights and obligations"], rules ["specific prescriptions or proscriptions for action"], and decision-making procedures ["prevailing practices for making and implementing collective choice"] around which actor's expectations converge in a given area of international relations" (but see Zacher with Sutton 1995: 14). Keohane and Nye (1977: 7) see them as those

est; and thus on the world's governability. Following a contextualizing discussion of globalization[6] and global governance, these competing perspectives are identified, and their implications are then explored.

Globalization, a frequently used term that, surprisingly, lacks a precise and commonly accepted definition, has a recurring theme: rapid developments in communications, technology and transportation during the latter years of the twentieth century. Jackson and Sorensen (1999) summarize these as the cross-border intensification of economic, social, and cultural relations, with the driving force of globalization being economics—the internationalization of production, trade, distribution, and finance. It can now be argued that modernization at the nation-state level is, in fact, a two-stage process. The first phase is integration into global trade and financial markets. The second phase then becomes unavoidable, as the economic imperatives imposed by market discipline inevita-

---

"networks of rules, norms and procedures that regularize behavior and control its effects." Jones (1996b: 424) considers them to be "norm-bound interactions relating to issues such as the global environment or human rights, in which states, international organizations, transnational corporations, individuals, and world wide pressure groups...all take part" (see also Nadelmann 1990). Young (1989: 13) defines them as those "more specialized arrangements that pertain to well-defined activities, resources, or geographic areas and often involve only some subset of the members of international society" (see also Nadelmann 1990). Keohane (1989: 4) suggests that in an international regime, there is a significant convergence among the states regarding norms, beliefs, rules, and procedures. Where a set of norms is common to a number of international regimes, Zacher and Sutton (1995: 4) speak of a *metaregime* (but see also Aggarawal 1986: 16–20). They (1995: 4, 30–33) identify four policy sectors relevant to international regimes: jurisdictional rights and obligations; damage control problems; technical and procedural barriers; and prices and market share. International regimes may have an authority structure because of the explicit powers delegated to them by their constituent cohorts of nation-states, or they may be the product of "a transnational process of consensus formation among the official caretakers of the global economy" (Cox 1992: 30; see also 1993). For a discussion of the formation of international regimes, see Keohane 1984; Little 2001; Young 1982, 1989.

[6] Higgott and Reich (1998) have identified four definitions of globalization that are in common use: as an historical epoch; as the confluence of economic phenomena; as the triumph of American values; and as a sociological and technological revolution. Cox (1997: 30, n. 1) observes that, etymologically, global has two meanings, merging to create the neologism globalization: the planet earth; and the array of factors that constitute a globalization process. Held et al. (1999) conceive globalization as a set of processes that transform the spatial organization of social relations and transcontinental or inter-regional transactions by stretching activities across borders, by intensifying interconnectedness, speeding up global interactions and processes, and deepening the impact of world-wide connectedness (see also Hirst and Thompson 1996, Jensen and de Sousa Santos 2000, Ohmae 1990). To Waters (1995: 5), globalization is "a social process in which the constraints of geography on social and cultural arrangements recede and in which people are becoming increasingly aware that they are receding." Contemporary globalization theory in sociology argues that globalization embraces two contradictory interactive processes of homogenization (*globalism*) and differentiation (*localism*), the product of which are powerful resistance movements against globalization processes (Marshall 1998: 258).

bly involve political and cultural integration (Cox 1986; but see also Picciotto 1991).[7]

The key trends that have provided the impetus, and need, for these new forms and patterns of relations and interdependencies, which consequently underpin much of the globalization discourse, are, however, broader than Jackson and Sorensen (1999) suggest. They are set out more fully in *States of Disarray: The Social Effects of Globalization* (UNRISD 1995; see also Bulcke and Verbeke 2001, Cuyvers 2001, Drabek 2001, Storm and Naastepad 2001). First, the liberal democracy is gradually becoming the dominant polity.[8] Second, the dominance of market forces and the integration of domestic economies into a global economy have facilitated the international integration of commodity and capital markets dominated by a number of multinational corporations, thereby creating a global capital market, which facilitates, if not actually actively encourages, the free movement of capital in and out of domestic economies. Third, an increasing number of transnational political, social, cultural, technological and environmental interdependencies have emerged, necessitating the transformation of domestic labor, capital and commodity markets. Fourth, the speed of technological change, and its pervasive influence, have accelerated. Finally, the media revolution and consumerism have forever changed expectations. At the nation-state level, the failure of governments to respond accordingly must raise concerns over their continuing ability to govern, as evidence would suggest that governments now find it more difficult to perform effectively, efficiently and legitimately (Kooiman 1993, 1999; Kooiman and Van Vliet 1995).

While discussion over governability at the global level has traditionally focused on the extreme examples provided by 'neo-states' and 'failed states,' the globalization-related erosion (whether real or perceived) of the effectiveness of governments in more advanced liberal democracies to perform those tasks essential to the orderly functioning of society is becoming increasingly apparent. This threat to societal governability is exemplified by the globalization of the world economy and its financial markets, in part a result of the application of modern communications and information technologies, which, by opening up borders, has limited the effectiveness of national economic policies in amelio-

---

[7] Dickens (1998) suggests that there has been a global shift in the form of a multi-dimensional movement in the patterns of economic activity from predominantly national to international, transnational and global levels. In this new setting, nation-states and international organizations appear as economic actors or as frameworks of economic action.

[8] Fukuyama's (1989) account of the 'end of history' posits that the processes of change in politics, of crisis and contradiction, are over because people everywhere have come to embrace democratic values. Indeed, surveying the global landscape in the late 1980s he sees a world in which ideology has been vanquished—"an unabashed victory of economic and political liberalism" (p. 3)—and neoliberal, capitalist democracy reigns supreme. Rustow (1990: 73) asserts that "a tide of democratic change is sweeping the world." Diamond et al. (1988: ix–x) focus on the "unprecedented growth of international concern for human rights…including the right to choose democratically the government under which one lives."

rating domestic problems (Hirst 1994). This threatens to undermine the stability not only of individual nation-states, but also of whole regions, and potentially, the entire world. It is, therefore, not surprising that the issue of global governability provides, at the start of the twenty-first century, one of the principal political challenges facing the global actors[9]—the national (or societal) governing elites, the global administrative elite,[10] the multinational business corporations managing elites, or global interest groups.[11]

The consequences of these globalization trends and developments must clearly raise questions about intergovernmental relationships and the need for global governance mechanisms that reflect not only the new forms and patterns of international relations and interdependencies, but also the emerging role of nonstate actors (Baylis and Smith 2001). The challenges facing the global actors in designing and implementing new and appropriate global governance mechanisms include how to address the following ten issues. The first is the increased economic interdependence among nation-states that has reduced their ultimate authority over people and institutions within their jurisdiction—their national sovereignty (Jouvenal 1957).[12] The second is the emergence of multinational business corporations, including financial institutions, whose activities cannot

---

[9] For a discussion of the role of globalizing elites in global transformations, see Gill 1994b, Gill and Law 1989.

[10] The *global administrative elite* comprises individuals who have been elected or appointed to administer global governance mechanisms. For a discussion of these transnational actors in relation to international organizations, see Willett 2001.

[11] The *global interest groups* comprise people in pressure groups, lobby groups, non-governmental organizations and social movements who are seeking to advance particular causes or sectional interests with respect to activities that cross national boundaries. Some operate on their own; others have chosen to form networks in order to share information and tasks, so as to enhance their impact (Commission on Global Governance 1995: 254). For a discussion of social movements and global change, see Ekins 1992 and Walker 1988.

[12] Bull (1977: 8) distinguishes (1) between a nation-state's *internal sovereignty* (its supremacy over all other authorities within its jurisdiction) and its *external sovereignty* (its independence from external authorities); and (2) between its *factual sovereignty* (legal or de jure sovereignty, akin to Keohane's (1991) *formal sovereignty*) and its *normative sovereignty* (the ability to exercise sovereignty by formulating, implementing and managing public policies, akin to Keohane's (1991) *operational sovereignty*) (see also Biersteker and Weber 1996). Jackson (1991: 26–31) distinguishes between *passive* and *active sovereignty* (the ability to act and collaborate both domestically and internationally). Globalization challenges a state's sovereignty: its *external sovereignty*, by requiring it to reduce its independence from external authorities in order to secure the benefits of cooperation; its *internal sovereignty*, by constraining the policy-making capacity of the state when confronted with globalized industries and markets); and thus its *operational sovereignty* (see Barkin and Cronin 1994; Cooper 1968; Lipodith 1992; Reinicke 1997, 1998; Ruggie 1983). Reinicke (1998: 218) concludes that international cooperation, if it is to generate concrete solutions to the challenge of globalization, requires more than just managing *external sovereignty*; internal cooperation must also be redefined so as to include the administration of *internal sovereignty*.

be effectively regulated by government. The third is the increased mobility of international trade and investment flows (Scholte 2001), which arguably limits national freedom to raise taxes for social programs. The fourth is the increased pressures on government to maintain international competitiveness, thereby to reduce the size of the public sector, to reduce (or at least not increase) taxation (especially direct taxes), and to reduce deficit financing and public debt. The fifth is the growing problem of structural unemployment in many industrialized countries. The sixth is the increasingly global nature of many environmental problems (Green 2001). The seventh is the rising and unacceptably high number of people living in absolute poverty (Thomas 2001, Wheeler and Bellamy 2001). The eighth is growing income disparities, both between richer and poorer countries, and between rich and poor within both developed and developing countries (Robinson and Tinker 1996). The ninth are the threats to, and posed by, least developed countries because they are being not only impoverished by the costs of globalization, but also excluded from its benefits, thus demonstrating the differential ways in which countries participate in the globalization process (Deacon et al. 1997). The final issue is the implication of the emergence of a 'global culture,'[13] giving rise to people increasingly defining themselves by their ethnicity and religion (Huntington 1997), a cultural polarization between the 'haves' and 'have nots,' and the emergence of a growing sense of isolation among those excluded from the benefits of globalization.[14]

Within the contemporary discourse surrounding global governance, the concept of 'governance without government' is especially relevant (Rosenau 1992a: 7; see also Ashley 1989, Rosenau 1987). The discourse has now moved well beyond the simplistic positing of a 'world government,' with a centralized decision-making authority orchestrating and overseeing intergovernmental relationships. It is recognized that the structures and processes of interactions among the global actors on any given global issue are always likely to be specific, unique and diverse, and that the patterns of relationships within these interactions are complex, with dynamic tensions ever present. Indeed, which of the global actors constitute the 'global governors'[15] and which are 'the governed' may well vary from one global governance issue to another.

---

[13] Giddens (1999) and Tomlinson (1999) put forward a sociological perspective on globalization in which a complex world culture is emerging as culture loosens its links to local nation states (through enforced proximity) and becomes deterritorialized. Mazrui (1976: 437) talks of "a process of normative convergence" that has taken place over recent centuries, based on Western values. For a Cultural Theory perspective on the mismatch between global networks and local cultures, see Thompson 2000a.

[14] Bauman (1998) posits the pessimistic view that large swathes of the world's population have had isolation forced upon them by globalization and are paying a heavy cultural, psychological and political price for the 'privilege.'

[15] The *global governors* are those individuals who seek to influence, guide, direct or control people in particular nation-state jurisdictions, multinational corporations, pressure groups, lobby groups, non-governmental organizations and social movements whose activities have a transnational impact.

Rosenau (1992a: 14) argues that global governance can be conceived as activities at three levels. The first is the ideational or intersubjective level: what people sense, perceive, or understand to be the arrangements through which global affairs are conducted (see also Biersteker 1992: 102). The second is the behavioral or objective level: what people routinely and regularly do, knowingly or otherwise, to maintain existing global arrangements. The third is the aggregate or political level: where governance mechanisms enact and implement the policies inherent in ideational and behavioral patterns. He concludes (Rosenau 1992a: 15) that the degree of orderliness achieved is the product of activity at all these levels. The implications of this for the design and implementation of the appropriate global governance mechanisms are clearly significant.

THE GLOBAL INTEREST: WHO SHOULD DETERMINE IT?

Adherents to each of the competing *social solidarities* have rival perceptions on whether the global interest is knowable and on the appropriate role in its identification of the global actors. Thus they have different perspectives on global governance capacity. They would accept that the world is governable, but only if their distinctive approach to identifying the global interest is adopted. They would, inevitably, resist the global interest propositions advanced by adherents to a competing *social solidarity*. As a consequence, the extent to which the governed resist the global governors' processes with respect to defining the global interest is determined by the extent to which they adhere to the same *social solidarity* and thus share a common view on what constitutes the global interest.

Hierarchist Perspective

The global interest, to hierarchists, would be knowable and grounded in the notion of the common good of the *international society*[16]—the global good—articulated as a set of national interests[17] of the constituent nation-states that are

---

[16] Hierarchists would readily accept the (neo)realists' perception (Buzan 1996c, Dunne and Schmidt 2001, Lamy 2001) that the world is a community of nation-states—an *international society* (Carr 1946, Morgenthau 1948, Waltz 1979; see also Armstrong 1993, Boucher 1998, Jackson 1991, Stern 1995; but compare Baldwin 1993, Kegley 1995, Keohane 1986). They would also readily accept that relations between states are power driven and emphasize competition and conflict, because the international society's anarchic structure provides few, if any, constraints on the pursuit of power (Buzan 1996c). *International society* was created by nation-states agreeing to establish commonly agreed rules and institutions under which they would conduct their relations, and recognizing their common interests in maintaining these arrangements (Buzan 1996b). It is also referred to as the Westphalia system, so-named after the 1648 Treaty of Westphalia, which recognized the state, rather than the Roman Catholic Church, as the sovereign power within national boundaries.

[17] (Neo)realists use the term *national interest* to indicate what is best for a nation-state in terms of its relationship with other states, which places considerable emphasis on the role of the state as the embodiment of the nation's interest, and which emphasizes not

prioritized and integrated by the global ruling elite.[18] They would expect people, whether individually or in interest groups, corporations or nation-states, to make whatever voluntary sacrifices or voluntary contributions to collective action are deemed to be for the common good of *international society*. Hierarchists would do so because of their preoccupation with retaining the protection of a hierarchical social order that is based on positional authority derived from the relative coercive and economic power of the dominant nation-states.

To hierarchists, then, the global interest would be knowable and can be intentionally and instrumentally promoted and protected—and thus, the world is governable—but only if there is continuity between the past, present and future. Such a continuity can only be ensured by the global ruling elite, who understand what is for the common good of *international society*, and who can best articulate the global interest propositions to be promoted and protected by the *international society's* global governance mechanisms.

Enclavist Perspective

The global interest is, to enclavists, knowable and embraces an inclusive set of categorical interests.[19] This would reflect the shared values[20] and define the

---

only the threats posed by international anarchy, but also the external constraints on its sovereignty (Byrd 1996).

[18] The *global ruling elite* comprises a fluid group of individuals, drawn from the *societal governing elites* of the dominant nation-states, who seek to take responsibility for influencing, guiding, directing or controlling some aspect of *international society*. This is consistent with Thomson's (1992: 198–99) proposition that whether international activities are defined as 'legitimate' or 'illegitimate' depends on state power and the material interests of state leaders. The basic assumption is that policy reflects the nation-state's primary interest in maintaining or building its power relative to any internal or external challenges to its authority. Thus, a transnational practice is 'deligitimated' only when strong states perceive it as a threat to their internal or external authority, thereby placing it on the international agenda for cross-national coordination or control (see also Krasner 1983, 1984). Hierarchists would see no serious tension between the views of the neorealists and the neoliberal institutionalists in the relative significance they place on the role of international institutions in this context. Cornett and Caporaso (1992: 233) demarcate the respective positions:

In Waltz's [neorealistic] estimation, international organizations "are barely once-removed" from the wishes and capacities of the predominant powers. They merely reflect power distribution at best, and add to the power of the powerful at worst. By contrast, neoliberal institutionalism claims that rules provide a determinant of behavior lying outside capabilities (excluding organizational capabilities) and preferences. In saying this, they do not imply that the power and interests of the major actors are irrelevant to the creation of rules and institutions. They do suggest, however, that once formed, the "rules of the game" rarely mirror the pattern of interests and capabilities from which they originate.

[19] Enclavists would readily accept Haas' (1964: 46) neofunctionalist proposition that "there is no common good other than that perceived through the interest-tainted lenses worn by international actors." Czempiel (1992: 256) talks of globalists and transnationalists for whom the world has become a *global society*, where the antagonistic issue-area of security still exists, but the issue-area of economic wellbeing has acquired salience, so strengthening the processes of compromise, cooperation, and integration (see

identity of global interest groups,[21] operating within a *global society*[22] (Banks 1948) based on the idea that all people have a shared identity, as determined by

---

also Beitz 1979, Buzan 1991, Buzan et al. 1998, Duffield 2001, Keohane and Nye 1977, Maghroori and Ramberg 1982). Indeed, enclavists would view favorably a broadening of the concept of security to one that links human with transnational security, thereby acknowledging that military-strategic threats can threaten fundamental human values such as the right to life, employment, private property, a sustainable and clean environment and legal protection (Knight 2000: 169; see also Krouse and Williams 1996).

[20] Enclavists would readily concur with the communitarianist's (Brown 1992, J. Thompson 1992) vision of a world in which self-determination is constrained by shared or communal values, in the universal moral order tradition; and in which there is a correct course of action independent of state interests and desire (Boucher 1998: 36; see also Part I). They would thus share the perception of the world as a transnational community of humanity, where the coincidence of the people's interests casts a universalist perspective (Boucher, 1998: 15). Thus, they would generally accept that people throughout the world not only share an underlying set of beliefs, ideas and values and a sense of human identity, which form a common context in which everyone lives their lives, but also feel themselves to constitute a unified and distinct entity, notwithstanding the all-too-evident extant human diversity. Enclavists would, no doubt, concur with the vision of the Commission on Global Governance's (1995: 4): "We believe that all humanity could uphold the core values of respect for life, liberty, justice and equality, mutual respect, caring and integrity" and with Linklater's (1990: 201) perception of a desirable global political order as one where people have inalienable rights as human beings. They would, however, argue that the identification of transnational values must be balanced by a respect for differences. Enclavists would have empathy with Green's (1899: 247) proposition that people's moral obligations to others expand as they expand the membership of the group of people—neighbors—with whom they have extensive and intimate attachments and share a set of beliefs about morality and behavior. This *moral community* begins, historically, with the family, then extends to the tribe, the nation, the state and finally to humanity. Donelan (1990: 10–11) argues, from a Natural Law perspective (Mackinnon 1966), that everyone is part of a world moral community and that obligations to humanity are innate, albeit perhaps unrecognized and unacknowledged. Nadelmann (1990: 1) talks of *nonstate transnational moral entrepreneurs* who, on the grounds of moral unacceptability, place the prohibition of particular international activities and practices (such as drugs, piracy and privateering) on the international political agenda, and then establish the norms that underpin their international prohibition regimes on the basis of moral principles and normative values. The emergence of transnational shared values could well undermine what Zacher (1992: 61) describes as two of the five pillars of the traditional international system, by providing the foundation for a global ideology that competes with the constituent nation-state's ideologies for people's political loyalty, and by diminishing the nation-state's perceived ability to provide its people with important values, such as the protection of life and economic welfare.

[21] Enclavists would accept the constructionist proposition that subnational groups in one nation-state are networking with their counterparts in others, thereby creating a dense web of relationships that constitutes a new global order (Slaughter 1997: 184; see also Smith 2001), in an effort to satisfy what they consider to be those important needs and interests that nation-states are unable to satisfy. In so doing, complex and multilayered relationships are established, which, over time, build shared attitudes, and common beliefs that, in turn, build commitments, expectations and loyalties that ultimately engender

consensus-seeking values discourse. Enclavists would presume that once people, whether individually or in interest groups, corporations or nation-states, agree about what is in the 'global interest,' they would make whatever voluntary sacrifices or voluntary contributions to collective action that are mutually agreed upon by an inclusive set of global actors.

To enclavists, then, the global interest would be knowable and can be promoted and protected—and thus, the world is governable—but only if it is assumed that the survival, stability and wellbeing of the world depends on the negotiation by an inclusive set of global actors of a set of categorical interests to be promoted and protected in the 'global interest'. This must be the product of interpersonal interactions and negotiations that take place on the basis of mutual trust, in order to build a shared commitment to its joint promotion and protection by the global civil society's inclusive global governance mechanisms.[23]

Individualist Perspective

The global interest, to individualists, is knowable only through people's revealed market preferences; it is the summation of all private interests in the global marketplace.[24]

---

transnational organizations beyond state control (see, for example, Mitrany 1933, 1966; see also Lindberg and Scheingold 1970). This has increased the importance of nonstate actors (see, for example, Groom and Taylor 1975, Haas 1964, Rosenau 1990; but compare Clark 1995, Herz 1969, Spiro 1995, Thomson and Krasner 1989, Weiss and Gordenker 1996), which has led to a power shift within the international system that challenges the states' traditional monopoly over global governance (Mathews 1997: 51) and now requires them to seek the active cooperation of nonstate actors (Reinicke, 1998: 219).

[22] For a discussion of the related concepts of a *global civil society*, see Edwards 1999, Kendig 1999, Knut 1997, Scholte 1999; *global citizenship*, see Falk 1992a, 1992b, 1994 and 1995; and the virtual *network community*, see Castells 1996, 1997, 1998; Frederic 1992.

[23] This brings into focus the neofunctionalist proposition that the goals being sought by the global actors, and their underlying beliefs and values, may change because of variations in consensual knowledge and perceptions of interests. Transnational institutions can bring about such goal shifts by directly altering the ideas, expectations and inclinations of the national governing elites, or by engaging with national interest groups to bring pressure to bear on national governing elites. As Nye (1988: 239) concludes: "In short, [neofunctionalists] emphasize the political process of learning and redefining national interests, as encouraged by institutional frameworks and regimes" (see also Haas 1964, Lindberg and Scheingold 1970).

[24] Individualists would empathize with the cosmopolitanists, who posit a *world community* of self-interested individuals—*còsmopolitan citizenship* (Delanty 20000)—and would subscribe, standing in the long utilitarian shadow of Jeremy Bentham, to the universalist-cosmopolitanist principle of the greatest happiness of the "citizens of the world" (Boucher 1998: 31, also Part 1; see also Bentham [1802] 1987: 128–36; Brown 1992, 1995; Thomson 1992). In so doing, they would become neoliberal advocates of the neoclassical economic theory proposition that social benefits inevitably follow from ef-

Individualists would presume that people, whether individually or in interest groups, corporations or nation-states, would be unwilling to make voluntary sacrifices or voluntary contributions to any collective action, in the so-called 'global interest,' unless it was in their private interest to do so.

To individualists, then, the global interest would be knowable and can be promoted and protected—and thus, the world is governable—but only when the global market is left to govern itself. This requires the role of global governance mechanisms to be limited to ensuring the safety and security of people, financial, physical and natural resources, and commodities, and to determining a transnational legal framework that defines and enforces property rights, so as to ensure the successful conduct of global market transactions, thereby enabling law-abiding corporate governing elites to satisfy revealed market preferences.

Fatalist Perspective

The global interest, to fatalists, is unknowable, because of capriciousness and uncertainty.

Fatalists would presume that people would be unable or unwilling to identify with any conception of a global community and would be unwilling to make any voluntary sacrifices, or voluntary contributions to any collective action, in the so-called 'global interest,' unless it was in their personal survival interest to do so.

To fatalists, then, the global interest cannot be intentionally and instrumentally promoted and protected. The world is, nevertheless, still governable, but only if the global powers that be can exercise the coercive power required to govern as they see fit.

GOOD GLOBAL GOVERNANCE: WHAT IS IT?

Cultural Theory postulates that what constitutes the best configuration of global governance modes, policies and regulatory instruments intended to protect and promote the global interest, depends on what people accept as the appropriate limitations that should be placed on their autonomy. This, in turn, depends on which of the four *social solidarities* they adhere to. The governed's response to the global governors' processes—the global governance structures and processes that identify, promote and protect the global interest—depends on the legitimacy and authority they give them.

Adherents to each of the four *social solidarities* have a distinctive perspective on global governance based on their preferred balance between, on the one hand, the autonomy of individuals in their own right (or as members of interest groups, corporations and nation-states), and, on the other, control by the global collective. Each of the four *social solidarities* legitimizes and gives authority to a distinctive set of mutually exclusive, and competing, modes of global governance.

---

forts to liberate the global market from political obstacles to exchange, which, they assert, should be the driving force of the relations between nation-states (see also Soros 1998).

Adherents to each *social solidarity* consider only their preferred approach to global governance to be legitimate and authoritative. They would, inevitably, resist the global governance structures and processes advanced by a competing *social solidarity*. As a consequence, the extent to which the governed resist the global governors' processes is determined by the extent to which they adhere to the same *social solidarity*, and thus share a common view on the appropriate individual autonomy-collective control balance that legitimizes the global governance system used to identify, promote and protect the global interest.

Hierarchist Perspective

Hierarchists would see the global sphere as being clearly demarcated from the national sphere.[25] As they believe that authority is derived from a hierarchi-

---

[25] Hierarchists would no doubt agree with the (neo)realists' argument that national interests are paramount within *international society* (Boucher 1998: 30; see also Part I) and that in political life power is the prime motivation or driving force (Buzan 1996c). For (neo)realists, the analytical focus is the group rather than the individual, with the key group being the state, which is presumed to be a unitary rational actor operating under conditions of uncertainty and imperfect information. *International society* regulates relations between states by means of four institutions: *international law* (often a codification of well-established customary practice); *recognition or legitimacy* (thereby acknowledging internal sovereignty and accepting the principle of noninterference); a constant *diplomatic presence* and continuing dialogue; and *limited war* (as a means of adjusting power imbalances) (Boucher 1998: 308; see also Mayall 1990, Miller 1990, Wright 1977). Bull (1977) characterizes this traditional international system as the *anarchical society* because there is no purposive order, no global government able to direct the conduct of nation-states, by force if necessary. Under these conditions, nation-states, of necessity, give priority to security and independence, a point on which realists and neorealists differ (Zacher with Sutton 1995: 18), joining together to oppose any threat to their sovereignty or survival. Realists would argue that this is the only basis for cooperation; neorealists would permit other important mutual interests to be a basis for cooperation (Zacher with Sutton 1995: 18, 19–21). The primary concern of both realists and neorealists is, however, with interdependence and transnational relations within *international society* in relation to power (Isakovic 2000), security, conflicts and alliances, with a focus on dominance and dependence. They postulate that interests and expediency are the criteria of state action, so emphasizing the competitive and conflictive side of international relations. (Neo)realists maintain that nation-states learn by responding to structural changes in their environment (Nye 1988: 238–39). Czempiel (1992: 257) uses a billiard ball metaphor to describe how (neo)realists treat nation-states in their world-of-states global model. Waltz (1979: 102; see also Nye 1988, Waltz 1990) argues that the anarchical structure of the international system, combined with the distribution of nation-state capabilities, determines the behavior of its constituent nation-state members that leads them inevitably to a balance-of-power policy and defines both the prerequisites and the limits of transnational cooperation. Thus, nation-states with uneven and varying capabilities (see, for example, Kugler and Domke 1986, Organski and Kugler 1978), including uneven military capabilities with changing potentials for destructiveness, pursue their survivalist goals, within an anarchical environment, by exercising the power needed to modify or change the behavior of other nation-states, using force, coercion, manipulation or persuasion, which makes the distribution of capabilities focal (Cornett and Caporasa

cal pattern of 'international order,'[26] hierarchists would prefer the balance-of-power (hierarchical) mode of global governance. This is because it offers the means by which a balance of power can be achieved among nation-states.[27] It is a stable and elitist governance mode, one dominated by the more powerful of the nation-states, the governing elites of which seeks to secure *international society's* agreement on preferred ends and required means, but would be willing to use force or coercion to direct and control noncompliant nation-states.[28] Hierarchists would be attracted to the idea of hierarchical global governance mechanisms that provide a broad mandatory governance framework that embraces all members of *international society* and a wide range of specific issues.[29] Thus, the

---

1992: 238). Hence, nation-states are reluctant to become interdependent and are willing to engage in transnational cooperation only if it gives them relatively greater gains or protects their existing power position. This is because they are concerned more with relative than with absolute gains from such cooperation, and because they are concerned about nation-states cheating on the transnational cooperative arrangements in order to gain a comparative advantage over the compliant. (Neo)realists posit, therefore, that only strong international institutions can monitor compliance and impose sanctions on the violating or cheating nation-states that diminish the acceptance of any such cooperation (Zacher with Sutton 1995: 19–20).

[26] Bull (1977: 3–6) differentiates between *international order* (a particular historically limited system of nation-states) and *world order* (the transhistorical order prevailing without reference to the manner in which humankind is institutionalized). The *international order* is effectively defined, more concretely, by Knight (2000: 195) (who, confusingly, prefers to call it *world order*) as "the political, economic, social, ideological, and cultural structures that define the behavior and power relationships among human groups." Carr (1946: 107) has suggested: "To internationalize government in any real sense means to internationalize power; and internationalized government is, in effect, government by the state which supplies the power necessary for the purposes of governing."

[27] Hierarchists would agree with the (neo)realist argument that there is only one device for governing *international society*: the balance of power among nation-states acting in favor of security and military predominance (Waltz 1979; see also Beitz 1979). As Holsti (1992: 32) remarks, "balances…are the automatic consequences of the interactions of functionally similar units operating in an anarchy." Thus, the balance of power becomes the principle by which nation-states regulate their relations (Buzan 1996a).

[28] Hierarchists would be sympathetic the *international society* (Buzan 1996d). They would incline to the view that war, or at least the threat of war, is a legitimate strategy in the context of a nation-state pursuing its national interest (see Clark 1989).

[29] Hierarchists would certainly stop short of advocating a world government independent of the global ruling elite. Indeed they would accept Righter's (1995) judgment that the United Nations was never synonymous with global governance, and Knight's (2000: 158) conclusion that it was established so as to protect nation-state sovereignty from the encroachment of centralized global governing mechanisms. But they would also, no doubt, agree with McNeill's (1990: 170) expectation that there should be a greater degree of piecemeal coordination and negotiation among the states and transnational private and public organizations. In answering the question Rosenau (1992b: 286) posited more generally as to whether they would be best served through the collective goals of a larger, territorially based transnational community or through the more nar-

lacunae between international regimes and interregimes—overlaps and conflicts—would be addressed.[30] To hierarchists, then, good global governance would be based on hierarchy.

Hierarchists would accept as obvious that the global ruling elite would presume themselves to be the guardians of the common good of *international society*, because of the authority they derive from their nation-state's dominant position in *international society's* hierarchy.[31] Hierarchists would expect them to select those who administer global governance mechanisms from among the global experts nominated by their national (societal) administrative elites. Selection would be on the basis of their specialized technical knowledge, skills, experience and the personal attributes they would bring to the global governance process. Hierarchists, would, of course, also expect the global administrative elite to remain loyal and obedient to the global ruling elite. The design of global governance strategies and their implementation would, wherever possible, be assigned to the national administrative elites, who would have the best interests of their national governing elites uppermost in mind. Hierarchists would, however, presume that the sovereign nation-states would know and accept their relative position in *international society's* hierarchy, and would thus voluntarily delegate to global governance mechanisms the power needed to address agreed transnational governance issues that have been deemed by the global ruling elite to be in the 'common interest' of *international society*.

The hierarchists would prefer global governance mechanisms that have decision-making processes that give greater weight to the more powerful member nation-states[32] and that involve the global administrative elite using functional-analytic policy analysis to derive objective facts that would facilitate satisficing decision making intent on producing incremental policy changes.

The appeal to hierarchists of distributive, redistributive, constituency and regulatory policies to promote and protect the global interest would depend on the extent to which they threaten the national interest of constituent national governing elites. Distributive policies would have a strong appeal, as they would enable global governing mechanisms to reinforce the institutionalized inequalities that exist among member nation-states when making allocative decisions. Regulatory policies would also have a strong appeal, as they would enable the global governing mechanisms to design and oversee, if not implement, regulatory regimes that proscribe or prescribe the behaviors of individuals or groups up to the nation-state level. Constituent policies would have rather less

---

rowly defined considerations of globalizing subgroups, hierarchists would place greater emphasis on the global collective goals as determined by the global ruling elite.

[30] Hierarchists would, certainly, want to bring purposive order to the global political system, which has been characterized by Jacobson (1984: 516) as "states entangled in webs of international organizations."

[31] This justifies the use of legitimate, positional, coercive, manipulative and persuasive power (Allison 1996b).

[32] Perhaps the scale would be defined in terms of budget contribution (for a discussion, see Wallensteen 1994).

appeal, as they only give the global governing mechanisms influence over individual or group behavior up to the national level. In contrast, redistributive policies would appeal only if they enhance the stability and security of *international society*, and did not radically threaten the institutionalized inequalities that exist among member nation-states.

The regulatory mode preferred by hierarchists would be hierarchical, whereby regulations are designed, authorized and implemented by global governing mechanisms, but administered, wherever possible, by national administrative elites. They would be predisposed to regulatory instruments that enhance the national interest of constituent national governing elites, particularly the global ruling elite. Command-and-control instruments would have a strong appeal, because they permit global governing mechanisms to establish and oversee, if not implement, processes that would permit the punishment of undesirable, deviant individual or group behaviors at the interest group, corporate and nation-state levels, with international regulatory compliance dependent on the ease of violation detection, the probability of sanctions being imposed on violators, and the magnitude of the imposed sanctions (Young 1992: 176; see also Fisher 1981, O. R. Young 1979). Such instruments would include collective security policies designed to maintain world peace and security by soliciting the collective support of all nation-states to oppose and punish acts of aggression, whether military aggression, state-sanctioned terrorism, or acts of terrorism by interest groups or sectarian organizations (Berridge 1992, Crocker and Hampson 1996, Holsti 1991, Kaldor 1999). Information and economic instruments, in contrast, would have only limited appeal because, despite the fact that, in the hands of global governing mechanisms, they can be used to influence behavior, their regulatory effectiveness depends, in the absence of sanctions, on people (whether individually or in interest groups, corporations or nation-states) voluntarily changing their behavior in the ways needed to achieve the desired regulatory outcomes.

When confronted with any global regulatory instruments, hierarchists would, axiomatically, comply because of their cognitive commitment derived from their rational calculations made in the context of the structural processes, such as legitimately prescribed rules and procedures. This may well be reinforced by a deontological moral code that builds commitment to the global ruling elite, the power of whom they consider to be legitimate because of their nation-state's superior position in *international society*. They would also expect others to comply on the same basis.

The salient global governance risk for hierarchists is the global ruling elite's loss of control or trust because it is repeatedly unable to understand the nature and causation of global governance problems, which follows from their adherence to naturalist epistemology, or why global ruling elite's solutions are unable to secure compliance from free individuals, which follows from their adherence to structuralist ontology. This risk stems from the explanatory weaknesses of the naturalist-structuralist methodology. In the absence of such trust and control, hierarchists would not be able to apportion blame for any global governance failure (Dixon and Dogan 2000c) to the deviants who failed to comply with a global governance mechanism's rules and regulations.

Hierarchists, if faced with the prospect that the global ruling elite is unable to correct hierarchical governance failure, would, in the first instance, express loyalty (Hirschman 1970), in the hope that solutions will eventually emerge, and then blame noncompliant deviants. Their acts of loyalty would probably include suppressing any information that is critical of the global ruling and administrative elites' governance performance, and punishing those who threaten to make disclosures critical of their interpretation of the causes of, and solutions to, the hierarchical governance failure. Their envisaged solution would be to strengthen hierarchical controls. This is because their structuralist ontology induces them to presume that people are motivated by cognitive commitment to the collective, and because their naturalist epistemology convinces them that they can identify social reality through the observation of patterns in, and correlations between, forms of social behavior, which reflect and represent structural constraints on their behavior. This solution could include setting aside or modifying rules and regulations; using publicity and persuasion to encourage compliance; strengthening disincentives; making noncompliance physically more inconvenient, difficult or impossible; and pursuing and punishing rule violators and deviant behavior with heavier sanctions, including military action or the threat of it.

Enclavist Perspective

Enclavists would see the global sphere as having blurred boundaries with the national sphere, which should be expanded if they conceal any unequal power relations at the nation-state level.[33] They would inevitably see the global sphere

---

[33] Enclavists would find appealing the functionalist explanation for the creation and growth of transnational cooperation in terms of two nineteenth-century historical inclinations: the widening and deepening of political participation within the state; and technological advancement (see, for example, Mitrany 1933, 1966; see also Haas 1964, Rosenau 1990). These inclinations, functionalists argue, have created both political pressure and technological opportunities for increasing international cooperation. According to Cornett and Caporaso (1992: 237–38):

Functionalism's system-transforming theory is based on two simple propositions: first, societies are composed of sectors that can be separated from one another for initial cooperative purposes; and second, intersectional linkages ensure that initial cooperative successes can be transmitted to related sectors. These two propositions imply an action strategy: (1) identify areas of society where people can cooperate; (2) arrange cooperative behavior functionally—not along territorial lines; and (3) take advantage of intersectoral imbalances to extend cooperative arrangements into related areas once initial cooperation has taken root. The final stages of integration involve cooperation on many different fronts along with appropriate political institutions....The key to the process-level component of functionalist theory lies in the concept of spillover. This refers to the purported self-expansive tendency of integration within pluralistic socioeconomic environments.

Thus, nation-states, however reluctantly, will become interdependent and willing to engage in transnational cooperation only after learning has taken place and interests have been transformed. This occurs only when many and varied groups realize the benefits of

as always being at risk of being amoral, if not immoral, and corrupt,[34] so it would have to be treated with constant vigilance.[35] This would require people to be participative,[36] and to give their consent to decisions made on their behalf. Enclavists would thus be attracted by the idea of people being active, responsive and obligated members of *global society*.

Enclavists would give support to the 'bottom-up' or *subsidiarity* approach to global governance (Knight 2000: 161, 170; see also Emiliou 1992, Falk 1994, Knight 1996), as the world moves beyond modernity, with its preoccupation with human-centered worlds of meaning; accent on individuality, reason and mastery over circumstances; and fixation with method and material prosperity (Onuf 1991: 425–26; see also Giddens 1990, 1991; Held 1991). This constructionist approach would involve sharing the tasks of governance among central, regional and local authorities in a way that would reconstruct the prevailing social order by providing retooled global institutional arrangements so as to enable them to address the global disorder effectively and efficiently, with a minimum amount of alienation (Knight 2000: 171–72; see also Reinicke 1998: 221, 1997; Ruggie 1993).

---

cooperation and when the policy debates on sovereignty lose force (Cornett and Caporaso 1992: 237).

[34] Enclavists would demand, as does Cable (1999: 102–7), that global governance mechanisms have a high degree of *transparency* (both in terms of actor behavior and the availability of information on governance requirements and processes), *accountability* (mandatory reporting and disclosure to those they seek to govern), *subsidiarity* (decisions made at the lowest possible level of a global governance hierarchy subject to being able to achieve the required governance objectives), *legitimacy* (a broad acceptability to its global stakeholders), and *epistemology* (knowledge relevant to global governance needs to become both more extensive and more intensely reflected upon) (see also Kratochwil and Ruggie 1986).

[35] Rosenau (1992b: 273–74) pointedly observes that in an era of rapid and profound global transformations:

too many of the squares of the world's cities have latterly been filled with large crowds who make a variety of demands, who return again and again even in the face of brutal government efforts to repress them, who thus escalate conflicts and solidify stalemates with a frequency indicating contagion effects that are transforming problems of domestic order into processes of global order—to note only the more obvious dynamics—to ignore the possibility that the micro level ["individuals and face-to-face groups"] is a source as well as a consequence of global change.

[36] The enclavists' presumption is that people want to be involved in the management of global issue-areas where governments are unable or unwilling to act, made possible by the development of new communication technologies that convey information broadly and enable people to interact across national borders, thereby encouraging "a global associational revolution" (Commission on Global Governance 1995: 523). Rosenau (1992b: 275–76) identifies five reasons why people have been empowered in the emergent global order: the erosion and dispersal of the power of state and societal institutions; global television; the emergence of transnational interdependencies that affect individual welfare and finances (such as AIDS, currency crises, terrorism); information technology; and the growing realization that individual actions can impact on world affairs.

Enclavists would prefer the global society (interactive) mode of global governance, because it offers the means to balance the diverse categorical interests of an inclusive set of global actors by enabling their broad participation in the design and conduct of global governance mechanisms. This governance mode would involve a significant degree of transnational cooperation,[37] which would go beyond traditional intergovernmentalism by having elements of supranationality. Because they would have a preference for an inclusive set of global actors to work together, voluntarily, to identify, promote and protect their categorical interests in the 'global interest,' their preferred global governance mechanisms would be voluntary transnational cogovernance networks, which they would see as having a greater capacity to cope with decision making in differentiated transnational settings. These would be expected to focus on the specific issue-areas in which enclavists foresee catastrophic, irreversible and inequitable global developments, which would, if left unchallenged, threaten their perceptions of equality, the dignity and rights of the individual, the sense of fellowship and community, and negative freedom.

Enclavists would expect the voluntary transnational cogovernance networks to enable broad participation in deliberative power.[38] They would preferably

---

[37] Enclavists would agonize before answering the question posited by Rosenau (1992b: 286) more generally about whether they would be best served through collective goals of a larger, territorially based transnational community or through the more narrowly defined considerations of globalizing subgroups, but they would opt for a coordinated set of globalizing subgroups. As a matter of principle, they may well agree with Rosenau's (1992a: 12) conception of the global order being all-encompassing, and thereby embracing every region, country, international relationship, interest group and corporation that engages in activities across national boundaries. But their distrust of all types of authority, and their unyielding commitment to promoting their categorical interests, would make them sympathetic to the functionalist proposition that international governmental organizations "should be designed to achieve transnational cooperation of specific technical issues, mediated by interest groups" (Jacobson et al. [1986] 1997: 58; see also Gallarotti [1991] 1997: 378, 403, n. 10). Enclavists would also agree with Reinicke's (1998: 220) proposition that international organizations should foster and facilitate the emergence of global policy networks, but they would disagree that the purpose of such actions should be limited merely to generating better knowledge that anticipates issues that demand global public responses, and to acting as intermediaries between the public and private sectors, so as to ensure that adequate information is available to meet global challenges. The conspiracy-theory inclination of enclavists would interpret such actions as manipulation, designed to ensure that their network's interactional processes generate a set of shared values and categorical interests that are more in line with those of the global ruling elite. Enclavists would demand nothing less than shared power in the form of a coordinated system of global cogovernance networks. They would expect national governing elites to compromise, voluntarily, their external and internal sovereignty by ceding authority to global governance mechanisms in issue-areas where action at the national level cannot adequately address mutually agreed transnational problems or issues.

[38] Enclavists would be attracted to the idea of a forum of *civil society* consisting of civil society organizations, or an assembly of the people, as a deliberative body to com-

involve decision-making processes that operate on the basis of one actor, one vote, and would presume that policy is the outcome achieved by balancing the competing interests of diverse interest groups,[39] using communicative-value policy analysis,[40] so as to produce consistent, congruent and cogent decisions.[41]

As enclavists believe that authority rests on the acceptance of normative patterns of order,[42] they would only endorse those global patterns of order that reflect their own idiosyncratic set of values and beliefs. As they would focus, almost uncompromisingly, on the specific, threatening and zero-sum global issue-areas, they would expect to be in dissent with those who do not share their

---

plement the United Nation's General Assembly, which is representative of governments (Commission on Global Governance 1995: 257–60). An example of such popular participation in a transnational polity is the European Parliament, which has, since 1979, been directly elected by residents in constituent European Union countries (Bromley 2001, Dinan 1999, McCormick 1999, Nugent 1999, Urwin 1995). Indeed, Underhill (1996: 168) concludes: "The EP [European Parliament] is…slowly evolving as a legislature in the traditional meaning of the word, paralleling the evolution of the EC [the European Community, now the European Union] towards something 'state-like' in the international system as the role of member states diminishes through successive reforms."

[39] Dahl's (1971) concept of *polyarchy*, which captures the idea that representative democracy should involve a substantial degree of interest group influence, has been used by Brown (1988: 245) to describe the state of world politics: "The forces now ascendant appear to be leaning toward a global society without a dominant structure of cooperation and conflict—a polyarchy in which nation-states, subnational groups, and transnational special interests and communities are all vying for the support and loyalty of individuals and conflicts need to be resolved primarily on the basis of ad hoc bargaining among combinations of these groups that vary from issue to issue." For a discussion of the importance of domestic coalitions and interest formation in international regimes, see Putman 1988.

[40] Reinicke (1998: 220) argues that by engaging with nonstate policy actors, a more efficient and effective global policy process that generates greater acceptability and legitimacy of global public policies will be achieved, because these actors have better information, knowledge and understanding of the increasingly complex, technology-driven and fast-changing public policy issues.

[41] Haas (1964: 64) denoted the style of decision making under conditions of supranationality as one that encourages a cumulative pattern of accommodation, because participants refrain from unconditionally vetoing proposals, preferring to attain agreement by compromises, and thereby enhance shared interests. Subsequently, he argued (Haas 1980: 393) that participants learn when the bargaining positions are tied to consensual goals, and when concessions are seen as instrumental, thereby realizing joint gains. Implicit in this bargaining process of accommodation is the notion of trust (see Barber 1983).

[42] This legitimizes only the use of persuasive power (Allison 1996b) by means of personal, referent, normative or integrative power (Boulder 1990, French and Raven 1959, Hales 2001). They would have some sympathy with the proposition advanced by universal moral order tradition (Boucher 1998 Part II) that right actions are determined by moral absolutes, although most would probably prefer, in the tradition of historical reason (Boucher 1998: Part III), Rorty's (1989: 59) proposition that morality is "the voice of ourselves as members of a community, speakers of a common language."

beliefs and values.[43] But this would not, however, prohibit them from engaging with voluntary transnational cogovernance networks, so as to ensure that their values and beliefs, if not made the basis of action, are at least heard.

The appeal to enclavists of distributive, redistributive, constituency and regulatory policies to promote and protect the global interest depends on whether they promote their categorical interests. Redistributive policies would have a strong appeal, because they would contribute to the removal of distinctions between people. In contrast, distribution policies only reinforce institutionalized inequalities. Constituency policies would appeal only if they impose desirable and necessary controls over individuals or groups. Regulatory policies would appeal only if they stimulate and facilitate voluntary behavior change.

The regulatory mode preferred by enclavists would be network coregulation, whereby regulations are designed, authorized and implemented by inclusive voluntary transnational cogovernance networks, with no powers of compulsion, a low noncompliance tolerance, and a capacity both to reward and to punish. They would be predisposed to regulatory instruments that acceptably promote their categorical interests. Information instruments would have a strong appeal because they stimulate and facilitate voluntary behavior change that suggests a commitment to the desired global governance outcomes. Economic instruments would have only limited appeal because the financial incentives and disincentives involved may create differentiations and may cause any voluntary behavior changes to be attributable to self-interest rather than a commitment to mutually agreed governance outcomes. Command-and-control instruments, including military action or the threat of it, would have no appeal because, axiomatically, rules can be enforced by sanctions when voluntary transnational cogovernance networks create global governance mechanisms, and, in any event, compliance built upon moral commitment is preferable.

When confronted with any regulatory instruments, enclavists would comply only if by so doing they did not compromise their moral commitment to their categorical interests and to those with whom they share common values and beliefs. They would expect others to comply on the same basis.

The salient global governance risk faced by enclavists, which stems from the inherent relativism of the hermeneutic-structuralist methodology, is that the global actors cannot agree among themselves on a set of common interests that needs to be jointly protected and promoted in the 'global interest'. In the absence of interactive global governance mechanisms that are harmonious, trustworthy and codetermining, enclavists would not be able to externalize blame for any global governance failure onto particular risk takers or particular secret enemies within the global governance processes.

---

[43] George and Campbell (1990) use critical social theory to explore the differences evident from the patterns of dissent in international relations, which they see as a cause for celebration. Kratochwil and Ruggie (1986) argue that the different interpretations given to global governance problems and their solution, require an interpretive (hermeneutic) epistemological perspective to be used in the study of international regimes (see also Smith et al. 1996).

Enclavists, if faced with the prospect that people cannot construct mutual understandings and acceptable joint perspectives that evoke moral commitment to the identification and correction of global governance failure, would, in the first instance, voice (Hirschman 1970) blame, accusing the risk takers and the secret enemies within the global governance mechanisms who do not share their commitment to interactive governance success for agreeing to accept too many risks that were too high. They would, no doubt, threaten to leave the global governance process if confronted with a values conflict over how best to correct the governance failure. Their envisaged solution would be to demand the removal of the risk takers and the secret enemies within the governance mechanisms, and then the empowerment of more and different people to engage fully in interactive global governance processes. This solution is prescribed by their structuralist ontology, which predisposes them to believe that people are motivated by moral commitments to collectively agreed processes and outcomes; and by their hermeneutic epistemology, which supports the presumption that people are willing and able to engage in reasoning that is intersubjective and values-based, which involves critically reflective communications that enable them to make and question arguments, and thereby determine the validity of normative judgments. Implementing this envisaged solution would entail developing strategies that would not only correct the governance failure, but also evoke a moral commitment to interactive governance success.

Individualist Perspective

Individualists would see the global sphere as a set of opportunities for exploitation by the private sphere. They would question whether there is any basis upon which any configuration of people can claim legitimate authority to impose, unilaterally, purposive global order,[44] as they can take no intentional or instru-

---

[44] This is not to suggest, however, that economic cooperation, among nation-states cannot, and does not, occur voluntarily. Neoliberals argue that interaction among nation-states that facilitates learning by national policymakers and bureaucrats (Axelrod 1984, Oye 1986) will, under certain circumstances, lead to cooperation among states (Reinicke 1998: 59–61). They posit that nation-states seek to maximize their absolute gains in the international system, which means that gains by other states are not an impediment to cooperation. Transnational cooperation agreements are thus premised on, and rationalized by, a comparable reduction in the external sovereignty of all participating nation-states, so ensuring that the principle of "cooperative competition" (Reinicke 1998: 60)—or "competitive cooperation" (p. 73)—is embedded in international governance mechanisms. This occurs because the corporate interests of dominant domestic business coalitions in each nation-state are embedded in international negotiations and the multilateral agreements by compliant governments (Grieco 1988; Keohane 1982, 1986, 1989; Reinicke 1998; Taylor 1987, 1990; Tollison and Willett 1979). Thus nation-states are willing to trade off their sovereign autonomy for the absolute economic benefits of cooperation, because of "the network of formal and informal institutions in world politics that facilitates the negotiation of mutually beneficial accords, promotes greater transparency in states' compliance with agreements, and helps states coordinate sanctions in some cases" (Zacher with Sutton 1995: 22, also 21). This means, of course, that the major im-

mental actions that will enhance individuals' wellbeing, because they cannot know people's preferences. To individualists, good global governance would be based on permitting law-abiding buyers and sellers in the marketplace to be self-regulating,[45] for all imposed global governance mechanisms are inherently rent seeking and are presumed to be ineffective.[46]

Individualists would prefer the international economic process (market) mode of global governance, because it offers the means by which the global marketplace can be self-regulating within a minimalist regulatory environment.[47] This would involve a set of imposed global governance mechanisms[48] that are concerned only with facilitating the successful conduct of global market transactions.[49] They would provide an international exchange framework[50] that,

---

pediment to transnational cooperation is the free-rider problem, which occurs when nation-states are willing to renege on agreements to reduce and limit their external sovereignty in order to gain a strategic advantage.

[45] This legitimizes only the use of persuasive power (Allison 1996b) by means of reward, resource, economic and exchange power (Boulder 1990, French and Raven 1959, Hales 2001).

[46] Individualists would readily accept Young's (1992) critical variables for international institution effectiveness: *transparency* (the ease of compliance monitoring and verification); *robustness* (the ability of the chosen social-choice mechanism that generates consensus to withstand and to adjust to disturbances to that consensus); *transformation rules* (the ease with which governance changes can be made); *capacity of governments* (the capacity of governments to implement the chosen governance strategies); *distribution of power* (the asymmetries of the distribution of power within the international institution); *interdependencies* (the level of interdependencies among participants in the international institutions); and *intellectual order* (the viability of the intellectual premises underpinning the actions of international institutions and their justification). For a public-choice perspective on the ineffectiveness of international governmental organizations, see, for example, Conybeare 1980, Ruggie 1972, Vaubel 1986, Wijkman 1982; but compare Gallarotti [1991] 1997; Payer 1974, 1982; Pitt and Weiss 1986; and on the ineffectiveness of international regimes, see Birnie 1989, Hass 1989, Young 1992.

[47] This follows from two propositions. The first is that private goods require less supranational regulation than public goods (Ruggie 1972; see also Conybeare 1980, Wijkman 1982). The second is the classic Olsonian rational choice treatment of collection action, which suggests that global governance mechanisms with limited membership are better able to eradicate public bads and generate public goods (Conybeare 1984, Snidal 1985, Stein 1982, Wagner 1983). For a discussion of global public goods, see Kaul et al. 1999.

[48] In answering the question posited by Rosenau (1992b: 286) more generally about whether they would be best served through collective goals of a larger, territorially based transnational community or through the more narrowly defined considerations of globalizing subgroups, individualists would undoubtedly opt for a coordinated set of globalizing subgroups, placing greater emphasis on those that best promote their own particular self-interest.

[49] International trade is the market transaction most closely associated with economic interdependence, and trade liberalization is the desired outcome, facilitated, some would argue, by the increased role of multinational business corporations in the world economy (see, for example, Cox 1987, Milner 1988). At the state macroeconomic level,

particularly, defines and enforces private property rights; that ensures the safety and security of people, financial, physical and natural resources, and commodities; and that creates global market opportunities for commercial exploitation.[51]

---

however, Biersteker (1992: 108–9) has identified the following array of items on the neoliberal global economic reform agenda: the reduction and transformation of state economic intervention (such as price controls, government subsidies, state marketing boards); increased reliance on market mechanisms (including privatization); more frequent use of monetarist instruments; greater public support for, and reliance on, the private sector; labor market reforms (such as abolishing wage indexation); greater export promotion at the expense of import substitution; exchange rate adjustments; trade liberalization; and financial reforms. He (Biersteker 1992: 105) talks of the "'triumph' of neoclassical economics," in much the same way as Ruggie (1982: 413) talks of "the resurgent ethos of liberal capitalism." This has prompted Gill (1997: 207) to observe that the "Anglo-American Lockeian self-regulating principle" (see also Pijl 1989), have increasingly becomes the global model for emulation (see also Gill 1992, 1994a; Frank 1991; Gill and Law 1988, 1989). Or, as Biersteker (1992: 105, n. 5) notes: "international political economy...has tended to reflect the general idea that a limited degree of convergence in economic policy is a prerequisite for effective participation in the world economy." Gilpin (1987: 67) states the position in stronger terms: "Inefficient actors are forced to adjust their behavior and to innovate or else face economic extinction." This has produced a transnational consensus formation regarding the needs or requirements of the world economy, which has converted the state, according to Cox (1992: 31), into the vehicle for adjusting national economic policies and practices to meet the perceived imperatives of the global economy. This means that state power has become concentrated in those agencies most closely associated with the global economy. In this competitive context, Porter (1990) has identified how the competitive advantages of nation-states can be demarcated; Charney (1991) has analyzed the competition between nations—'the race to the bottom'—to attract and keep corporate registrations by the formulating of ever more favorable corporate law rules; and Salacuse (1991) has analyzed the basis on which global deals are negotiated.

[50] Building a consensus on such a governance framework is facilitated by the transnational convergence of foreign and domestic economic policies. Keohane (1884) postulates that international cooperation is less problematic between countries that share common interests and where "the benefits of international cooperation may be easiest to realize" (pp. 6–7).

[51] This focuses attention on two issues. The first is the underpinning neoliberal assumptions that there will be continuous competition within global governance mechanisms over access to scarce resources; that decision-making processes in those mechanisms "modify the dictates of rationality;" and that their appeal depends upon their ability to lower transaction costs or to offer incentives to encourage transnational cooperation (Knight 2000: 13). The second issue is the international market failures caused by the uncertainty surrounding costs and commercial opportunities. These failures are associated with (1) the transaction costs involved (including the costs incurred, for example, because of different governmental structures, domestic laws, economic organizations, state-society relations, national goals and communication habits); (2) the impediment to the flow of factors of production; (3) supply and price collusion; (4) natural monopolies; (5) negative externalities; (6) scarce common property resources (located in international space); and (7) the existence of public goods (the free-rider issue resulting from nonex-

Such global governance mechanisms as are necessary should focus on the efficient conduct of global market exchanges and should have undisputed sovereignty over the global marketplace, while others, with nonmarket objectives, should be designed to be weak, unobtrusive and small, empowered more to create opportunities for entrepreneurial exploitation than to impose inhibiting constraints on positive freedom.

All imposed global governance mechanisms would preferably have decision-making processes that give more weight to the global administrative elite who understand that global market transactions must take place within an environment free of political obstacles, and who use instrumentally and synoptically rational policy analysis, premised on the self-interest motivation of all global actors. This would facilitate optimal decision making by global governance mechanisms, however their members are appointed, which minimize the adverse consequences for the global economy of their inevitably misguided governance intentions.

The appeal to individualists of imposed distributive, redistributive, constituency and regulatory policies to promote and protect the so-called global interest depends on the extent to which they promote their self-interests. Distributive policies appeal only if they do not create more competition in the marketplace or create exploitable business opportunities. Constituency policies appeal only if they do not constrain negative freedom or limit global business opportunities. Regulatory policies appeal only if they help maintain international confidence in the global marketplace. In contrast, redistributive policies have no appeal, as they tend to stifle the wealth-accumulation ambitions of those in countries that win, while reducing the wealth-accumulation capacities of those in countries that lose.

The regulatory mode preferred by individualists is market self-regulation, conducted within a globalized exchange framework, and achieved by means of contracts embodying a zero tolerance of noncompliance and full restitution as the ultimate sanction. Individualists would thus not be predisposed toward any imposed regulatory instruments. Economic instruments, however, would have the most appeal because of the incentives and disincentives embodied, provided those who design them understand the global marketplace. Command-and-control instruments would have appeal only if they are designed by those who understand what the market consequences are likely to be in order to maintain public confidence in the global marketplace. The information instruments would appeal only if they close down opportunities for competitors or create new opportunities for market exploitation.

When confronted with any regulatory instruments, individualists would respond with instrumental compliance, based on calculations of compliance costs and benefits. This means that they would find ways of minimizing, if not avoiding, any changes that did not promote their own self interests. They would expect others to comply on the same basis.

---

cludability and jointness of supply) (Zacher with Sutton 1995: 27–28; see also Cornett and Capoaso 1992: 226).

The salient global governance risk faced by individualists are two principal-agent problems. The first is not being able to specify completely and comprehensively the implicit and explicit contracts they have with their agents because of uncertainty and opportunism. The second is not being able to enforce the executed contracts with a zero noncompliance tolerance and full restitution as the ultimate sanction. This risk stems from the incapacity of the naturalist-agency methodology to identify causal relationships, a consequence of the naturalist epistemology, and structural imperatives, a consequence of the agency ontology. In the face of these problems, they would be unable either to attribute the cause of market self-governance failure to non-market factors, or to determine a market solution to global governance failure.

Individualists, if faced with the prospect of a market self-regulation malfunction because law-abiding buyers and sellers are unable to specify completely enforceable contracts, would, in the first instance, blame either bad luck, rogue buyers and sellers, or the global ruling or administrative elites. The latter would be blamed for failing to establish the international legal, judicial or regulatory environments needed for the global market to operate efficiently. Their envisaged solution would be to strengthen global market self-regulation by more stringent drafting, execution and enforcement of contracts that have full restitution as the sanction. This solution is the product of their agency ontology, which justifies their presumption that people are motivated by personal incentives rather than collective commitments, and of their naturalist ontology, which underpins the presumption that they can make reliable predictions about the consequences of human behavior by observing patterns in, and correlations between, forms of social behavior. The expected outcome would be to initiate the economic calculations needed to induce the instrumental compliance necessary to correct governance failure. Then, if their prospects for material success are threatened, they would exit (Hirschman 1970) by withdrawing from the global marketplace in order to renegotiate their relationships.

Fatalist Perspective

Fatalists would not discriminate between the global and the national sphere, both of which they would see as being capricious and fearful realms. The global interest to be the will of the unknowing, untrustworthy and indifferent global powers that be, and thus irrelevant, for they do not expect them to address life's inevitable vicissitudes.

The least alienating form of global governance to fatalists would be one that does not require people's constructive engagement.[52] Thus, fatalists would be

---

[52] In answering the question posited by Rosenau (1992b: 286) more generally about whether they are best served through collective goals of a larger, territorially based transnational community or through the more narrowly defined considerations of globalizing subgroups, fatalists would say that neither serves their needs. They would not expect their survival interests to be of any concern to the global elites. They would not be surprised by Zacher's (1992: 78) reflection that environmental interdependencies are going to generate conflict between those who are significantly harmed (mostly in the Third World)

attracted to the idea of global governance processes that maximize the distance between the hapless governed and the self-seeking global powers that be, who are always attempting to initiate exploitative collective action against them. They would also wish to constrain the potential of the powers that be to take collective action that may, at times, be benign in intent but is inevitably malevolent in action, so as to make them less intrusive and less coercive.[53] Fatalists would also require the powers that be to adopt decision-making processes that are not dominated by untrustworthy vested interests, who assert the truthfulness of facts and the sanctity of abstract values, but who deny the limits of human cognition.

The appeal to fatalists of distributive, redistributive, constituency and regulatory policies that could be used to promote the global interest, depends on the extent to which they advance their survival interests, although they would have no confidence that the so-called global experts would get it right. Distributive policies would have a strong appeal to them because they, at least, have a chance of being included as beneficiaries. Constituency policies would appeal, but only if they do not permit or facilitate their abuse and exploitation. Regulatory policies would appeal, if they offer some protection against abuse and exploitation. Redistributive policies would have no appeal, as they would expect that the untrustworthy and unknowing global powers would inevitably cast them among the losers.

Fatalists would not be predisposed to any regulatory mode or to any form of regulatory instrument. Hierarchical command-and-control instruments would, however, have some appeal if they offer some protection against their abuse and exploitation. Economic instruments, however administered, would have some appeal if they create an opportunity for them to be rewarded for doing what is in their own survival interest. Information however administered, would have no appeal because the experts cannot be trusted to get anything right, and, even if by chance they did, the information would probably be ignored by those who are abusing and exploiting them.

When confronted with any regulatory instruments, fatalists would respond with alienative compliance, born of fear of force, threat and menace in the belief that the power being exercised has no legitimacy. This means that they would find ways of minimizing, if not avoiding, any changes that were contrary to

---

and those who are not harmed or are actually helped (mostly in the developed world) (see also Caldwell 1990, M'Gonigle and Zacher 1979). Nor would they be surprised by the proposition that economic reforms have been forced on debt-dependent political regimes, particularly in Latin America, against the wishes of the vast majority of their skeptical people, who have yet to see any material accomplishments that would suggest that the tangible economic success promised will eventuate (see, for example, Biersteker 1992, Paster 1987).

[53] As fatalists would not voluntarily comply with the wishes of the global powers that be, they would expect them to exercise physical, coercive and threat power, thereby achieving only alienative compliance (Boulder 1990, French and Raven 1959).

their own survival interests. They would expect others to comply on the same basis.

The salient global governance risk faced by fatalists is that their self-chosen isolation has been in vain. This stems from their presumption that the global interest cannot be intentionally and instrumentally promoted and protected, as no one is able to establish that the social world is knowable. This is premised on the inherent relativism of the hermeneutic-agency methodology and its inability to identify causal relationships and structural imperatives.

Fatalists, if faced with the prospect that the global interest can be intentionally and instrumentally promoted and protected, would, in the first instance, deny that such a proposition can be proven, and then blame fate for letting their self-chosen isolation be in vain. Their envisaged solution would be to leave well enough alone, because their hermeneutic epistemology predisposes them to presume that people can only contestably know the subjective social world as what they believe it to be, and because their agency ontology leads them to presume that people's actions are constrained by their subjective perceptions of social reality. This solution would involve resisting vigorously any fate-tempting global governance innovation, which would only make matters worse. Then, if their survival interests are threatened, they would exit (Hirschman 1970) by disengaging from global governance processes.

GLOBAL GOVERNANCE ANTAGONISMS

Because adherents to one *social solidarity* would resist the flawed approaches to global governance advanced by any competing *social solidarities*, trench warfare is inevitable.

Hierarchists, if trapped in, or subject to, a failing global governance mode posited by another *social solidarity*, would, in the 'global interest', and seeing themselves as the rational saviors of global good as articulated by the global ruling elite, seek to impose formal, hierarchical, elitist and stable global governance mechanisms that reflect the balance of power among the nation-states. These would be empowered to protect and promote *international society's* common good by means of a set of agreed distribution, constituency and regulatory policies, the latter involving command-and-control regulations (embracing collective security policies designed to maintain world order, peace and security) administered with a zero noncompliance tolerance and substantial sanctions.

Enclavists in such a situation would, in the 'global interest', and seeing themselves as passionate saviors of their categorical interests, demand that voluntary transnational networks with broad participation be empowered to design and operationalize global governance mechanisms. These would be intended to balance the diverse interests of an inclusive set of global actors and would administer redistribution and regulatory policies, the latter involving regimes that permit discretion, a low noncompliance tolerance, and a capacity both to reward and to punish.

Individualists in a similar situation would, in the 'global interest', and seeing themselves as commonsense saviors of their own self-interest, take the necessary steps to ensure that the global marketplace becomes self-regulating. Thus, they would seek to reduce the power of global governance mechanisms, restricting their role to ensuring the safety and security of people, financial, physical and natural resources and commodities; and to providing the legal framework that defines and enforces property rights.

Fatalists in such a situation would, seeing themselves as victims of the global powers that be, feel vindicated, because they correctly anticipated the so-called global experts getting it wrong, and so would become prophets of doom.

CONCLUSION

The self-imposed constraints that the global governors place on their ability to manipulate or constrain the behavior of those they seek to affect, because of their adherence to a particular set of the global governance truths (Dixon and Dogan 2002c), limit their governance capacity. The extent of these constraints on global governance capacity depends on the extent to which their actions violate or reinforce the global governance truths of those whose behavior they are seeking to affect. Adherents to each of the four *social solidarities* have a distinctive, but flawed, perspective on what constitutes good global governance.

Hierarchists, who would argue that the global interest is knowable only as a set of prioritized and integrated national interests deemed by the global ruling elite to be for the common good of *international society*, would have faith only in the hierarchical mode of global governance. This would involve hierarchical governance mechanisms that are elitist and stable, reflecting the balance of power among nation-states, and thereby soliciting behavioral compliance because of a cognitive commitment to the global governing elite. Good global governance is based on strong distributive and constituent policies, and hierarchically administered command-and-control regulatory instruments, all for the purpose of enhancing the global ruling elite's dominance over *international society*, particularly over rogue nation-states and over violating global interest groups, social movements and multinational business corporations.

Enclavists, who see the global interest as an inclusive set of negotiated categorical interests, would prefer people to be active, responsive and obliged members of *global society*, would thus have faith in subsidiarity-oriented global governance mechanisms created by voluntary transnational cogovernance networks. This reflects their desire to share power among an inclusive set of global actors, and thereby achieve genuine behavioral compliance by building a moral commitment to a common cause. Good global governance is thus based on strong redistributive policies and cogovernance networks administering information regulatory instruments, all for the purpose of empowering people and enhancing their categorical good.

Individualists, who would argue that the global interest is only knowable as people's revealed market preferences, would not prefer any imposed global governance mechanisms to be minimalist. They would be concerned only with facilitating the successful conduct of global market transactions, and thereby solicit instrumental compliance. Good global governance is thus a self-regulating marketplace. The best of the misguided global governance policies and regulatory instruments are those that most enhance their self-interest, namely distributive policies, which create exploitable business opportunities, and regulatory policies, which help maintain people's confidence in the global marketplace. This is should be done by means of economic instruments, which both reward desirable and punish undesirable behaviors. Such instruments, however, must be designed by those who understand how the global marketplace works, what the market response is likely to be, and thus, what the market consequences are likely to be.

Fatalists, who would deny the knowability of the global interest, would resignedly accept whatever the global powers that be decide to do. The world is thus governable, but only if the powers that be are willing and able to exercise the required coercive power necessary to govern as they see fit. Global governance mechanisms may well be sometimes benign in their intent, but, inevitably, they are malevolent in their actions. The idea that global governance should be less coercive and less intrusive would thus be attractive, but they expect to be alienated from the global powers that be, so their engagement with them can only be on the basis of alienative compliance. Good societal governance is based on distributive policies that advance their survival interests and economic regulatory instruments that inhibit their coercion and exploitation, but they expect the global experts to get it all wrong.

Adherents to each *social solidarity* thus accept that the world is governable, but only if their preferred mode of global governance is adopted. Adherents to one *social solidarity* consider their balance between individual, corporate and national autonomy and global control to be the only legitimate one. Thus, they consider their approach to the identification, promotion and protection of the global interest to be the only acceptable one. They would, inevitably, resist the global interest identification, promotion and protection propositions advanced by adherents to competing *social solidarities*. As a consequence, the extent to which the processes of those who seek to govern the world are resisted by those whose behavior they are seeking to affect is determined by the extent to which they adhere to the same *social solidarity*. If they do, they would share a common view not only of what the global interest is, but also of the best enabling environment that will ensure its proper identification, promotion and protection—the global governance mechanisms' most appropriate structures, processes, strategies and tactics. If they do not, the result will be global governance disillusionment, even despair, among the governed, which may lead to their withdrawal from, or rebellion against, the global governors' processes. It is to this theme that attention is now turned.

Appendix 5.1
The Competing Social Solidarities on the Global Interest and Global Governance

Dimensions	Hierarchist	Enclavist	Fatalist	Individualist
Global sphere:	The realm of the global ruling elite, focused on dominance and dependence, where power is the driving force in political life. An *international society* of nation-states.	A realm with boundaries that should be expanded if they conceal unequal power relations either within or between nation-states. Must be treated with constant vigilance if it is to be benevolent. A global *civil society* as a community of interests.	A capricious and fearful realm that is untrustworthy and indifferent to human needs. Engagement with this sphere is pointless and thus to be avoided at all costs.	A realm full of business opportunities for exploitation, which should be liberated from any political interference that places inhibiting constraints on positive freedom. A *world community* of self-interested individuals
Salient global power:	The state (exercising legitimate force, coercive, manipulative and persuasive power).	Global interest groups (exercising personal, referential, normative power).	The state, interest groups and multinational corporations (exercising physical or coercive power).	Multinational corporations (exercising resource, reward, exchange or economic power).

Dimension	Hierarchist	Enclavist	Fatalist	Individualist
Predisposition toward:				
national governing elites:	Presumed to know and accept their nation-state's relative position in *international society*'s hierarchy, and to be willing to delegate to global governance mechanisms the authority needed to address transnational governance issues.	Expected to compromise, voluntarily, their external and internal sovereignty by ceding authority to global governance mechanisms in issue-areas where action at the nation-state level cannot adequately address mutually agreed transnational issues.	Unknowing, untrustworthy and indifferent to survival needs and thus not expected to address life's inevitable vicissitudes.	Pedantic rent-seekers, without any legitimate authority to impose, unilaterally, purposive global order.
global administrative elite:	Chosen by the global ruling elite, from among those nominated by national governing elites. Expected to remain loyal and obedient to the global ruling elite.	However chosen, are always at risk of being immoral and corrupt.	Unknowing, untrustworthy and indifferent to people's survival needs and thus not expected to address life's inevitable vicissitudes.	Pedantic rent seekers, who will not be able to avoid the adverse global economic consequences of their inevitably misguided global governance interventions.

Appendix 5.1 (cont'd)

Dimension	Hierarchist	Enclavist	Fatalist	Individualist
Predisposition toward (cont'd):				
multinational business:	Global ruling elite knows what is in their best interests.	Untrustworthy and are always at risk of being amoral, immoral or corrupt.	Self-interested, exploitative and untrustworthy.	Must be given free rein to conduct their business affairs in a global market environment free of political obstacles.
global interest groups:	Global ruling elite knows what is in their best interests.	Should be fully engaged in the creation and functioning of global governance mechanisms and empowered to mediate transnational cooperation.	Unknowing, untrustworthy and indifferent to their survival needs and thus not expected to address life's inevitable vicissitudes.	Pedantic rent seekers who have no role in the global market place.
The global interest:	Knowable and grounded in the notion of the common good of *international society*, articulated as a set of national interests by constituent nation-states and prioritized and integrated by a global ruling elite.	Knowable and embraces an inclusive set of categorical interests that reflects shared values and defines the identity of global interest groups, as determined by consensus-seeking values discourses.	Unknowable, because of capriciousness and uncertainty, and thus cannot be intentionally and instrumentally promoted and protected.	Knowable only through people's preferences revealed in the global marketplace.

Dimension	Hierarchist	Enclavist	Fatalist	Individualist
Governance mode:	Balance of power (hierarchical).	World society (interactional).	No preferences, as none can make any difference.	International economic processes (market).
Governance decision making:	Gives greater weight to the more powerful member nation-states; and uses functional-analytic analysis to facilitate satisficing decision making to achieve incremental policy changes.	Respects the one actor, one vote, principle, must enable broad participation in deliberative power, and must seek to balance diverse interests, using communicative-value analysis to produce consistent, congruent and cogent decisions.	Autocratic and involves garbage can-like decision processes, dominated by unknowing and untrustworthy vested interests, and utilizing nonrational analysis to facilitate timely decision making.	Gives more weight to the global administrative elite who understand the global marketplace, and who use instrumentally and synoptically rational policy analysis, premised on self-interest motivation, to facilitate optimal decision making.
Global governability:	World is governable, but only if a global ruling elite, operating through a global administrative elite, is given the authority needed to address transnational governance issues agreed to by constituent nation-states.	World is governable, but only if an inclusive set of global actors can build a shared commitment to the survival, stability and wellbeing of the world.	World is governable, but only if the powers that be exercise the required coercive power to govern as they see fit.	World is governable, but only if the global market is left to govern itself in an environment free of political obstacles.

Appendix 5.1 (cont'd)

Dimension	Hierarchist	Enclavist	Fatalist	Individualist
Governance challenge:	To establish global governance mechanisms that a global ruling elite of the *international society* can dominate.	To establish global governance mechanisms that facilitate the codetermination, protection and promotion of categorical interest in the *global society*.	To establish global governance mechanisms that do not require people's constructive engagement.	To establish global governance mechanisms that will enable the market to govern itself.
Governance salient threat:	The inability of global ruling and administrative elites to identify, protect and promote the global interest.	The inability of people engaged in interactive global governance processes to make consensus decisions that identify, protect and promote their categorical interests.	The ability of anyone intentionally and instrumentally to promote and protect the global interest, so revealing that their self-chosen isolation has been in vain.	The inability of those operating in the global marketplace to understand the nature and causation of, and solutions to, systemic failures in the global marketplace.
Policy arenas:				
distributive:	Strong appeal.	No appeal.	Strong appeal.	Appeals only for public goods.
redistributive:	No appeal.	Strong appeal.	No appeal.	No appeal.
constituency:	Strong appeal.	Appeals only if no controls imposed.	Appeals only if they do not facilitate abuse and exploitation.	Appeals only if negative freedom not constrained.

Dimension	Hierarchist	Enclavist	Fatalist	Individualist
Policy arenas (cont'd):				
regulatory	Strong appeal.	Appeals only if voluntary behavior change rewarded.	Appeals only if they offer some protection against abuse and exploitation.	Appeal only if they help maintain confidence in the market.
Regulatory mode:	Hierarchical.	Network coregulation.	None preferred.	Market.
Regulatory instruments:				
command-and-control:	Appeals.	No appeal.	Appeals, provided they offer protection against abuse and exploitation.	Appeals only if market confidence promoted, and if they reflect an understanding of the marketplace.
information:	Appeals.	Appeals.	No appeal.	Appeals, particularly if they reduce market opportunities for competitors.
economic:	Appeals.	Appeals only if they are negotiated.	Appeals, if they can be rewarded for doing what is in their survival interests.	Appeals, because they provide incentives, but only if they reflect an understanding of the market.

Appendix 5.1 (cont'd)

Dimension	Hierarchist	Enclavist	Fatalist	Individualist
Regulatory enforcement levels and modes:	Through formal regulatory regimes with a zero tolerance of noncompliance and substantial sanctions.	Through discretionary regulatory regimes that have a low noncompliance tolerance and a capacity to reward and punish.	Through regulatory regimes with a high tolerance of noncompliance and constrained sanctions.	Through enforceable contracts with a zero tolerance of noncompliance and full restitution as the sanction.
Compliance:	Follows a cognitive commitment.	Follows a moral commitment.	Alienative compliance.	Instrumental compliance.
Response to regulatory instrument imposition:				
command-and-control:	Would axiomatically do what the global ruling elite expects.	Would seek to find ways of minimizing any changes that are inconsistent with their categorical interests.	Would seek to find ways of avoiding or minimizing any change that threatens their survival.	Would seek to find ways of avoiding or minimizing any change that involves a net compliance cost.
information:	Would axiomatically do what the global ruling elite expects.	Would ignore any information that is inconsistent with their categorical interests.	Would ignore any information that threatens their survival.	Would ignore any information unless it threatens or creates a market opportunity.

Dimension	Hierarchist	Enclavist	Fatalist	Individualist
Response to regulatory instrument imposition (cont'd):				
economic:	Would axiomatically do what the global ruling elite expects.	Would seek to find ways of minimizing any changes that are inconsistent with their categorical interests.	Would seek to find ways of avoiding or minimizing any change that threatens their survival.	Would seek to find ways of avoiding or minimizing any change that involves a net compliance cost.
Response to the failure of their preferred global governance mode:	Express loyalty toward the global ruling elite, in expectation of a solution being found, and then blame deviants.	Voice blame, accusing the risk takers and the secret enemies within, demand their removal, and then engage more interest groups in inclusive cogovernance networks that design and empower global governance mechanisms.	No response, as they have no preference.	Blame bad luck, the incompetence of rogue buyers and sellers, or the incompetent global ruling and administrative elites, then, if their prospects for material success are diminished, exit by disengaging from the global marketplace.

Appendix 5.1 (cont'd)

Dimension	Hierarchist	Enclavist	Fatalist	Individualist
Response if trapped in, or subject to, a failing global governance mode posited by another *social solidarity*:	Would see themselves as the rational saviors of the common good of *international society*, and would impose hierarchical global governance mechanisms that reflect the balance of power among the nation-states.	Would see themselves as passionate saviors of their categorical interests, and would demand that interest groups be permitted to establish, and engage fully with, voluntary transnational cogovernance networks to design and empower global governance mechanisms.	Would see themselves as the vindicated victims of the global powers that be, and would become prophets of doom.	Would each see themselves as commonsense saviors of their self-interest, and would take the necessary steps to ensure that the global market becomes self-regulating, by limiting the power and role of global governance mechanisms.

6

Antagonism, Disillusionment and Despair: The Challenges

INTRODUCTION

The extent to which the governed resist the governors' processes is determined by the extent to which they share a common allegiance to a mode of governance. Compliance follows when both sides share such a commitment. Resistance follows the buildup of antagonism when they do not. The purpose of this chapter is to examine the implications of the interaction between the governed and their governors for corporate, societal and global governance capacity and, thus, governability.

GOVERNANCE ANTAGONISM

Adherents to a particular *social solidarity*—hierarchist, enclavist, individualist or fatalist—argue that corporations, societies and, indeed, the world are governable, but only if their preferred governance mode is adopted. The governance antagonisms among them are the product of mutually incompatible sets of epistemological, ontological, rationalistic and nomological assumptions that underpin the four *social solidarities*. These sets of assumptions give rise to mutually incompatible sets of idiosyncratic governance truth propositions, or truths, that provide the foundations for the competing governance modes.

Antagonism over Philosophical Perspectives

The competing *social solidarities* offer incompatible contentions about what does or can exist in the social world—the nature of being—and what is knowable in that world. As naturalists, hierarchists and individualists believe that the social world is knowable as objective truth by application of the scientific method; but hierarchists, as structuralists, believe that ordered social interrelationships—social structures—exercise power upon agency by molding people's thoughts about their social world and their actions in it; whereas individualists, as agentists, believe that people take action in the social world only after actively interpreting their social reality from the perspective of their own self-interest, unconstrained by any group norms. In contradistinction, as hermeneuticists, enclavists and fatalists believe that the social world cannot be objectively explained from without, since it can only be understood subjectively from within by acquiring knowledge of how people construct it and by making sense of what others say and do; but enclavists, as structuralists, believe that people take action in the social world after actively interpreting their social reality as mutually constructed; whereas fatalists, as agentists, believe that agency is defined by their subjective perceptions of the true social reality of ordered social relationships, as it seems to them.

If, then, social action is the result of structural processes, as hierarchists and enclavists believe, then good governance requires strategies that enable these processes to be modified in order to achieve desirable governance outcomes. This creates a problem for hierarchists because their naturalist epistemology does not have the capacity to identify causal relationships, hence establishing the nature of the connection between structural-process change and governance outcomes becomes problematic. For enclavists, the problem is that their hermeneutic epistemology provides knowledge of the social world that is relativist and dynamic, and thus unable to offer reliable predictions as to whether structural process changes will generate the desired governance outcome. Structuralist-based governance strategies will, of course, fail to address the imperatives that motivate free individuals because they cannot explain or predict those imperatives.

If, alternatively, social action rests on individual human motivation, as individualists and fatalists believe, then good governance requires strategies that enable these individual aspirations to be addressed. This causes problems for individualists because their naturalist epistemology is unable to identify definitively cause-and-effect relationships, which makes establishing the connection between self-interest enhancing strategies and governance outcomes problematic. For fatalists, the problem is that their hermeneutic epistemology does not give them the means for reliable predictions as to whether changes intended to enhance agency will generate the desired governance outcomes. Agency-based governance strategies will, of course, fail to address the structural imperatives that constrain and influence individual behavior because they cannot explain or predict those imperatives.

In essence, supporters of the competing modes of governance categorically deny the existence not only of either structure or agency, thereby making them unable to understand and address problems that stem from the excluded ontology, but also of either hermeneutics or naturalism, thereby making them unable understand and address problems that stem from the excluded epistemology. Under these circumstances, antagonism born of inevitable governance failure is unavoidable.

Antagonism over Reasoning Perspectives

The competing *social solidarities* offer incompatible contentions about the forms of reasoning that should be the basis for thought and action. Hierarchists prefer functionally analytical reasoning capable of producing satisficing decisions, arguing that the intellect is constrained, not least by hierarchically determined values and beliefs. Enclavists prefer reasoning that is critical, communicative and values-based, using processes that only embrace all committed and engaged actors who are empowered and enabled to make and question arguments, which makes good argument and the validity of normative judgments the final authority. Individualists prefer reasoning that is instrumental, functional, synoptical and strategic, with purposeful action only following decisions made on the basis of self-interest. Fatalists prefer to engage in reasoning that is non-rational, since reality can never be known, only made plausible and credible by the application of intuition and rolling hindsight.

In essence, supporters of the competing modes of governance categorically assert the validity only of their preferred forms of reasoning, thereby making them unable to deal with governance problems that can only be analyzed and addressed by means of an excluded form of reasoning. Under these circumstances antagonism born of inevitable governance failure is unavoidable.

Antagonism over Nomological Perspectives

The competing *social solidarities* have incompatible contentions about how people behave or are inclined to behave in given situations. Hierarchists believe that behavior is predictable because a person makes choice decisions on the basis of reasoning constrained by given and known hierarchical expectations. Enclavists believe that behavior is predictable because a person makes choice decisions on the basis of reasoning constrained by known socially constructed collective expectations. Individualists believe that behavior is predictable because a person makes choice decisions on the basis of reasoning processes constrained only by self-interest, and thus without reference to any group norms. Fatalists believe that behavior is unpredictable because a person's choice decisions are made on the basis of reasoning processes constrained by what they believe to be the true social reality, which is ever changing and always contestable.

In essence, supporters of the competing modes of governance categorically assert the validity only of their preferred contentions about human behavior, thereby making them unable to deal with governance problems that can only be understood and addressed by reference excluded human-behavior contentions. Under these circumstances, antagonism born of inevitable governance failure is unavoidable.

THE GOVERNED'S ANTAGONISM TOWARD THE GOVERNORS

When the governed and the governors do not share an adherence to the same epistemological, ontological, rationalistic and nomological assumptions, and thus to the same governance truths that they underpin, then they would hold mutually incompatible core governance values, attitudes, and opinions. As a consequence, they would prefer different governance modes. Hierarchists would prefer hierarchical governance structures and processes, with enforceable command-and-control regulations administered with a zero noncompliance tolerance and substantial sanctions. Enclavists would prefer voluntary interactive governance structures and processes that permit and empower people to engage fully in the process of balancing a diverse set of categorical interests, and that administer regulatory regimes that permit discretion and have a low noncompliance tolerance and a capacity to reward. Individualists would prefer the market to be self-regulating, facilitated by the imposition of minimal governance structures and processes. Fatalists would feel least alienated by a governance mode that ignores them, and certainly does not require their constructive engagement.

The governors would be seen antagonistically by those among the governed who disagree with them, because 'they' are adopting the 'wrong' solutions to governance failures, because 'they' cannot or will not see the 'correct' cause of governance failures, and thus see that 'their' solutions are the only 'correct' ones. Governance change would thus be demanded by those among the governed who feel trapped in, or subject to, what they perceive to be a failing governance mode. The governors and their supporters, who deny that their governance mode is fundamentally failing, despite apparent evidence to the contrary, would demand the maintenance of the governance status quo.

Two groups drawn from among the governed would feel governance antagonism. One contains those who feel trapped in, or subject to, what they perceive to be a failing governance mode that the governors deny is fundamentally failing, and indeed, are strengthening so as to enhance compliance in order to correct governance failure. The other group contains those who feel threatened because they are subject to a governance mode that they believe is not fundamentally failing yet is being changed because the governors believe that it is fundamentally failing. Continuing antagonism by the governed inevitably increases their resistance to the governors' processes, which, in turn, inevitably solicits a counter response from the governors. The extent to which the mutual annoyance, frustration and even anger are felt by the governed and the governors depends, crucially, on how rigidly and inflexibly they both hold onto their governance truths, and thus their governance values, attitudes, and opinions. Insights into this can be gleaned from Olli's (1995, 1999) three models of the individual.

Olli's (1999: 60) "consistent, solid and single-minded," or intransigent *coherent individuals,* would be intolerant of widely differing degrees of *group*- and *grid*-grip, and thus would have a restricted and rigid set of *social-control comfort zone* boundaries because they have strongly held, almost immutable, core governance values, slow-to-adapt governance attitudes and slow-to-change governance opinions. The very idea that reality might actually be otherwise than they take it to be is a proposition that they find difficult, if not impossible, to take seriously, no matter how compelling the arguments may be. Indeed, it would be easier for them to push these arguments aside, unaddressed, than to renounce their ways of looking at the world. To them, their worldview must be accepted as self-evidently right. They would, thus, readily not only deny that their preferred governance mode could ever be fundamentally failing, but also reject the governance truths of the competing *social solidarities*. They would either not notice the contrary evidence, or it would initiate from them Hirschman's (1991: 168) "rhetoric of intransigence," so reinforcing their faith in their preferred governance mode. They would expect the governors to adopt only their hard-line solutions to any governance failures. They would be intolerant, probably to the point of frustration, if any alternative solutions were to be proposed, and angry if their imposition were to move them out of their *social-control comfort zone*. Disillusionment with their preferred governance mode would be slow in coming, but disillusionment with the governors with whom they did not share governance truths would be very readily forthcoming.

Olli's (1999: 60) adaptable *sequential individuals* would be tolerant of a wide degree of *group-* and *grid-*grip, and thus would have an expansive and flexible set of *social-control comfort zone* boundaries falling within their preferred *social solidarity*, because they hold core governance values that they are willing to change, albeit slowly, governance attitudes that they are more readily willing to adapt, and governance opinions that they are quite willing to change. Hence they would have the willingness to at least consider substituting a set of governance truths proffered by a competing *social solidarity*. They would readily accept evidence that their preferred governance mode could be fundamentally failing, but their initial response may well be denial, so reinforcing their faith in that governance mode, preferring to procrastinate, agonizingly, as they grapple with the process of coherently changing their governance opinions, attitudes and values. They would also expect the governors to consider a range of solutions to any governance failures. They would be tolerant if any alternative solutions were to be proposed, but annoyed, perhaps to the point of frustration, if their imposition were to move them out of their existing *social-control comfort zone* before they were ready. Disillusionment with their preferred governance mode would be quick in coming, but disillusionment with the governors with whom they did not share governance truths would not be so readily forthcoming.

Olli's (1999: 60) flexible *synthetic individuals* would be tolerant of very wide degrees of *group-* and *grid-*grip, and thus would have a *social-control comfort zone*, the boundaries of which could well marginally overlap two or more *social solidarities*, because they hold core governance values that they are willing and able to change relatively quickly, governance attitudes that they are readily willing to adapt, and governance opinions that they are willing to change as needed. They thus have the ability not only to reconcile the ambiguities of incompatible governance truths, but also to accept any evidence that their largely preferred governance mode could be fundamentally failing. Their initial response may well be denial, so reinforcing their faith in their largely preferred governance mode, and procrastination, as they grapple, thoughtfully, with the process of reconciling the new governance ambiguities created by the evidence of governance failures. They would also expect the governors to consider seriously adopting their solutions to any governance failures, but they would be tolerant if any alternative solutions were to be proposed, but annoyed, at worst, if their imposition were to move them out of their existing *social-control comfort zone* before they were ready. Disillusionment with their preferred governance mode would be very quick in coming, but disillusionment with the governors with whom they did not share governance truths would rarely eventuate.

Governance Disillusionment

Those who deny, in the face of contrary evidence, that their preferred governance mode is fundamentally failing, would only be inclined to change their governance attitudes when they have reached the point where the cumulative effect of belief-challenging governance failure facts begin to challenge their governance truths by disconfirming or disproving their beliefs on what constitutes good governance. For only then are they beginning to experience a level of cognitive dissonance that demands, in the first instance, that the validity of their good governance postulates be questioned because they seem no longer to be capable of delivering on their expectations. Ultimately, however, a new set of governance truths may be needed to modify those good governance belief patterns, so as to bring them into alignment with their perceptions of governance reality.

On Crossing the Governance Disillusionment Threshold

Most people would, no doubt, find the process of crossing the governance disillusionment threshold a demanding one. They would have to slough off their current governance mode allegiance, requiring them to be absolutely convinced that it is wrong, and thus incapable of stemming the flow of governance failures. They would also have to cultivate a new set of governance truths, so as to be able to justify to themselves their adherence to a new governance mode. This would require them to adopt different perspectives on what can exist and has causal capacity and what is knowable in the social world, different forms of reasoning, and different assumptions about human behavior. They would also have to adapt how they relate to other people, how they gain their self-esteem, and their metalife-goal.

For Olli's (1999: 60) intransigent *coherent individuals*, a change of governance mode allegiance would require almost a personality change. This would particularly be so if they had previously strongly rejected the governance truths underpinning all the competing governance modes. They would thus be dilatory in the extreme about accepting any evidence that threatens their governance mode convictions, forever seeking evidence that supports their apportioning of blame for its failures and their preferred hard-line solutions. They would thus procrastinate on the condemning of their preferred governance mode, giving themselves time to satisfy themselves that a change of governance mode allegiance is both unthinkable and undesirable.

For Olli's (1999: 60) adaptable *sequential individuals*, crossing the governance disillusionment threshold would not be so traumatic, for they would readily accept the possibility that their preferred governance mode could be fundamentally failing. But the prospect of having to adopt new ways of seeing themselves, their relationship with others, and the world around them might well reinforce their faith in what only *might be* a failing governance mode. They would accept any disconfirming evidence generated by the flow of governance failures that challenges their governance mode convictions. They would, however, feel the need to satisfy themselves that there is no evidence that enabled them to apportion blame for the governance failures on those they are inclined to blame, or that supported their belief that their preferred governance solutions would eventually work. They would thus procrastinate on condemning their preferred governance mode, giving themselves time to be satisfied that a change of governance mode allegiance is really necessary.

For Olli's (1999: 60) flexible *synthetic individuals* a governance disillusionment threshold transition would be readily facilitated by their ability to see the competing governance truths as puzzle pieces that can solve the governance failure conundrum and by their capacity to justify to themselves apparently incompatible governance truth propositions. They would readily accept any disconfirming evidence generated by the flow of governance failures that requires a modification of their governance mode convictions. They would, however, procrastinate on condemning their preferred pattern of governance mode allegiances, giving themselves time to consider how best to reconfigure the governance truths so as to recast appropriately their composite governance mode allegiances.

Governance Despair

Governance despair would come from two sources. One is the alienation that flows from the unremitting antagonism felt by the governed when governors of a different ilk are forever adopting the wrong solutions to governance failures, because they steadfastly refuse to accept that their solutions are the correct ones. The second source is the alienation that flows from undiminished cognitive dissonance experienced by those who, despite being adaptable in their governance mode allegiance, have been unable to modify their good governance belief patterns in a way that aligns them with their perceptions of governance reality, because each of the governance modes is inherently flawed by the philosophical limitations of its epistemological and ontological foundations, so none of their cognitive maps of governance reality can deliver on their expectations. Under what conditions, then, would such alienation and disillusionment take the governed to their governance despair threshold?

Alienation Born of Unremitting Antagonism

Olli's (1999: 60) intransigent *coherent individuals* would be sufficiently convinced of the rightness of their governance truths to be alienatingly antagonistic ones toward governors who incessantly adopt the wrong solutions to governance failures. For them to cross the threshold of governance despair would require the realization that wrong-headed governors will never voluntarily adopt their preferred governance mode, because it would inevitably incite resistance by those who are antagonistic to it, despite any efforts they may make to win acceptance and compliance. This realization requires two preceding realizations. One is that other people can be just as firmly committed to competing governance modes as they can; just as convinced that other governance modes are fundamentally flawed as they can; and just as antagonistic to, and, eventually, as alienated from, a governance process that they consider to be fundamentally flawed as they can. The second realization is that other people can be just as resistant to governance mode allegiance conversion as they can, because they can be just as firmly committed to their set of governance truths as they can.

Alienation Born of Undiminished Cognitive Dissonance

Despair follows the realization that substituting any alternative governance modes will not reduce cognitive dissonance ones. Adaptable *sequential individuals* would find despair after agonizingly grappling with the sequential process of coherently changing their governance opinions, attitudes and values in search of viable solutions to continuing governance failure. Flexible *synthetic individuals* would find despair following the realization that their eclectic governance failure solutions would certainly raise antagonisms, and thus solicit resistance from two sources. One would be those who are intransigently committed to particular governance modes, because they do not have the capacity to adopt a set of different governance truths. The second source would be other *synthetic individuals* who build their eclectic governance failure solutions on different configurations of governance truths.

Responses to Alienation

There are two responses open to the governed once they have crossed the threshold of governance despair: to withdraw or to rebel.

Withdrawal: The Response of the Chameleonic Disillusioned. Adaptable *sequential* and *synthetic individuals* would abandon all hope that a solution to the continued flow of governance failures will, somehow, finally emerge, as they increasingly lose faith in all the governance truths that justify the governors' *group-* and *grid*-grip on them. This would make them increasingly intolerant of the governors' failing governance processes, and thus inclined to withdraw from any engagement with the governors, so becoming *hermits*.[1]

Withdrawal from governance processes could manifest itself in a variety of ways. At the corporate level, shareholders could sell their shares; employees,

---

[1] The path to seclusion can only be through those *social solidarities* that impose the weakest degrees of social control, namely, fatalists, egalitarians and, most particularly, individualists. Indeed, Douglas's (1978: 42) original inclination, it must be remembered, was to co-locate *hermits* with individualists at the minimum *grid-group* grip point.

managers and directors could resign; strategic stakeholders could withdraw from, or not renew, their contractual relationships (such as creditors foreclosing on debts, financiers refusing to refinance or reschedule debts); and stakeholders could withdraw from commitments made to a corporation (such as environmental or community groups withdrawing public support for proposed initiatives). At the societal level, residents could emigrate, perhaps becoming political refugees; those qualified to vote in elections for political office could decline to vote (or vote informally in the event of compulsory voting); members of network governance mechanisms could withdraw from their engagement; and corporate elites could withdraw from particular product lines or market segments at the national or a particular subnational jurisdictional level. At the global level, national political elites, interest groups or multinational corporate elites could withdraw from their engagement in, or withdraw their support for, transnational governance negotiations; national political elites could withdraw their country from participation in particular (or even all) international organizations or regimes; and multinational corporate elites could withdraw from particular product lines or regional market segments in the global marketplace.

Rebellion: The Response of the Intransigent Disillusioned. Intransigent *coherent individuals* would find their antagonism toward hostile governors eventually becoming more resentful, even more revengeful. Their response would be to rebel against the governors' power and authority, using whatever means is necessary. Camus (1971: 19) captures the essence of rebellion:

In every act of rebellion, the man [sic] concerned expresses not only a feeling of revulsion at the infringement of his rights but also a complete and spontaneous loyalty to certain aspects of himself. Up to the present he has, at least, kept quiet and, in desperation, has accepted a condition to which he submits even though he considers it unjust.

These acts of rebellion may be instrumental or noninstrumental.[2] Instrumental rebellion would involve arguing against, resisting and refusing allegiance to the governors, with a view to changing governance processes in the implacable belief that the flow of governance failures will only be stemmed by the imposition of their correct solutions. Noninstrumental rebellion would be intent on wreaking havoc on the governors, motivated simply by the need to

---

[2] Those social psychologists who use the *locus of control* construct to ascertain people's perceptions of the relative importance of internally derived and externally imposed sources of control over their behavior argue (Levenson 1981: 49-52) that *instrumental militant behavior* is most likely to come from *internalists* (those who tend to accept responsibility for their actions and consider they are in control of their lives and destinies, largely through their own personal effort, ability, and initiative), arguably enclavists and individualists; while *noninstrumental militant behavior* is most likely to come from *externalists* (those who tend to see control as external to themselves, residing in other people, social structures, luck or fate), arguably fatalists and hierarchists.

express their hostility so as to relieve the acrimony and frustration[3] that builds up with unremitting antagonism.

The Differentiated Response of the Governed to Governance Failure

All but the most intransigent adherents to any *social solidarity* are capable of being surprised by a flow of governance failures. Some may be willing to consider transferring their allegiance to a competing governance mode. A few might actually change their allegiance. Despair might well eventually effects some of them, eliciting rebellious responses from the more intransigent among them.

Hierarchists. Hierarchists would be surprised if hierarchical elites could not correct hierarchical governance mode failures by strengthening controls and sanctions. This would reveal that they do not understand the causes of governance failures and their correction, and that their presumptions about the behavioral responses of the governed are inadequate, which means that they cannot effectively manage hierarchical governance.

Hierarchists would be attracted to interactive governance only if it became apparent to them that hierarchical governance failure could only be corrected if they voice their concerns about the limitations of the hierarchical elite and demand the introduction of interactive governance processes that engage with those who are expected to change their behavior. This means that they would have to be convinced that governance success requires the governed to be morally committed to the governance outcomes sought, so necessitating their engagement in the construction of mutually acceptable governance failure solutions that evoke moral commitment, which is achieved through norming and forming discourses on contestable values standards. It would also mean that they would have to reject their faith in the scientific method and the objectivity of reality, and their belief that behavior is predictable on the basis of reasoning processes that are constrained by given and known hierarchical group norms. They would also have to confront their reluctance to act without the approval of authority figures, and be willing to negotiate their relationships with other people as equals; to demonstrate continually their commitment to the common governance cause; to determine their interpersonal relationships without reference to authority figures; and to accept that the recognition and acclaim of those who are committed to a common cause is more important than the approval of authority figures.

Hierarchists would be attracted to market self-regulation only if it became apparent to them that hierarchical governance failure could only be corrected by the removal of governance structures that are inherently coercive, intrusive and inefficient, and that contain pedantic rent seekers, who do not permit people to negotiate freely their own contractual relationships as they see fit. This would enable the market to be self-regulating by means of enforceable contracts with a

---

[3] Dollard et al. (1939) long ago offered the Freudian proposition that aggressive behavior occurs when purposeful behavior is interrupted.

zero noncompliance tolerance and with full restitution as the ultimate sanction. They would thus have to be convinced that law-abiding buyers and sellers, who conduct their affairs in accordance with their contractual obligations and a sense of personal responsibility, can correct governance failure without the expert assistance of the hierarchical elite. It would also mean that they would have to reject their belief that structure molds behavior and makes it predictable on the basis of reasoning processes that are constrained by given hierarchical group norms. They would have to become networking risk takers seeking conspicuous material success; to confront not only their reluctance to determine their interpersonal relationships without reference to authority figures, but also their fear of being excluded from the paternalistic protection of the hierarchy if they act without the approval of authority figures; and to accept that the recognition and acclaim of materially successful people is more important than the approval of authority figures.

Disillusioned hierarchists would be attracted to a governance mode that does not expect people's constructive engagement, only if it became apparent to them that no amount of such engagement with any governance mechanisms contributes to the correction of hierarchical governance failure. This means that they would have to be convinced of the improbability of anybody's constructive engagement contributing to the reversal of governance failures. It would mean that they would have to reject the objectivity of reality, their faith in the scientific method, and their belief that behavior is predictable on the basis of reasoning processes that are constrained by given and known hierarchical group norms. They would also have to be willing to abandon their structured and orderly existence in a paternalistic hierarchy and become loners and survivors; to confront their reluctance to act without the approval of authority figures; and to accept that seeing themselves as survivors, despite the odds that fate decrees, is more important than gaining the approval of authority figures.

Most hierarchists would find it difficult to cross the governance disillusionment threshold and accept a new set of governance truths if they had to adapt not only the way in which they relate to other people and gain their self-esteem, but also their metalife-goal. Some would be willing to cross the threshold as a step toward the reconciliation of their governance perceptions with governance reality, in the hope of finding temporary relief from the cognitive dissonance that first brought them to the governance despair threshold. Eventually, perhaps, they would decide to disengage from the governance process. Others would not even question their governance views; they may simply confront their governance despair.

Intransigent hierarchists,[4] with their implacable belief that they have a duty to the hierarchical elite to stem the flow of governance failures, would seek to

---

[4] Adorno and et al.'s (1950; but see Madge 1962) enunciation of the authoritarian personality is insightful. Authoritarians are characterized by their extreme conformity; their submissiveness both to authority and to the collective's moral authority; their rigid adherence to conventional values; their readiness to punish; their arrogance toward those

impose a well-run hierarchy governance mode on the collective. Their inclination would thus be toward the assumption of power by whatever means. At the corporate level, this could manifest itself as a management buyout or a hostile corporate takeover contrived by disgruntled managing elites of collaborating corporations, joint venture partners, or consortia or federation members; or it could manifest itself as managing elites engaging in backward integration to acquire control of a strategically important supplier. At the societal level, it could involve a military coup d'état or a civil war, perhaps involving guerrilla warfare; the nationalization of a privately owned industry or corporation; or the imposition of state-sanctioned regulatory regimes on previously self-regulating professional occupational groups (such as medical practitioners, lawyers and social workers). At the global level, it could involve war (whether total, limited, or cold) or the threat of military intervention by a global ruling elite to change the behavior of, or to remove from a position of power, rogue national political elites or interest groups that unacceptably seek, by the use of force, coercion (perhaps involving state-sponsored terrorism) or manipulation, to sabotage, direct or control another country's affairs.

As *instrumental rebels*, intransigent hierarchists would plan in detail their seizure of power, leaving nothing to chance. They would assert that they are exercising power for the common good of the collective, believing that stemming the flow of governance failures requires that collective claims override the claims of its individual members. Their primary concern would be to protect the collective's future by constraining both negative and positive freedoms.

The governance structures imposed by intransigent hierarchical *rebels* would embody a set of roles, rules and regulations, so that everyone knows precisely what is expected of them. For, in order to stem the flow of governance failures, they must discipline deviants who do not know their place or who are not willing to operate within the rules, because their inclination is to avoid obligations wherever possible. Individual sacrifices would, undoubtedly, be expected in the collective interest, out of a sense of duty, and reinforced by the threat of expulsion.

Intransigent hierarchists would be intent on establishing correct governance procedures, on the grounds that efficiently ordered and appropriate action produces the right results and that the required manipulation of control, constraint and leverage factors can be built into implementation plans. They would use ritualism and sacrifice to support the underpinning deontological moral code. They would expect people to acquire quickly the habit of obedience to command, with a sense of obligation that does not question the judgments of the command-issuing authority, because they presume that people's reasoning processes are constrained by hierarchically determined behavior norms and thus that behaviorial compliance follows cognitive commitment. Apathy would be encouraged. They would also tightly control all information, so as to avoid worrisome contradictions and incompatibilities.

---

they consider inferior; their capacity for prejudice; and their unwillingness to tolerate ambiguity.

Hierarchical *instrumental rebels* would countenance no contesting of their governance objectives or values standards on moral or political grounds. These they would readily justify by reference to some extrapersonal ideal (such as the corporate, national or global interest). They would insist that the experts, who can be trusted to manage successfully the risk environment, make all critical governance decisions.

Only if a grab for power is deemed by the experts to be unachievable, would intransigent hierarchists consider resorting to noninstrumental rebellion. At all levels this could manifest itself as the hierarchical elite sanctioning or sponsoring acts of sabotage (such as undermining future plans by the timely public disclosure of sensitive information); violence (ranging from disorderly conduct, criminal lawlessness, riotous behavior, to frenzied mob behavior aimed at property and authority figures); even life-threatening or life-taking actions (terrorism or assassination).

Enclavists. Enclavists would be surprised if, having removed from the interactive governance processes those who do not share their common governance values, those who are left are unable to engage in harmonious discourse that builds, by consensus, a set of governance understandings that provides the basis for determining mutually acceptable solutions to governance failure. Such a failure would mean that they cannot ensure that genuine compliance, based on a moral commitment to interactive governance success, will emerge from the norming and forming discourses on contestable governance values standards. This would mean that the interactive governance mode cannot be effectively managed by those who are engaged with it.

Disillusioned enclavists would be attracted to the hierarchical governance mode only if it became apparent to them that interactive governance failure could be corrected by adopting the hierarchical governance prescriptions. They would thus have to be convinced that a hierarchical elite have demonstrated their ability to understand and correct governance failure in a way that is compatible with their values. It also means that they would have to reject their faith in critical and values-based reasoning and their beliefs that people take action only after actively interpreting their mutually constructed social reality, and that behavior is predictable on the basis of socially constructed group regulatory norms. They would also have to disengage from their personally negotiated egalitarian relationships with like-minded people and reengage with a group that is structured, orderly and paternalistic; to confront their true feelings in support of inequality and differentiation; and to accept that the approval of authority figures is more important than the recognition and acclaim of those who are committed to the common cause they once valued.

Enclavists would be attracted to the market self-regulation mode of governance only if it became apparent to them that interactive governance failure can be corrected by the market being left to regulate itself by means of enforceable contracts with a zero noncompliance tolerance and with full restitution as the ultimate sanction. It also means that they would have to reject their faith in critical and values-based reasoning, and their beliefs that people take action only after actively interpreting their mutually constructed social reality so making behavior predictable on the basis of socially constructed group regulatory norms. They would have to be convinced that law-abiding buyers and sellers, who conduct their affairs on the basis of enforceable contracts with a sense of personal responsibility, have demonstrated that they are able to understand governance problems and have found appropriate market solutions that are compatible with their values framework. They would also have to abandon their personally negotiated egalitarian relationships with like-minded people in order to become networking risk takers seeking conspicuous material success; to confront their suppressed true feelings in support of their commitment to themselves and to self-interest; and to accept that the recognition and acclaim of materially successful people is more important than the recognition and acclaim of those who are committed to the interactive governance cause they once valued.

Enclavists would be attracted to a governance mode that does not expect people's constructive engagement only if it became apparent to them that no amount of such engagement in any governance mechanism can contribute to the correction of interactive governance failure. This means that they would have to be convinced of the implausibility of anybody's constructive engagement contributing to the correction of governance failure. It also means that they would have to reject their faith in critical and values-based reasoning, and their beliefs that people take action only after actively interpreting their mutually constructed social reality, and that behavior is predictable on the basis of socially constructed group regulatory norms. They would also have to disengage from their personally negotiated egalitarian relationships with like-minded people and become loners and survivors who are detached from any values discourse; to confront their suppressed true feelings in support of the fact that they are no longer committed to anyone, including themselves, or to any cause; and to accept that being survivors, despite the odds that fate decrees, is more important than the recognition and acclaim of those who are committed to the common cause they previously valued.

Most enclavists would probably find it difficult to cross the governance disillusionment threshold and change their governance mode allegiance, as this would mean disengaging from their extant personal relationships and ethical commitments. Some would, of course, be willing to do so under the duress of having no choice. Others would not even bother to question their governance views; they may simply confront their governance despair.

Intransigent enclavists, with their implacable sense of justice, equality and fairness that gives them the moral obligation to reverse the iniquities caused by the flow of governance failures, would demand the imposition of an interactive governance mode on the collective. Their first inclination would thus be toward instrumental rebellion to rid the governance system of all evils, so that it can contribute to human fulfilment and wellbeing. At all levels, this could involve interest groups engaging in oppositional rhetoric; orchestrating disobedience (Rai 1996), in order either to gain rights, achieve publicity, or force reconsiderations, or as an expression of conscientious objection (Singer 1973: Part II). This could be achieved by means of passive resistance, perhaps involving the disobeying of laws and regulations (such as the public disclosure of information about governance failure, so as to raise public awareness of the need for broader participation in governance processes, or whistle-blowing on unethical behavior) in order to place moral pressure on the governors; threats of withdrawal from governance processes in which interactive governance reform is not forthcoming (for example, stakeholders of strategic importance could threaten to withdraw their services or their support for strategically important initiatives); demagogy (Canetti [1960] 2000, Mackay [1852] 1995, Rudé [1981] 1995), involving acts of protest (such as interest group protests at governance meetings); or illicit rebellion intended to transfer authority and transform the nature of power (such as, labor unions engaged in militant industrial relations campaigns, freedom fighters engaged in guerrilla warfare or wars of liberation, and environmental justice activists engaged in militant global campaigns against the inappropriate dumping of hazardous wastes and the use of environmentally damaging toxic substances).

As *instrumental rebels*, enclavists would stress the importance of fraternal and sororal cooperation, believing that people have the capacity for real moral progress, once they have been isolated from the corrupting influences of past market or hierarchical social formations; those concrete economic, political and ideological relations that, when bound together, give a society a particular character. People would be expected to engage in public governance discourses, persuasive governance discourses with targeted individuals, and consciousness-raising governance discourses with fellow adherents, in order to find solutions to stem the flow of governance failures in the hope of governance reform. They would, then, be intent on engaging people in intersubjective communications, in order to construct mutual governance understandings that build consensus views on the sensible reality of governance failures.

They would demand that decisions on how best to stem the flow of governance failures should be fair, equitable and philosophically justified. This, they would assert, is only possible if there is complete consensus among those committed to the interactive governance cause. This requires acceptance of the propositions that authority rests only with those engaged in the interactive governance process, and that each decision maker must have the ability and an equal chance to expound truth claims, challenge statements, express attitudes, feelings and emotions, and, most crucially, to permit and forbid. Their concern would be with enhancing positive freedom by imposing necessary constraints on negative freedom. Once a set of governance rules, embodying agreed governance beliefs, has been negotiated as the long-term solution to governance failure, compliance and the necessary voluntary sacrifices for the collective would be expected on the basis of moral commitment.

Intransigent enclavist *rebels* would see governance failures as correctable, but only if their solutions are accepted by all to be the only right ones, which means that those who oppose them must have their governance values, attitudes and opinions changed. Intransigent enclavists would thus seek to punish or convert those holding different governance views. To this end they would demand that all governance information be openly and readily available. Should their opponents become intransigent, then intransigent enclavists would adopt a defiant posture and, gradually, compromise would become more unthinkable; negotiations more impossible; and violence more likely.

When incited by the behavior of intransigent outsiders, intransigent enclavists could well resort to noninstrumental rebellion, which would be a natural development from their dissident inclinations.[5] This proclivity is born of their determination to resist actively all types of power and authority, fed by the paranoia that comes from ceaseless conspiracy theorizing and from endless suspicion of infiltration or betrayal. At all levels, noninstrumental rebellion could manifest itself as rogue interest groups (whether environmental or economic millenarians, or moral, religious or political fanatics) sanctioning or sponsoring acts of sabotage (such as undermining future plans by the timely public disclosure of sensitive information, and damaging, disabling or destroying property, resources and technology); violence (ranging from disorderly conduct, criminal lawlessness, riotous behavior, to frenzied mob behavior aimed at property and authority figures); and terrorism or assassination by zealots.

Fatalists. Fatalists would be surprised if anyone is, repeatedly, able to anticipate and explain governance failure. This would mean that the social world they thought to be capricious is, indeed, knowable to an acceptable degree of probability, and thus can be effectively managed, which means that their isolation has been in vain.

Disillusioned fatalists would be attracted to hierarchical governance if it became apparent to them that correcting governance failure is important and could only be achieved by adopting the hierarchical governance prescriptions espoused by an hierarchical elite. They would need to have decided to abandon their isolationism. They would also have to be convinced that a hierarchical elite has demonstrated that it is able to understand the causes of governance problems and has found appropriate solutions. It would also mean that they would have to reject their faith in nonrationality, and their belief that people take unpredictable action in the light of how they make sense of what others say and do. They would also have to abandon their indifference to authority and be willing to become members of a structured, orderly and paternalistic hierarchy; to confront their inability to engage personally with a hierarchically ordered social environment; and to accept that gaining the approval of new authority figures is more important than seeing themselves as survivors despite the odds that fate decrees.

Fatalists would be attracted to interactive governance if it became apparent to them that correcting governance failure is important and could only be achieved by them voicing their concerns and demanding the introduction of interactive governance processes that engage with those who are expected to change their behavior. They would need to have decided to abandon their isolationism. They would also have to be convinced that governance success requires

---

[5] Writers as diverse as Koestler (1967), Arendt (1963, 1963b) and Milgram (1963) have come to the conclusion that people are capable of destroying themselves, others and even the planet in order to gain social approval or in loyalty to their in-group.

the governed to be morally committed to the governance outcomes sought, so necessitating their engagement in the construction of mutually acceptable governance failure solutions that evoke moral commitment. It would also mean that they would have to reject their faith in nonrationality, and their belief that people take predictable action in the light of how they make sense of what others say and do. They would also have to abandon their indifference to values discourse; to confront their inability to engage personally with an egalitarian social environment, so as to be able to negotiate their relationships with other people as equals and engage with them on issues of common concern; to confront their inability to relate to their human environment closely enough to be able to engender and demonstrate, continually, their commitment to the common cause; and to accept that gaining the recognition and acclaim of those who are committed to their new governance cause is more important than seeing themselves as survivors despite the odds that fate decrees.

Fatalists would be attracted to market self-regulation only if it became apparent to them that correcting governance failure is important and could only be achieved by the market being left to regulate itself by means of enforceable contracts with a zero noncompliance tolerance and with full restitution as the ultimate sanction. They would need to have decided to abandon their isolationism. They would also have to reject their faith in nonrationality, and their belief that people take predictable action in the light of how they make sense of what others say and do. They would have to be convinced that law-abiding buyers and sellers, who conduct their affairs in accordance with their contractual obligations and a sense of personal responsibility, can correct governance failures. They would also have to abandon their indifference to material success, and be willing to become networking risk takers seeking conspicuous material success; to confront their inability to relate personally to their human environment closely enough to identify exploitable entrepreneurial opportunities; and to accept that gaining the recognition and acclaim of materially successful people is more important than seeing themselves as survivors despite the odds that fate decrees.

Most fatalists would probably find it very difficult to cross the governance disillusionment threshold. Most would turn a blind eye to the flow of governance failures, shrugging them off as none of their business. A few might find such apathy more problematic, forcing them to confront their governance despair.

Intransigent fatalists, with their implacable sense of the human condition—as existential, isolated, normless and self-estranged—that confirms their belief that governance events can never be controlled, would see no point in changing their governance mode allegiance. This disposition would make instrumental rebellion pointless and noninstrumental rebellion a nihilistic act,[6] one that fol-

---

[6] Nihilism is a philosophy of negation, rejection or denial of some or all aspects of thought and life (Crosby 1988, Levine 1988). Morally, nihilists reject the possibility of justifying or criticizing moral judgments, on the grounds that such morality is a cloak for egoistic self-seeking. Epistemologically, nihilists deny the possibility of justifying or

lows the failure of apathy as a coping strategy and reflects their belief that there is nothing to approve of in the established governing order.

As *noninstrumental rebels*, fatalists, who can make no sense of governance reality, would lash out, perhaps ritualistically, at the unpredictable and malevolent powers that be, whom they blame for all the undesirable governance outcomes they experience. They would see themselves as being subject to binding governance prescriptions, which inevitably frustrate any steps they might wish to take toward greater self-determination, with their compliance born of an alienating fear of force, threat and menace. At all levels, noninstrumental rebellion could manifest itself as rogue individual acts of sabotage (such as damaging, disabling or destroying property, resources and technology); violence (ranging from protests, criminal lawlessness, to riotous behavior toward property and authority figures); or even terrorism or assassination.

Individualists. Individualists would be surprised if market operators cannot specify completely, and enforce, their implicit and explicit contracts, with a zero noncompliance tolerance and full restitution as the ultimate sanction. This would reveal that buyers and sellers cannot enhance their own self-interests, which means that the market cannot be left to self-regulate its transactions.

Disillusioned individualists would be attracted to interactive governance only if it became apparent to them that market self-governance failure could only be corrected by them voicing their concerns about the inability of the market to regulate itself, and demanding the introduction of governance processes that engage with those who are expected to change their behavior. They would have to be convinced that governance success requires those involved to have a commitment to the governance outcomes being sought. It also means that they would have to reject their faith in the objectivity of reality and in synoptical, instrumental, functional and strategic reasoning, as well as their belief that people take predictable action in the social world because they interpret their social reality from the perspective of their own self-interest. They would also have to abandon their actively self-interested preference for networked, spontaneous exchange relationships and be willing to engage with people who share their concerns; to confront their suppressed true feelings in favor of making the necessary values commitment concomitant with a group engagement that continually demands that they demonstrate their commitment to their new-found interactive governance cause; and to accept that gaining the recognition and acclaim of those who are committed to their new interactive governance cause is more important than gaining the recognition and acclaim of materially successful people.

---

criticizing knowledge claims, on the grounds that there are no infallible universal truths by which they can be judged. Politically, nihilists call for the destruction of existing political institutions. Thus nihilists are willing to engage in what some people regard as immoral actions "against those whom they believe to be their enemies; in this regard their moral consciences are dulled by the fanatical zeal with which they seek to realize their purely negative, destructive aims....They are indifferent to promises, treaties, or agreements, to the needs, rights, and lives of human beings" (Stack 1977: 186–87, n. 54).

Individualists would be attracted to hierarchical governance only if it became apparent to them that market self-governance failure could only be corrected by adopting the hierarchical governance prescriptions espoused by a hierarchical elite. They would have to be convinced that the hierarchical elite has demonstrated that it is able to understand how a market operates, its problems, and their solutions. It also means that they would have to reject their belief that people take predictable action in the social world only after actively interpreting their social reality from the perspective of their own self-interest. They would also have to abandon their actively self-interested preference for networked, spontaneous exchange relationships and become members of a structured, orderly and paternalistic hierarchy; to confront their true feelings in favor of engagement with groups with hierarchically determined inequalities and differentiations; and to accept that gaining the approval of authority figures is more important than gaining the recognition and acclaim of materially successful people.

Individualists would be attracted to a governance mode that does not expect people's constructive engagement, only if it became apparent to them that no amount of such engagement in any governance mode can contribute to the correction of market self-governance failure. This means that they would have to be convinced of the improbability of anybody's constructive engagement contributing to the reversal of governance failures. It also means that they would have to reject their faith in the objectivity of reality and in synoptical, instrumental, functional and strategic reasoning, as well as their belief that people take predictable action in the social world because they actively interpret their social reality from the perspective of their own self-interest. They would also have to abandon their actively self-interested preference for networked, spontaneous, exchange relationships, and become loners and survivors who are indifferent to material success; to confront their suppressed true feelings about no longer being committed to themselves; and to accept that seeing themselves as survivors despite the odds that fate decrees is more important than gaining the recognition and acclaim of materially successful people.

Most individualists would, no doubt, find it difficult to cross the governance disillusionment threshold and change their governance mode allegiance, for it would mean abandoning their commitment to themselves. Some would, of course, be willing to do so if they saw no other way of fulfilling that commitment. Others would not even bother to question their governance views; they may simply confront their governance despair.

Intransigent individualists, with their implacable sense of what is in their self-interest, would feel confident that they should facilitate the imposition of market self regulation on the collective.[7] Their first inclination would thus be toward instrumental rebellion targeted on procuring control over, or at least

---

[7] Intransigent individualists would have sympathy with the German philosopher Max Stirner's view, expressed in *The Ego and His Own* (1845), that the authority of all social and political institutions must be rejected, along with all moral principles, because they are obstacles to freedom of individual ego and will (see K. Taylor 1996a).

gaining the strategic support of, the governors. At the corporate level, this could manifest itself as active shareholders building corporate voting support to gain board control or to reform corporate governance processes (such as the adoption of a code of ethical conduct); hostile corporate takeovers contrived by disgruntled institutional shareholders; shareholder groups engaging in oppositional rhetoric, orchestrating passive resistance (such as boycotts of corporate goods and services, or disclosing information about corporate failures). At the societal and global levels, it could involve the use of legitimate economic incentives (such as loans and job-creating investments) or acts of bribery.

As *instrumental rebels*, individualists would subscribe to the belief that the imposition of market self-regulation is such an unexceptionable goal that it justifies whatever means are necessary to achieve it. They would see no moral or ethical risks involved, for the market will is sacrosanct. They would seek to shift vital governance decisions away from formalized decision-making systems and on to informal networks, where they would stress the importance of having maximum freedom to negotiate implicit contractual terms on ends and means of governance reform, without any constraints on their private dealings. They would see the governors as self-seeking and malleable, whose efforts can be focused and channeled to achieve mutually beneficial outcomes (Rose-Ackerman 1978). Thus, they would negotiate with the governors to determine which governance failure problems should be solved and by what means, so as to identify which governance goals should be sought on the basis of how best to create short-term opportunities for their self-interested exploitation. Individualist *instrumental rebels* would presume that the governors, by accepting the personal and other benefits specified in their implicit contracts, have given their implicit consent to the governance solutions adopted to stem the flow of governance failures. They would demand that information on governance reform arrangements be treated in a highly pragmatic and utilitarian way, thereby ensuring that consensual apathy is the popular response.

Only in the event of the governors being unresponsive to their overtures would intransigent individualists consider resorting to noninstrumental rebellion, with the intent of undermining, or even destroying, the governors' power. They would do this by engaging in hostile predatory actions intended to maximize their short-term self-interested outcomes without any reference to the short- and long-term costs borne by the governors. They would do so being concerned only for their bottom lines, utterly indifferent to the consequences of their actions on others, for which they would not accept contractual responsibility, preferring to lay the blame at the feet of the rogue governors who are not prepared to compromise. At all levels, this could manifest itself as individual acts of sabotage (such as during a hostile corporate takeover bid selling equity to a corporate bidder, criminal lawlessness, and riotous behavior toward property and authority figures); or even terrorism or assassination.

GOVERNORS' COUNTERRESPONSES

The response of governors to any resistance to their governance processes by those they seek to govern, who have crossed the governance despair threshold, depends on two considerations. The first is whether the resistance manifested itself as acts of withdrawal or acts of rebellion. The second relates to the governance truths they hold. If governors have an incorrect definition of the causes of governance failures they are responding to, because of their flawed governance truths, then their governance responses could elicit new behaviors from the despairing governed. These could make their incorrect understanding of the governance situation come true—thus becoming a self-fulfilling prophecy—and thereby reinforcing in their minds the correctness of their original understanding, and thus of their governance responses. This could well exacerbate any paranoiac tendencies they may have. If, further, the governors are inclined to explain the resistance to their governance processes in terms of the despairing governed being in a state of false consciousness,[8] then the reinforced correctness of their solution to governance failure may well lead them to draw the further lesson that they must redouble their efforts to impose that 'correct' solution. This would then exacerbate any paranoiac tendencies the increasingly despairing governed may have. If, still further, the governors are inclined to label those who resist their 'correct' governance processes as "folk devils," and thereby showing the governed "which [deviant] roles should be avoided...[so becoming] visible reminders of what we should not be" (S. Cohen 1972: 67), then they may well further strengthen the intransigence of counterresponses, thereby initiating a reinforcing series of polarizing self-fulfilling prophecies.[9]

Hierarchist Governors' Responses

Hierarchist governors, who seek to understand the social world by looking through a naturalist-structuralist lens, would see the despairing as nonconformists who do not understand the nature of, or refuse to accept the reality of, a structured social world.[10] They would initially see those who have withdrawn—

---

[8] A false consciousness implies "a misconception of reality, or one's relationship to the world of which one is a part" (Apperley 1996a: 176).

[9] The labeling of people whose behavior is considered deviant, as part of a social control process, can induce an amplification of that deviant behavior (S. Cohen 1972). Social control measures that stigmatize and isolate deviants, and perhaps even give rise to a sense of persecution, encourage them, as a means of defense, attack or adjustment to the situation they find themselves in, to define themselves in terms of the deviant identity implied by the labeling, and to associate with others who are so labeled. In so doing they are exposing themselves to reinforcing stereotyping and stereotypical beliefs. This could well initiate further paranoid reactions from those who consider them to be threatening, which can be mobilized to contribute to the achievement of the desired degree of social control (Adorno et al. 1950).

[10] Hierarchical governors with an authoritarian personality (Adorno et al. 1950) would demand conformity and submission to authority, would be arrogant toward any nonconformists, and would be ever ready to punish them rather than to tolerate the ambi-

the *hermits*—as a challenge rather than a threat, as they would take their apathy to mean consent. They would use their expert or knowledge power to try and convince them that they know best. Hierarchical governors would also use their manipulative power over economic and social institutions to transform their behavior, perhaps calling upon their sense of duty to a benevolent hierarchical order. If, however, continual withdrawal becomes a threat to hierarchical order, they would feel justified, for the common good of the collective, in exercising of their legitimate physical or coercive power to make it increasingly more difficult, and ultimately impossible, for people to achieve or to sustain withdrawal. In a corporate setting, shareholders can be stopped from selling their shares. In a societal setting, emigration can be stopped by physical force or coercion, and perhaps even state terror. In a global setting, those seeking to disengage from one international organization or regime can be stopped from doing so by the threat of physical or economic retaliation.

In contrast, hierarchical governors would immediately recognize that the hostility, resentfulness and revengefulness of *rebels* make them a threat to their hierarchical order. They would use their legitimate power to coerce or force from the *rebels* the necessary behavioral conformity.[11] Their interests can never be permitted to override the collective's, in fear of the hierarchical governors losing control or public trust. In exercising their authority, hierarchical governors would strengthen controls to make noncompliance more difficult, and ultimately impossible. This they could do by imposing, or threatening to impose, ever more stringent formal negative sanctions, and by using ritual and sacrifice to support their moral code. These punitive restraints may well be reinforced by informal social controls, initiated perhaps by the governors' pejorative labeling of deviant behavior, which both feeds, and feeds upon, any extant paranoia that is the product of a perceived personal threat. The response the governors would ultimately expect would be compliance induced by cognitive commitment derived from a rational calculation in the context of structural processes, such as prescribed rules and regulations. Then, the *rebels* would be ready to have instilled in them a deontological moral code that builds an affirmative attitude to hierarchical power and authority, one that is based on trust, loyalty and obedience in return for security and safety. They would then expect the *rebels* to change their attitudes and behavior as they come to understand and accept the appropriate hierarchical behavior and attitude norms. Such an approach is unlikely to convince those who see knowledge as a social construct or who deny the causal capability of social structures. If, ultimately, they fail to achieve cal-

---

guity they connote. These traits would be amplified if a paranoid reaction follows the perception of the nonconformist as a personal threat.

[11] They would take comfort from Skinner's (1971) derogation of free will. He believes that people must relinquish their belief in free will and self-determination, and come to accept that forces outside themselves control them. Only then will they become more responsive to those controlling forces that reinforce what is naturally acceptable to people, namely, more orderly and mannerly behaviors. This would bring to an end the normlessness and unpredictability of the relatively random world they live in.

culative compliance, then force or coercion would be used to make noncompliance impossible. At the corporate level, this could involve dismissal or threats of dismissal. At the societal level, it could mean imprisonment. At the global level, it could mean war.

Enclavist Governors' Responses

Enclavist governors, who seek to understand the social world by looking through a hermeneutic-structuralist lens, would see the despairing as lacking in moral commitment because they lack a sense of belonging, an unfortunate product of past social formations. They would believe that, given an opportunity, they would definitely have a capacity for real moral progress. They would see *hermits* as a threat because their apathy can be contagious, so threatening to undermine the desire of others to engagement in real participation. In contrast, they would see *rebels* as a real challenge to their capacity to convert outsiders. In both instances they would exercise personal, persuasive and integrative power to induce the engagement of both *hermits* and *rebels* in interactive governance processes, in the expectation of achieving their authentic conformity because of their moral commitment to the norms of interactive governance. This would enable enclavist governors to engage with them, with a view to developing a set of belief-based governance rules and standards to which all can be morally committed. They would expect this to elicit their willingness to make voluntary sacrifices for the collective. Such an approach, however, is unlikely to convince those who see knowledge as objective, or who deny the causal capacity of social discourse. If continual refusal to engage becomes a threat to the enclavist governors' ability to manage successfully the interactive governance process, then they would feel themselves justified in expelling and disempowering any *rebels* who refuse to engage with them, in order to sustain the consensus achieved. At all levels, those who are expelled or withdraw from an interactive governance mechanism can be stopped from disclosing details of the governance failures caused by inappropriate governance norms and standards, and prohibited from having any involvement with those remaining under its jurisdiction.

Individualist Governors' Responses

Individualist governors, who seek to understand the social world by looking through a naturalist-agency lens, would see the despairing as lacking in self-interest motivation. They would consider that, given the opportunity, they would embrace a desire for material success, and thus their efforts can be focused and channeled by appropriate incentives, even disincentives.[12] They would see *hermits* as a threat, because their indifference to material success can be contagious, undermining the willingness of others to engage in market trans-

---

[12] Those individualist governors with narcissist tendencies would be inclined toward punishing those who threaten their highly favorable view of themselves (Bushman and Baumeister 1998).

actions even if the benefits exceed the costs of so doing. In contrast, they would see *rebels* as a real challenge to their capacity to negotiate a contractual relationship that produces an agreement on which governance failure problems should be solved and how, on the basis of creating short-term opportunities for mutual exploitation. In both instances they would increasingly exercise reward, exchange or economic power to induce instrumental compliance, on the basis of net compliance cost calculations, to a set of governance rules and standards that entail rights. This would enhance their negative freedom, albeit as well as their duties, but any sacrifices they would be expected to make for the collective would be minimized. Such an approach is unlikely to convince those who view knowledge as socially constructed, or who deny the causal capability of individual intention. If failure to achieve instrumental compliance becomes a threat to the individualist governors' ability to manage self-governance processes, then they would exit and seek to renegotiate all the affected contractual relationships.

THE DESPAIRING GOVERNED'S REACTION

Governors' responses to resistance to their governance processes shown by the despairing governed will, of course, solicit counterresponses from them. If, indeed, the despairing governed also have an incorrect understanding of the governance failure they are responding to, because of their flawed governance truths, then their responses could evoke new behaviors from the governors that could make their incorrect understanding of the governance situation come true. This would further reinforce the apparent correctness of their solutions to governance failure, and thus the appropriateness of their counterresponses to the governors' responses. This, in turn, could well exacerbate any paranoiac tendencies they may have. The consequence is a self-fulfilling prophecy that could make them even more intolerant of the governors and their processes.

Hermits' Reaction

Any calls for reengagement with unconscionable governors would fall on deaf ears and solicit an apathetically dismissive response from *hermits*. If governors become persistent with their use of coercive, persuasion or reward powers to induce such a reengagement, because they have defined the cause of any resistance to their governance processes in terms of *hermits* being nonconformists (if they are hierarchists), lacking in moral commitment (if they are enclavists) or lacking in self-interest motivation (if they are individualists), then they should not be surprised if the behavior solicited by their decision to strengthen controls over them (if they are hierarchists), to disempower them (if they are enclavists) or to increase incentives for them (if they are individualists), induces *hermits* to be apathetic and dismissive. The governors would, of course, draw the conclusion that *hermits* are, indeed, nonconformists, or lacking in moral commitment or in self-interest motivation, so justifying a hardening of their respective positions. From the *hermits'* perspective, if they define the governance situation in the light of the governors' responses as one of harassment, because they are being forced, cajoled or bribed into reengagement, then the governors' further, hardened, responses to their dismissive and apathetic reactions would only confirm that interpretation, so justifying further withdrawal. This would initiate further sanctions, perhaps labeling and even more paranoia from the governors, thus worsening the governance resistance of the *hermits*, perhaps even inciting them into a rebellious reengagement with the governors.

Intransigent Hierarchists' Reaction

With their strong sense of trust and confidence in, and thus commitment to, the hierarchical elite, intransigent hierarchists would define the unconscionable governors' responses as either intellectually absurd or institutionally naïve, or possibly both. If enclavist or individualist governors have defined the cause of resistance to their governance processes in terms of, respectively, a lack of moral commitment, or a lack of self-interest motivation, then they should not be surprised if the behaviorial response induced from intransigent hierarchists is to plot and plan further a seizure or assumption of power. This they would do believing that they still have a duty, for the common good of the collective, to impose hierarchical governance structures and processes through the exercising of physical or coercive power, if necessary. Governors would, of course, draw the conclusion that intransigent hierarchists are, indeed, lacking in moral commitment or in self-interest motivation, thus justifying a further hardening of their respective positions. From the intransigent hierarchists' perspective, if they define the governance situation in the light of the governors' responses as an affront to their sense of obligation to the hierarchical elite, because they are being threatened with disempowerment or bribed to gain their compliance to a governance process that they are implacably opposed to, then the governors' further hardened responses to their more defiant reactions only confirm that interpretation. This would justify even more instrumental rebellion, which, in turn, would initiate further sanctions, perhaps labeling, and even more paranoia from, thus hardening even further the governance resistance of intransigent hierarchists. If such a seizure of power is deemed by the experts to be unachievable, then they would resort to acts of noninstrumental rebellion.

Intransigent Enclavists' Reaction

With their strong sense of moral indignation, intransigent enclavists would define the unconscionable governors' responses as an unacceptable affront to their socially constructed, belief-based governance norms, rules and standards. If hierarchist or individualist governors have defined the cause of resistance to their governance processes in terms of, respectively, an unwillingness to conform or a lack of self-interest motivation, then they should not be surprised if the behaviorial response induced from intransigent enclavists is to adopt a more defiant posture, which makes compromise more unthinkable and negotiations more impossible. The governors would, of course, draw the conclusion that the intransigent enclavists are, indeed, nonconformists or lacking in self-interest motivation, thus justifying a further hardening of their respective positions. From the intransigent enclavists' perspective, if they define the governance situation in the light of the governors' responses as an affront to their sense of justice, because they are being threatened with force by those in hierarchical citadels of privilege, or offered bribes by rapacious, self-centered people to gain their compliance to a governance process to which they are implacably opposed, then the governors' further hardened responses to their more defiant reactions only confirm that interpretation, thus justifying even more and stronger instrumentally rebellious responses. This would initiate further sanctions, perhaps labeling, and even more paranoia from the governors, thus worsening the governance resistance of intransigent enclavists even further. Their proclivity for noninstrumental rebellion would be enhanced by the recalcitrant, hard-line behavior of intransigent governors, which is fed by their suspicions of infiltration or betrayal born of their predilection for conspiracy theories.

Intransigent Individualists' Reaction

With their strong sense of what is in their own self-interest, intransigent individualists would define the unconscionable governors' responses as an unacceptable affront to their self-interest. If hierarchist or enclavist governors have defined the cause of resistance to their governance processes in terms of, respectively, an unwillingness to conform or the lack of moral commitment, then they should not be surprised if the behaviorial response induced from intransigent individualists is to seek out those governors in front of whom they could dangle "the golden bait of avarice" (Miller 1845: 6), in order to negotiate an acceptable way of achieving mutually beneficial agreement on how best to address governance failure. The governors would, of course draw the conclusion that the intransigent individualists are, indeed, nonconformists or lacking in moral commitment, thus justifying a hardening of the governors' respective positions. From the intransigent individualists' perspective, if they define the governance situation in the light of the governors' responses as an affront to their self-interest, because they are being threatened with force or disempowerment to gain their compliance to a governance process that they are implacably opposed to, then the governors' further hardened responses to their more persistent reactions only confirm that interpretation, thus justifying a response that undermines or destroys the power of the governors. This would initiate further sanctions, perhaps labeling, and even more paranoia from the governors, thus worsening the governance resistance of intransigent individualists even further.

Intransigent Fatalists' Reaction

Because they reject the philosophical premises to any of the modes of governance, intransigent fatalists would consider the governors' threats of force or disempowerment, or offers of inducements, to gain their compliance to be pointless. If governors have defined the cause of resistance to their governance processes in terms of deviance and nonconformity (if they are hierarchists), the lack of moral commitment (if they are enclavists) or the lack of self-interest motivation (if they are individualists), then they should not be surprised if the behavioral response induced from intransigent fatalists is to plunge enthusiastically into more acts of nihilistic rebellion. By so doing, they are showing the governors that they are, indeed, nonconformists, or lacking in moral commitment or self-interest motivation, thus justifying a hardening of the governors' respective positions. From the intransigent fatalists' perspective, if they define the governance situation in the light of the governors' responses as inevitably alienating, because they expect to be threatened with force or disempowerment, or bribed, to gain their compliance to a governance process that they see no point in, then the governors' further hardened responses to their rebellious acts only confirm that interpretation. This, in turn, justifies even more extreme acts of nihilistic rebellion, which would initiate further sanctions, perhaps labeling, and even more paranoia, from the governors, thus worsening the governance resistance of intransigent fatalists even further.

ON GOVERNABILITY

The ability of governors to govern is inversely related to their ability to see beyond their own governance truths, for that determines the degree to which there is an *unresponsive dialogue*—one voice drowning out all the others—because of the polarization of governance truths underpinning the governance mode that dominates a governance process; a *dialogue of the deaf* (Hirschman 1991)—all the voices talking but none listening and thus no engagement because of the polarization of governance truths underpinning the governance modes competing for dominance of a governance process; or a *constructive dialogue*, where those who govern create enabling and empowering processes that enhance tolerance of competing governance truths (Thompson 2000b).

Unresponsive Governance Dialogues

The domination of a governance process by governors who accept only the governance truths of one *social solidarity*, or of an incomplete coalition,[13] is unsustainable. The explanations offered for the inevitable instances of governance failure induce hard-line responses from the threatened governors. This makes them increasingly more detached from their chameleonic supporters and thus increasingly in need of the endorsement of their intransigent supporters. Once a threat to the governors' hegemony can be identified, their inclination would be to strengthen the governance structures and process by adopting a

---

[13] This is a coalition that excludes adherents to at least one of the *social solidarities*. Wildavsky (1998) argues that *social solidarities* that do not share a dimensional position on the *social map* attract, while those that do, repel. Thus, he argues that hierarchists and individualists are inclined to enter into coalitions, as are enclavists and fatalists. Of crucial importance is the organization of interaction patterns between the coalition partners, which may well identify the plurality patterns that provide more or less effective governance in a particular relational situation.

harder line toward those who are unwilling to comply because of their intolerance. The threatened governors would deny, with increasing vehemence, any evidence that their governance mode is fundamentally failing. They would also eagerly accept any evidence in support of their preferred apportioning of blame for governance failure and of their preferred solutions. They would forever seek to retrench and abate any governance discourse by their blinkered recourse to fermenting support for simplified solutions. This would, of course, exacerbate governance disillusionment and despair among the governed. Those who are disillusioned would have more reason to reconsider their governance mode allegiance. Those experiencing undiminished cognitive dissonance have even more reason to withdraw from the governance process. The intransigent would have even more reason to engage in acts of rebellion. In response to these threats of withdrawal or rebellion, threatened governors would increasingly strengthen their governance processes, which, in turn, would increasingly incite resistance from those whose behavior they are seeking to change. Thus, threatened governors would have, simultaneously, maintained their dominance of the governance process but diminished their capacity to govern. Ungovernability would undoubtedly follow with time.

Governance Dialogues of the Deaf

A governance process in which adherents to each of the *social solidarities* compete aggressively for the dominance of their governance truths is unsustainable, for their cognitive maps can only provide explanations for the inevitable instances of governance failures that induce intolerant responses, from the threatened or trapped adherents to competing governance modes. Once the trapped governed or the threatened governors (and their supporters) become intransigent, they would inevitably become even more convinced of the rightness of their solutions to governance failure. The trapped governed would accept, with increasing vehemence, any evidence that supports their belief that their governance mode is fundamentally failing. They would also deny any evidence that threatens the efficacy of their solutions to governance failure. The threatened governors (and their supporters) would deny, with similarly increasing vehemence, any evidence that their governance mode is fundamentally failing. They would also wholeheartedly accept any evidence in support of their preferred apportioning of blame for governance failures and of their preferred solutions.

The inclination on all sides would be to become increasingly more insistent that they, and they alone, have the right solution to the unabated flow of governance failures. Each would thus become increasingly more polarized, more isolated. Everyone engaged with the governance process would be seeking to relocate the governance discourse in a way that makes their simplified solutions to governance failures more attractive, in order both to address the threat of their supporters being poached and in the hope of poaching new ones.

This polarization of views would, of course, exacerbate governance disillusionment and despair among the governed. Those who are disillusioned would have more reason to reconsider their governance mode allegiance, but they would find it more difficult to recast their allegiance to one or more of the polarizing governance modes, making withdrawal from the governance process a more attractive option. Those experiencing undiminished cognitive dissonance would have every reason to withdraw from the governance process. The intransigent would have more reason to engage in acts of rebellion.

In response to these threats of withdrawal or rebellion, the threatened governors would strengthen their governance processes. This, in turn, would incite greater resistance from those whose behavior they are seeking to change. Thus, the threatened governors would have, simultaneously, reduced their dominance of the governance process and diminished their capacity to govern. The expected outcome would be a governance process that vacillates, with power shifts within the ranks of potential governors, between the polarizing governance truths. This would inevitably result in the underrecognition and overarticulation of one or more of them in the governance process, and thus in an ever diminishing capacity to resolve conflicts between them. Ungovernability would certainly follow with time.

Constructive Governance Dialogues

A governance process in which governors embrace *communicative rationality*[14] (Habermas 1968, 1971, 1975, 1984, 1986, 1987, 1996a; see also Barnes 1974, Feyerabend 1976, Knorr-Certina 1981, Kuhn 1970) would create enabling and empowering processes[15] that can facilitate the constructive engagement of adherents to all the competing governance truths present,[16] and thereby en-

---

[14] Dryzek (1987: 434) defines *communicative rationality* as:

[A form of social interaction that] is free from domination (the exercise of power), strategic behavior by the actors involved, and (self) deception. Further, all actors should be equally and fully capable of making and questioning arguments (that is, they should be communicatively competent). There should be no restrictions on the participation of these competent actors. Under these conditions, the only remaining authority is that of a good argument, which can be advanced on behalf of the veracity of empirical description, explanation, and understanding, and just as importantly, the validity of normative judgments.

Habermas's (1968) fundamental contention is that through language, communications involves, necessarily, the raising of validity claims, distinguished as truth, rightness and sincerity. The contested status of these can only be resolved, ultimately, through discussion in an ideal speech situation, which he defines as a discourse, with the aim of achieving a consensus (see also Cooke 1994).

[15] Follet ([1940] 1973: 255) rightly observed, with considerable, simple, profundity: "We want worked out a relation between leaders and led which will give each the opportunity to make creative contributions to [a] situation....The best leader knows how to make his (her) followers actually feel power themselves, not merely acknowledge his (her) power."

[16] This raises a contentious issue in Cultural Theory: whether all the *social solidarities* are (as distinct from ought to be) represented in every relational situation (from the family unit, to corporations and societies, through to global organizations and regimes) or

hancing tolerance,[17] especially among the more chameleonic adherents. This would permit and facilitate common recognition, or perhaps even common acceptance, of the validity of competing governance truths. By so doing, boundaries would be placed around governance conflicts, whether occurring among or within adherents to competing governance truths, which could otherwise lead to polarization and, ultimately, ungovernability. The strongest form of this plurality principle[18] holds that consensus is necessary on a specific governance issue, albeit for quite different reasons, if it is to have robustness. This, of course, would give the intransigent of any ilk the power of veto. In its weaker form, this principle holds that agreement among the more chameleonic adherents to competing governance truths present on a general governance approach, or, at least, its more salient strategies, would make it robust enough to survive the con-

---

whether social scale is limiting in this regard. The degree of variety is taken here to be context dependent: the larger the social scale of the relational situation, the greater the probability of adherents to all *social solidarities* being present. What matters, of course, is that the governors need to engage with all adherents to *social solidarities* that are present in a particular relational situation, in order to provide the necessary checks and balances, so as to control their mutual tendencies toward self-destruction, and thereby ensure the closest possible fit with the changing governance environment in which they are seeking to operate viably.

[17] Follett (1918: 212) makes another insightful, pertinent point: "We must remember that most people are not for or against anything; the first object of getting people together is to make them respond somehow, to overcome inertia. To disagree, as well as to agree, with people brings you closer to them."

[18] An underdeveloped tenet of Cultural Theory is its *requisite variety condition*. Thompson (2000b) argues that if, as he sees it, Cultural Theory is about self-organizing social organizations, then the application of the cybernetic law of requisite variety (which holds that to be complete, a control system's complexity must correspond, but not necessarily synoptically mirror, the complexity of the system under its control) can be applied (Ashby 1956, 1960). This, Thompson (2000b) argues, is a necessary, but not sufficient, condition for organizational viability, as measured (Perri 201b) by an organization's (1) "effective capacity to (i.e. it actually does, and it does so not accidentally...) reproduce its basic character and institutions over a cycle of distinct periods", and (2) "effective capacity to...withstand external shocks other than *force majeure*." It means that in any social organization, all, or perhaps a context-dependent mix of, adhertents to each *social solidarities* must be constructively engaged and have their voices heard. This is because of the particular positive net contributions that the *social solidarities* can make to organizational viability. They can each compensate for the weaknesses of another *social solidarity* by, for example, being a reflector of frustrations (as enclavists can be), a producer of resources (as individualists can be), a reproducer of institutions (as hierarchists can be), or an inhibitor of exhausting hyperactivism (as fatalists can be). Cultural Theory identifies the conditions under which (1) adherents to each *social solidarity* should be listened to or ignored and (2) whether a particular mix of *social solidarity* adherents contributes to cultural viability or causes cultural dysfunctionism (Swedlow 2001). Tansay (2001) sums up the situation, with appropriate and considerable apologies to P. T Barnum: "You can probably screw each of the solidarities some of the time; you can screw several of the solidarities for a period of time; but you can't screw any of the solidarities indefinitely, and you certainly can't screw several of them all the time."

flictual reactions of the more intransigent adherents; those who would seek to change it by coup d'etat (if they are intransigent hierarchists), by destabilizing public, persuasive and consciousness-raising governance discourses (if they are intransigent enclavists), by inducements and bribery (if they are intransigent individualists), or by nihilistic acts of destruction (if they are intransigent fatalists).

Reflexive, culturally pluralized governance structures, to the extent that they can draw from, and integrate, the wisdom of all competing governance truths to stem the flow of governance failures, would diminish the tendency toward governance radicalization and polarization. This makes withdrawal from the governance process or acts of rebellion less attractive options, thereby increasing their capacity to govern. Greater cultural plurality would also be likely to stimulate and facilitate creative lateral thinking about governance problems among the more chameleonic adherents to particular governance truths.

CONCLUSION

When the governed and the governors hold mutually incompatible core governance values, attitudes, and opinions, and, as a consequence, prefer different governance modes, they do so because they also not accept the same (flawed) epistemological and ontological assumptions and concomitant rationalistic and nomological predispositions, and thus the same (flawed) governance truths that they underpin. The governed resist their governors' processes because they do not agree on the causes of, and solutions to, incidences of governance failure. Thus conflict is inevitable. This follows a build up of antagonism that leads to disillusionment and, eventually, to despair among the governed, the response to which is withdrawal or rebellion.

Should the governors' responses be premised on an incorrect definition of the causes of governance failure, because their governance truths are incorrect, then they could well elicit new behaviors from the despairing governed, which reinforce in their minds the correctness of their solution. This may well lead them to increased their efforts to impose that 'correct' solution, thereby further strengthening the intransigence of counterresponses of the despairing governed. A reinforcing series of polarizing self-fulfilling prophecies is the likely outcome. Ungovernability would undoubtedly follow with time.

The ability of the governors to govern is inversely related to their ability to see beyond their own governance truths, for that determines the degree to which there is, between governed and governors, an *unresponsive dialogue, dialogue of the deaf,* or a *constructive dialogue,* the latter being one in which the governors create enabling and empowering processes that enhance tolerance. Culturally pluralized governance structures diminish the tendency toward governance radicalization and polarization, and makes either withdrawal from a governance process or acts of rebellion less attractive options, thereby increasing governance capacity.

Appendix 6.1
The Competing Social Solidarities on Antagonisms, Disillusionment and Despair

Dimension	Hierarchist	Enclavist	Fatalist	Individualist
Perspectives on:				
epistemology:	Naturalism.	Hermeneutics.	Hermeneutics.	Naturalism.
ontology:	Structuralism	Agency.	Structuralism.	Agency.
rationality:	Bounded, functional-analytic.	Communicative-value.	Nonrational, inspirational-strategic.	Instrumental, synoptic, functional-strategic.
nomology:	Behavior predictable on the basis of rational thought constrained by group norms.	Behavior predictable on the basis of group-constructed understandings.	Behavior unpredictable.	Behavior predictable on the basis of rational choice.
What would initiate a shift in governance allegiance to:				
hierarchical mode:	If hierarchical governance failure can only be corrected by the minimizing governance structures and processes.	If interactive governance failure can only be corrected by adopting the hierarchical governance prescriptions that reflect an acceptable set of values.	If governance failure can be corrected by adopting the hierarchical governance prescriptions.	If market self-governance failure can only be corrected by adopting the hierarchical governance prescriptions that reflect an understanding of the marketplace.
self-regulation mode:		If interactive governance failure can only be corrected by marketplace being left to regulate itself.	If governance failure can only be corrected by the market being left to regulate itself.	

Dimension	Hierarchist	Enclavist	Fatalist	Individualist
What would initiate a shift in governance allegiance to (cont'd):				
interactive mode:	If hierarchical governance failure can only be corrected by voicing concerns and demanding interactive governance processes that engage with those effected.		If governance failure can only be corrected by them voicing concerns and demanding interactive governance processes that require engagement.	If market self-governance failure can only be corrected by voicing concerns and demanding interactive governance processes that engage with those effected.
no expected constructive governancer engagement:	If no amount of constructive engagement with hierarchical governance mechanisms addresses governance failure.	If no amount of constructive engagement with interactive governance mechanisms addresses governance failure.		If no amount of constructive engagement with market self-regulation addresses governance failure.
Ungovernability accepted:	If their safety and security needs can never be met.	If categorical interests can never be protected.	If survival needs can never be met.	If material wellbeing can never be achieved.
Sources of governance despair:				
cognitive dissonance:	Experienced by chameleonic disillusioned hierarchists.	Experienced by chameleonic disillusioned enclavists.	Experienced by chameleonic disillusioned fatalists.	Experienced by chameleonic disillusioned individualists.
alienation:	Experienced by intransigent hierarchists.	Experienced by intransigent enclavists.	Experienced by intransigent fatalists.	Experienced by intransigent individualists.
Response to governance despair of the chameleonic disillusioned:	Become *hermits*.	Become *hermits*.	Become *hermits*.	Become *hermits*.

Appendix 6.1 (cont'd)

Dimension	Hierarchist	Enclavist	Fatalist	Individualist
Response of the intransigent disillusioned to governance despair:	Instrumental rebellion: a grab for power. Noninstrumental rebellion: only if a power grab is deemed unachievable.	Instrumental rebellion: expel risk takers and traitors. Noninstrumental rebellion: only if incited by intransigent outsiders.	Instrumental rebellion: pointless. Noninstrumental rebellion: nihilistic acts justified.	Instrumental rebellion: procure governors' support by incentives and bribes. Noninstrumental rebellion: only if the governors are intransigent.
As governors, their reaction to:				
those experiencing governance despair:	Obviously, deviants.	The unfortunate products of their past social formations.	Would never be governors.	Lacking in self-interest motivation.
hermits:	Their apathy interpreted as consent initially, but if apathy spreads then they become a threat, justifying use of legitimate physical and coercive power to stop withdrawal.	Their apathy makes them a threat, justifying the use of personal, persuasive and integrative power to induce re-engagement.	Would never be governors.	Their apathy makes them a threat, justifying the use of reward, exchange and economic power to induce re-engagement.
rebels:	Their hostility makes them a threat, justifying use of legitimate physical and coercive power to achieve behavioral conformity.	Their hostility makes them a real challenge, justifying the use of personal, persuasive and integrative power to induce authentic conformity.	Would never be governors.	Their hostility makes them a real challenge, justifying the use of reward, exchange and economic power to induce instrumental conformity.

Dimension	Hierarchist	Enclavist	Fatalist	Individualist
As intransigents, their responses to the governors' reactions would be to:	Redouble efforts to plan and carry out a grab for power.	Carry out acts of noninstrumental rebellion, incited by moral indignation.	Plunge enthusiastically into ever more acts of nihilistic rebellion.	Redouble efforts to seek out those governors whose support can be attained by incentives and bribes, if unsuccessful destroy their power base.
The hermits' reactions to governors' responses would be dismissive. Any persistent use of power would turn them into intransigent rebels.				

7

Conclusion

Quot homines, tot sententiae

Publius Terentius Afer (Terence),
second century BC

"Many men, many opinions." So wrote Terence, the slave who became a great Roman comic dramatist, with a masterly economy of words. Those words neatly capture the essence of the never-ending search by philosophers for truth, which lies at the heart of this book.

The governed's responses—compliant or antagonistic—to their governors' processes of corporate, societal and global governance depend on how they justify, to themselves and to others, the limitations that the governors seek to place on their autonomy. To understand the implications of this for governance capacity, good governance and governability requires a subtle analysis of the governed's plurality of responses to the governors' differentiated processes. Cultural Theory provides such a construct, one that permits a manageable classification and analysis of the opposing sets of beliefs that underlie the behavior observable in both the governed and the governors.

Cultural Theory posits four *social solidarities* that are associated with the four types of social beings: hierarchists, enclavists, fatalists and individualists. Each draws upon a distinctive set of flawed epistemological and ontological propositions, with concomitant rationalistic and nomological predispositions. Each thus offers an idiosyncratic set of flawed governance truths, which inevitably stand in contradistinction to the governance truths posited by the other *social solidarities*. Each stands opposed, as competitor, forever seeking converts. People's allegiance to a particular *social solidarity* in a particular relational situation is determined by the attractiveness of these truths.

Adherents to each of the four *social solidarities* have a distinctive, albeit flawed, perspective on what constitutes good governance. They each accept that corporations, societies and the world are governable, but only if their preferred mode of governing is adopted. They each consider their balance between individual autonomy and collective control to be the only legitimate one; and their approach to the resolution of conflicting claims to be the only acceptable one. They would, inevitably, resist governance processes based on the truths of competing *social solidarities*. As a consequence, the extent to which the governed resist their governors' processes is determined by the extent to which they adhere to the same *social solidarity*.

One product of this governance antagonism between adherents to competing *social solidarities* is governance disillusionment, even despair, a consequence of an accumulation of surprises caused by becoming cognizant of unexpected governance failures. Alienation is source of this governance despair, and it has two origins. The first is the alienation that flows from the unremitting antagonism felt by the governed when governors of a different ilk are forever adopting the 'wrong' solutions to governance failure, because they steadfastly refuse to accept that their solutions are the 'correct' ones. The second is the alienation that flows from the undiminished cognitive dissonance experienced by those who have been unable to modify their good-governance belief patterns so as to align them with their perceptions of governance reality.

Once they have crossed the threshold of governance despair, two responses are open to the governed: to withdraw or to rebel. The chameleonic disillusioned are increasingly inclined toward withdrawal, so becoming *hermits*. They become increasingly intolerant of the governors' failing governance processes, as the realization dawns upon them that each of the governance modes is underpinned by a flawed set of governance truths, causing them to abandon gradually all hope that solutions can be found to the continual flow of governance failures. The intransigent disillusioned, who find themselves becoming more and more hostile toward the governors, are increasingly inclined toward acts of instrumental or noninstrumental rebellion against the powers that be and their authority.

The governors could choose to take steps to reduce the threat to governability posed by disillusionment and despair by stopping the governed from withdrawing or rebelling. Their responses to any resistance to their governance processes depends on whether that resistance manifests itself as acts of withdrawal or acts of rebellion, and on the strength of adherence to their governance truths. If their response is one of intransigence, then they may well be strengthening the intransigence of the governed's counterresponses, thereby initiating a reinforcing series of polarizing, self-fulfilling prophecies. The governors face threats to the soundness of their governance process from the intransigent, who, they believe, can be bought, cajoled or coerced into abandoning rebellion. The governors, however, face a real threat to their power by those who have disempowered them by withdrawing from their sphere of influence; the shareholders who sell their equity in a failing corporation, the political émigré who flees a failing state, a maverick national political elite that withdraws its state from a failing global governance mechanism. In responding to these threats to their power, the governors need to be mindful of the Nietzschean proposition that "Power as the pursuit of power inevitably founders in the void that lies behind. The Will to Power begets the problem of nihilism....Power for power's sake, no matter how far the power has extended, leaves always the dread of the void beyond" (Barrett 1958: 181).

The ability of the governors to govern is inversely related to their ability to see beyond their own fundamentally flawed governance truths, and thus to build a new governance consensus around a configuration of governance truths drawn from the epistemological and ontological wisdom underpinning all the *social solidarities* (see Dixon and Dogan 2002a, 2002b and 2002c).

The contemporary philosophy of social sciences offers a way forward in the face of the incompatible contentions of the epistemological and ontological dichotomies, through the diverse philosophical and methodological work of Archer (1990, 1995, 1996), Bourdieu (1998), Bhaskar (1975, 1998), Giddens (1979, 1981, 1984, 1990) and Habermas (1969, 1971, 1975, 1984). They herald a very clear attempt to address both the epistemological limitations of naturalism and hermeneutics, resulting in the *trancendental realism* synthesis (Bhaskar 1998), and the ontological inadequacies of structure and agency, resulting in the *(post)structuration* synthesis (Archer 1995; Bourdieu 1998; Giddens 1984, 1993).

Trancendental realism is concerned with the factual description of the real world, and offers a process by which its causal mechanisms can be described (Bhaskar 1998). It makes two fundamental claims. The first is that the real world operates at three levels: the *actual* (events or processes as they are), the *empirical* (the perceived nature of those events or processes open to the observer) and the *deep* (the underlying mechanisms or imperatives that cause these events or processes) (Baert 1998: 191). Bhaskar (1998: 11) draws a distinction between the *transitive objects* or phenomena (objects or phenomena as they are experienced) and the *intransitive objects* or phenomena (objects or phenomena as they are in reality). Thus, knowledge of the real world rests on unreliable empirical perceptions of the *actual* world, which is quite removed from any *deep* explanations of it. He (Bhaskar 1998: 11) explains the difference: "It is clearly a condition of intelligibility of scientific discovery that, in the intransitive dimension, what is discovered, exists independently of its discovery; and that, in the intransitive dimension, it is not known prior to its discovery."

The second claim made by *trancendental realism* is that knowledge of the real world is a cumulative process of hermeneutics-based, imaginative model building, whereby transitive knowledge is used to postulate hypothetical causal mechanisms that, if they exist, would explain any intransitive phenomenon under investigation. Thus, science involves the identification of a phenomenon, the postulation of its explanation, the empirical corroboration of this explanation, and the discovery of its intransitive generative mechanism, which, in turn, becomes a new phenomenon to be explained. This leads progressively to deeper levels of explanation. As Bhaskar (1998: 12) observes, "science must construct and test its explanations with the cognitive resources and physical tools at its disposal, which in the process are themselves progressively formed, modified and refined."

Transcendental realism does not overcome the uncertainties of naturalism— the problems of induction and the theory-laden nature of observation (Popper [1959] 2000)—but Bhaskar's recognition of the contingent nature of scientific explanation releases him from the constraints of strict falsification and from the need to preclude the sustainability of apparently falsified theories. It also potentially reconciles the hermeneutics aspects of scientific discovery identified by Kuhn (1970) with an empirical-based approach to choosing the hypothesis or theory that best explains available data (retroduction or abduction), that is, to inference to the best explanation (see Wendt 1999: 62–63).

The challenge of reconciling the ontological inadequacies of structure and agency has been the *(post)structuration* synthesis. Giddens (1984, 1993) asserts that there is an identity (duality rather than (analytical) dualism) relationship between structure and agency. He argues that social structures exist "only in so far as forms of social conduct are reproduced chronically across time and space" (1984, p. xxi); and that human agents "have, as an inherent aspect of what they do, the capacity to understand what they do while they do it" (1984, p. xxii). "The reflexive capacities of the human actor are characteristically involved in a continuous manner with the flow of day-to-day conduct in the contexts of social activity" (1984, p. xxiii). He thereby conflates structure and agency, which involves, as Archer (1996: 687) explains, "a decentering of the subject…because human beings become people…only through drawing upon structural properties to generate social practices, [and] there is an equivalent demotion of structure, which becomes real…only when instantiated by agency…neither structure nor agency have independent or autonomous features, but only properties which are manifest in, and reproduced or transformed through, social practice." This creates, according to Archer (1982: 457; see also 1995), "an image of society, not as a series of acts, but as a continuous flow of conduct which changes or maintains a potentially malleable social world," one that is populated by actors who are "hyperactive" and able to "enjoy very high degrees of freedom" (Archer 1990: 77) and who "cannot escape contributing to reproduction [of structures] as every bit of their behavior is implicated in it" (Parker 2000: 78–79).

Archer's (1996: 680) *poststructurationist* ontological synthesis places structure and agency in an analytically dualist or morphogenetic relationship, which means that, with time (Archer 1996) and power (Bourdieu (1998), structure is both a cause and a consequence of agency. Analytical dualism (or morphogeneses) asserts that " the relationship between agency and structure is one of historical alternation between the conditioning of agents by structures and the elaboration of structure by interacting agents. Given time, systems can be both cause and caused, as can agency" (Parker 2000: 74–75).

The combination of these epistemological and ontological syntheses suggests a fifth methodological position. This presumes a social world in which structures and agency have properties that are manifest in, and reproduced or transformed through, social practice, but in which events or processes actually exist, the nature of which can be only unreliably and contestedly perceived by observers. The knowledge gained through social practice can be used to generate hypothetical causal explanations for the observed events or processes, for which empirical corroboration needs to be sought. The discovery of intransitive generative mechanisms, however, becomes a new phenomenon that needs, itself, to be explained. Progressively, this methodology generates deeper explanations of the social world.

When applied to governance this synthesized methodology facilitates, progressively, the reaching of deeper levels of understanding of governance events and processes, permits more subtle explanations of governance problems, and facilitates the enhancement of organizational learning through the reflexive capacities of those it empowers.

In seeking to understand the causation of governance failure, transcendental realists would accept that governance events and processes exist, but they would be skeptical of any empirical generalizations about their causation derived from naturalist methods, which they would treat only as preliminary working hypotheses. They would search for a deep understanding of the underlying causation mechanism or imperatives. This would require them to engage with other relevant actors in acts of reflexive interpretation of governance problems, so as to ensure that they have an appropriate contextualization of meaning. This would involve the application of hermeneutics methods enabling them to identify perspective reciprocities that result from acts of ideation resting on intersubjectively shared symbols. This cumulative process of hermeneutics-based imaginative governance model building involves transitive knowledge being used to postulate hypothetical causal mechanisms that would explain, if any can be demonstrated to exist, the relevant intransitive governance phenomena. This would involve a search for empirical corroboration. If such confirmation is possible, then new intransitive generative mechanisms would have been discovered, which, in turn, become new phenomena that need to be explained. Transcendental realism thus leads progressively to deeper levels of explanation of governance events or processes, thereby permitting more subtle explanations of governance problems.

In seeking to identify how best to deal with governance problems for which subtle explanation has been found and agreed on, *(post)structurationists* would accept that people engaged in governance processes have the necessary reflexive capacities to solve governance problems, but that it can only be actualized, so becoming meaningful human action, when people are empowered and enabled to draw on the structural properties of governance mechanisms. This reflexive capacity is the embodied understanding that people gain by engaging with governance practice, thereby enabling them to learn by trial and error and from the mistakes made by others, so as to determine the relevance of general principles (such as rules, recipes, formal procedures and judgmental criteria). By this means they are able to garner the understanding needed to solve governance problems as they conduct their affairs with, and within, governance mechanisms. The resultant social practice, mobilized as it is in a continuous manner with the flow of day-to-day conduct, will, in turn, transform the enabling structural properties. This creates the potential for further governance problems, thus necessitating the prospect of further organizational learning as a byproduct of the continuing search for problem explanation and solution.

The governance process is a bumpy road along which there are precious few signposts. The message that both Cultural Theory and social theory offers to the governors is a simple one: to nurture the constructive dynamic plurality of governance propositions needed to build a consensus on, at least, the salient dimensions of good governance. The governance process must be seen as an environment in which competing governance desires are confronted, assessed and integrated. This means a freeing of both the governors and the governed from their self-imposed, fundamentally flawed, epistemological and ontological straightjackets, with the prospects of increased governance capacity thereby enhanced.[1] This may well require what Thompson (1993, 2001) describes as "clumsy institutions."[2] In such organizations, governors would accept the following propositions.

First, adherents to competing governance truths will never agree because they are based on mutually incompatible sets of epistemological, ontological, rationalistic and nomological assumptions. Second, there are no correct (or failure proof) governance truths, merely governance suppositions. Third, governance problems may not be solvable but they must be managed. Fourth, good governance is an essentially contested concept that can only be clarified through constructive and inclusive discourses. Fifth, constructive governance discourses, rather than being a threat to the power and authority of governors, are creative opportunities for people with disparate governance perspectives to find solutions to threatening governance problems. Sixth, the governors need to be able to establish ways of ensuring intelligent and creative dialogical relationships between the slow learners (hierarchists and enclavists) and fast learners (fatalists and individualists). Seventh, the governors must learn to comprehend and evaluate the intended meaning of the arguments coming from adherents to competing governance truths, which requires the governors to be able to cull and integrate arguments based on a diversity of methodological perspectives. Eighth, conflict is normal and necessary, with the degree of tolerable conflict determined by the willingness and ability of the more chameleonic adherents to competing governance truths to join together to deflect and resist any con-

---

[1] Habermas (1975) argues that a fair, equitable and philosophically justified decision is achieved only in an ideal speech situation in which each individual has an equal chance to expound truth claims; to challenge statements, to express attitudes, feelings and emotions; and to permit and forbid norms (so as to exclude unilateral norms); authority is sourced only in the speakers themselves; and complete consensus is achieved.

[2] Thompson (1993, 2001) talks of "clumsy institutions" (citing Schapiro 1988) as those institutions that are willing and able to maintain and nurture dynamic requisite plurality. He (Thompson 1993: 4) explains and illustrates this proposition by drawing on the experiences of a Himalayan village: "transactions are parceled out to what seem to be the appropriate culture modes and, if circumstances change, some of those transactions can be switched to a more appropriate mode. It is this combination of plurality and flexibility that confers such a high level of resilience on the Himalayan village."

flictual responses of the more intransigent. Ninth, the best outcomes that they can expect from constructive governance discourses are sets of achievable governance goals, implementable governance strategies, and tolerable levels of conflict, because the goals and strategies derived provoke the greatest acquiescence from the more chameleonic adherents to competing governance truths and the least hostility from the more intransigent ones. Tenth, achieving good governance is an iterative process that involves learning-by-doing and learning-from-experience about what is the right thing to do and how to do things right. Finally, the essence of good governance is in its contestation.

Confrontation and integration require tolerance on the part of both governors and the governed. There must also be a willingness to settle competing governance truth claims with consistency and without recourse to intentional activities and motivated processes that enable self-deception or self-delusion, and thereby allow the avoidance of unpleasant truths or issues. Such avoidance produces the mental states of ignorance, false belief, unwarranted attitudes and inappropriate emotions (Haight 1980). The challenge faced by both sides is to accept Heidegger's proposition that thinking only begins at the point when reason, which has been glorified for centuries, is instead acknowledged to be the most obstinate adversary of thinking (Barrett 1977: 184). As Barrett 1958: 247) observes, "the centuries-long evolution of human reason is one of man's greatest triumphs, but it is still in process, still incomplete, still to be."

Clearly, then, over the centuries the quest for the meaning of good governance in its many manifestations has gone hand in hand with the search for the philosopher's stone. As the twenty-first century advances, the question that must be asked is whether modernism and its successors—postmodernism and neomodernism—have brought anything to distil the wisdom of the ancients. That seems highly problematic, as the governance questions posed more than two thousand years ago remain the challenging ones. But the fact that there is a continuing search for enlightenment must carry the hope for succeeding generations to be able not only to provide fresh governance answers, but also to deal with the challenge of new governance questions.

Bibliography

Aberle, D. F. (1966). *The Peyote Religion among the Navajo.* Chicago, IL: Aldine Publishing Company.
Ackerman, R. and Bauer, R. 1976. *Corporate Social Responsibility.* Reston, Manitoba, Canada: Reston Publishing.
Ackrill, J. L. 1981. *Aristotle the Philosopher.* Oxford: Oxford University Press.
Adams, G. B. and Ingersoll, V. H. 1990. "Culture, Technical Rationality and Organizational Culture." *American Review of Public Administration* 20 (4): 285–302.
Adams, J. S. 1965. "Inequality in Social Exchange." In Berkowitz, L. (ed.), *Advances in Experimental Psychology* (Vol. 2). New York: Academic Press.
Adler, A. 1938. *Social Interest.* London: Faber and Faber.
Adorno, T., Frenkel-Bruns, E., Levinson, D. J. and Sanford, R. N. 1950. *The Authoritarian Personality.* New York: Harper.
Aggarawal, V. 1986. *Liberal Protectionism: International Politics of Organized Textile Trade.* Berkeley, CA: University of California Press.
Aggarawal, V. and Samwick, A. A. 1999. "The Other Side of the Trade: The Impact of Risk on Executive Compensation." *Journal of Political Economy* 107 (1): 65–105.
Aiken, M. and Hague, J. 1968. "Organizational Interdependence and Intra-organizational Structure." *American Sociological Review* 33: 912–30.
Alcentara C. 1998. "Uses and Abuses of the Concept of Governance." *International Social Science Journal* 50 (1): 105–13.
Alchian, A. A. and Demsetz, H. 1972. "Production, Information Costs and Economic Organization." *American Economic Review* 62 (4): 777–95.
Alderfer, C. P. 1972. *Existence, Relatedness, and Growth.* New York: Free Press.
Aldrich, H. A. 1979. *Organizations and Environments.* Englewood Cliffs, NJ: Prentice-Hall.
Aldrich, H. A. and Whetten, D. A. 1981. "Organization-Sets, Action-Sets and Networks: Making the Most Out of Simplicity." In Nystrom, P. C. and Starbuck, W. H. (eds.), *Handbook of Organizational Design.* Oxford: Oxford University Press.
Alexander, J. C. 1982. *Positivism, Presupposition, and Current Controversies.* London: Routledge & Kegan Paul.

Alexander, R. D. 1987. *The Biology of Moral Systems*. New York: Aldine de Gruyter.
Alexander, Y. (ed.). 1976. *International Terrorism: National, Regional and Global Perspectives*. New York: Praeger.
Allison, L. 1996a. "Critical Theory." In McLean, I. (ed.), *The Concise Oxford Dictionary of Politics*. Oxford: Oxford University Press.
Allison, L. 1996b. "Power." In McLean, I. (ed.), *The Concise Oxford Dictionary of Politics*. Oxford: Oxford University Press.
Alston, W. P. 1989. *Epistemic Justification: Essays in the Theory of Knowledge*. Ithaca, NY: Cornell University Press.
Altman, Y. and Baruch, Y. 1998. "Cultural Theory and Organizations: Analytical Methods and Cases." *Organizational Studies* 19 (5): 769–85.
Aman, A. C., Jr. 1995. "A Global Perspective on Current Regulatory Reform: Rejection, Relocation, or Reinvention?" *Indiana Journal of Global Legal Studies* 2: 429–64.
Analytica 1992. *Board Directors and Corporate Governance: Trends in the G7 Countries over the Next Ten Years*. Oxford: Analytica.
Andersen, E. S. 1994. *Evolutionary Economics: Post-Schumpeterian Contributions*. New York: Pinter.
Andriessen, E. J. H. and Coetsier, P. L. 1984. "Industrial Democratization." In Drenthe, P. J. D. et al. (eds.), *Handbook of Work and Organizational Psychology*. Chichester, W Susx., UK: Wiley.
Anthony, P. D. 1994. *Managing Culture*. Buckingham, Bucks., UK: Open University.
Apperley, A. 1996a. "False Consciousness." In McLean, I. (ed.), *The Concise Oxford Dictionary of Politics*. Oxford: Oxford University Press.
Apperley, A. 1996b. "Public Interest." In McLean, I. (ed.), *The Concise Oxford Dictionary of Politics*. Oxford: Oxford University Press.
Aquinas, St. T. [1264] 1974. *Selected Political Writings* (ed. d'Entreves, A. P.). Oxford: Blackwell.
Archer, M. S. 1982. "Morphogenesis versus Structuration: On Combining Structure and Agency." *British Journal of Sociology* 33 (4): 455–83.
Archer, M. S. 1990. "Human Agency and Social Structure: A Critique of Giddens." In Clark, J., Modgil, C. and Modgil, S. (eds.), *Anthony Giddens: Consensus and Controversy*. Basingstoke, Hamp., UK: Falmer Press.
Archer, M. S. 1995. *Realist Social Theory: A Morphogenetic Approach*. Cambridge: Cambridge University Press.
Archer, M. S. 1996. "Social Integration and System Integration: Developing the Distinction." *Sociology* 30 (4): 679–99.
Archibugi, D. and Held, D. 1995. *Cosmopolitan Democracy*. Cambridge: Polity.
Ardrey, R. 1967. *The Territorial Imperative*. London: Collins.
Arendt, H. 1958. *The Human Condition*. Chicago, IL: University of Chicago Press.
Arendt, H. 1963a. *On Revolution*. New York: Penguin.
Arendt, H. 1963b. *Adolf Eichmann in Jerusalem: A Report on the Banality of Evil*. New York: Viking Press.
Argyris, C. 1985. *Strategy, Change and Defensive Routines*. Boston, MA: Pitman
Argyris, C. and Schön, D. 1978. *Organizational Learning: A Theory of Action Perspective*. Reading, MA: Addison-Wesley.
Armstrong, D. 1993. *Revolution and World Order: The Revolutionary State in International Society*. Oxford: Clarendon.
Arnhart, L. 1998. *Darwinian Natural Right: The Biological Ethics of Human Nature*. Albany, NY: State University of New York Press.
Arrow, K. J. 1954. *Social Choice and Individual Values*. New York: Wiley.

Arrow, K. J. 1984. *Individual Choice under Certainty and Uncertainty*, Oxford: Blackwell.
Arrow. K. J. 1994. "Methodological Individualism and Social Knowledge." *American Economic Review* 89 (2): 1–9.
Ashby, W. R. 1956. *An Introduction to Cybernetics*, London: Chapman and Hall.
Ashby, W. R. 1960. *Design for the Brain: The Origins of Adaptive Behavior* (2nd ed.). London: Chapman and Hall.
Ashley, R. K. 1989. "Imposing International Purpose: Notes on a Problematic of Governance." In Czempiel, E.–O. and Rosenau, J. N. (eds.), *Global Change and Theoretical Challenges: Approaches to World Politics for the 1990s*. Lexington, MA: Lexington Books.
Atkins, R. A. 1991. *Egalitarian Community: Ethnography and Exegesis*. Tuscaloosa, AL: University of Alabama Press.
Atkinson, M. M. and Coleman, W. D. 1989. "Strong States and Weak States: Sectoral Policy Networks in Advanced Capitalist Economies." *British Journal of Political Science* 19: 747–67.
Axelrod, R. 1984. *The Evolution of Cooperation*. New York: Basic.
Ayres, I. and Braithwaite, J. 1992. *Responsive Regulation: Transcending the Deregulation Debate*. Oxford: Oxford University Press.
Baert, P. 1998. *Social Theory in the Twentieth Century*. Cambridge: Polity.
Bakhtin, M. 1981. *The Dialogic Imagination*. Austin, TX: University of Texas Press.
Baldwin, A. (ed.) 1993. *Neorealism and Neoliberalism: The Contemporary Debate*. New York: Columbia University Press.
Bale, T. 1999. "Broad Churches, Big Theory and One Small Example: Cultural Theory and Intra-party Politics." In Thompson, M., Grendstat, G. and Selle, P. (eds.), *Cultural Theory as Political Science*. London: Routledge.
Bancaire 1996. *Two-tier Structure and Corporate Governance: A Special Report by Compagnie Bancaire*. Paris: Compagnie Bancaire.
Banfield, E. C. 1958. *The Moral Basis of a Backward Society*. New York: Free Press.
Banks, M. (ed.), 1948. *Conflict in World Society: A New Perspective on International Relations*. New York: St Martin's Press.
Barber, B. 1983. *The Logic and Limits of Trust*. New Brunswick, NJ: Transaction Books.
Barber, B. 1984. *Strong Democracy: Participator Politics for a New Age*. Berkeley, CA: University of California Press.
Bardach, E. and Kagan, R. A. 1982. *Going by the Book*. Philadelphia, PA: Temple University Press.
Barker, E. 1945. *Reflections on Government*. Oxford: Oxford University Press.
Barkin, J. S. and Cronin, B. 1994. "The State and the Nation: Changing Norms and Rules of Sovereignty in International Relations." *International Organization* 48 (1): 107–30.
Barkow, J. H., Cosmides, L. and Tooby, J. (eds.) 1992. *The Adapted Mind: Evolutionary Psychology and the Generation of Cultures*. New York: Oxford University Press.
Barnard, C. 1938. *The Functions of the Executive*. Cambridge, MA: Harvard University Press.
Barnes, B. 1974. *Scientific Knowledge and Sociological Theory*. London: Routledge & Kegan Paul.
Barnet, R. and Cavanagh, J. 1994. *Global Dreams: Imperial Corporations and the New World Order*. New York: Simon and Schuster.
Barnet, R. and Muller, R. E. 1974. *Global Reach: The Power of Multinational Corporations*. New York: Simon and Schuster.

Barney, J. B. and Ouchi, W. G. (eds.) 1986. *Organizational Economics: Towards a New Paradigm for Understanding and Studying Organizations.* San Fransisco, CA: Jossey-Bass.

Barrett, W. 1958. *Irrational Man: A Study in Existential Philosophy.* Westport, CT: Greenwood.

Barth, F. 1966. *Models of Social Organization* (Occasional Paper 25). London: Royal Anthropological Institute.

Bauman, Z. 1998. *Globalization: The Human Consequence.* New York: Columbia University Press.

Baumeister, R. 1993. *Self-Esteem.* New York: Plenum Press.

Baylis, J. and Smith, S. (eds.) 2001. *The Globalization of World Politics: An Introduction to International Relations* (2nd ed.). Oxford: Oxford University Press.

Baysinger, B. and Hoskisson, R. 1990. "The Composition of Boards of Directors and Strategic Control: Effects on Corporate Strategy." *Academy of Management Review* 15: 72–87.

Beck, U. 1992. *Risk Society: Towards a New Modernity* (tr. Ritter, M.). London: Sage.

Becker, L. C. 1977. *Property Rights: Philosophic Foundations.* London and Boston, MA: Henley in conjunction with Routledge & Kegan Paul.

Beckstrom, J. H. 1993. *Darwinism Applied: Evolutionary Paths to Social Goals.* New York: Praeger.

Beitz, C. R. 1979. *Political Theory and International Relations.* Princeton, NJ: Princeton University Press.

Benedict, R. 1935. *Patterns of Culture.* Boston, MA: Houghton Mifflin.

Benson, J. K. 1975. "The Interorganizational Network or a Political Economy." *Administrative Science Quarterly* 20 (2): 229–49.

Benson, J. K. 1982. "A Framework for Policy Analysis." In Rodgers, D. L. and Whetten, D. A. (eds.), *Interorganizational Co-ordination: Theory, Research, and Implementation.* Ames, IA: Iowa State University Press.

Bentham, J. [1789] 1970. *An Introduction to the Principles of Morals and Legislation.* London: Athlone.

Bentham, J. [1802]1987. "A Plan for an Universal and Perpetual Peace." In Kainz, H. P. (ed.), *Philosophical Perspectives on Peace.* London: Macmillan.

Beran, H. 1987. *The Consent Theory of Political Obligation.* London: Croom Helm.

Berger, P. and Luckmann, T. 1966. *The Social Construction of Reality: A Treatise in the Sociology of Knowledge.* New York: Doubleday.

Berle, A. A., Jr. and Means, G. C. 1932. *The Modern Corporation and Private Property.* New York: Macmillan.

Berlin, I. 1969. *Four Essays on Liberty.* Oxford: Oxford University Press.

Bernholz, P. 1993. "Constitutions as Governance Structures: The Political Foundations of Secure Markets." *Journal of Institutional and Theoretical Economics* 149: 312–20.

Bernstein, M. H. 1955. *Regulating Business by Independent Commission.* Princeton, NJ: University of Princeton Press.

Bernstein, P. 1980. *Workplace Democratization: Its Internal Dynamics.* New Brunswick, NJ: Transaction Books.

Berquist, W. 1993. *The Postmodern Organization: Mastering the Art of Irreversible Change.* San Francisco, CA: Jossey-Bass.

Berridge, G. R. *International Politics: States, Power and Conflict since 1945* (2nd. ed.). Hemel Hempstead, Herts., UK: Harvester.

Bhaskar, R. 1975. *A Realist Theory of Science*, Leeds, W York., UK: Leeds Books.

Bhaskar, R. 1998. *The Possibility of Naturalism: A Philosophical Critique of the Contemporary Human Sciences* (3rd ed.). London and New York: Routledge.

Biersteker, T. J. 1992. The 'Triumph' of Neoclassical Economics in the Developing World: Policy Convergence and Bases of Governance in the International Economic Order." In Rosenau, J. N. and Czempiel, E.–O. (eds.), *Governance Without Government Order and Change in World Politics.* Cambridge: Cambridge University Press.

Biersteker, T. J. and Weber, C. (eds.) 1996. *State Sovereignty as a Social Construct.* New York: Cambridge University Press.

Birnie, P. W. 1989. "International Legal Issues in the Management and Protection of the Whale: A Review of Four Decades of Experience." *Natural Resources Journal* 29 (3): 903–34.

Bittner, E. 1963. "Radicalism and the Organization of Social Movements." *American Sociological Review* 28: 928–40.

Blair, M. M. 1995. *Ownership and Control.* Washington, DC: The Brooking Institute.

Blake, R. R. and Mouton, J. S. 1982. *The Versatile Manager: A Grid Profile.* Homewood, IL: Richard D. Irwin.

Blake, R. R. and Mouton, J. S. 1984. *The Managerial Grid III* (3rd ed.). Houston, TX: Gulf Publishing.

Blanchard, E. B. and Scarboro, M. E 1972. "Locus of Control, Political Attitudes, and Voting Behavior in a College Age Population." *Psychology Reports* 30: 529–30.

Blank, R. 1995. "The Changing Nature of Human Nature." In Somit, A. and Losco, J. (eds.), *Research in Biopolitics, 3: Human Nature and Politics.* Greenwich, CT: JAI Press.

Blasi, J. R. 1988. *Employee Ownership.* Cambridge, MA: Ballinger.

Blauner, R. 1964. *Alienation and Freedom.* Chicago, IL: University of Chicago Press.

Blom-Hansen, J. 1998. "A 'New' Institutional Perspective on Policy Networks." *Public Administration* 75 (4): 669–93.

Bloor, D. 1982. "Polyhedra and the Abominations of Leviticus: Cognitive Styles in Mathematics." In Douglas, M. (ed.), *Essays in the Sociology of Perception.* London: Routledge & Kegan Paul.

Bloor, D. 1984. *Wittgenstein: A Social Theory of Knowledge.* New York: Macmillan.

Blumberg, P. 1968. *Industrial Democracy: The Sociology of Participation.* London: Constable.

Blumer, H. 1969. *Symbolism Interactionism: Perspective and Method.* Englewood Cliff, NJ: Prentice Hall.

Boje, D., Gephart, R. and Thatchkery, T. J. 1996. *Postmodern Management and Organizational Theory.* Newbury Park, CA: Sage.

Börzel, T. A. 1997. What's so Special about Policy Networks? An Exploration of the Concept and Its Usefulness in Studying European Governance. Mimeo, European University, Florence.

Börzel, T. A. 1998. "Organizing Babylon—on the Different Conceptions of Policy Networks." *Public Administration* 76: (2): 253–73.

Bott, E. 1957. *Family and Social Network: Roles, Norms, and External Relationships in Ordinary Urban Families.* London: Tavistock.

Boucher, D. 1998. *Political Theories of International Relations: From Thucydides to the Present.* Oxford: Oxford University Press.

Boulder, K. 1990. *Three Faces of Power.* Newbury Park, CA: Sage.

Bourdieu, P. 1998. *Practical Reason.* Cambridge: Polity.

Bourdieu, P. 1999. "Rethinking the State: Genesis and Structure of the Bureaucratic Field." In Steinmetz, G. (ed.), *State/Culture: State Formation after the Culture Turn*. Ithaca, NY: Cornell University Press.
Bovens, M. and t'Hart, P. 1990. *Policy Fiascos*. New Brunswick, NJ: Transaction Books.
Bovens, M., t'Hart, P. and Peters, B. G. 2001. *Success and Failure in Public Governance*. Cheltenham, Gloucs., UK: Edward Elgar.
Bowen, H. 1953. *Social Responsibilities of the Businessman*. New York: Harper.
Bradach, J. L. and Eccles, R. G. 1991. "Price, Authority and Trust: From Ideal Types to Plural Forms." In Thompson, G., Frances, J., Levacic, R. and Mitchell, J. (eds.) 1991. *Markets, Hierarchies and Networks: The Coordination of Social Life*. London: Sage and Open University Press.
Brand, M. and Walton, D. (eds.) 1976. *Action Theory*. Dordrecht, Netherlands: Reidel.
Brans, M. 1997. "Challenges to the Practice and Theory of Public Administration in Europe." *Journal of Theoretical Politics* 9 (3): 389–415.
Brans, M. and Rossbach, S. 1997. "The Autopoiesis of Administrative Systems: Niklas Luhmann on Public Administration and Public Policy." *Public Administration* 75: 417–39.
Braverman, H. 1974. *Labor and Monopoly Capitalism: The Degradation of Work in the Twentieth Century*. New York: Monthly Review Press.
Brech, E.F.L. and Urwick, L. 1945. *The Making of Scientific Management*. London: Management Publications Trust.
Brennan, H. G. and Buchanan, J. H. 1985. *The Reason for Rules*. Cambridge: Cambridge University Press.
Breton, A., Galeotti, G., Salmon, P. and Wintrobe, R. 2001. *Political Extremism and Rationality*. Cambridge: Cambridge University Press.
Brickman, R. 1984. "Science and the Politics of Toxic Chemicals Regulations: US and European Contrasts." *Science, Technology and Human Values* 9: 107–11.
Brink, D. 1989. *Moral Realism and the Foundations of Ethics*. Cambridge: Cambridge University Press.
Bromley, S. (ed.) 2001. *Governing Europe: Governing the European Union*. London: Sage and the Open University.
Brown, C. 1992. *International Relations Theory: New Normative Approaches*. Hemel Hempsted, Herts., UK: Harvester Wheatsheaf.
Brown, C. 1995. "International Political Theory and the Idea of an Old Community." In Booth, K. and Smith, S. (eds.), *International Relations Theory Today*. Cambridge: Polity.
Brown, C. C. (ed.) 1970. *World Business*. New York: Macmillan.
Brown, P. 1994. *Restoring the Public Trust*. Boston, MA: Beacon Press.
Brown, S. 1988. *New Forces, Old Forces, and the Future of World Politics*. Glenview, IL: Scott Foresman.
Bruyn, S. T. 1991. *A Future for the American Economy: The Social Market*. Palo Alto, CA: Stanford University Press.
Buechler, S. M. 1999. *Social Movements in Advanced Capitalism: The Political Economy and Cultural Construction of Social Activism*. New York: Open University Press.
Bulcke, D. van and Verbeke, J. (eds.) 2001. *Globalisation and the Small Open Economy*. Cheltenham, Gloucs., UK: Edward Elgar.
Bull, H. 1977. *The Anarchical Society: A Study of Order in World Politics*. New York: Columbia University Press.

Burnham, P. 1996. "State." In McLean, I. (ed.), *The Concise Oxford Dictionary of Politics*. Oxford: Oxford University Press.

Burns, T. 1966. "On the Plurality of Social Systems." In Lawrence, J. R. (ed.), *Operational Research and the Social Sciences*. London: Tavistock.

Burns, T 1999. "The Evolution of Parliaments and Societies in Europe: Challenges and Prospects." *European Journal of Social Theory* 2 (2): 184–215.

Burns, T. and Stalker, G. M. 1961. *The Management of Innovation*. London: Tavistock.

Burrough, B. and Helyar, J. 1990. *Barbarians at the Gate: The Fall of RJR Nabisco*. New York: Harper and Row.

Burton, R. [1621] 2001. *The Anatomy of Melancholy* (ed. Faulkner, T.) (6 vols.). Oxford: Clarendon.

Buschardt, S. C., Toso, R. and Schnake, M. E. 1986. "Can Money Motivate?" In Dale, T. A. (ed.), *Motivation of Personnel*. New York: KEND.

Bushman, B. and Baumeister, R. 1998. "Threatened Egoism, Narcissism, Self-esteem, and Direct and Displaced Aggression: Does Self-love and Self-hate Lead to Violence." *Journal of Personality and Social Psychology* 75: 219–29.

Buzan, B. P. 1991. *People, States and Fear: An Agenda for International Security Studies in the Post-Cold War Era*. Hemel Hempsted, Herts., UK: Harvester Wheatsheaf.

Buzen, B. 1996a. "Balance of Power." In McLean, I. (ed.), *The Concise Oxford Dictionary of Politics*. Oxford: Oxford University Press.

Buzan, B. 1996b. "International Society." In McLean, I. (ed.), *The Concise Oxford Dictionary of Politics*. Oxford: Oxford University Press.

Buzan, B. 1996c. "Realism." In McLean, I. (ed.), *The Concise Oxford Dictionary of Politics*. Oxford: Oxford University Press.

Buzan, B. 1996d. "War." In McLean, I. (ed.), *The Concise Oxford Dictionary of Politics*. Oxford: Oxford University Press.

Buzan, B., Waever, O. and de Wilde, J. 1998. *Security: New Framework for Analysis*. Boulder and London: Lynne Reinner.

Byrd, P. 1996. "National Interest." In McLean, I. (ed.), *The Concise Oxford Dictionary of Politics*. Oxford: Oxford University Press.

Cable, V. 1999. *Globalization and Global Governance* (Chatham House Papers). London: Pinter in conjunction with the Royal Institute of International Affairs.

Cadbury Committee 1992. *Report on the Financial Aspects of Corporate Governance*. London: Gee Publishing.

Caldwell, L. K. 1990. *International Environmental Policy: Emergence and Responses*. Durham, NC: Duke University Press.

Campbell, D. T. 1972. "On the Genetics of Altruism and the Counterhedonic Components in Human Culture." *Journal of Social Issues* 28 (3): 21–37.

Campbell, D. T. and Cziko, G. A. 1990. "Comprehensive Evolutionary Epistemology Bibliography." *Journal of Social and Biological Structures* 13 (1): 41–81.

Camus, A. 1971. *The Rebel*. London: Penguin.

Camus, A. [1942] 1982. *The Outsider* (tr. Laredo, J.). London: Penguin.

Canetti, E. [1960] 2000. *Crowds and Power*. London: Phoenix Press.

Cantor, R., Henry, S. and Rayner, S. 1992. *Making Markets: An Interdisciplinary Perspective on Economic Exchange*. Westport, CT: Greenwood.

Caplan, A. L. (ed.) 1978. *The Sociobiology Debate: Readings on Ethical and Scientific Issues*. New York: Harper and Row.

Carlsson, L. 2000. Policy Networks as Collective Action." *Policy Studies Journal* 28 (3): 502–20.

Carr, H. E. 1946. *The Twenty Years' Crisis, 1919–1939*. London: Macmillan.

Carroll, A. 1979. "A Three-Dimensional Model of Corporate Social Responsibility." *Academy of Management Review* 4 (2): 497–505.
Castells, M. 1983. *The City and the Grassroots*. Berkeley, CA: University of California Press.
Castells, M. 1996. *The Information Age: 1, The Rise of the Network Society*. Oxford: Blackwell.
Castells, M. 1997. *The Information Age: 2, The Power of Identity*. Oxford: Blackwell.
Castells, M. 1998. *The Information Age: 3, End of the Millenium*. Oxford: Blackwell.
Cawson, A. (ed.) 1985. *Organized Interests and the State: Studies in Mesa-Corporatism*. London: Sage.
Cawson, A. 1986. *Corporatism and Political Theory*. Oxford: Blackwell.
Chai, S.–K. and Wildavsky, A. 1994. "Culture, Rationality and Violence." In Coyle, D. J. and Ellis, R. J. (eds.), *Politics, Policy and Culture*. Boulder, CO: Westview.
Chamberlain, F. 1973. *The Limits of Corporate Responsibility*. New York: Basic Books.
Champlin, J. R. (ed.) 1971. *Power*. New York: Atherton.
Chandler, A. D., Jr. 1962. *Strategy and Structure*. Cambridge, MA: MIT Press.
Charkham, J. 1994. *Keeping Good Company: A Study of Corporate Governance in Five Countries*. Oxford: Claredon.
Charny, D. 1991. "Competition among Jurisdictions in Formatting Corporate Law Rules: An American Perspective on the 'Race to the Bottom' in the European Communities." *Harvard International Law Journal* 32 (1): 30–54.
Chia, R. 1995. "From Modern to Postmodern Organizational Analysis." *Organizational Studies* 16 (4): 580–604.
Child, J. 1969. *The Business Enterprise in Modern Industrial Society*. London: Collier-Macmillan.
Child, J. 1972. "Organizational Structure and Strategies of Control: A Replication of the Aston Study." *Administrative Science Quarterly* 17 (2): 163–77.
Cisero [44BC] 1971. *De Fato [On Fate]* (tr Sharples, R. W.). Warminister, Wilts., UK: Aris & Phillips.
Clark, I. 1989. *The Hierarchy of States: Reform and Resistance in the International Order*. Cambridge: Cambridge University Press.
Clark, M. 1995. "Nongovernmental Organizations and their Influence on International Society (Transcending National Boundaries)." *Journal of International Affairs* 48 (2): 507–25.
Clark, P. and Wilson, J. 1961. "Incentive Systems: A Theory of Organizations." *Administrative Science Quarterly* 6 (1): 129–66.
Clayton, A. (ed.) 1993. *Governance, Democracy and Conditionality: What Role for NGOs?* Oxford: INTRAC.
Clegg, S. 1990. *Modern Organizations: Organizational Studies in the Postmodern World*. Newbury Park, CA: Sage.
Coglianese, G. 1997. "Assessing Consensus: The Promise and Performance of Negotiated Rulemaking." *Duke Law Journal* 46: 1255–1350.
Cohen, J. 1989. "Deliberation and Democratic Legitimacy." In Hamlin, A. S. and Pettit, P. (eds.), *The Good Polity*. Oxford: Blackwell.
Cohen, J. and Rogers, J. 1992. "Secondary Associations and Democratic Governance." *Politics and Society* 20 (4): 393–472.
Cohen, M., March, J. and Olsen, J. 1972. "A Garbage Can Model of Organizational Choice." *Administrative Science Quarterly* 17 (1): 1–23.
Cohen, R. 1972. "Altruism: Human, Cultural, or What?" *Journal of Social Issues* 28 (3): 39–57.

Cohen, S. 1972. *Folk Devils and Moral Panics: The Creation of the Mods and Rockers, Sociology and the Modern World.* London: MacGibbon and Kee.
Colebatch, H. and Lamour, P. 1993. *Markets, Bureaucracy and Community.* London: Pluto.
Collier, P. 1997. "Audit Committees in Smaller Listed Companies." In Keasey, K. and Wright, M. (eds.), *Corporate Governance: Responsibilities, Risks and Remuneration.* Chichester, W Susx., UK: Wiley.
Collins, R. 1981. "On the Micro Foundations of Macrosociology." *American Journal of Sociology* 86 (4): 938–65.
Commission on Global Governance 1995. *Our Global Neighborhood.* New York: Oxford University Press.
Congdon, T. 1997. "How Britain Benefits from Short-termism." In *Stakeholding and Its Critics.* London: Institute of Economic Affairs, Health and Welfare Unit.
Conti, R. F. and Warner, M. 1996. "Technology, Teams and Theories of the Firm." *Human System Management* 15: 101–12.
Conybeare, J. 1984. "Public Goods, Prisoners' Dilemmas and the International Political Economy." *International Studies Quarterly* 28 (1): 5–22.
Conybeare, J. 1980. "International Organization and the Theory of Property Rights." *International Organization* 34 (2): 299–315.
Cook, F. L. and Skogan, W. G. 1991. "Convergent and Divergent Voice Models of the Rise and Fall of Policy Issues." In Protess, D. L. and McCombs, M. (eds.), *Agenda Setting: Readings on Media Public Opinion and Policy Making.* Hillsdale, NJ: Lawrence Erlbaum.
Cook, K. S. 1977. "Exchange and Power in Networks of Interorganizational Relations." *The Sociological Quarterly* 18 (1): 62–82.
Cooke, M. 1994. *Language and Reason: A Study of Habermas' Pragmatics.* Cambridge, MA: MIT Press.
Cooper, R. N. 1968. *The Economics of Interdependence: Economic Policy in the Atlantic Community.* New York: McGraw-Hill.
Cooperrider, D. L. and Srivastva, S. 1987. "Appreciative Inquiry in Organizational Life". In Woodman, R. and Pasmore, W. (eds.), *Research in Organizational Change and Development; 1.* Greenwich, CT: JAI Press.
Cornett, L. and Caporaso, J. A. 1992. "'And Still it Moves!' State Interests and Social Forces in the European Community." In Rosenau, J. N. and Czempiel, E.-O. (eds.), *Governance Without Government Order and Change in World Politics.* Cambridge: Cambridge University Press.
Coser, L. 1974. *Greedy Institutions: Patterns of Undivided Commitment.* New York: Free Press and Collier Macmillan.
Coughlan, R. P. B. 1994. "Conceptualizing and Operationalizing Cultural Theory." In Coyle, D. J. and Ellis, R. J. (eds.), *Politics, Policy and Culture.* Boulder, CO: Westview.
Coughlin. R. and Lockhart, C. 1998. "Grid-group Theory and Political Ideology: A Consideration of Their Relative Strengths and Weaknesses for Explaining the Structure of Mass Belief Systems." *Journal of Theoretical Politics* 10 (1): 33–58.
Cox, R. W. 1986. "Social Forces, States, and World Orders: Beyond International Relations Theory" (with Postscript). In Keohane, R. O. (ed.), *Neorealism and Its Critics.* New York: Columbia University Press.
Cox, R. W. 1987. *Production, Power and World Order: Social Forces in the Making of History.* New York: Columbia University Press.
Cox, R. W. 1992. "Global *Perestroika*." In Miliband, R. and Panitch, L. (eds.), *Socialist Register 1992.* London: Merlin Press.

Cox, R. W. 1993. "Structural Issues for Global Governance: Implications for Europe." In Gill, S. (ed.), *Gramsci's Historical Materialism and International Relations.* Cambridge: Cambridge University Press.

Cox, R W. 1997. "A Perspective on Globalization." In Mittelan, J. H. (ed.), *Globalization: Critical Reflections.* Boulder, CO: Lynne Riener.

Coyle, D. J. 1997. "A Cultural Theory of Organizations." In Ellis, R. J. and Thompson, M. (eds.), *Culture Matters: Essays in Honor of Aaron Wildavsky.* Boulder, CO: Westview.

Coyle, D. J. and Ellis, R. J. (eds.) 1994. *Politics, Policy and Culture.* Boulder, CO: Westview.

Crider, K. A. 1999. *The Strategic Implications of Culture: A Historical Analysis of China's Culture and Implications for US Policy* (a Research Report) (AU/ACSC/031/1999–04). Maxwell, AL: Air Command and Staff College.

Crocker, C. A. and Hampson, F. O. 1996. *Managing Global Chaos: Sources of and Responses to International Conflict.* New York: US Institute of Peace Press.

Crosby, D. A. 1988. *The Specter of the Absurd: Sources and Criticisms of Modern Nihilism.* Albany, NY: State University of New York Press.

Cross, M. J. R. 2001. *Communities of Individuals: Liberalism, Communitarianism and Sartre's Anarchism.* Aldershot, Hants., UK: Ashgate.

Crowley, J. 1994. "Social Complexity and Strong Democracy." *Innovation: The European Journal of Social Sciences* 7 (3): 309–20.

Crozier, M. 1964. *The Bureaucratic Phenomenon.* London: Tavistock and University of Chicago Press.

Crozier, M. and Friedberg, E. 1968. *Actors and Systems.* Chicago, IL: University of Chicago Press.

Crozier, M., Huntington, S. P. and Watanuki, J. 1975. *The Crisis of Democracy: Report on the Governability of Democracies to the Trilateral Commission.* New York: New York University Press.

Cutting, B. and Kouzmin, A. 1997. "Towards an Ontological Understanding of Good Governance Based on a Synthesis of Weber's Concept of 'Ideal Types' and the Enneagram Typology." *Indian Journal of Public Administration* 2 (2): 85–112.

Cutting, B. and Kouzmin, A. 1999. "From Chaos to Patterns of Understanding: Reflections on the Dynamics of Effective Government Decision-Making." *Public Administration* 77 (3): 475–508.

Cutting, B. and Kouzmin, A. 2000a. "The Emerging Patterns of Power in Corporate Governance: A Hermeneutic Analysis of Institutional Archetyping and Its Capacity to Improve Corporate Performance." *Journal of Management Psychology* 15 (5): 477–511.

Cutting, B. and Kouzmin, A. 2000b. "Formulating a Metaphysic of Governance: Explaining the Dynamics of Governance Using the New JEWAL Synthesis Framework." *Journal of Management Development* 20 (6): 526–64.

Cutting, B. and Kouzmin, A. 2001. "A Synthesis of Knowing and Governance: Making Sense of Organizational and Governance Polemics." Paper presented at the Fifth International Research Symposium on Public Management, University of Barcelona, Spain, April.

Cuyver, L. (ed.) 2001. *Globalisation and Social Development: European and Southeast Asian Evidence.* Cheltenham, Gloucs., UK: Edward Elgar.

Cyert, R. M. and March, J. G. [1963] 1992. *A Behavioral Theory of the Firm.* Oxford: Blackwell.

Czempiel, E.-O. 1992. "Governance and Democratization." In Rosenau, J. N. and Czempiel, E.-O. (eds.), *Governance Without Government Order and Change in World Politics.* Cambridge: Cambridge University Press.
Dahl, R. A. 1957. "The Concept of Power." *Behavioral Sciences* 2: 201–5.
Dahl, R. A. 1968. "Power." In *The International Encyclopaedia of the Social Sciences.* New York: Macmillan.
Dahl, R. A. 1971. *Polyarchy: Participation and Opposition.* New Haven, CT: Yale University Press.
Dahl, R. A. 1982. *Dilemmas of Pluralist Democracy: Autonomy versus Control.* New Haven, CT: Yale University Press.
Dahl, R. A. 1985. *A Preface to Economic Democracy.* Cambridge: Polity.
Dahl, R. A. 1999. "The Anti-reflexive Revolution: On the Affirmation of the New Right." In Featherstone, M. and Lash, S. E. (eds.), *Spaces of Culture: City, Nation, World.* London: Sage.
Dahl, R. A. and Lindblom, C. E. 1976. *Politics, Economics and Welfare.* New York: Harpers.
D'Andrade, R. G. 1984. "Cultural Meaning Systems." In Shweder, R. A. and LeVine, R. A. (eds.), *Culture Theory: Essays on Mind, Self, and Emotion.* New York: Cambridge University Press.
Davidson, D. 1984. *Inquiries into Truth and Interpretation.* Oxford: Oxford University Press.
Davies, S. 1996. *Short-termism and the State We're In* (Economic Research Paper). London: Institute of Directors.
Davis, S. M. and Lorsch, J. W. 1977. *Matrix.* Reading, MA: Addison-Wesley.
Dawkins, R. 1976. *The Selfish Gene.* Oxford: Oxford University Press.
Deacon, B. with Hulse, M. and Stubbs, P. 1997. *Global Social Policy: International Organizations and the Future of Welfare.* London: Sage.
de Board, R. 1978. *The Psychoanalysis of Organizations: A Psychoanalytic Approach to Behavior in Groups and Organizations.* London: Tavistock.
De Bruijn, J. A. and Ringeling, A. B. 1997. "Normative Notes: Perspectives on Networks." In Kickert, W. J., Klijn, J. and Koppenjan, J. (eds.), *Managing Complex Networks.* London: Sage.
de Grazia, A. 1960. "The Science and Values of Administration: 1." *Administrative Science Quarterly* 5: 421–47.
de Haven-Smith, L. 1988. *Philosophical Critiques of Policy Analysis.* Gainesville, FL: University of Florida Press.
Delanty, G. 2000. *Modernity and Postmodernity: Knowledge, Power and Self.* London: Sage.
de Leon, P. 1978. "Public Policy Termination: An End and a Beginning." *Policy Analysis* 4 (3): 369–92.
de Leon, P. 1983. "Policy Evaluation and Program Termination." *Policy Studies Review* 2 (4): 631–47.
Demb, A. and Neubauer, F. F. 1992. "The Corporate Board: Confronting the Paradoxes." *Long Range Planning* 25 (3): 9–20.
Denham, R. and Porter, M. E. 1995. *Lifting all Boats* (Report of the Capital Allocation Subcouncil to the Competitive Policy Council). Washington, DC: Competitive Policy Council.
Diamond, L., Linz, J. and Lipset, S. M. 1988. *Democracy in Developing Countries, 1: Persistence, Future, and Renewal.* Boulder, CO: Lynne Riener.
Dickens, P. 1998 *Global Shift: Transforming the World Economy.* New York: Guilford Press.

Diehl, P. F. 1989. *The Politics of International Organizations: Patterns and Insights.* Chicago, IL: Dorsey Press.

Dinan, D. 1999. *Ever Closer Union* (2nd ed.). Basingstoke, Hamp., UK: Macmillan.

Dixit, A. 1997. "Indo-Nepal Water Resources Development: Cursing the Past or Moving Forward." In Ray, J. K. (ed.), *Indo-Nepal Cooperation Broadening Measures* (History Department, University of Calcutta, Monograph 13, K. P.). Calcutta: Bagchi and Company.

Dixon, J. and Dogan, R. 2002a. "Hierarchies, Networks and Markets: Responses to Societal Governance Failures." *Administrative Theory and Praxis* 24 (1): 175–196.

Dixon, J. and Dogan, R. 2002b. "Corporate Governance Failure: Philosophical Antagonisms and Corporate Governability." *The Journal of the Philosophy of Management* forthcoming.

Dixon, J. and Dogan, R. 2002c. "A Philosophical Investigation of the Problem of Global Governance Failure." *European Journal of Political Theory* forthcoming.

Dixon, J. and Dogan, R. 2002d. "Organization and Management: A Philosophical Investigation." *Organizational Studies* forthcoming.

Dixon, J., Sanderson, A. and Dogan, R, 2002. "The Communitarian Vision and Community Reality: A Philosophical Investigation." *European Journal of Social Theory* forthcoming.

Dogan, R. 2001. Personal communications. March.

Dollard, J., Doob, L. W., Mowrer, O. H. and Sears, R. R. 1939. *Frustration and Aggression.* New Haven, CT: Yale University Press.

Domahidy, M. R. and Gilsinan, J. F. 1992. "The Back Stage is not the Back Room: How Spatial Arrangements Affect the Administration of Public Affairs." *Public Administration Review* 52 (6): 588–93.

Donagan, A. 1987. *Choice: The Essential Element of Human Action.* London: Routledge & Kegan Paul.

Donahue, R. 1989. *The Privatization Decision: Public Ends, Private Means.* New York: Basic.

Donald, G. 1942. "A Study of a Consumer's Cooperative." *Applied Anthropology* 2 (1): 22–28.

Donaldson, I. 1990. "The Ethereal Hand: Organizational Economics and Management Theory." *Academy of Management Review* 15 (3): 369–81.

Donaldson, I. and Davis, J. H. 1994. "Boards and Company Performance—Research Challenges the Conventional Wisdom." *Corporate Governance: An International Review* 2 (3): 151–60.

Donaldson, I. and Preston, L. E. 1995. "The Stakeholder Theory of the Corporation: Concepts, Evidence, and Implications." *Academy of Management Review* 20 (1): 65–91.

Donelan, M. 1990. *Elements of International Political Theory.* Oxford: Oxford University Press.

Dorff, H. 1996. "Democratization and Failed States: the Challenge of Ungovernability." *Parameters* 26 (2): 17–31.

Douglas, J., Douglas, M. and Thompson, M. 1983. *Social Choice and Cultural Bias* (Collaborative Paper 83–84). Laxenberg, Austria: International Institute of Applied Systems Analysis.

Douglas, M. 1970. *Natural Symbols: Explorations in Cosmology.* London: Barry and Rockliff.

Douglas, M. 1972. "Environments at Risk." In Benthall, J. (ed.), *Ecology: The Shaping Enquiry.* London: Longman.

Douglas, M. 1978. *Cultural Bias* (Occasional Paper 35). London: Royal Anthropological Institute of Great Britain and Ireland.
Douglas, M. (ed.) 1982a. *In the Active Voice*. London: Routledge & Kegan Paul.
Douglas, M. 1982b. "Cultural Bias." In Douglas, M. (ed.), *In the Active Voice*. London: Routledge & Kegan Paul.
Douglas, M. 1982c. *Essays in the Sociology of Perception*. London: Routledge & Kegan Paul.
Douglas, M. 1983. "Perceiving Low Probability Events." In Douglas, J., Douglas, M. and Thompson, M. (eds.), *Social Choice and Cultural Bias* (Collaborative Paper 83–84). Laxenberg, Austria: International Institute of Applied Systems Analysis.
Douglas, M. 1985. *Risk Acceptability According to the Social Sciences*. New York: Russell Sage Foundation.
Douglas, M. 1986a. *How Institutions Think*. Syracuse, NY: Syracuse University Press.
Douglas, M. 1986b. *Risk Acceptability*. Berkeley, CA: University of California Press.
Douglas, M. 1987. "Wants." In *The New Palgrave Dictionary of Economics*. London: Macmillan.
Douglas, M. 1989. "Culture and Collective Action." In Freilich, M. (ed.), *The Relevance of Culture*. New York: Bergin and Garvey.
Douglas, M. 1991. "The New Wave of Austerity: Effects of Culture on Environmental Issues." In *L'Association Descartes*. Paris: L'Association Descartes.
Douglas, M. 1992a. "In Defense of Shopping." In Eisendle, A. and Miklautz, E. (eds.), *Produktulturen: Dynamik und Bedeutungswandel des Konssums*. Frankfurt am Main, Germany: Campus Verlag.
Douglas, M. 1992b. "The Person in an Enterprise Culture." In Hargreaves Heap, S. and Ross, A. (eds.), *Understanding the Enterprise Culture*. Edinburgh, C Edin., UK: University of Edinburgh Press.
Douglas, M. 1994. *Risk and Blame: Essays in Culture Theory*. London: Routledge.
Douglas, M. 1995. "Converging on Autonomy: Anthropology and Institutional Economics," In Williamson, O. E. (ed.), *Organizational Theory: From Chester Barnard to the Present and Beyond* (expanded ed.). New York: Oxford University Press.
Douglas, M. 1996. "Prospects for Asceticism." In Douglas, M. (ed.), *Thought Style: Critical Essays on Good Taste*. London: Sage.
Douglas, M. 1998. Grid-group.listserv@uea.ac.uk, March 10.
Douglas, M. 1999. "Four Cultures: The Evolution of a Parsimonious Model." GeoJournal 47 (3): 411–15.
Douglas, M. 2001. Grid-group listserv@uea.ac.uk, August 6.
Douglas, M. and Calvez, M. 1990. "The Self as Risk Taker: A Culture Theory of Contagion in Relation to AIDS." *The Sociological Review* 38 (3): 445–64.
Douglas, M. and Isherwood, B. 1979. *The World of Goods: Towards an Anthropology of Consumption*. London: Allen Lane.
Douglas, M. and Ney, S. 1998. *Missing Persons: A Critique of the Social Sciences*. Berkeley, CA: University of California Press.
Douglas, M. and Wildavsky, A. 1982. *Risk and Culture: An Essay on the Selection of Technical and Environmental Dangers*. Berkeley, CA: University of California Press.
Douglas, M., Gasper, D., Ney, S. and Thompson, M. 1997. "Human Needs and Wants." In Rayner, S. and Malone, E. L. (eds.), *Human Choice and Climate Change, 1: The Societal Framework*. Columbus, OH: Battelle Press.
Downie, R. S. and Telfer, E. 1969. *Respect for Persons*. London: Allen & Unwin.
Downs, A. 1967. *Inside Bureaucracy*. Boston, MA: Little, Brown.

Doyal, L. and Gough, I. 1991. *A Theory of Human Need*. London: Macmillan.
Draaisma, D. 2000. *Metaphors and Memory: A History of Ideas about the Mind*. Cambridge: Cambridge University Press.
Drabek, Z. (ed.) 2001. *Globalisation under Threat: The Stability of Trade Policy and Multilateral Agreements*. Cheltenham, Glos.: Edward Elgar.
Drake, K. 1991. "Orienting Dispositions in the Perception of Risk: An Analysis of Contemporary Worldviews and Cultural Biases." *Journal of Cross-Cultural Psychology* 22 (1): 61–82.
Drake, K. and Thompson, M. 1993. "The Meaning of Sustainable Development: Household Strategies for Managing Needs and Resources." In Wright, S. D., Dietz, T., Borden, R., Young, G. and Guagnano, G. (eds.), *Human Ecology: Crossing Boundaries*. Fort Collins, CO: The Society for Human Ecology.
Drake, K. and Thompson, M. 1999. "Making Ends Meet, in the Household and on the Planet." *GeoJournal* 47 (3): 417–24.
Drake, K. And Wildavsky, A. 1991. "Individual Differences in Risk Perception and Risk-taking Preferences." In Garrick, B. J. and Gekler, W. C. (eds.), *The Analysis, Communication and Perception of Risk*. New York: Plenum.
Dror, Y. 1968. *Public Policy Re-examined*. Scranton, PA: Chandler.
Dror, Y. 1976. "Some Features of a Meta-model for Policy Studies." In Gregg, P. (ed.), *Problems of Theory in Policy Analysis*. Englewood Cliffs, NJ: Prentice Hall.
Dror, Y. 1994. *La Capacidad de Governar: Informe al Club de Roma*. Barcelona: Circulo de Lectores and Galaxia Gutenberg.
Dryzek, J. S. 1987. "Complexity and Rationality in Public Life." *Political Studies* 35: 424–42.
Duffield, M. 2001. *Global Governance and the New Wars: The Merging of Development and Security*. London: Zed.
du Gay, P. 2000. *In Praise of Bureaucracy: Weber—Organization—Ethics*. London: Sage.
Dumont, L. 1970. *Homo Hierarchus*. Chicago, IL: University of Chicago Press.
Dunleavy, P. and O'Leary, B. 1987. *The Theories of the State: The Politics of Liberal Democracy*. Basingstoke, Hamp., UK: Macmillan Education.
Dunne, T. and Schmidt, B. C. 2001. "Realism." In Bayless, J. and Smith, S. (eds.), *The Globalization of World Politics: An Introduction to International Relations* (2nd ed.). Oxford: Oxford University Press.
Dunning, J. 1993. *Multinational Enterprises and the Global Economy*. Wokingham, Berks, UK: Addison Wesley.
Dunsire, A. 1996. "Tipping the Balance: Autopoiesis and Governance." *Administration and Society* 28 (3): 299–334.
Durkheim, E. [1897] 1952. *Suicide: A Study in Sociology*. London: Routledge & Kegan Paul.
Dworkin, G. 1988. *The Theory and Practice of Autonomy*. Cambridge: Cambridge University Press.
Dye, T. R. 1972. *Understanding Public Policy* (2nd ed.). Englewood Cliffs, NJ: Prentice-Hall.
Eckhoff, T. 1974. *Justice: Its Determinants in Social Interaction*. Rotterdam, Netherlands: Rotterdam University Press.
Eckstein, H. 1988. "A Culture Theory of Political Change." *American Political Science Review* 82 (3): 789–804.
Eckstein, H. 1997. "Social Science as Cultural Science, Rational Choice as Metaphysics." In Ellis, R. J. and Thompson, M. (eds.), *Culture Matters: Essays in Honor of Aaron Wildavsky*. Boulder, CO: Westview.

Edelman. G. M. 1992. *Bright Air, Brilliant Fires: On the Matter of the Mind*. London: Penguin.
Edelman, M. 1964. *The Symbolic Uses of Politics*, Champaign-Urbana IL: University of Illinois Press.
Edelman, M. 1988. *Constructing the Political Spectacle*. Chicago, IL: University of Chicago Press.
Edvardsen, U. 1997. "A Cultural Approach to Understanding Modes of Transition to Democracy." *Journal of Theoretical Politics* 9 (2): 211–34.
Edwards, M. 1999. *Future Positive: International Cooperation in the 21st Century*. London: Earthscan and Sterling.
Eilon, S. 1974. "The Board: Functions and Structure." *Management Decisions* 12 (2): 167–190.
Eilstein, H. 1995. "The Virus of Fatalism." In Gavrogulu, A., Stachel, J. and Wartofsky, M. (eds.), *Science, Mind and Art*. Dordrecht, Netherlands: Kluwer.
Ekins, P. 1992. *A New World Order: Grassroots Movements for Global Change*. London: Routledge.
Elder, N., Thomas, A. and Arter, D. 1982. *The Consensular Democracies? The Government and Politics of Scandinavian States*. Oxford: Martin Robertson.
Eldredge N. 1986. *Time Frames: the Rethinking of Darwinian Evolution and the Theory of Punctuated Equilibria*. Princeton, NJ: Princeton University Press.
Ellis, R. J. 1991. "Explaining the Occurrence of Charismatic Leadership in Organizations." *Journal of Theoretical Politics* 3 (3): 305–20.
Ellis, R. J. 1992a. "Rival Visions of Equality in American Political Culture." *Review of Politics* 54: 253–80.
Ellis, R. J. 1992b. "Radical Locheanism in American Political Culture." *Western Political Quarterly* 45 (4): 825–50
Ellis, R. J. and Thompson, F. 1997a. "Culture and the Environment in the Pacific Northwest." *American Political Science Review* 91 (4): 885–97.
Ellis, R. J. and Thompson, F. 1997b. "Seeing Green: Cultural Biases and Environmental Preferences." In Ellis, R. J. and Thompson, M. (eds.), *Culture Matters: Essays in Honor of Aaron Wildavsky*. Boulder, CO: Westview.
Ellis, R. J. and Thompson, M. 1997a. "Introduction." In Ellis, R. J. and Thompson, M. (eds.), *Culture Matters: Essays in Honor of Aaron Wildavsky*. Boulder, CO: Westview
Ellis, R. J. and Thompson, M. (eds.) 1997b. *Culture Matters: Essays in Honor of Aaron Wildavsky*. Boulder, CO: Westview.
Ellis, R. J. and Wildavsky, A. 1989. *Dilemmas of Presidential Leadership, From Washington through Lincoln*. New Brunswick, NJ, and Oxford: Transaction Books.
Ellis, R. J. and Wildavsky, A. 1990. "A Cultural Analysis of the Role of Abolitionists in the Coming of the Civil War." *Comparative Studies of Society and History* 31–2: 89–116.
Elster, J. 1985a. *Making Sense of Marx*. Cambridge: Cambridge University Press.
Elster, J. 1985b. *Sour Grapes: Studies in the Subversion of Rationality*. Cambridge: Cambridge University Press
Elster, J. 1991a. *The Cement of Society: A Study of Social Order*. Cambridge: Cambridge University Press.
Elster, J. 1991b. "The Possibility of Rational Politics." In Held, D. (ed.), *Political Theory Today*. Oxford: Oxford University Press.
Emery, F. E. and Trist, E. L. 1965. "The Causal Texture of Organizational Environments." *Human Relations* 18 (1): 21–32.

Emiliou, N. 1992. "Subsidiarity: An Effective Barrier against 'the Enterprise of Ambition.'" *European Law Review* 17: 383–407.
Epstein, E. J. 1986. *Who Owns the Corporation? Management or Shareholders.* New York: Priority Press.
Epstein, R. A. 1985. *Takings: Private Property and the Power of Eminent Domain.* Chicago, IL: University of Chicago Press.
Etzioni, A. 1961. *A Comparative Analysis of Complex Organizations.* New York: Free Press.
Ermarth, E. D. 1992. *Sequel to History: Postmodernism and the Crisis of Representational Time.* Princeton, NJ: Princeton University Press.
Etzioni, A. 1965. "Organizational Control Structure." In March, J. G. (ed.), *Handbook of Organizations.* Chicago, IL: Rand-McNally.
Etzioni, A. 1968. *The Active Society: A Theory of Societal and Political Processes.* New York: Free Press.
Etzioni, A. 1988. *The Moral Dimension: Towards a New Economics.* New York: Free Press.
Etzioni, A. 1993. *The Spirit of Community: Rights, Responsibilities and the Communitarian Agenda.* New York: Crown Publishers.
Etzioni, A. 1994. "Who Should Pay for Care?" *The Sunday Times* (London), 3 July.
Etzioni, A. 1995. *New Communitarian Thinking: Persons, Virtues, Institutions, and Communities.* Charlottsville, VA: University of Virginia Press.
European Commission 1983. *The Employee's Right to Know* (SEC/B24/83, 11 August). Brussels, Belgium: European Commission.
Evan, W. M. 1972. "An Organizational-set Model of Interorganizational Relations." In Tuite, M. F., Radnor, M. and Chisholm, R. K. (eds.), *Interorganizational Decision-Making.* Chicago, IL: Aldine-Atherton.
Evans, D. A. and Alexander, S. 1970. "Some Psychological Correlates of Civil Rights Activity." *Psychology Reports* 26: 899–906.
Ezzamel, M. and Watson, R. 1997. "Executive Remuneration and Corporate Performance." In Keasey, K. and Wright, M. (eds.), *Corporate Governance: Responsibilities, Risks and Remuneration.* Chichester, W Susx., UK: Wiley.
Falk, R. 1992a. "Democratizing, Internationalizing and Globalizing: A Collage of Blurred Images." *Third World Quarterly* 13 (4): 627–40.
Falk, R. 1992b. "The Making of Global Citizenship." In Brecher, J. et al. (eds.), *Global Visions: Beyond the New World Order.* Boston, MA: South End Press.
Falk, R. 1994. "From Geopolitics to Geogovernance: WOMP and Contemporary Political Discourse." *Alternatives* 19 (2): 145–54.
Falk, R. 1995. *On Humane Governance: Towards a Global Politics.* Cambridge: Polity.
Falk Moore, S. 1983. *Law as a Process: An Anthropological Approach.* London: Routledge & Kegan Paul.
Fama, F. and Jensen, M. 1983a. "Separation of Ownership and Control." *Journal of Law and Economics* 26: 301–26.
Fama, F. and Jensen, M. 1983b. "Agency Problems and Residual Claims." *Journal of Law and Economics* 26: 327–49.
Fardon, R. 1999. *Mary Douglas: An Intellectual Biography.* London: Routledge.
Fayol, H. [1916] 1949. *General and Industrial Management* (tr. Stoors, C.). Boston, MA: Pitman.
Feld, W. J. and Pfaltzgraff, R. L., with Hurwitz, L. 1988. *International Organizations: A Comparative Approach.* New York: Praeger.

Feldman, M. S. and Khademain, A. M. 2000. "Managing for Inclusion: Balancing Control and Participation." *International Public Management Journal* 3 (2): 149–167.

Fernandes, P. 1986. *Managing Relations between Government and Public Enterprises: A Handbook for Administrators and Managers* (Management Development Series, 25). Geneva: International Labor Office

Ferrero, G. 1942. *The Principles of Power* (tr. Jaeckel, T.). New York: Putnam.

Festinger, L. 1957. *A Theory of Cognitive Dissonance.* Evanston, IL: Row, Peterson.

Fetzer, J. H. (ed.) 1985. *Sociobiology and Epistemology.* Dordrecht, Netherlands: D. Reidel.

Feuerbach, L. A. [1841] 1893. *The Essence of Christianity* (tr. Evans. M.) (3rd ed.). London: Kegan Paul and Trench Trubner.

Feyerabend, P. K. 1976. *Against Method.* New York: Humanities Press.

Fischel, W. A. 1995. *Regulatory Takings: Law, Economics, and Politics.* Cambridge, MA: Harvard University Press.

Fischer, F. and Forester, J. 1993. "Introduction." In Fischer, F. and Forester, J. (eds.) *The Argumentative Turn in Policy Analysis and Planning.* London: UCL Press.

Fisher, G. 1988. *Mindsets: The Role of Culture and Perception in International Relations.* Yarmouth, ME: Intercultural Press.

Fisher, R. 1981. *Compliance with International Law.* Charlottesville, VA: University Press of Virginia.

Fiskin, J. 1991. *Democracy and Deliberation.* New Haven, CT: Yale University Press.

Fitzmaurice, J. 1991. *Austrian Politics and Society Today*, London: Macmillan.

Flathman, R. E. 1980. *The Practice of Political Authority: Authority and the Authoritative.* Chicago, IL: University of Chicago Press.

Fletcher, J. 1966. *Situational Ethics.* Philadelphia, PA: Westminster Press.

Follett, M. P. 1918. *The New State: Group Organization the Solution of Popular Government.* New York: Longmans, Green.

Follett, M. P. [1940] 1973. *Dynamic Administration: The Collected Papers of MaryParker Follett* (eds. Fox, E. M. and Urwick, L.). London: Pitman.

Fontana, B. (ed.) 1994. *The Invention of the Modern Republic.* Cambridge: Cambridge University Press.

Forbes, G. 1989. *Language of Possibility.* Oxford: Oxford University Press,

Forester, J. 1989. *Planning in the Phase of Power.* Berkeley, CA: University of California Press.

Foucault, M. [1966] 1970. *The Order of Things* (tr. Sheridan, A.). New York: Random House.

Foucault, M. 1976. *The Archaeology of Knowledge and the Discourse on Language.* New York: Harper Colophon.

Foucault, M. 1978. *The History of Sexuality, Vol. 1: An Introduction* (tr. Hurley, R.). New York: Pantheon.

Foucault, M. 1980. *Power/Knowledge: Selected Interviews And Other Writings 1972–1977* (cd. Gordon, C.). New York. Harvester Wheatsheaf.

Foucault, M. 1984. "Nietzsche, Genealogy, History." In Rabinow, P. (ed.), *The Foucault Reader.* New York: Pantheon.

Foucault, M. 1991. "Governmentality." In Burchaell, G., Gordon, C. and Miller, P. (eds.), *The Foucault Effect: Studies In Governability.* Hemel Hempstead, Herts. UK: Harvester Wheatsheaf.

Foy, N. 1980. *The Yin and Yang of Organizations: A Scintillating Guide to the Best in Current Management Thinking.* London: Grant McIntyre.

Francis, A., Turk, J. and Willman, P. (eds.) 1983. *Power, Efficiency and Institutions.* London: Heinemann Educational.
Frank, A. G. 1991. "No Escape from the Laws of World Economics." *Review of African Political Economy* 50 (1): 20–31.
Frederic, H. 1992. "Computer Networks and the Emergence of Global Civil Society." In Harasim, L. M. (ed.), *Global Networks: Computers and International Communication.* Pacific Grove, CA: Cole.
Freeman, R. E. 1984. *Strategic Management: A Stakeholder Approach.* Boston, MA: Pitman.
Freeman, R. E. and Evans, W. M. 1990. "Corporate Governance: A Stakeholder Interpretation." *Journal of Behavioral Economics* 19: 357–59.
French, J. R. P. and Raven, B. 1959. "The Bases of Social Power." In Cartwright, D. (ed.), *Studies in Social Power.* Ann Arbor, MI: University of Michigan Press.
Fried, C. 1978. *Right and Wrong.* Cambridge, MA: Harvard University Press.
Friedman, M. 1970. *Capitalism and Freedom.* Chicago, IL: University of Chicago Press.
Friere, P. 1972. *Pedagogy of the Oppressed.* Harmondsworth, Gt. Lon., UK: Penguin.
Friese, H. and Wagner, P. 1999. "Not All that is Solid Melts into Air: Modernity and Contingency." In Featherstone, M. and Lash, S. E. (eds.), *Spaces of Culture: City, Nation, World.* London: Sage.
Frooman, J. 1997. "Social Irresponsibility and Illegal Behaviour and Shareholder Wealth: A Meta-Analysis of Event Studies." *Business and Society* 36 (3): 221–49.
Frost, M. 1996. *Ethics in International Relations: A Constitutive Theory.* Cambridge: Cambridge University Press.
Fukuyama, F. 1989. "The End of History." *National Interest* 16 (Summer): 3–18.
Fukuyama, F. 1995. *Trust.* London: Hamish Hamilton.
Funk, W. 1997. "Bargaining Towards the New Millenium: Regulatory Negotiation and the Subversion of the Public Interest." *Duke Law Journal* 46: 1351–88.
Furnham, A. 1984. "Many Sides of the Coin: The Psychology of Money Usage." *Personality and Individual Differences* 5: 501–9.
Gallarotti, G. M. [1991] 1997. "The Limits of International Organization: Systematic Failure in the Management of International Relations." *International Organization,* 45 (2). Reprinted in Diehl, P. F. (ed.), *The Politics of Global Governance: International Organizations in an Interdependent World.* Boulder, CO: Lynne Riener.
Gallie, W. B. 1955. "Essentially Contested Concepts." *Proceedings of the Aristotelian Society* 567: 167–98.
Gambetta, D, (ed.) 1988a *Trust: Making and Breaking.* Oxford: Oxford University Press.
Gambetta, D, 1988b. "Can We Trust?" In Gambetta, D. (ed.), *Trust: Making and Breaking.* Oxford: Oxford University Press.
Garen, J. E. 1994. "Executive Compensation and Principal-Agent Theory." *Journal of Political Economy* 102 (4): 1175–99.
Garfinkel, H. [1967] 1984. *Studies in Ethnomethodology.* Oxford: Blackwell.
Garland, D. 1997. "'Governmentality' and the Problem of Crime: Foucault, Criminology." Sociology." *Theoretical Criminology* 1 (2): 173–214.
Garvin, D. 1983. "Can Industry Self-regulation,Work?" *California Management Review* 25 (4): 42–51.
Geertz, C. 1973. *The Interpretation of Culture.* New York: Basic.
Geertz, C. 1983. "The Way We Think Now: Towards an Ethnography of Modern Thought." In Geertz, C. (ed.), *Local Knowledge.* New York: Basic.

Gellerman, S. W. 1968. *Management by Motivation*. New York: American Management Association.
George, J. and Campbell, D. 1990. "Patterns of Dissent and the Celebration of Differences: Critical Social Theory and International Relations." *International Studies Quarterly* 34 (2): 269–94.
Gergen, K. 1994. *Realities and Relationships: Soundings in Social Construction*. Cambridge, MA: Harvard University Press.
Gergen, K. J. 1999. *An Introduction to Social Construction*. London: Sage.
Gergen, K. J. 2001. *Social Construction in Context*. London: Sage.
Gergen, K. J. and Thatchenkey, T. J. 1998. "Organizational Science in Postmodern Context." In Chia, R. C. H. (ed.), *In the Realm of Organization: Essays for Robert Cooper*. London: Routledge.
Gershuny, J. I. 1978. "Policymaking Rationality: A Reformulation." *Policy Sciences* 9: 295–316.
Gerth, H. H. and Mills, C. W. (eds.) 1948. *From Max Weber: Essays in Sociology*. London: Routledge & Kegan Paul.
Giddens, A. 1979. *Central Problems in Social Theory*. London: Macmillan.
Giddens, A. 1981. *A Contemporary Critique of Historical Materialism*. London: Macmillan.
Giddens, A. 1984. *The Constitution of Society*. Cambridge: Polity.
Giddens, A. 1990. *The Consequences of Modernity*. Cambridge: Polity.
Giddens, A. 1991. *Modernity and Self-Identity: Self and Society*. Cambridge: Polity.
Giddens, A. 1999. *Runaway World: How Globalization is Reshaping Our Lives*. London: Profile Books.
Giddens, A. 2001. *Sociology* (4th ed.). Cambridge: Polity.
Gierke, O. von 1990. *Community in Historical Perspective* (ed. Black, A.). Cambridge: Cambridge University Press.
Gilbert, N. and Gilbert, B. 1989. *The Enabling State*. Oxford: Oxford University Press.
Gill, S. 1992. "Economic Globalization and the Internationalization of Authority: Limits and Contradictions." *Geoforum* 23: 269–83.
Gill, S. 1994a. "Knowledge, Power and Neo-liberal Political Economy." In Stubbs, R. and Underhill, G. (eds.), *Political Economy and the International System: Global Issues, Regional Dynamics and Political Conflict*. Toronto, ON: McLelland and Stewart.
Gill, S. 1994b. "The Global Political Economy and Structural Change: Globalizing Elites in the Emerging World Order." In Sakamoto, Y. (ed.), *Global Transformation*. Tokyo: UN University Press.
Gill, S. 1997. "Globalization, Democratization, and the Politics of Indifference." In Mittelman, J. H. (ed.), *Globalization: Critical Reflections*. Boulder, CO: Lynne Riener.
Gill, S. and Law, D. 1988. *The Global Political Economy*. Baltimore, MD: Johns Hopkins University Press.
Gill, S. and Law, D. 1989. "Global Hegemony and the Structural Power of Capital." *International Studies Quarterly* 33: 475–99.
Gilpin, R. 1987. *The Political Economy of International Relations*. Princeton, NJ: Princeton University Press.
Goffman, E. 1974. *Frame Analysis*. Cambridge, MA: Harvard University Press.
Goodin, R. E. 1992. "The Green Theory of Agency." In Goodin, R. E. (ed.) *Green Political Theory*. Cambridge: Polity.
Goodman, N. 1965. *Fact, Fiction and Forecast*. Indianapolis, IN: Boobs-Merrill.

Gootnick, A. T. 1974. "Locus of Control and Political Participation of College Students: A Comparison of Unidimensional and Multidimensional Approaches." *Journal of Consulting and Clinical Psychology* 42: 54–58.

Gore, P. S. and Rotter, J. B. 1963. "A Personality Correlate of Social Action." *Journal of Personality* 31: 58–64.

Gormley, W. T., Jr. 1994. "Privatization Revisited." *Policy Studies Review* 13 (3/4): 215–34.

Gouinlock, J. 1972. *John Dewey's Philosophy of Value*. New York: Humanities Press.

Gould, S. J. 1989. *Wonderful Life: The Burgess Shale and the Nature of History*. New York: Norton.

Granovetter, M. 1985. "Economic Action and Social Structure: The Problem of Embeddedness." *American Journal of Sociology* 91: 481–510.

Grant, W. (ed.) 1985. *The Political Economy of Corporatism*. London: Macmillan.

Grant, W. 1996a. "Interest Groups." In McLean, I. (ed.), *The Concise Oxford Dictionary of Politics*. Oxford: Oxford University Press.

Grant, W. 1996b. "Social Movements." In McLean, I. (ed.), *The Concise Oxford Dictionary of Politics*. Oxford: Oxford University Press.

Grauer, M., Wiezbicki, A. and Thompson, M. 1985. *Plural Rationality and Interactive Decision Processes* (Lecture Notes in Economics and Mathematical Systems, 248). Berlin: Springer-Varlag.

Graves, R. [1955] 1996. *The Greek Myths* (vol. 1). London: The Folio Society.

Gray, B. 1989. *Collaborating: Finding Common Ground for Multi-Party Collaboration*. San Francisco, CA: Jossey-Bass.

Gray, P. 1998. *Policy Disasters*. London: Routledge.

Green, O. 2001. "Environmental Issues." In Bayless, J. and Smith, S. (eds.), *The Globalization of World Politics: An Introduction to International Relations* (2nd ed.). Oxford: Oxford University Press.

Green, T. H. 1899. *Prolegomena to Ethics*. Oxford: Clarendon.

Greenberg, J. 1987. "Reactions to Procedural Injustice in Payment Distribution: Do the Means Justify the Ends?" *Journal of Applied Psychology* 72 (1): 55–61.

Greif, A. 1994. "Cultural Beliefs and the Organization of Society: A Historical and Theoretical Reflection on Collectivist and Individualist Societies." *Journal of Political Economy* 102 (5): 912–50.

Grendstad, G. 1999. "A Political Map of Europe: A Survey Approach." *GeoJournal* 47 (3): 463–75.

Grendstad, G. 2000. "Grid-Group Theory and Political Orientation: Effects of Cultural Biases in Norway in the 1990s." *Scandinavian Political Studies* 23 (3): 217–44.

Grendstad, G. 2001. "Nordic Cultural Baselines: Accounting for Domestic Convergence and Foreign Policy Divergence." *Journal of Comparative Policy Analysis* 3 (1): 5–30.

Grendstad, G. and Selle, P. 1995. "A Culture Theory and the New Institutionalism." *Journal of Theoretical Politics* 7 (1): 5–27.

Grendstad, G. and Selle, P. 1997. "Culture Theory, Postmaterialism and Environmental Attitudes." In Ellis, R. J. and Thompson, M. (eds.), *Culture Matters: Essays in Honor of Aaron Wildavsky*. Boulder, CO: Westview.

Grendstad, G. and Selle, P. 1999. "The Formation and Transformation of Preferences: Cultural Theory and Postmaterialism Compared." In Thompson, M., Grendstat, G. and Selle, P. (eds.), *Cultural Theory as Political Science*. London: Routledge.

Grendstad, G. and Selle, P. 2000. "Cultural Myths of Human and Physical Nature: Integrated or Separated?" *Risk Analysis* 20 (1): 27–39.

Groom, A. J. R. and Taylor, P. (eds.) 1975. *Functionalism: Theory and Practice of International Relations.* New York: Crane, Russak.

Gross, B. M. 1964. *The Managing of Organizations: The Administrative Struggle,* Vol. II. London: The Free Press of Glencoe.

Gross, J. and Rayner, S. 1985. *Measuring Culture: A Paradigm for the Analysis of Social Organizations.* New York: Colombia University Press.

Gundfest, J. 1990. "Subordination of American Capital." *Journal of Financial Economics* 27: 89–114.

Gunningham, N. and Grabosky, P. 1998. *Smart Regulation: Designing Environmental Policy.* New York: Oxford University Press.

Gunningham, N. and Sinclaire, D. 1999. "Regulatory Pluralism: Designing Policy Mixes for Environmental Protection." *Law and Policy* 21 (1): 49–76.

Gutherie, J. and Turnbull, S. 1995. "Audit Committees: Is There a Role for Corporate Senates and/or Stakeholder Councils?" *Corporate Governance: An International Review* 3 (2): 78–89.

Gyawali, D. 1999. "Institutional Forces Behind Water Conflict in the Ganga Plains." *GeoJournal* 47 (3): 443–52.

Gyawali, D. 2000a. "Nepal-India Water Resource Relations." In Zartman, I. W. and Rubin, J. Z. (eds.), *Power and Negotiation.* Ann Arbor, MI: University of Michigan Press.

Gyawali, D. 2000b. *Re-orienting Water Resources in Nepal: Evolving New Roles for a Changing Context* (Occasional Paper 8). Kathmandu, Napal: Royal Academy of Science and Technology.

Haas, E. B. 1964a. *Beyond the Nation-State: Functionalism and International Organization.* Stanford, CA: Stanford University Press.

Haas, E. B. 1964b. "Technocracy, Pluralism and the New Europe." In Graubard, S. R. (ed.), *A New Europe.* Boston, MA: Houghton Mifflin.

Haas, E. B. 1980. "Why Collaborate? Issue Linking and International Regimes." *World Politics* 32 (3): 390–406.

Haas, E. B. 1990. *When Knowledge is Power: Three Models of Change in International Organizations.* Berkeley, CA: University of California Press.

Habermas, J. 1968. *Knowledge and Human Interest.* Boston, MA: Beacon Press.

Habermas, J. 1971. *Towards a Rational Society.* Boston, MA: Beacon Press.

Habermas, J. 1975. *Legitimation Crisis.* Boston, MA: Beacon Press.

Habermas, J. 1984. *The Theory of Communicative Action, 1: Reason and the Rationalization of Society.* Boston, MA: Beacon Press.

Habermas, J. 1986. "Hannah Arnedt's Communications Concept of Power." In Lukes, S. (ed.), *Power.* New York: New York University Press.

Habermas, J. 1987. *The Theory of Communicative Action, Vol. 2: Lifeworld and System: A Critique of Functional Reason.* Boston, MA: Beacon Press.

Habermas, J. 1996a. *Between Facts and Norms: Contributions to a Discourse Theory of Law and Democracy.* Cambridge: Polity.

Habermas, J. 1996b. "The Normative Models of Democracy." In Benhabib, S. (ed.), *Democracy and Difference: Contesting the Boundaries of the Political.* Princeton, NJ: Princeton University Press.

Hague, D. C., Mackenzie, W. J. M. and Barker, A. S. 1975. *Public Policy and Private Interest.* London: Macmillan.

Hague, H. 1978. *The Organic Organization and How to Manage It.* London: Associated Business Press.

Hahlweg, K. and Hooker, C. A. (eds.) 1989. *Issues in Evolutionary Epistemology.* New York: State University of New York Press.

Haight, M. R. 1980. *A Study of Self-Deception*. London: Humanities Press.
Hajer, M. A. 1993. "Discourse Coalitions and the Institutionalization of Practice." In Fischer, F. and Forester, J. (eds.), *The Argumentative Turn in Policy Analysis and Planning*. London: UCL Press.
Hales, C. 2001. *Managing through Organization: The Management Process, Forms of Organisation and the Work of Managers*. London: Business Press.
Hampel Committee on Corporate Governance 1998. *Final Report*. London: Gee Publishing.
Hampton, J. 1986. *Hobbes and the Social Contract Tradition*. Cambridge: Cambridge University Press.
Hancock, M. D. 1989. *West Germany: The Politics of Democratic Corporatism*. Chatham, NJ: Chatham House.
Hancock, M. D., Logue, J. and Schiller, W. (eds.) 1991. *Managing Modern Capitalism: Industrial Renewal and Workplace Democracy in the United States and Western Europe*. Westport, CT: Greenwood.
Handy, C. 1976. *Understanding Organisations*. Harmondsworth, Gt. Lon., UK: Penguin.
Handy, C. 1979. *The Gods of Management*. London: Souvenir Press.
Hannan, M. T. and Freeman, J. 1989. *Organizational Ecology*. Harvard, MA: Harvard University Press.
Hanson, N. R. 1958. *Patterns of Discovery*. Cambridge: Cambridge University Press.
Hart, O. 1995. "Corporate Governance: Some Theory and Implications." *Economic Journal* 105: 678–89.
Harter, P. 1982. "Negotiating Regulations: A Cure for Malaise." *The Georgetown Law Journal* 71 (1): 1–113.
Harvey, D. 1992. *The Condition of Postmodernism: An Enquiry*. Oxford: Oxford University Press.
Hass, P. M. 1989. "Do Regimes Matter? Epistemic Communities and Mediterranean Pollution Control." *International Organization* 43 (2): 377–403.
Hassard, J. 1994. "Postmodern Organizational Analysis: Towards a Conceptual Framework." *Journal of Management Studies* 31 (3): 303–24.
Hatherly, D. J. 1994. "The Case for the Shareholder Panel in the UK." *European Accounting Review* 4 (3): 535–53.
Haubrich, J. G. 1994. "Risk Aversion, Performance Pay and the Principal-Agent Problem." *Journal of Political Economy* 102 (1): 65–105.
Hawley, J. P. and Williams, A. T. 1996. *Corporate Governance in the United States: The Rise of Fiduciary Capitalism* (Working Paper). Los Angeles: Saint Mary's College of California, School of Economics and Business Administration.
Hay, C. 1998. "The Tangled Web We Weave: The Discourse, Strategy and Practice of Networking." In Marsh, D. (ed.) *Comparing Policy Networks*. Buckingham, Bucks., UK: Open University Press.
Hayek, F. A. 1960. *The Constitution of Liberty*. London: Routledge & Kegan Paul.
Hayek, F. A. 1978. *New Studies in Philosophy, Politics, Economics and the History of Ideas*. Chicago, IL: University of Chicago Press.
Hayek, F. A. 1979. *Legislation, Liberty, 3: The Political Order of a Free People*. Chicago, IL: University of Chicago Press.
Hayek, F. A. 1991. "Spontaneous ('Grown') Order and Organized ('Made') Order." In Thompson, G., Francis, J., Levacic, R. and Mitchell, J. (eds.), *Markets, Hierarchies and Networks: The Coordination of Social Life*. London: Sage.
Heald, M. 1970. *The Social Responsibilities of Business: Company and Community, 1900–1960*. Cleveland, OH: The Press of Case Western University.

Hechter, M. 1994. "The Role of Values in Rational Choice Theory." *Rationality and Society* 6 (July): 318-33.
Hechter, M. 2000. *Containing Nationalism*. Oxford: Oxford University Press.
Heclo, H. 1972. "Review Article: Policy Analysis." *British Journal of Political Science* 2 (1); 83-108.
Heclo, H. 1978. "Issue Networks and the Executive Establishment." In King, A. (ed.), *The New American Political System*. Washington, DC: American Enterprise Institute.
Held, D. 1980. *Introduction to Critical Theory*. Berkeley and Los Angeles, CA: University of California Press.
Held, D. 1987. *Models of Democracy*. Cambridge: Cambridge University Press.
Held, D. 1991. "Democracy and Globalization." *Alternatives* 16 (2): 119-74.
Held, D., McGrew, A., Goldblatt, D. and Perraton, J. 1999. *Global Transformation: Politics, Economics and Culture*. Cambridge: Polity.
Held, V. 1984. *Rights and Goods: Justifying Social Action*. New York and London: Free Press.
Hempel, C. G. 1966. *Philosophy of Natural Science*. Englewood Cliffs, NJ: Prentice Hall.
Hendriks, F. 1994. "Cars and Culture in Munich and Birmingham: The Case for Cultural Pluralism. In Coyle, D. J. and Ellis, R. J. (eds.) 1994. *Politics, Policy and Culture*. Boulder, CO: Westview.
Hendriks, F. and Zouridis, S. 1999. "Cultural Biases and New Media for the Public Domain: Cui Bono." In Thompson, M., Grendstat, G. and Selle, P. (eds.), *Cultural Theory as Political Science*. London: Routledge.
Hershey, P. and Blanchard, K. H. 1969. "Life Cycles Theory of Leadership." *Training and Development Journal* 23 (5): 26-34
Hershey, P. and Blanchard, K. H. 1993. *Management of Organizational Behavior* (6th ed.). Englewood Cliffs, NJ: Prentice-Hall.
Herz, J.H. 1969. "The Territorial State Revisited: Reflections on the Future of the Nation-State." In Rosenau, J. N. (ed.), *International Politics and Foreign Policy: A Reader in Research and Theory* (2nd ed.). New York: Free Press.
Herzberg, F. 1966. *Work and the Nature of Man*. New York: World Publishing.
Herzberg, F., Mausner, B. and Snyderman, B. 1959. *The Motivation to Work*. New York: Wiley.
Herzel, L. and Shepro, R. W. 1990. *Bidders and Targets*. Cambridge, MA: Basil Blackwell.
Higgott, R. and Reich, S. 1995. *Globalisation and Sites of Conflict: Towards Definition and Taxonomy* (CSGR Working Paper No. 01/98). Coventry, W Mids., UK: Economic and Social Research Council Centre for the Study of Globalization and Regionalization (CSGR), Warwick University.
Hill, C.W.I. and Jones, T. M. 1992. "Stakeholder-Agency Theory." *Journal of Management Studies* 29 (2): 131-54.
Hillier, B. 1997. *The Economics of Asymmetric Information*. London: Macmillan Press.
Hilmer, F. G. 1993. *Strictly Boardroom*. Melbourne, Vic., Australia: Information Australia.
Hirschman, A. O. 1970. *Exit, Voice and Loyalty: Responses to Decline in Firms, Organizations and States*. Cambridge, MA: Harvard University Press
Hirschman, A. O. 1991. *The Rhetoric of Reaction: Perversity, Futility, Jeopardy*. Cambridge, MA: Harvard University Press.
Hirst, P. 1994. *Associative Democracy: New Forms of Economic and Social Governance*. Cambridge: Polity.

Hirst, P. and Thompson, G. 1996. *Globalization in Question: The International Economy and the Possibilities of Governance*. Cambridge: Polity.
Hobbs, T, [1651] 1991. *Leviathan* (ed. Tuck, R.). Cambridge: Cambridge University Press.
Hochschild, A. 1979. "Emotional Work, Feeling Rules, and Social Structure." *American Journal of Sociology* 85: 551–75.
Hofstede, G. 1980. *Culture's Consequences*. Newbury Park, CA: Sage.
Hofstede, G. 1991. *Cultures and Organizations: Software of the Mind*. New York: McGraw-Hill.
Holland, J. 1994. "Bank Lending Relationships and the Complex Nature of Bank-Corporate Relations." *Journal of Business Finance and Accounting* 21 (3): 367–93.
Holling, C. S. 1986. "The Resilience and Vulnerability of Eco-systems." In Clark, W. C. and Munn, R. E. (eds.), *The Sustainable Development of the Biosphere*. Cambridge: Cambridge University Press.
Hollingsworth, J. R. and Lindberg, L. N. 1985. "The Governance of the American Economy: The Role of Markets, Clans, Hierarchies, and Associative Behaviours." In Streeck, W. and Schmitter, P. C. (eds.), *Private Interest Government: Beyond Markets and State*. London: Sage.
Hollingsworth, J. R., Schmitter, P. C. and Streeck, W. 1994. "Capitalism, Sectors, Institutions, and Performance." In Hollingsworth, J. R., Schmitter, P. C. and Streeck, W. (eds.), *Governing Capitalist Economies*. London: Oxford University Press.
Hollis, M. 1994. *The Philosophy of Social Science*. Cambridge: Cambridge University Press.
Hollis, M. and Lukes, S. (eds.) 1982. *Rationality and Relativism*. Cambridge, MA: MIT Press.
Holsti, K. J. 1991. *Peace and War: Armed Conflict and International Order, 1648–1989*. Cambridge: Cambridge University Press.
Holsti, K. J. 1992. "Governance Without Government Polyarchy in Nineteenth-Century European International Politics." In Rosenau, J. N. and Czempiel, E.–O. (eds.), *Governance Without Government Order and Change in World Politics*. Cambridge: Cambridge University Press.
Hood, C. 1986. *Administrative Analysis: An Introduction to Rules, Enforcement and Organizations*. Brighton, E. Susx., UK: Wheatsheaf Books.
Hood, C. 1998. *The Art of the State: Culture, Rhetoric, and Public Management*. Oxford: Clarendon.
Hoppe, R. 1993. "Political Judgement and the Policy Cycle: The Case of Ethnicity Policy Arguments in the Netherlands." In Fischer, F. and Forester, J. (eds.) *The Argumentative Turn in Policy Analysis and Planning*. London: UCL Press.
Hoppe, R. 1999. "Culture Theory and the Study of Public Policy." Paper presented at the Symposium on Theory, Policy and Society, Leiden University, Netherlands, June 24–25.
Hoppe, R. 2000. "Grid-Group Culture Theory and the Politics of Problem Definition." Paper presented at the 8th Biennial Jerusalem Conference in Canadian Studies, Hebrew University of Jerusalem, Israel, June 25–29.
Hoppe, R. and Grin, J. 1999. "Pollution through Traffic and Transport: A *Praxis* of Cultural Pluralism in Parliamentary Technology Assessment." In Thompson, M., Grendstat, G. and Selle, P. (eds.) *Cultural Theory as Political Science*. London: Routledge.
House, R. J. and Mitchell, T. R. 1974. "Path-goal Theory of Leadership." *Journal of Contemporary Business* 3: 81–97.
Howard, L. (ed.) 1992. *Terrorism: Roots, Impact, Responses*. New York: Praeger.

Hudson, B., Hardy, B., Henwood, M. and Wistow, G. 1999. "In Pursuit of Inter-Agency Collaboration in the Public Sector." *Public Management* 1(2): 235–60.
Hulsink, W. 1996. *Do Nations matter in a Globalising Industry? The Restructuring of Telecommunications Governance Regimes in France, the Netherlands and the United Kingdom*. Delft, Netherlands: Eburon.
Hult, K. and Walcott, C. 1990. *Governing Public Organizations*. Pacific Grove, CA: Brooks/Cole.
Hume, D. [1748] 1920. *An Enquiry Concerning Human Understanding* (ed. Selby-Biggs, L. A.). Oxford: Clarendon.
Humphrey, C., Moizer, P. and Turley, S. 1993. "The Audit Expectations Gap in Britain: An Empirical Investigation." *Accounting and Business Research* 23: 395–411.
Huntington, S. P. 1997. *The Clash of Civilizations and the Remaking of World Order*. New York: Simon and Schuster.
Hurd, J. P. (ed.) 1996. *Investigating the Biological Foundations of Human Morality*. New York: Edwin Mellon.
Hutcheon, L. 1989. *The Politics of Postmodernism*. London and New York: Routledge.
Hurka, T. 1993. *Perfectionism*. New York: Oxford University Press.
Hutchings, K. 1999. *International Political Theory: A Critical Investigation*. London: Sage.
Hutter, B. M. 1997. *Compliance: Regulation and Environment*. Oxford: Clarendon.
Huxham, C. 1991. "Facilitating Collaboration: Issues in Multi-Organizational Group Decision Support in Voluntary, Informal Collaborating Settings." *Journal of Operational Research* 42 (12): 1037–45.
Huxham, C. (ed.) 1996. *Creating Collaborative Advantage*. London: Sage.
Huxham, C. 2000. "The Challenge of Collaborative Governance." *Public Management* 2 (3): 337–58.
Huxham, C. and Macdonald, D. 1992. "Introducing Collaborative Advantage." *Management Decision* 30 (3): 5–17.
Huxham, C. and Vangen, S. 2000. "Ambiguity, Complexity and Dynamics in the Membership of Collaboration." *Human Relations* 53 (6): 771–806.
Hyde, M and Dixon, J. 2001. "Welfare Ideology, the Market and Social Security: Towards a Typology of Market-Oriented Reform." In Dixon, J, and Hyde, M. (eds.) *The Marketization of Social Security*. Westport, CT: Quorum Books.
Illich, I. 1977. *Mediaeval Nemesis: The Expropriation of Health*. Harmondsworth, Gt. Lon., UK: Penguin.
Inglehart, R. 1990. "Values, Ideology, and Cognitive Mobilization in New Social Movements." In Russell, J. D. and Kuechler, M. (eds.), *Challenging the Political Order: New Social and Political Movements in Western Democracies*. Cambridge: Polity.
Institute of Directors 1982. *A Code of Practice for the Non-executive Director*. London: Institute of Directors, Non-Executive Director Appointment Service.
In't Veld, R. J., Schaap, L., Termeer, C. J. A. M. and van Twist, M. J. W. (eds.) 1991. *Autopoiesis and Configuration Theory: New Approaches to Societal Steering*. Dordrecht, Netherlands: Kluwer.
Isakovic, Z. 2000. *Introduction to a Theory of Political Power in International Relations*. Aldershot, Hants., UK: Ashgate.
Jackson, R. H. 1991. *Quasi-States: Sovereignty, International Relations and the Third World*. Cambridge: Cambridge University Press.
Jackson, R. H. and Sorensen, G. 1999. *Introduction to International Relations*. Oxford: Oxford University Press.

Jacobson, H. K. 1984. *Networks of Interdependence: International Organizations and the Global Political System* (2nd ed.). New York: Alfred A Knopf.

Jacobson, H. K., Reisinger, W. M. and Mathers, T. [1986] 1997. "National Entanglements in International Governmental Organizations." *American Political Science Review* 80 (1). Reprinted in Diehl, P. F. (ed.), *The Politics of Global Governance: International Organizations in an Interdependent World*. Boulder, CO: Lynne Riener.

Jamieson, A. 1995. *Terrorism.* New York: Thomson Learning.

Janakiraman, S. N., Lambert, R. A. and Larcker, D. F. 1992. "An Empirical Investigation of the Relative Performance Evaluation Hypothesis." *Journal of Accounting Research* 30 (1): 53–69.

Janis, L. L. 1972. *Groupthink: Psychological Policy Decisions and Fiascoes*. Boston, MA: Houghton Mifflin.

Jaques, E. 1976. *A General Theory of Bureaucracy*. London: Heinemann.

Jeffcutt, P. 1994. "From Interpretation to Representation in Organizational Analysis: Postmodernism, Ethnography and Organizational Symbolism." *Organizational Studies* 15 (2): 241–74.

Jenkins-Smith, H. C. and Smith, W. K. 1994. "Ideology, Culture and Risk Perception." In Coyle, D. J. and Ellis, R. J. (eds.), *Politics, Policy and Culture*. Boulder, CO: Westview.

Jensen, J. and de Sousa Santos, B. 2000. *Globalizing Institutions: Case Studies in Regulation and Innovation*. Aldershot, Hants., UK: Ashgate.

Jensen, L. 1998. "Cultural Theory and Democratising Functional Domains." *Public Administration* 76 (1): 117–39.

Jensen, L. 1999. "Images of Democracy in Danish Social Housing." In Thompson, M., Grendstat, G. and Selle, P. (eds.), *Cultural Theory as Political Science*. London: Routledge

Jensen, M. C. and Meckling, W. H. 1976. "Theory of the Firm: Managerial Behavior, Agency Costs and Ownership Structure." *Journal of Financial Economics* 3: 305–60.

Jensen, M. C. and Murphy, K. L. 1990. "Performance Pay and Top-Management Incentives." *Journal of Political Economy* 98 (1): 255–65.

Jessop, B. 1979. "Corporatism, Parliamentarism and Social Democracy." In Schmitter, P. C. and Lehmbruch, G. (eds.), *Trends towards Corporatist Intermediation*. London: Sage.

Jessop, B. 1990. *State Theory: Putting Capitalist States in Their Place*. Cambridge: Polity.

Jessop, B. 1997. Capitalism and Its Future: Remarks on Regulation, Government and Governance. *Review of International Political Economy* 4 (3): 561–607.

Jessop, B. 2001. *Regulatory Theory and the Crisis of Capitalism* (5 vols). Cheltenham, Glos., UK: Edward Elgar

Johnson, G. 1995. "The Evolutionary Origins of Government and Politics." In Somit, A. and Losco, J. (eds.), *Research in Biopolitics, 3: Human Nature and Politics*. Greenwich, CT: JAI Press.

Johnson, S., Rickwood, C. and Greenfield, S. 1993. *Accounting Control and Management Philosophies*. London: CAEW, Research Board.

Johnston, H. and Klandermans, B. 1995. "The Cultural Analysis of Social Movements." In Johnston, H. and Klandermans, B. (eds.), *Social Movements and Culture*. London: UCL Press.

Jones, C. 1996a. "Idealism." In McLean, I. (ed.), *The Concise Oxford Dictionary of Politics*. Oxford: Oxford University Press.

Jones, C. 1996b. "Regime." In McLean, I. (ed.), *The Concise Oxford Dictionary of Politics*. Oxford: Oxford University Press.
Jones, C. 1996c. "Multinational Corporation." In McLean, I. (ed.), *The Concise Oxford Dictionary of Politics*. Oxford: Oxford University Press.
Jones, G. N. 1991. "Education and Training in Public Administration: Transference of Segmenting Organizational Behavior." *International Journal of Public Administration* 14 (2): 197–235.
Jordan, G. 1990. "Sub-governments, Policy Communities and Network Labels." *Journal of Theoretical Politics* 2 (3): 319–38.
Jordan, G. and Schubert, K. 1992. "A Preliminary Ordering of Policy Network Labels." *European Journal of Political Research* 21 (1–2): 7–27.
Jouvenel, B., de. 1957. *Sovereignty*. Cambridge: Cambridge University Press.
Julius, D. 1990. *Global Companies and Public Policy: The Growing Challenge of Foreign Direct Investment*. London: Pinter in conjunction with the Royal Institute of International Affairs.
Julius, D. 1997. "Globalization and Stakeholder Conflicts: A Corporate Perspective." *International Affairs* 73 (3): 435–668.
Kahn, R. L. 1974. "Organizational Development: Some Problems and Prospects." *The Journal of Applied Behavioral Science* 10 (4): 485–502.
Kakabadse, A. and Kakabadse, N. 2001. *The Geopolitics of Governance: The Impact of Contrasting Philosophies*. Basingstoke, Hamp., UK: Palgrave.
Kaldor, M. 1999. *New and Old Wars*. Cambridge: Polity.
Kant, I. [1781-87] 1963. *Critique of Pure Reason* (tr. Kemp Smith, N.). London: Macmillan.
Kanter, R. M. 1984. *The Change Masters: Corporate Entrepreneurs at Work*. London: Allen & Unwin.
Kanter, R. M. 1989. *When Giants Learn to Dance*. New York: Simon and Schuster.
Kateb, G. 1963. *Utopia and Its Enemies*. New York: Free Press.
Katz, D. and Kahn, R. 1966. *The Social Psychology of Organizations*. New York: Wiley.
Katzenstein, P. J. 1996. "Introduction: Alternative Perspectives on National Security." In Katzenstein, P. J. (ed.), *The Culture of National Security: Norms and Identity in World Politics*. New York: Columbia University Press.
Kaufman, H. 1976. *Are Governmental Organizations Immortal?* Washington, DC: Brooking Institution.
Kaul, I., Grundberg, I. and Stern, M. A. (eds.) 1999. *Global Public Goods: International Cooperation in the 21st Century*. New York: Oxford University Press.
Kaviraj, S. and Khilnani, S. 2001. *Civil Society: History and Possibilities*. Cambridge: Cambridge University Press.
Kazancigil, A. 1998. *Governance and Science: Market-like Modes of Managing Society and Producing Knowledge*. Paris: UNESCO.
Keasey, K. and Wright, M. 1993. "Corporate Governance: Issues and Concerns." *Accounting and Business Research* 23: 301–13.
Keasey, K. and Wright, M. (eds.), 1997. *Corporate Governance: Responsibilities, Risks and Remuneration*. Chichester, W Susx., UK: Wiley.
Kegley, C. (ed.) 1995. *Controversies in International Relations Theory: The Neorealism and the Neoliberal Challenge*. New York: St Martin's Press.
Kendig, K. 1999. *Civil Society, Global Governance and the United Nations*. Tokyo: United Nations University.
Kenis, P. and Schneider, V. 1991. "Policy Networks and Policy Analysis: Scrutinizing a New Analytical Toolbox." In Marin, B. and Mayntz, R. (eds.), *Policy Networks: Empirical Evidence and Theoretical Considerations*. Boulder, CO: Westview.

Keohane, R. 1982. "The Demand for International Regimes." *International Organization* 34 (2): 325–56.
Keohane, R. O. 1984. *After Hegemony: Cooperation and Discord in the World Political Economy*. Princeton, NJ: Princeton University Press.
Keohane, R. O. (ed.) 1986. *Neorealism and Its Critics*. New York: Columbia University Press.
Keohane, R. O. 1989. "Neoliberal Institutionalism: A Perspective on World Politics." In Keohane, R. O. (ed.), *International Institutions and State Power*. Boulder, CO: Westview.
Keohane, R. O. 1991. *Sovereignty, Interdependence, and International Institutions* (Working Paper 1). Cambridge, MA: Harvard University.
Koehane, R. O. and Nye, S. J., Jr. 1977. *Power and Interdependence: World Politics in Transition*. Boston, MA: Little, Brown.
Kester, W. C. 1992. "Industrial Groups as Systems of Contractual Governance." *Oxford Review of Economics Policy* 8 (3): 24–44.
Kettl, D. F. 1993. *Sharing Power: Public Governance and Private Markets*. Washington, DC: Brooking Institution.
Keynes, J. M. 1926. *Essays in Persuasion*. London: Macmillan.
Kickert, W. J. 1993. "Autopoiesis and the Science of (Public) Administration." *Organizational Studies* 14 (3): 261–78.
Kickert, W. J. 1993. "Complexity, Governance and Dynamics: Conceptual Explorations of Public Network Management." In Kooiman, J. (ed.), *Modern Governance: New Government-Society Interactions*. Newbury Park, CA: Sage.
Kickert, W. J., Klijn, J. and Koppenjan, J. 1997. *Managing Complex Networks*. London: Sage.
Kindleberger, C. P. (ed.) 1970. *The International Corporation*. Cambridge, MA: MIT Press.
Kingdon, J. W. 1984. *Agendas, Alternatives and Public Policies*. Boston, MA: Little, Brown.
Kirkham, R. L. 1992. *Theories of Truth: A Critical Introduction*. Cambridge, MA: MIT Press.
Kitcher, P. 1985. *Vaulting Ambition: Sociobiology and the Quest for Human Nature*. Cambridge, MA: MIT Press.
Klijn, E. H. and Koppenjan, J. F. M. 2000. "Public Management and Policy Networks: Foundations of a Network Approach to Governance." *Public Management* 2 (2): 135–58.
Klijn, E. H., Koppenjan, J. F. M. and Terrier, C. J. M. 1995. "Managing Networks in the Public Sector." *Public Administration* 73 (3): 437–54.
Knight, W. A. 1996. "Towards a Subsidiarity Model for Peacemaking and Preventive Diplomacy: Making Chapter VIII of the UN Charter Operational." *Third World Quarterly* 17 (1): 31–52.
Knight, W. A. 2000. *A Changing United Nations: Multilateral Evolution and the Quest for Global Governance*. New York: Palgrave.
Knorr-Cetina, K. D. 1981. *The Manufacture of Knowledge*. Oxford: Pergamon.
Knut, R. 1997. *Globalization and Civil Society: NGO Influence in International Decision-making*. Geneva: UNRISD.
Kochan, N. and Syrett, M. 1991. *New Directions in Corporate Governance*. London: Business International.
Koestler, A. 1967. *The Ghost in the Machine*. London: Hutchinson.
Kolaja, J. 1965. *Workers' Councils: The Yugoslav Experience*. London: Tavistock.

Kooiman, J. (ed.) 1993. *Modern Governance: New Government-Society Interactions*. Newbury Park, CA: Sage.
Kooiman, J. 1997. "Social-Political Governance." Paper presented at the Ross Priority Conference on the Theories of Governance, University of Strathclyde, Glasgow, UK, October.
Kooiman, J. 1999. "Social-Political Governance: Overview, Reflection and Design." *Public Management* 1 (1): 67–92.
Kooiman, J. 2000. "Societal Governance: Levels, Modes and Orders of Social-Political Interaction." In Pierre, J. (ed.), *Debating Governance: Authority, Steering and Democracy*. Oxford: Oxford University Press.
Kooiman, J. 2001. *Interactive Governance*. London: Routledge.
Kooiman, J. and Van Vliet, M. 1993. "Governance and Public Management." In Eliassen, K. and Kooiman, J. (eds.), *Managing Public Organisations* (2nd ed.). London: Sage.
Kooiman, J. and Van Vliet, M. 1995. "Riding Tandem: The Case of Co-governance." *Demos* 7: 44–5.
Kooiman and Associates 1997. *Social-Political Governance and Management* (Report Series 33, 34 and 35). Rotterdam, Netherlands: Erasmas University, Rotterdam School of Management.
Kooiman, J. and Van Vliet, M. 2001. "Self-governance as a Mode of Societal Governance." *Public Management* 2 (3): 360–77.
Korac-Kakabadse, N., Kakabadse, A. and Kouzmin, A. 2001. "Board Governance and Company Performance: Any Correlations." *Corporate Governance* 1 (1): 24–30.
Kothari, R. 1987. "On Human Governance." *Alternatives* 12 (3): 275–93.
Krasner, S. D. 1983. "Structural Causes and Regime Consequences: Regimes as Intervening Variables." In Krasner, S. D. (ed.), *International Regimes*. Ithaca, NY: Cornell University Press.
Krasner, S. D. 1984. "Approaches to the State." *Comparative Politics* 16 (1): 223–46.
Krasner, S. D. 1985. *Structural Conflict: The Third World against Global Liberalism*. Berkeley, CA: University of California Press.
Kratochwil, F. and Ruggie, J. G. 1986. "International Organization: A State of the Art or an Art of the State." *International Organization* 40 (4): 735–75.
Krause, K. and Williams, M. 1996. "Broadening the Agenda for Security Studies: Politics and Methods." *Mershan International Studies Review* 40 (2 Supplement): 9–54.
Kressel, N. J. 2001. *Mass Hate: The Global Rise of Genocide and Terror*. Boulder, CO: Westview.
Kugler, J. and Domke, W. 1986. "Comparing the Strength of Nations." *Comparative Political Studies* 19 (1): 39–69.
Kuhn, T. S. 1970. *The Structure of Scientific Revolutions* (2nd ed.). Chicago, IL: University of Chicago Press.
Kunreuther, H. C., Linnerooth, J., Lathrop, J., Atz, H., Macgill, S., Mandl, C., Schwartz, M. and Thompson, M. 1983. *Risk Analysis and Decision Processes: The Siting of Liquefied Energy Gas Facilities in Four Countries*. Berlin: Springer-Verlag.
Kymlicka, W. 1990. *Contemporary Political Philosophy: An Introduction*. Oxford: Oxford University Press.
Laitin, D. and Wildavsky, A. 1988. "Political Culture and Political Preferences." *American Political Science Review* 82 (2): 589–97.
Lakoff, G. and Johnston, M. 1980. *Metaphors We Live By*. Chicago, IL: University of Chicago Press.
Lamy, S. L. 2001. "Contemporary Mainstream Approaches: Neo-Realism and Neo-Liberalism." In Bayless, J. and Smith, S. (eds.), *The Globalization of World Politics:*

An Introduction to International Relations (2nd ed.). Oxford: Oxford University Press.
Lasch, C. 1978. *The Culture of Narcissism: American Life in an Age of Diminishing Expectations*. New York: Norton.
Lasswell. H. D. 1930. *Psychopathology and Politics*. Chicago, IL: University of Chicago Press.
Lasswell. H. D. 1948. *Power and Personality*. New York: W. W. Norton.
Lasswell, H. D. 1958. *Politics: Who Gets What, When, How* (2nd ed.). Cleveland, OH: Meriden Books.
Lasswell, H. D. and Kaplan, A. 1950. *Power and Society*. New Haven, CT: Yale University Press.
Laumann, E. O. and Knoke, D. 1987: *The Organizational State*. Madison, WI: University of Wisconsin Press.
Laurence, P. R. and Lorsch, J. W. 1967. *Organization and Environment*. Cambridge, MA: Harvard University Press.
Lecher, W., Negal, B. and Platzer, H.–W. 1999. *The Establishment of European Works Councils: From Information Committee to Social Actor*. Aldershot, Hants., UK: Ashgate.
Legge, K . 1994. "Managing Culture: Fact or Fiction." In Sisson, K. (ed.), *Personnel Management: A Comprehensive Guide to Theory and Practice in Britain*. Oxford: Blackwell.
Leibenstein, H. 1976. *Beyond Economic Man*. Cambridge, MA: Harvard University Press.
Leonardi, R. 1995. "Regional Development in Italy: Social Capital and the Mezzogiorno." *Oxford Review of Economic Policy* 11 (2): 165–79.
Lepore, E. (ed.) 1986. *Truth and Interpretation*. Oxford: Blackwell.
Lerry, W. and Taket, A. 1994. "The Death of the Expert." *Journal of Operational Research* 45: 733–48.
Levenson, H. 1981. "Differentiating among Internality, Powerful Others, and Chance." In Lefcourt, H. M. (ed.), *Research with the Locus of Control Construct, 1: Assessment Methods*. Orlando, FL: Academic Press.
Levi, M. D. 1990. *International Finance: The Markets and Financial Management of Multinational Business*. New York: McGraw-Hill.
Levine, A. 1993. *The General WIL: Rousseau, Marx, Communism*. Cambridge: Cambridge University Press
Levine, D. M. 1988. *The Opening of Vision: Nihilism and the Postmodern Situation*. New York and London: Routledge.
LeVine, R. A. 1984. "Properties of Culture: An Ethnographic View." In Shweder, R. A.and LeVine, R. A. (eds.), *Culture Theory: Essays on Mind, Self, and Emotion*. New York: Cambridge University Press
Levine, S. and White, P. E. 1961. "Exchange as a Conceptual Framework for the Study of Interorganizational Relationships." *Administrative Science Quarterly* 5: 583–601.
Lewin, K. 1948. "Experimenting in Social Space." In Lewin, G. W. (ed.), *Resolving Social Conflicts*. New York: Harper and Row.
Lewin, K. 1952. "Defining the Field at a Given Time." in Cartwright, D. (ed.), *Field Theory in Social Sciences: Selected Theoretical Papers*. London: Tavistock.
Lewin, K. 1972. "Needs, Force and Violence in Psychological Fields" In Hollander, E. P. and Hunt, R. G. (eds.), *Classic Contributions to Social Psychology*. London: Oxford University Press.
Lewis, D. (ed.) 1999. *International Perspectives on Voluntary Action: Reshaping the Third Sector*. London: Earthscan.

Lewis, O. 1961. *Children of Sanchez*. New York: Random House.
Lewontin, R. C., Rose, S. and Kamin, L. J. 1984. *Not in Our Genes: Biology, Ideology, and Human Nature*. New York: Pantheon.
Ley, W. A. R. and Perry, C. 1959. *Philosophy and the Public Interest*. Chicago, IL: Committee to Advance Original Work in Philosophy.
Likert, R. 1961. *New Patterns of Management*. London: McGraw-Hill.
Likert, R. 1967. *The Human Organization: Its Management and Value*. New York: McGraw-Hill.
Lindberg, L. N. and Scheingold, S. A. (eds.) 1970. "Special Issue: Regional Integration: Theory and Research." *International Organization* 24 (4).
Lindblom, C. E. 1959. "The Science of Muddling Through." *Public Administration Review* 19 (1): 78–88.
Linklater, A. 1990. *Men and Citizens in the Theory of International Relations* (2nd ed.). London: Macmillan.
Linnerooth-Bayer, J. 1999. "Climate Change and Multiple Views of Fairness." In Toth, P. L. (ed.), *Fair Weather? Equity Concerns in Climate Change*. London: Earthscan.
Linnerooth-Bayer, J. and Fitzgerald, K. B. 1996. "Conflicting Views on Fair Siting Processes." *Risk, Health, Safety and Environment* 7 (2): 119–34.
Lipjhart, A. 1984. *Democracies: Patterns of Majoritarian and Consensual Government in Twenty-One Countries*. New Haven, CT: Yale University Press.
Lipodith, R. 1992. "Sovereignty in Transition." *Journal of International Affairs* 45 (2): 325–46.
Lister, R. 1995. "Dilemmas in Engendering Citizenship." *Economy and Society* 24 (1): 1–40.
Lister, R. 1997. *Citizenship: Feminist Perspectives*. London: Macmillan.
Lister, R. 1998. "Citizenship and Difference: Towards a Differentiated Universalism." *European Journal of Social Theory* 1 (1): 71–90.
Little, R. 2001. "International Regimes." In Bayless, J. and Smith, S. (eds.), *The Globalization of World Politics: An Introduction to International Relations* (2nd ed.). Oxford: Oxford University Press.
Locke, E. A. 1968. "Towards a Theory of Task Motivation and Incentives." *Organizational Behavior and Human Performance* 7 (2): 157–89.
Locke, E. A. and Latham, G. P. 1990. *A Theory of Goal Setting and Task Performance*. New York: Prentice Hall.
Locke, J. [1689] 1959. *An Essay Concerning Human Understanding* (ed. Fraser, A. C.). New York: Dover.
Lockhart, C. 1997. "Political Culture and Political Change." In Ellis, R. J. and Thompson, M. (eds.), *Culture Matters: Essays in Honor of Aaron Wildavsky*. Boulder, CO: Westview.
Lockhart, C. 1998. "Cultural Contributions to Explaining Institutional Form, Political Change, and Rational Decisions." *Comparative Political Studies* 32: 862–93.
Lorsch, J. W. and McIver, E. 1989. *Pawns and Potentates: The Reality of American Corporate Boards*. Boston, MA: Harvard Business School Press.
Loughlan, M. and Scott, C. 1997. "The Regulatory State." In Dunleavy, P., Gamble, A., Holliday, A. and Peele, G. (eds.), *Developments in British Politics 5*. Basingstoke, Hamp., UK: Macmillan.
Lowe, S. 1986. *Urban Social Movements: The City after Castells*. London: Macmillan.
Lowi, T. J. 1964. "American Business, Public Policy, Case Studies and Political Theory." *World Politics* 16: 677–93.
Lowi, T. J. 1969. *The End of Liberalism*. New York: Norton.

Lowi, T. J. 1972. "Four Systems of Policy, Politics and Choice." *Public Administration Review* 32: 298–310.
Lowndes, V. and Skelcher, C. 1998. "The Dynamics of Multi-Organizational Partnerships: An Analysis of Changing Modes of Governance." *Public Administration* 76 (2): 313–33.
Lucas, J. R. 1993. *Responsibility*. Oxford: Oxford University Press.
Lucey, K. 1996. *On Knowing and the Known*. Buffalo, NY: Prometheus.
Luhmann, N. 1988. "Familiarity, Confidence and Trust: Problems and Alternatives." In Gambetta, D. (ed.), *Trust: Making and Breaking*: Oxford: Oxford University Press.
Lukes, S. 1974. *Power: A Radical View*. London: Macmillan.
Lumsden, C. J. and Wilson, E. O. 1981. *Genes, Mind and Culture: The Coevolutionary Process*. Cambridge, MA: Harvard University Press.
Lyotard, J.–F. 1979. *The Postmodern Condition: A Report on Knowledge* (tr. Bennington, G and Massumi, B.). Minneapolis, MN: University of Minnesota Press.
Maassen, G. F. 1999. *An International Comparison of Corporate Governance Models*. Amsterdam, Netherlands: Spencer Stuart.
Mace, M. L. 1971. *Directors: Myth and Reality* (Harvard Business School Classics). Boston, MA: Harvard Business School Press.
Macfarlane, A. 1978. *The Origins of English Individualism: The Family, Property and Social Transition*. Oxford: Basil Blackwell.
Machiavelli, N. [1513] 1961. *The Prince* (tr. Bull, G.). Harmondsworth, Gt.Lon., UK: Penguin.
Machiavelli, N. [1513] 1977. *The Prince* (ed. and tr. Adams, R. M.). New York: W. W. Norton.
Machiavelli, N. [1519] 1970. *The Discourses* (ed. Crick, B., tr. Walker, L. J., rev. Richardson, B.) London: Penguin.
Mackay, C. [1852] 1995. *Extraordinary Popular Delusions and the Madness of Crowds*. Ware, Herts., UK: Wordsworth Editions.
Mackie, J. L.1977. *Ethics: Inventing Right and Wrong*. London: Penguin.
Mackinnon, D. M. 1966. "Natural Law." In Butterfield, H. and Wight, M. (eds.), *Diplomatic Investigations: Essays in the Theory of International Relations*. London: Allen & Unwin.
MacMillan, I., Bruce, A. and Buck, T. 1996. "Venture Capitalists Involvement in Their Investments: Extent and Performance." *Journal of Business Venturing* 4 (1): 27–47.
Madge, J. 1962. *The Origins of Scientific Sociology*. New York: Free Press of Glencoe.
Maghroori, R. and Ramberg, B. (eds.) 1982. *Globalism versus Realism*. Boulder, CO: Westview.
Main, B., Bruce, A. and Buck, T. 1996. "Total Board Remuneration and Corporate Performance." *Economic Journal* 106: 1627–44.
Majone, G. 1989. *Evidence, Argument and Persuasion in the Public Policy Process*. New Haven, CT: Yale University Press.
Majone, G. 1994. "The Rise of the Regulatory State in Europe." *West European Politics* 17 (3): 77–101.
Majone, G. 1997. "From the Positive to the Regulatory State: Causes and Consequences of Changes in the Mode of Governance." *Journal of Public Policy* 17 (2): 139–67.
Mak, H. J. 1982. *Subsidiary Boards in Transition* (Research Report for the Business Associates Program). Geneva: International Management Institute.
Mamadouh, V. 1999a. "Grid-Group Culture Theory: An Introduction." *GeoJournal* 47: 395–409.

Mamadouh, V. 1999b. "National Political Cultures in the European Union." In Thompson, M., Grendstat, G. and Selle, P. (eds.), *Cultural Theory as Political Science*. London: Routledge.

Mansbridge, J. 1983. *Beyond Adversary Democracy* (rev. ed.). Chicago, IL: Chicago University Press.

March, J. G. 1988. *Decisions and Organizations*. Oxford: Blackwell.

March, J. G. 1994. *A Primer on Decision-Making*. New York: Free Press.

March, J. G. 1999. *The Pursuit of Organizational Intelligence*. Malden, MA: Blackwell.

March, J. G. and Olsen, J. P. 1976. *Ambiguity and Change in Organizations*. Bergen, Norway: Universitets Forlaget.

March, J. G. and Olsen, J. P. 1989. *Rediscovering Institutions*. New York: Free Press.

Marin, B. and Mayntz, R. (eds.) 1991. *Policy Networks: Empirical Evidence and Theoretical Considerations*. New York: Free Press.

Marks, J. (ed.) 1986. *The Way of Desire*. Chicago, IL: Precedent.

Mars, G. 1982. *Cheats at Work: An Anthropology of the Workplace*. London: Allen & Unwin.

Mars, G. and Mars, V. 1993. "Two Contrasting Dining Styles: Suburban Conformity and Urban Individualism." In Mars, G. and Mars, V. (eds.), *Food, Culture and History*. London: London Food Seminar.

Marsh, D. 1998. "The Development of the Policy Network Approach." In Marsh, D. (ed.), *Comparing Policy Networks*. Buckingham, Bucks., UK: Open University Press.

Marsh, P. 1990. *Short-termism on Trial*. London: Institutional Fund Managers Association.

Marshall, G. (ed.) 1998. *A Dictionary of Sociology* (2nd ed.). Oxford: Oxford University Press.

Marwell, G. and Ames, R. F. 1981. "Economists Free Ride, Does Anyone Else?" *Journal of Public Economics* 15: 295–310.

Marx, K. 1967. "Economic and Philosophical Manuscripts." In Easton, L. D. and Guddat, K. H. (eds.), *Writings of the Young Marx on Philosophy and Society*. New York: Doubleday.

Maslow, A. 1970. *Motivation and Personality* (2nd ed.). New York: Harper Row.

Masters, R. D. 1989. *The Nature of Politics*. New Haven, CT: Yale University Press.

Mathews, J. 1996a. "Holonic Organizational Architecture." *Human Systems Management* 15: 24–54.

Mathews, J. 1996b. "Organizational Foundations of Economic Learning." *Human Systems Management* 15: 113–24.

Mathews, J. T. 1997. "Power Shifts." *Foreign Affairs* 76 (1): 50–66.

Matthews, J. 1989. *The Age of Democracy*. Melbourne, Vic. Australia: Oxford University Press

May, P. 1986. "Politics and Policy Analysis." *Political Science Quarterly* 101 (1): 109–25.

Mayall, J. 1990. *Nationalism and International Society*. Cambridge: Cambridge University Press.

Mayer, C. 1996. "There is a Direct Relationship between a Country's System of Corporate Governance and Its Economic Success." In *Enterprise and Governance: Proceedings of a Conference*. London: Institute of Directors.

Mayntz, R. 1993. "Governing Failure and the Problem of Governability: Some Comments on a Theoretical Paradigm." In Kooiman, J. (ed.) *Modern Governance: New Government-Society Interactions*. London: Sage.

Mazrui, A. A. 1976. A *World Federation of Cultures: An African Perspective*. New York: Free Press.
McClelland, D. C. 1961. *The Achieving Society*. Princeton, NJ: Van Nostrand.
McCelland, D. C., Atkinson, J. W., Clark, R. A. and Lowell, E. L. 1953. *The Achievement Motive*. New York: Appleton-Century-Crofts.
McCormick, J. 1999. *Understanding the European Union: A Concise Introduction* (4th edit.). Basingstoke, Hamp.: Macmillan.
McGregor, D. 1960. *The Human Side of Enterprise*. New York: McGraw-Hill.
McGregor, D. 1967. *Leadership and Motivation*. Cambridge, MA: MIT Press.
McGregor, P. (ed.) 1980. *Two Tier Boards: Proceedings of the Joint Anglo-German Foundation and Corporate Policy Group Conference* (PP1/80). Oxford: The Corporate Policy Group.
McKinney, J. C. 1966. *Constructive Typologies and Social Theory*. New York: Meredith.
McKinney, J. P. 1981. "The Construct of Engagement Style: Theory and Research." In Lefcourt, H. M. (ed.), *Research with the Locus of Control Construct, 1: Assessment Methods*. Orlando, FL: Academic Press.
McLean, I. "Chaos Theory." In McLean, I. (ed.), *The Concise Oxford Dictionary of Politics*. Oxford: Oxford University Press.
McLeod, K. C. D. 1982. The Political Culture of the Warring States in China." In Douglas, M. (ed.), *Essays in the Sociology of Perception*. London: Routledge & Kegan Paul.
McMahon, R. 1979. *Human Beings: The World of Jean-Paul Sartre*. Chicago, IL: Chicago University Press.
McMillan, C. J. 1973. "Corporations without Citizenship: The Emergence of Multinational Enterprise." In Salaman, G. and Thompson, K. (eds.), *People and Organisations*: London: Longman, for the Open University Press.
McNeill, W. H. 1990. "Winds of Change." *Foreign Affairs* 69 (1): 165–79.
M'Gonigle, R. M. and Zacher, M. W. 1979. *Pollution, Politics, and International Law: Tankers at Sea*. Berkeley, CA: University of California Press.
Mead, G. H. 1934. *Mind, Self and Society: From the Standpoint of a Social Behaviorist*. Chicago, IL: University of Chicago Press.
Mènard, C. 2000. *Institutions, Contracts and Organizations: Perspectives from New Institutional Economics*. Cheltenham, Glos., UK: Edward Elgar.
Merrien, F-X. 1998. "Governance and Modern Welfare States." *International Social Science Journal* 50 (1): 57–67.
Merton, R. K. 1957. *Social Theory and Social Structure* (rev. ed.). Glencoe, IL: Free Press.
Messner, D. 1997. *The Network Society: Economic Development and International Competitiveness as Problems of Social Governance*. London: Frank Cass.
Middlemas, K. 1979. *Politics and Industrial Society*. London: Andrè Deutsch.
Migdal, J. 1988. *Strong Societies and Weak States*. Princeton, NJ: University Press.
Miles, R. E. and Snow, C. C. 1978. *Organizational Strategy, Structure and Process*. New York: McGraw-Hill.
Milgram, S. 1963. "Behavioral Study of Obedience." *Journal of Abnormal and Social Psychology* 67: 371–78.
Mill, J. S. [1863] 1968. *Utilitarianism, Liberty and Representative Government*, London: Everyman.
Miller, D. 1991. *Anarchism*. London: Dent.
Miller, D. (ed.) 1991. *Liberty*. Oxford: Oxford University Press.

Miller, J. 1845. *An Interesting Historical Account of the South Sea Scheme, 1720.* London: S. Gilbert.

Miller, L. H. 1990. *Global Order: Values and Power in International Politics.* Boulder, CO: Westview.

Miller, P. and Rose, N. 1990. "Governing Economic Life." *Economy and Society* 19 (1): 3–25.

Millett, J. D. 1954. *Management in the Public Service: The Quest for Effective Performance.* New York: McGraw-Hill.

Mills, R.W. 1997. "Internal Control Practices within Large UK Companies." In Keasey, K. and Wright, M. (eds.), *Corporate Governance: Responsibilities, Risks and Remuneration.* Chichester, W Susx., UK: Wiley

Millstein, I. M. and Katsh, S. M. 1981. *The Limits of Corporate Power: Existing Constraints on the Exercise of Corporate Discretion.* New York: Collier Macmillan with the Columbia School of Business.

Milner, C. 1991. "Interest Groups and Policy Formulation." In Greenaway, D., Bleaney, M. and Stewart, I. (eds.), *Companion to Contemporary Economic Thought.* London: Routledge.

Milner, H. V. 1988. *Resisting Protectionism: Global Industries and the Politics of International Trade.* Princeton, NJ: Princeton University Press.

Milward, H. B. and Francisco, R. A. 1993. "Subsystem Politics and Corporatism in the United States." *Policy and Politics* 11 (3): 273–93.

Mintzberg, H. 1989. *Mintzberg on Management.* New York: Free Press.

Mitchell, D. 1999. *Governmentality: Power and Rule in Modern Society.* London: Sage.

Mitnick, B. M. 1980. *The Political Economy of Regulation.* New York: Columbia University Press.

Mitrany, D. F. 1933. *The Progress of International Government.* New Haven, CT: Yale University Press.

Mitrany, D. F. 1966. *A Working Peace System.* Chicago, IL: Quadrangle.

Mitroff, I. I. 1983. *Stakeholders of the Organizational Mind.* San Francisco, CA: Jossey-Bass.

Moir, L. 2001. "What Do We Mean by Corporate Social Responsibility." *Corporate Governance: The International Journal of Effective Board Performance* 1 (2): 16–22.

Molenaers, N. and Thompson, M. 1999. "The Cultural Conditions for Democracy and Their Implications for Transitional Societies." In Thompson, M., Grendstat, G. and Selle, P. (eds.), *Cultural Theory as Political Science.* London: Routledge.

Monks, R. A. G. 1994. "Relationship Investing." *Corporate Governance: An International Review* 2 (2): 58–76.

Monks, R. A. G. 1996. "The American Corporation at the End of the 20th Century: Outline of Ownership-based Governance." The Arthur Andersen Lecture. The Judge Institute, University of Cambridge, 8 July (available on line at http://www.Lens-inc-com).

Monks, R. A. G. and Minnow, N. 1991. *Power and Accountability.* New York: HarperCollins.

Monks, R. A. G. and Minnow, N. 1995. *Corporate Governance.* Oxford: Blackwell.

Montgomery, A. H. 2000. *Cultural Limitations to Civilian Fissile Material Protection.* Stanford, CA: Stanford University, Center for International Security and Cooperation.

Morçol, M. 1996. "Fuzz and Chaos: Implications for Public Administration Theory and Research." *Journal of Public Administration Research and Theory* 6 (2): 315–25.

Moran, M. 2000. "The Frank Stacey Memorial Lecture: From Command State to Regulatory State?" *Public Policy and Administration* 15 (4): 1–13.
More, T. [1516] 1989. *Utopia* (eds. Logan, G. M. and Adams, R. M.). Cambridge: Cambridge University Press.
Morgan, G. 1983. *Beyond Method: Strategies for Social Research*. Newbury Park, CA: Sage.
Morgan, G. 1986. *Images of Organizations*. Newbury Park, CA: Sage.
Morgan, G., Krisernsen, P. H. and Whitley, R. 2001. *The Multinational Firm*. Oxford: Oxford University Press.
Morgenthau, H. J. 1948. *Politics among Nations*. New York: Knopf.
Morris, P. 1987. *Power: A Philosophical Analysis*. Manchester, Gt Man.: Manchester University Press.
Morrow, P. 1983. "Concept Redundancy in Organizational Research: The Case of Work Commitment." *Academy of Management Review* 8: 486–500.
Moser, P. K. 1989. *Knowledge and Evidence*. Cambridge: Cambridge University Press.
Mouzelis, N. 1989. "Restructuring Structuration Theory." In Mouzalis, N. (ed.), *Back to Sociological Theory*. Basingstoke, Hamp.: Macmillan.
Mulgan, G. 1988. "New Times: The Power of the Weak." *Marxism Today* December: 24–31.
Murray, R. 1971. "The Internationalization of Capital and the Nation State." *New Left Review* 67 (May–June): 84–108.
Myers, G. E. 1986. *William James: His Life and Thought*. New Haven, CT: Yale University Press.
Nadelmann, E. A. 1990. "Global Prohibition Regimes: The Evolution of Norms in International Society." *International Organizations* 44 (3): 480–505.
Nader, R. and Green, M. 1979. "Public Citizens Congress Watch." *New York Times*, 28 December.
Nader, R., Green, M. and Seligman, J. 1976. *Corporate Power in America*. New York: Norton.
Narango, C. 1990. *Enna-type Structures: Self-analysis for the Seeker*. Nevada City: Gateways/IDHHB.
Nardin, T. 1983. *Law, Morality and the Relations of States*. Princeton, NJ: Princeton University Press.
Natanson, M. (ed.) 1963. *Philosophy of the Social Sciences*. New York: Random House.
Negandhi, A. R. (ed.) 1975. *Interorganization Theory*. Lawrence, KA: University Press of Kansas.
Nelson, R. R. and Winter, S. G. 1982. *An Evolutionary Theory of Economic Change*. Cambridge, MA: Harvard University Press.
Neufield, E. P. 1971. *The Global Corporation*. Toronto, ON; University of Toronto Press.
Ney, S. and Molnaers, N. 1999. "Culture Theory as a Theory of Democracy." *Innovation* 12 (4): 489–509.
Ney, S. and Thompson, M. 1999. "Consulting then Frogs: The Normative Implications of Culture Theory." In Thompson, M., Grendstat, G. and Selle, P. (eds.), *Cultural Theory as Political Science*. London: Routledge.
Ney, S. and Thompson, M. 2000. "Cultural Discourses in the Global Climate Change Debate." In Jochem, E., Sathaye, J. and Bouille, D. (eds.), *Society, Behavior and Climate Change Mitigation*. Dordrecht, Netherlands: Kluwer.
Nichols, J. R. 1986. "Congruent Leadership." *Leadership and Organizational Development Journal* 7 (1): 27–31.

Nightingale, D. J. and Cromby, J. 1999. *Social Constructionist Psychology: A Critical Analysis of Theory and Practice*. Buckingham, Bucks., UK: Open University Press.
Nozick, R. 1974. *Anarchy, State and Utopia*. New York: Basic.
Nozick, R. 1981. *Philosophical Explanations*. Oxford: Oxford University Press.
Nugent, N. 1999. *The Government and Politics of European Union*. Basingstoke, Hamp.: Macmillan.
Nye, J. S. Jr. 1988. "Neorealism and Neoliberalism." *World Politics* 40: 236–48.
Oakeshott, M. J. 1975. *On Human Conduct*. Oxford: Oxford University Press.
O'Brien, G. E. 1984. "Locus of Control, Work, and Retirement." In Lefcourt, H. M. (ed.), *Research with the Locus of Control Construct, Vol. 3: Extensions and Limitations*. Orlando, FL: Academic Press.
Offe, C. 1984. "Ungovernability: on the Renaissance of Theories of Crisis." In Habermas, J. (ed.), *Observations on the Spiritual Situation of the Age*. Cambridge, MA: Harvard University Press.
Ogden, S. and Watson, R. 1996. "Changes in Incentive Structures and Links with Performance Changes: Some Evidence from the Privatized Water Industry in England and Wales." *Journal of Business Finance and Accounting* 28 (5–6): 721–51.
Ohmae, O. 1990. *The Borderless World*. London: Collins.
Olli, E. 1995. *Cultural Theory Specified—the Coherent, Sequential and Synthetic Individual Approaches* (Paper 230). Bergen, Norway: University of Bergen: Department of Comparative Politics.
Olli, E. 1999. "Rejection of Cultural Biases and Effects on Party Preferences." In Thompson, M., Grendstat, G. and Selle, P. (eds.), *Cultural Theory as Political Science*. London: Routledge.
Olsen, M. 1965. *The Logic of Collective Action*. Cambridge, MA: Harvard University Press.
Olsen, M. 1982. *The Rise and Decline of Nations*. New Haven, CT: Yale University Press.
O'Malley, P., Weir, L. and Shearing, C. 1997. "Governmentality, Criticism, Politics." *Economy and Society* 26 (4): 501–17.
O'Neill, O. 1989. *Constructions of Reason: Explorations of Kant's Practical Philosophy*. Cambridge: Cambridge University Press.
Onuf, N. G. 1989. *World of Our Making: Rules and Rule in Social Theory and International Relations*. Columbia, SC: University of South Carolina Press.
Onuf, N. G. 1991 "Sovereignty: Outline of a Conceptual History." *Alternatives* 16 (4): 423–42.
Organski, A. F. K. and Kugler, J. 1978. "Davids and Goliaths: Predicting the Outcomes of International War." *Comparative Political Studies* 11 (2): 141–80.
Ortega y Gasset, J. 1970. "Man has no Nature." In Kaufman, W. (ed.), *Existentialism from Dostoevsky to Sartre*. New York: Meridian.
Ostrander, D. 1982. "One-and Two-dimensional Models of the Distribution of Beliefs." in Douglas, M. (ed.), *Essays in the Sociology of Perception*. London: Routledge & Kegan Paul.
Ostrom, E., Walker, J. and Gardner, R. 1992. "Covenants with and without a Sword: Self-governance is Possible." *American Political Science Review* 86: 404–17.
Ostrom, V. and Ostrom, E. 1997. "Cultures: Frameworks, Theories, and Models." In Ellis, R. J. and Thompson, M. (eds.), *Culture Matters: Essays in Honor of Aaron Wildavsky*. Boulder, CO: Westview.
O'Sullivan, M. 2001. *Contests for Corporate Control: Corporate Governance and Economic Performance in the United States and Germany*. Oxford: Oxford University Press.

Otley, D. 1988. "The Contingency Theory of Management Control." In Thompson, S. and Wright, M. (eds.), *Internal Organisation: Efficiency and Control.* Deddington, Oxon., UK: Philip Allan.

Ott, J. S. and Goodman, D, 1998. Government Reform or Alternative Bureaucracy? Thickening, Tides and the Future of Governing. *Public Administration Review* 58 (6): 540–45.

Ouchi, W. G. 1980. "Markets, Bureaucracies and Clans." *Administrative Science Quarterly* 25: 95–100.

Owen, D. E. 1982. "Spectral Evidence: the Witchcraft Cosmology of Salem Village in 1692." In Douglas, M. (ed.), *Essays in the Sociology of Perception.* London: Routledge & Kegan Paul.

Oye, K. A. (ed.) 1986. *Cooperation under Anarchy.* Princeton, NJ: Princeton University Press.

Packard, V. 1959. *The Status Seekers.* New York: David Mackay.

Panitch, L. 1977. "The Development of Corporatism in Liberal Democracies." *Comparative Political Studies* 10 (1): 61–90.

Panitch, L. 1980. "Recent Theorization of Corporatism." *British Journal of Sociology* 31 (2): 161–87.

Paris, D. C. and Reynolds, J. F. 1983. *The Logic of Policy Inquiry.* New York: Longman.

Parker, J. 2000. *Structuration.* Buckingham, Bucks., UK: Open University Press.

Parsons, T. 1951. *The Social System.* Glencoe, IL: Free Press.

Parsons, T. 1963. "On the Concept of Political Power." *Proceedings of the American Philosophical Society* 107: 232–62.

Parsons, T. 1964. "A Sociological Approach to the Theory of Organizations." In Parsons, T. (ed.), *Structure and Process in Modern Societies.* Glencoe, IL: Free Press.

Parsons, W. 1995. *Public Policy: An Introduction to the Theory and Practice of Policy Analysis.* Cheltenham, Glos., UK: Edward Elgar.

Passes, N. and Agnew, R. (eds.) 1997. *The Future of Anomie Theory.* Boston, MA: Northeastern University Press.

Paster, M. 1987. *The International Monetary Fund and Latin America: Economic Stabilization and Class Conflict.* Boulder, CO: Westview.

Payer, C. 1974. *The Debt Trap: The International Monetary Fund and the Third World.* New York: Monthly Review Press.

Payer, C. 1982. *The World Bank: A Critical Analysis.* New York: Monthly Review Press.

Pearce, F. and Tombes, S. 1998. *Toxic Capitalism: Corporate Crime and the Chemical Industry.* Aldershot, Hants., UK: Ashgate.

Pejovich, S. (ed.) 2001. *The Economics of Property Rights* (2 vols.). Cheltenham, Glos., UK: Edward Elgar.

Peltzman, S. 1976. "Towards a General Theory of Regulation." *Journal of Law and Economics* 19: 211–40.

Perri 2001b. Grid-group @ uea.ac.uk, June 18.

Perry. J. 1993. *The Problem of the Essential Indexical and Other Essays.* Oxford: Oxford University Press.

Peters, B. G. 1998. *Globalization, Institutions and Governance.* (Jean Monet Chair Paper RSC 98/51). Paris: European University Institute, Robert Schuman Center (RSC).

Peters, B. G. 1996. *The Future of Governing: Four Emerging Models.* Lawrence, KA: University Press of Kansas.

Peters, B. G. 1997. "Shouldn't Row, Can't Steer: What's a Government to do?" *Public Policy and Administration* 12 (2): 51–61.

Peters, B. G. and Savoie, D. J. (eds.) 1998. *Taking Stock: Assessing Public Sector Reforms* (Canadian Center for Management Development Series on Governance and Public Management, No. 2). Montreal: Canadian Center for Management Development and the McGill-Queen's University Press.

Peters, T. J. 1988. *Thriving on Chaos: A Handbook of Management Revolution*. New York: Macmillan.

Peters, T. J. 1994a. *The Pursuit of WOW*. New York: Macmillan.

Peters, T. J. 1994b. *The Tom Peters Seminar*. New York: Vintage.

Peters, T. J. and Waterman, R. H. 1982. *In Search of Excellence: Lessons from America's Best-Run Companies*. New York: Harper and Row.

Pettigrew, A. and McNulty, T. 1995. "Power and Influence in and Around the Boardroom." *Human Relations* 48 (8): 845–73.

Pfeffer, J. and Salancik, G. R. 1978. *The External Control of Organizations: A Resource Dependence Perspective*. New York: Harper and Row.

Phillips, A. 1960. "A Theory of Interfirm Organization." *Quarterly Review of Economics* 74: 602–13.

Phillips, A. 1995. *The Politics of Presence*. Oxford: Oxford University Press.

Picciotto. S. 1991. "The Internationalization of the State." *Capital and Class* 43 (special issue): 43–64.

Pierre, J. and Peters, B. G. 2000. *Governance, Politics and the State*. New York: St. Martin's Press.

Pijl, K. van der 1989. "Ruling Classes, Hegemony, and the State System." *International Journal of Political Economy* 19 (1): 7–35.

Pit, D. and Weiss, T. (eds.) 1986. *The Nature of the United Nations Bureaucracy*. Boulder, CO: Westview.

Pitt-Rivers, J. 1968. "Honor." In Stills, D. (ed.), *International Encyclopedia of the Social Sciences, 6.* New York: Macmillan.

Pizzorno, A. 1966. "Amoral Familism and Historical Marginality." *International Review of Community Development* 15: 55–60.

Plant, R. 1991. *Modern Political Thought*. Oxford: Basil Blackwell.

Plato [c380s] 1952. *Phaedras* (tr. Hackforth, R.). Cambridge: Cambridge University Press.

Polanyi, K. 1957. *The Great Transformation: The Political and Economic Origins of our Time*. Boston, MA: Beacon Press.

Polisar, D. and Wildavsky, A. 1989. "From Individual to System Blame: Analysis of Historical Change in the Law of Tort." *Journal of Policy History* 1 (2): 129–55.

Popkin, S. 1979. *The Rational Peasant: The Political Economy of Rural Society in Vietnam*. Berkeley, CA: University of California Press.

Popper, K. R. [1962] 1968. *Conjectures and Refutations*. New York: Harper and Row.

Porter, L. W. and Lawler, E. E. 1965. "Properties of Organizational Structure in Relation to Job Attitudes and Job Behavior." *Psychological Bulletin* 64: 22–51.

Porter, M. E. 1990. *The Competitive Advantage of Nations*. New York: Free Press.

Porter, M. E. 1992. *Capital Choices: Changing the Way America Invests in Industry* (Research Report Presented to the Council on Competitiveness). Boston, MA: Harvard Business School Press.

Portes, A. 1972. "Rationality in the Slum: An Essay on Interpretive Sociology." *Comparative Studies in Sociology and History* 14: 668–86.

Pound, J. 1992. "Beyond Takeovers: Politics Comes to Corporate Control." *Harvard Business Review* (March–April): 83–93.

Powell, V. 1987. *Improving Public Enterprise Performance: Concepts and Techniques* (Management Development Series 22). Geneva: International Labour Office.

Powell, W. W. 1990. "Neither Markets nor Hierarchy: Network Forms of Organization." *Research in Organizational Behavior* 12: 295–336.
Power, M. 1997. *The Audit Society: Rituals of Verification*. Oxford: Oxford University Press.
Power, M. 2000. "The New Risk Management." *European Business Forum* 1 (1): 60–61.
Prakash, S. 1998. "Fairness, Social Capital and the Commons: The Societal Foundations of Collective Action in the Himalayas." In Goldman, M. (ed.), *Privatizing Nature: Political Struggle for Global Commons*. London: Pluto.
Preston, L. E. 1996. *Redefining the Corporation: Stakeholder Theory in International Perspectives* (Occasional Paper 78). College Park, MD: University of Maryland at College Park, Center for International Business Education and Research.
Preston, L. E. and Post, J. 1975. *Private Management and Public Policy: The Principles of Public Responsibility*. Englewood, NJ: Prentice-Hall.
Preston, V. A. 1998. *Beyond the Market and State: Social Enterprises and Civil Democracy in a Welfare Society*. Aldershot, Hants., UK: Ashgate.
Price, M. and Thompson, M. 1997. "The Complex Life: Human Land Uses in Mountain Ecosystems." *Global Ecology and Biogeography Letter* 6: 77–90.
Pugh, D. S and Hickson, D. J. 1976. *Organizational Structure in its Context: The Aston Programme 1*. Aldershot, Hants., UK: Gower.
Pugh, D. S and Hickson, D. J. 1996. *Writers on Organizations* (5th. ed.). Harmondworth, Gt. Lon., UK: Penguin.
Punch, M. 1996. *Dirty Business: Exploring Corporate Misconduct, Analysis and Cases*. London: Sage.
Putman, R. 1988. "Diplomacy and Domestic Politics: The Logic of Two-Level Games." *International Organization* 42 (3): 427–60.
Pye, L. 1968. "Political Culture." In Sillis, D. L. (ed.), *International Encyclopedia of the Social Sciences*. New York: Macmillan and the Free Press.
Quade, E. S. 1976. *Analysis for Public Decisions* (3rd ed.). New York: Elsevier.
Rachels, J. 1990. *Created from Animals: The Moral Implications of Darwinism*. New York: Oxford University Press.
Radner, R. 1992. "Hierarchy: The Economics of Managing." *Journal of Economic Literature* 30: 1282–415.
Rai, S. 1996. "Civil Disobedience." In McLean, I. (ed.), *The Concise Oxford Dictionary of Politics*. Oxford: Oxford University Press.
Rashid, A. 2001. *Jihad: The Rise of Militant Islam in Central Asia*. New Haven, CT: Yale University Press.
Rawls, J. A. 1971. *A Theory of Justice*. Oxford: Oxford University Press.
Rayner, S. 1982. "The Perceptions of Time and Space in Egalitarian Sects: A Millenarian Cosmology." In Douglas, M. (ed.), *Essays in the Sociology of Perception*. London: Routledge & Kegan Paul.
Rayner, S. 1984. "Disagreement about Risk." In Hadden, S. (ed.), *Risk Analysis, Institutions and Public Policy*. New York: Associated Faculty Press.
Rayner, S. 1986. "Management of Radiation Hazards in Hospitals: Plural Rationalities in a Single Institution." *Social Studies of Science* 16: 573–91.
Rayner, S. 1987. "Risk and Relativism in Science Policy." In Johnson, B. B. and Covello, V. T. (eds.), *The Social and Cultural Construction of Risk: Essays on Risk Selection and Perception*. Dordrecht, Netherlands: D. Reidel.
Rayner, S. 1988. "The Rules That Keep Us Equal." In Flanagan, J. G. and Rayner, S. (eds.), *Rules, Decisions and Inequality*. Brookfield, VT: Avebury.
Rayner, S. 1991. "A Cultural Perspective on the Structure and Implementation of Global Environmental Agreements." *Evaluation Review* 15 (1): 75–102.

Rayner, S. 1992. "Cultural Theory and Risk Analysis." In Krimsky, S. and Golding, D. (eds.), *Social Theories of Risk*. Westport, CT: Praeger.

Rayner, S. and Cantor, R. 1987. "How Fair Is Safe Enough: The Cultural Approach to Technology Choice." *Risk Analysis: An International Journal* 7 (1): 3–9.

Rayner, S. and Malone, E. L. 1998. "What Have We Learned?" In Rayner, S. and Malone, E. L (eds.), *Human Choice and Climate Change*, Vol. 4. Columbus, OH: Battelle.

Raz, J. (ed.) 1990. *Authority*. Oxford: Oxford University Press.

Reason, P. and Rowan, J. (eds.) 1981. *Human Inquiry: A Sourcebook of New Paradigm Research*. Chichester, W Susx., UK: Wiley.

Reber, A. S. 1995. *Dictionary of Psychology* (2nd ed.). Harmondsworth, Gt. Lon., UK: Penguin.

Reeve, A. 1996a. "Alienation." In McLean, I. (ed.), *The Concise Oxford Dictionary of Politics*. Oxford: Oxford University Press.

Reeve, A. 1996b "Common Good." In McLean, I. (ed.), *The Concise Oxford Dictionary of Politics*. Oxford: Oxford University Press.

Reeve, A. 1996c. "Communitarianism." In McLean, I. (ed.), *The Concise Oxford Dictionary of Politics*. Oxford: Oxford University Press.

Reeve, A. 1996d. "Millenarianism." In McLean, I. (ed.), *The Concise Oxford Dictionary of Politics*. Oxford: Oxford University Press.

Rein, M. and Schön, D. A. 1993. "Reframing Policy Discourse." In Fischer, F. and Forester, J. (eds.) *The Argumentative Turn in Policy Analysis and Planning*. London: UCL Press.

Reinecke, W. H. 1997. "Global Public Policy.' *Foreign Affairs* 76 (6): 127–38.

Reinecke, W. H. 1998. *Global Public Policy: Governing without Government*. Washington, DC: Brookings Institution.

Rescher, N. 1983. *Risk: A Philosophical Introduction*. Washington, DC: University Press of America.

Rhodes, R. A. W. 1988. *Beyond Westminster and Whitehall: The Sub-central Governments of Britain*. London: Unwin Hyman.

Rhodes, R. A. W. 1990. "Policy Networks: A British Perspective." *Journal of Theoretical Politics* 2(3): 293–317.

Rhodes, R. A. W. 1996. "The New Governance: Governing Without Government." *Political Studies* 44 (4): 652–57.

Rhodes, R. A. W. 1997. *Understanding Governance: Policy Networks, Governance, Reflexivity and Accountability*. Buckingham, Bucks., UK: Open University Press.

Richards, P. 1998. *Fighting for the Rain Forest: War, Youth and Resources in Sierra Leone*. London and Oxford: James Curry, for the International African Institute.

Richards, P. 1999. "New Political Violence in Africa: Secular Sectarianism in Sierra Leone." *GeoJournal* 47: 433–42.

Richards, R. J. 1987. *Darwin and the Emergence of Evolutionary Theories of Mind and Behavior*. Chicago, IL: University of Chicago Press.

Richardson, J. J. (ed.) 1982, *Policy Styles in Western Europe*. London: Allen & Unwin.

Richardson, J. J. and Jordan, G. 1979. *Governing Under Pressure: The Policy Process in a Post-Parliamentary Democracy* (2nd ed.). Oxford: Martin Robinson.

Ridley, M. 1986. *Taking Darwin Seriously: A Naturalistic Approach to Philosophy*. Cambridge, MA: Blackwell.

Ridley, M. 1997. *The Origins of Virtue: Human Instincts and the Evolution of Cooperation*. New York: Viking.

Ridley, M. and Dawkins, R. 1981. "The Natural Selection of Altruism." In Rushton, J. P. and Sorrentino, R. M. (eds.), *Altruism and Helping Behavior: Social Personality and Developmental Perspectives*. Hillsdale, NJ: Lawrence Erlbaum.
Riesman, D. 1950. *The Lonely Crowd*. New Haven, CT: Yale University Press.
Righter, R. 1995. *Utopia Lost: The United Nations and World Order*. New York: Twentieth Century Fund.
Riker, W. H. 1964. "Some Ambiguities in the Notion of Power." *American Political Science Review* 58: 341–49.
Riker, W. H. 1982. *Liberalism against Populism: A Confrontation between the Theory of Democracy and the Theory of Social Choice*. San Francisco, CA: W. H. Freeman.
Ring, P. and Smith, S. 1997. "Processes Facilitating Reliance on Trust in Inter-Organizational Networks." In Ebers, M. (ed.), *The Formation of Inter-Organizational Networks*. Oxford: Oxford University Press.
Ripley, R. B. and Franklin, G. 1987. *Congress, the Bureaucracy and Public Policy* (rev. ed.). Homewood, IL: Dorsey.
Riso, D. R. 1987. *Personality Types: Using the Enneagram for Self-discovery*. Boston, MA: Houghton Mifflin.
Ritcher, F.-J. 1994. "The Emergence of Corporate Alliance Networks—Convention or Self-organization." *Human System Management* 13: 19–26.
Rizzello, S. 1999. *The Economics of the Mind*. Cheltenham, Glos., UK: Edward Elgar.
Robertson, B. A. 1996. "Islamic Fundamentalism." In McLean, I. (ed.), *The Concise Oxford Dictionary of Politics*. Oxford: Oxford University Press.
Robertson, R. 1992. *Globalization: Social Theory and Global Culture*. London: Sage Publications.
Robey, D. (ed.) 1973. *Structuralism: An Introduction*. Oxford: Oxford University Press.
Robinson, C. 1998. "Foreword." In Sternberg, E., *Corporate Governance: Accountability in the Marketplace*. London: Institute of Economic Affairs.
Robinson, J. and Tinker, J. 1996. "Reconciling Ecological, Economic and Social Imperatives: Towards an Analytical Framework." Paper prepared for the International Development Research Center.
Roe, E. M. 1996. "Sustainable Development and Culture Theory." *Sustainable Development and World Ecology* 3: 1–14.
Rolston, H. (ed.) 1995. *Biology, Ethics, and the Origins of Life*. Boston, MA: Jones and Bartlett.
Rorty, R. 1989. *Contingency, Irony and Solidarity*. Cambridge: Cambridge University Press.
Rosaldo, M. Z. 1984. "Towards an Anthropology of Self and Feeling." In Shweder, R. A. and LeVine, R. A. (eds.), *Culture Theory: Essays on Mind, Self, and Emotion*. New York: Cambridge University Press.
Rose, N. 1996. "The Death of the Social? Re-figurating the Territory of Government." *Economy and Society* 25 (3): 327-56.
Rose, R. 1994, "Postcommunism and the Problem of Trust," *Journal of Democracy* (July): 18–30.
Rose-Ackerman, S. 1978. "Bureaucratic Structure and Corruption." In Rose-Ackerman, S. (ed.), *Corruption: A Study in Political Economy*. New York: Academic Press.
Rosenau, J. N. 1987. *Governance Without Government Systems of Rule in World Politics*. Los Angeles: University of Southern California, Institute for Transnational Studies.
Rosenau, J. N. 1990. *Turbulence in World Politics: A Theory of Change and Continuity*. Princeton, NJ: Princeton University Press.

Rosenau, J. N. 1992a. "Citizenship in a Changing Global Order." In Rosenau, J. N. and Czempiel, E.-O. (eds.), *Governance Without Government Order and Change in World Politics*. Cambridge: Cambridge University Press.

Rosenau, J. N. 1992b. "Governance, Order, and Change in World Politics." In Rosenau, J. N. and Czempiel, E.-O. (eds.), *Governance Without Government Order and Change in World Politics*. Cambridge: Cambridge University Press.

Rosenau, J. and Czempiel, E. (eds.) 1992. *Governance Without Government Order and Change in World Politics*. Cambridge: Cambridge University Press.

Rosenkrantz, R. 1977. *Inference, Method, and Decision*. Boston, MA: Reidal.

Ross, S. 1973. "The Economic Theory of Agency: The Principal's Problem." *American Economic Review* 65 (1): 134–9.

Rothschild-Whitt, J. 1979. "The Collectivist Organization: An Alternative to Rational-Bureaucratic Models." *American Sociological Review* 14: 509–27.

Rousseau, J.-L. [1762] 1973. *The Social Contract*. Reprinted in Cole, G. D. H. (ed. and tr.), *The Social Contract and Discourses*. London: Dent.

Rudé, G. [1981] 1995. *The Crowd in History* (rev. ed.). London: Serif.

Rudwick, M. 1982. "Cognitive Styles in Geology." In Douglas, M. (ed.), *Essays in the Sociology of Perception*. London: Routledge & Kegan Paul.

Ruggie, J. G. 1972. "Collective Goods and Future International Collaboration." *American Political Science Review* 66 (3): 870–94.

Ruggie, J. G. 1982. "International Regimes, Transaction Bookss, and Change: Embedded Liberalism in the Post War Economic Order." *International Organization* 36 (3): 408–23.

Ruggie, J. G. 1983. "Continuity and Transformation in the World Polity: Towards a Neorealist Synthesis." *World Politics* 33 (2): 273–92.

Ruggie, J. G. 1993. "Territoriality and Beyond: Problematizing Modernity in International Relations." *International Organizations* 47 (1): 139–74.

Rushton, J. P. and Sorrentino, R. M. 1981. "Altruism and Helping Behavior: An Historical Perspective." In Rushton, J. P. and Sorrentino, R. M. (eds.), *Altruism and Helping Behavior: Social Personality and Developmental Perspectives*. Hillsdale, NJ: Lawrence Erlbaum.

Russell, B. 1948. *Human Knowledge: Its Scope and Its Limitations*. London: George Allan & Unwin.

Rustow, D. A. 1990. "Democracy: A Global Revolution?" *Foreign Affairs* 69 (1): 68–83.

Ruthven, M. 1997. *Islam: A Very Short Introduction*. Oxford: Oxford University Press.

Sacks, S. (ed.) 1979. *On Metaphor*. Chicago, IL: University of Chicago Press.

Sabatier, P. A. 1986. "Top-down and Bottom-up Approaches to Implementation Research: A Critical Analysis and Suggested Synthesis." *Journal of Public Policy* 6: 21–48.

Sabatier, P. A. 1987. "Knowledge, Policy-oriented Learning, and Policy Change: An Advocacy Coalition Framework." *Knowledge: Creation, Diffusion, Utilization* 8 (4): 649–92.

Sabatier, P. A. 1988. "An Advocacy Coalition Framework of Policy Change and the Role of the Policy-oriented Learning Therein." *Policy Sciences* 24: 129–68.

Sabatier, P. A. 1991. "Towards Better Theories of the Policy Process." *PS: Political Science and Politics* 24: 147–56.

Sabatier, P. A. 1993. "Policy Change Over a Decade or More." In Sabatier, P. A. and Jenkins-Smith, H. C. (eds.), *Policy Change and Learning: An Advocacy Coalition Approach*. Boulder, CO: Westview.

Salacuse, J. 1991. *Making Global Deals: Negotiations in the Global Marketplace*. Boston, MA: Houghton Mifflin.
Salancik, G. R. 1978. "Wanted: A Good Network Theory of Organization." *Administrative Science Quarterly* 40 (2): 345–49.
Sandbach, F. H. 1975. *The Stoics*. London: Chatto & Windus.
Sandel, M. 1982. *Liberalism and the Limits of Justice*. Cambridge: Cambridge University Press.
Sanderson, I. 1999. "Participation and Democratic Renewal: From 'Instrumental' to 'Communicative' Rationality." *Policy and Politics* 27 (3): 325–41.
Sartre, J.–P. [1938] 1948. *The Emotions: Sketch of a Theory* (tr. Frechtman, B.). New York: Philosophical Library.
Sartre, J.–P. [1943] 1957. *Being and Nothingness: An Essay of Phenomenological Ontology* (tr. Barnes, H. E.). London: Methuen.
Sartre, J.–P. [1946] 1973. *Existentialism and Humanism* (tr. Mairet, P.). London: Methuen.
Sarup, M. 1996. *Identity, Culture and the Postmodern World*. Edinburgh, C Edin, UK: University of Edinburgh Press.
Scanlon, J. N. 1948. "Profit-sharing under Collective Bargaining: Three Case Studies." *Industrial and Labour Relations Review* 2 (1): 58–75.
Scanlon, T. M. 1977. "Liberty, Contract, and Contribution." In Dworkin, G., Bermant, G. and Brown, P. G. (eds.), *Markets and Morals*: Washington, DC: Hemisphere Publishing.
Scarre, G. 1996. *Utilitarianism*. London: Routledge.
Schacht, R. *Nietzsche*. London: Routledge.
Schapiro, M. 1988. "Judicial Selection and the Design of Clumsy Institutions." *Southern California Law Review* 61: 1555–69.
Scharpf, F. W. 1991. *Crisis and Choice in European Social Democracy* (trs. Crowley, R. and Thompson, F). Ithaca, NY: Cornell University Press.
Scheffler, S. 1988. *Consequentialism and Its Critics*. Oxford: Oxford University Press.
Scheffler, S. 1992. *Human Morality*. Oxford: Oxford University Press.
Schein, E. H. 1978. *Career Dynamics: Matching Individual and Organizational Needs*. Reading, MA: Addison-Wesley.
Schein, E. H. 1980. *Organizational Psychology* (3rd ed.). Englewood Cliffs, NJ: Prentice-Hall.
Schein, E. H. 1985. *Organizational Culture and Leadership*. San Francisco, CA: Jossey-Bass.
Schein, E. H. 1991. "What is Culture?" In Frost, P. J. et al. (eds.), *Reframing Organizational Culture*. Newbury Park, CA: Sage.
Schmitter, P. C. 1974. "Still the Century of Corporatism." *Review of Politics* 36: 85–131.
Schmitter, P. C. and Lehmbruch, G. (eds.) 1979. *Trends towards Corporatist Intermediation*. London: Sage.
Schmutzer, M. 1994, Ingenium und Individuum: Eine Sozialwissenschaftliche Theorie von Wissenschaft und Technik. Vienna, Austria: Springer-Verlag.
Schmutzer, M. E. A. and Bandler, W. 1980. "Hi and Low—In and Out: Approaches to Social Status." *Journal of Cybernetics* 10: 283–99.
Scholte, J. A. 1999. *Global Civil Society: Changing the World*. London: University of Warwick, Department of Politics and International Studies.
Scholte, J. A. 2001. "Global Trade and Finance." In Bayless, J. and Smith, S. (eds.), *The Globalization of World Politics: An Introduction to International Relations* (2nd ed.). Oxford: Oxford University Press.

Schön, D. A. 1983. *The Reflective Practitioner: How Professionals Think in Action.* New York: Basic.
Schubert, G. 1960. *The Public Interest.* New York: Free Press.
Schubert, G. and Masters, R. D. 1991. *Primate Politics.* Carbondale, IL: University of Southern Illinois Press.
Schuchman, A. 1957. *Codetermination: Labor's Middle Way in Germany.* Washington, DC: Public Affairs Press.
Schuller, T. 1985. *Democracy at Work.* Oxford: Oxford University Press.
Schutz, A. [1932] 1967. *The Phenomenology of the Social World.* Evanston, IL: Northwestern University Press.
Schumpeter, J. A. 1976. *Capitalism, Socialism and Democracy.* New York: Harper and Row.
Schwarz, M. and Thompson, M. 1990. *Divided We Stand: Redefining Politics, Technology and Social Choice.* Philadelphia, PA: University of Pennsylvania Press.
Searle, J. R. 1983. *Intentionality.* Cambridge: Cambridge University Press.
Selle, P. 1991a. "Culture and the Study of Politics." *Scandinavian Political Studies*, 14: 97–124.
Selle, P. 1991b. "It Must Have Something to Do With 'Logic': A Rejoinder to Aaron Wildavsky." *Scandinavian Political Studies* 14: 97–124.
Selznick, P. 1957. *Leadership in Administration.* New York: Harper and Row.
Shackleton, M. 1991. "The European Union: Between Three Ways of Life." *Journal of Common Market Studies* 29 (6): 575–601.
Shanks, M. and Grantham, R. 1980. "The Role of the Employee and the Trade Unions." In *Control of the Corporations.* Oxford: Corporate Policy Group.
Shareef, R. 1994. "Subsystem Congruence: A Strategic Change Model for Public Organizations." *Administration and Society* 25 (4): 489–517.
Sher, G. 1987. *Desert.* Princeton, NJ: Princeton University Press.
Shleifer, A. and Summers, L. 1988. "Breach of Trust in Hostile Takeovers." In Auerbach, A. (ed.), *Corporate Takeovers: Causes and Consequences.* Chicago, IL: Chicago University Press.
Shleifer, A. and Vishny, R. W. 1996. *A Survey of Corporate Governance* (Working Paper 5554). Cambridge, MA: National Bureau of Economic Research.
Shonfield, A. 1965. *Modern Capitalism.* Oxford: Oxford University Press.
Shope, R. K. 1983. *The Analysis of Knowing: A Decade of Research.* Princeton, NJ: Princeton University Press.
Short, H. and Keasey, K. 1997. "Institutional Shareholders and Corporate Governance." In Keasey, K. and Wright, M. (eds.), *Corporate Governance: Responsibilities, Risks and Remuneration.* Chichester, W Susx., UK: Wiley.
Shughart, W. F., II and Razzolini, L. 2001. *The Elgar Companion to Public Choice.* Cheltenham, Glos., UK: Edward Elgar.
Shweder, R. A. and Bourne, E. J. 1984. "Does the Concept of Person Vary Cross-culturally?" In Shweder, R. A. and LeVine, R. A. (eds.), *Culture Theory: Essays on Mind, Self, and Emotion.* New York: Cambridge University Press
Shweder, R. A. 1984a. "Preview: A Colloquy of Culture Theorists." In Shweder, R. A. and LeVine, R. A. (eds.), *Culture Theory: Essays on Mind, Self, and Emotion.* New York: Cambridge University Press
Shweder, R. A. 1984b. "Anthropology's Romantic Rebellion Against the Enlightenment, or There's More to Thinking Than Reason and Evidence." In Shweder, R. A. and LeVine, R. A. (eds.), *Culture Theory: Essays on Mind, Self, and Emotion.* New York: Cambridge University Press

Sibeon, R. 1999. "Agency, Structure and Social Chance as Cross-Disciplinary Concepts." *Politics* 19 (3): 139–44.
Sibeon, R. 2000. "Governance and the Policy Process in Contemporary Europe." *Public Management* 2 (3): 289–309.
Sieber, S. 1981. *Fatal Remedies*. New York: Plenum.
Simon, H. 1957. *Models of Man: Social and Rational*. New York: Wiley.
Simon, H. A. 1960. *Administrative Behavior* (2nd ed.). New York: Macmillan.
Simon, H. A. 1962. "The Architecture of Complexity." *Proceedings of the American Philosophical Society* 106 (December): 467–82.
Simon, H. A. 1976. *Administrative Behavior* (3rd ed.). New York: Macmillan.
Simon, H. 1978. "Rationality as Process and as Product of Thought." *American Economic Review Papers and Proceedings* 68 (1): 1–16.
Simon, H. A., Smithburg, D. and Thompson, V. 1950. *Public Administration*. New York: Knopf.
Singer, P. 1973. *Democracy and Disobedience*, Oxford: Oxford University Press.
Singer, P. 1981. *The Expanding Circle: Ethics and Sociobiology*. New York: Farrar, Straus and Giroux.
Siven, E. 1995 "The Enclave Culture." In Marty, M. M. (ed.), *Fundamentalism Comprehended*. Chicago, IL: University of Chicago Press.
Skinner, B. F. 1971. *Beyond Freedom and Dignity*. New York: Knopf.
Skinner, G. 1996. "New Social Movements." In McLean, I. (ed.), *The Concise Oxford Dictionary of Politics*. Oxford: Oxford University Press.
Slaughter, A.–M. 1997. "The Real New World Order." *Foreign Affairs* 76 (1): 183–97.
Slevin, C. 1996a. "Anarchism." In McLean, I. (ed.), *The Concise Oxford Dictionary of Politics*. Oxford: Oxford University Press.
Slevin, C. 1996b. "General Will." In McLean, I. (ed.), *The Concise Oxford Dictionary of Politics*. Oxford: Oxford University Press.
Smelser, N. J. 1963. *Theory of Collective Behavior*. New York: The Free Press of Glencoe.
Smiles, S. [1859] 1968. *Self Help*. London: Sphere.
Smircich, L. 1983. "Concepts of Culture and Organizational Analysis." *Administrative Science Quarterly* 28: 339–58.
Smith, A. [1776] 1977. *The Wealth of Nations*. New York: Penguin.
Smith, M. 1993. "Changing Sociological Perspectives on Chance." *Sociology* 27 (3): 515–31.
Smith, M. J. 1993. *Pressure, Power and Policy: State Autonomy and Policy Networks in Britain and the United States*. Hemel Hempstead, Herts., UK: Harvester Wheatsheaf.
Smith, S., Booth, K. and Zalewski, M. (eds.) 1996. *International Theory: Positivism and Beyond*. Cambridge: Cambridge University Press.
Smith, S. 2001. "Reflectivist and Constructionist Approaches to International Theory." In Bayless, J. and Smith, S. (eds.), *The Globalization of World Politics: An Introduction to International Relations* (2nd ed.). Oxford: Oxford University Press.
Smuts, J. Ch. 1926. *Holism and Evolution*. London and New York: Macmillan.
Snidal, D. 1985. "Coordination Versus Prisoners' Dilemma: Implications for International Cooperation and Regimes." *American Political Science Review* 79 (4): 923–42.
Somit, A. and Peterson, S. A. 1995. "Darwinism, Dominance, and Democracy." In Somit, A. and Losco, J. (eds.), *Research in Biopolitics, 3: Human Nature and Politics*. Greenwich, CT: JAI Press.
Somit, A. and Peterson, S. A. 1997. *Darwinism, Dominance, and Democracy: The Biological Basis for Authoritarianism*. Westport, CT: Praeger.

Soros, G. 1998. *The Crisis of Global Capitalism: Open Society Endangered.* New York: Public Affairs.
Spalding, N. 1996. "The Tanzanian Peasant and Ujamaa: A Study of Contradictions." *Third World Quarterly* 17 (1): 89–108.
Spalding, N. 2000. "A Cultural Explanation of Collapse into Civil War: Escalation of Tension in Nigeria." *Culture and Psychology* 6 (1): 56–74.
Spiro, M. E. 1984. "Some Reflections on Cultural Determinism and Relativism with Special Reference to Emotion and Reason." In Shweder, R. A. and LeVine, R. A. (eds.), *Culture Theory: Essays on Mind, Self, and Emotion.* New York: Cambridge University Press.
Spiro, P. J. 1995. "New Global Communities: Nongovernmental Organizations in International Decisionmaking Institutions (Sovereignty at Bay)." *Washington Quarterly* 18 (1): 45–57.
Spitzer, R. J. 1987. "Promoting Policy Theory: Revising the Arenas of Power." *Policy Studies Journal* 15 (4): 675–89.
Stack, G. J. 1977. *Kierkegaard's Existential Ethics* (Studies in the Humanities, 16 Philosophy). Montgomery, AL: Alabama University Press.
Starr, P. 1992. "Social Categories and Claims in the Liberal State." In Douglas, M. and Hull, D. (eds.), *How Classifications Work.* Edinburgh, C Edin., UK: University of Edinburgh Press.
Stein, A. S. 1982. "Coordination and Collaboration: Regimes in an Anarchic World." *International Organization* 36 (2): 299–324.
Stern, G. 1995. *The Structure of International Society: An Introduction to the Study of International Relations.* London: Pinter.
Stern, N. H. 1995. *The Theory of International Public Goods and the Architecture of International Organizations* (United Nations Background Paper 7). New York: United Nations, Department for Economic and Social Information and Policy Analysis.
Sternberg, E. 1994. *Just Business: Business Ethics in Action.* New Brunswick, NJ: Transaction Books.
Sternberg, E. 1996a. "A Teleological Approach to Business Ethics." In Gasparski. W. W. and Ryan, L. V. (eds.), *Human Action in Business. Praxiology*, 5. London: Little, Brown.
Sternberg, E. 1996b. "Stakeholder Theory Exposed." *The Corporate Governance Quarterly* 2 (1): 4–18.
Sternberg, E. 1997a. "The Defects of Stakeholder Theory." *Corporate Governance* 5 (1): 3–10.
Sternberg, E. 1997b. "Stakeholder Theory: The Defective State It's In." In *Stakeholding and Its Critics* (Choices in Welfare 36). London: Institute of Economic Affairs Health and Welfare Unit.
Sternberg, E., 1998. *Corporate Governance: Accountability in the Marketplace.* London: Institute of Economic Affairs.
Sternberger, P. J. 1999. "Public and Private." *Political Studies* 47 (2): 292–313.
Stiglitz, J. E. 1987. "Principal and Agent." In Eatwell, J. M., Milgate, M. and Newman, P. (eds.), *The New Palgrave: A Dictionary of Economics.* London: Macmillan.
Stogdill, R. M. and Coons, A. (eds.) 1957. *Leadership Behavior: Its Description and Measurement* (Research Monograph, 88). Columbus, OH: Ohio State University, Bureau of Business Research.
Stoker, G. 1997. "Public-Private Partnerships and Urban Governance." In Pierrre (ed.), *Public-Private Partnerships in Europe and the United States.* London: Macmillan.

Stoker, G. 1998. "Governance as Theory: Five Propositions." *International Social Science Journal* 50 (1): 17–28.
Stokey, E. and Zeckhauser, R. 1978. *A Primer for Policy Analysis*. New York: W. W. Norton.
Storey, J. 1993. *An Introductory Guide to Cultural Theory and Popular Culture*. Hemel Hempsted, Herts., UK: Harvester Wheatsheaf.
Storm, S. and Naastepad, C. W. M. (eds.) 2001. *Globalisation and Economic Development: Essays in Honour of J. George Waardenburg*. Cheltenham, Glos., UK: Edward Elgar.
Strange, S. [1982] 1997. "*Cave! Hic Dragones*: A Critique of Regime Analysis." *International Organization*, 36 (2). Reprinted in Diehl, P. F. (ed.), *The Politics of Global Governance: International Organizations in an Interdependent World*. Boulder, CO: Lynne Riener.
Strauss, A. 1978. *Negotiations: Varieties, Contexts, Processes and Social Order*. San Francisco, CA: Jossey-Bass.
Strauss, A., Schatzman, L., Ehrlich, D., Bucher, R. and Sabshin, M. 1963. "The Hospital and Its Negotiated Order." In Friedson, E. (ed.), *The Hospital in Modern Society*. New York: Macmillan.
Strawson, G. 1986. *Freedom and Belief*. Oxford: Clarendon.
Streeck, W. 1991. "Interest Heterogeneity and Organizing Capacity—Two Class Logics of Collective Action." In Czada, R. and Windhoff-Heritier, B. (eds.), *Political Choice, Institutions, Rules and Limits of Rationality*. Frankfurt am Main, Germany: Campus Verlag.
Streeck, W. and Schmitter, P. C. 1991. "Community, Market, State—and Associations? The Prospective Contribution of Interest Governance to Social Order." In Thompson, G., Frances, J., Levacic, R. and Mitchell, J. (eds.), *Markets, Hierarchies and Networks: The Coordination of Social Life*. London: Sage and Open University Press.
Strickland, B. R. 1965. "The Prediction of Social Action from a Dimension of Internal-External Control." *Journal of Social Psychology* 66: 353–58.
Swedlow, B. 2001. Gridgroup@uea.ac.uk 13 June 2001.
Sztompka, P. 1996. "Trust and Emerging Democracy: Lessons from Poland." *International Sociology* 11 (1): 37–62.
Tanks, F. and Passkey, A. 1999. "Trust, Confidence and Voluntary Organizations: Between Values and Institutions." *Sociology* 33 (2): 257–74.
Tannenbaum, A. S. 1962. *Control in Organizations*. New York: McGraw-Hill.
Tannenbaum, K. and Schmidt, W. H. (1958). "How to Choose a Leadership Pattern." *Harvard Business Review* (March–April): 95–102.
Tansey, J. 2001. Grid-group @ uea.ac.uk, 2 August.
Tansey, J. and O'Riordan, T. 1999. "Culture Theory and Risk: A Review." *Health, Risk and Society* 1 (1): 71–90.
Taras, D. G. 1991. "Breaking the Silence: Differentiating Crises Agreements." *Public Administration Quarterly* 14 (4): 401–18.
Tawney, R. T. H. 1938. *Religion and the Rise of Capitalism: The Holland Memorial Lectures*. London: Penguin.
Taylor, C. 1975. *Hegel*. Cambridge: Cambridge University Press.
Taylor, F. W. [1911] 1947. *Scientific Management*. New York: Harper and Row.
Taylor, I. 1996. "Who is Enabled by Whom to do What, A Critique of the 'Enabling State' Concept." Paper presented at the International Research Symposium on Public Services Management, Astor University, Birmingham, UK, April.
Taylor, K. 1982. *The Political Ideals of the Utopian Socialists*. London: Frank Cass.

Taylor, K. 1996a. "Stirner, Max." In McLean, I. (ed.), *The Concise Oxford Dictionary of Politics*. Oxford: Oxford University Press.
Taylor, K. 1996b. "Utopianism." In McLean, I. (ed.), *The Concise Oxford Dictionary of Politics*. Oxford: Oxford University Press.
Taylor, M. 1987. *The Possibility of Cooperation*. New York: Cambridge University Press.
Taylor, M. 1990. "Cooperation and Rationality: Notes on the Collective Action Problem and Its Solution." In Cook, K. S. and Levi, M. (eds.), *The Limits of Rationality*. Chicago, IL: University of Chicago Press.
Taylor, P. 2001. "The United Nations and International Order." In Bayless, J. and Smith, S. (eds.), *The Globalization of World Politics: An Introduction to International Relations* (2nd ed.). Oxford: Oxford University Press.
Teubner, G. 1993. *Law as an Autopoietic System*. Oxford: Blackwell.
Thomas, C, 2001. "Poverty, Development, and Hunger." In Bayless, J. and Smith, S. (eds.), *The Globalization of World Politics: An Introduction to International Relations* (2nd ed.). Oxford: Oxford University Press.
Thomas, W. I. and Znaniecki, F. 1918–20. *The Polish Peasant in Europe and America* (2 vols.) (2nd ed.). New York: Dover.
Thompson, G., Frances, J., Levacic, R. and Mitchell, J. (eds.) 1991. *Markets, Hierarchies and Networks: The Coordination of Social Life*. London: Sage and Open University Press.
Thompson, J. 1992. *Justice and World Order: A Philosophical Inquiry*. London: Routledge.
Thompson, J. D. 1967. *Organizations in Action*. New York: McGraw-Hill.
Thompson, K. A. 1973. "The Religious Organization." In McKinlay, J. (ed.), *Processing People: Case Studies in Organizational Behavior*. New York: Holt, Reinhart and Winston.
Thompson, M. 1982a. *Among the Energy Tribes: The Anthropology of the Current Policy Debate* (Working Paper WP-82-59). Laxenburg, Austria: International Institute for Applied Systems Analysis.
Thompson, M. 1982b. "A Three-Dimensional Model." In Douglas, M. (ed.), *Essays in the Sociology of Perception*. London: Routledge & Kegan Paul.
Thompson, M. 1982c. The Problem of the Center: An Autonomous Cosmology." In Douglas, M. (ed.), *Essays in the Sociology of Perception*. London: Routledge & Kegan Paul.
Thompson, M. 1983a. "Postscript: A Cultural Basis for Comparisons." In Kunreuther, H. C., Linnerooth, J., Lathrop, J., Atz, H., Macgill, S., Mandl, C., Schwartz, M. and Thompson, M., *Risk Analysis and Decision Processes: The Siting of Liquefied Energy Gas Facilities in Four Countries*. Berlin, Germany: Springer-Varlag.
Thompson, M. 1983b. The Aesthetics of Risk: Culture or Context." In Swing, H. C. and Albers, W. (eds.), *Societal Risk Assessment*. New York: Plenum.
Thompson, M. 1984. "Among the Energy Tribes, A Cultural Framework for the Analysis and Design of Energy Policy." *Policy Sciences* 17 (3): 321–39.
Thompson, M. 1989a. "Surprises from Systems, Natural or Cultural." *Speculations in Science and Technology* 12 (4): 299–306.
Thompson, M. 1989b. "Engineering and Anthropology: Is There a Difference." In Brown, J. (ed.), *Environmental Threats: Perceptions, Analysis and Management*. London: Belhaven.
Thompson, M. 1992. "The Dynamics of Culture Theory and their Implications for the Enterprise Culture." Hargreaves Heap, S. and Ross, A. (eds.), *Understanding the Enterprise Culture*. Edinburgh, C Edin., UK: University of Edinburgh Press.

Thompson, M. 1993. "The North Stars to Catch up with the South: The Himalayan Village as a Clumsy Institution and Its Lessons for Policy." Paper presented to the Workshop on Risk and Fairness, sponsored by the International Academy of the Environment, Laxenburg, Austria.

Thompson, M. 1996. *Inherent Relationality: An Anti-dualist Approach to Institutions* (LOS Center Report). Bergen, Norway: University of Bergen, LOS Center.

Thompson, M. 1997a. "Cultural Theory and Integrated Assessment." *Environmental Modeling and Assessment* 2: 139–50.

Thompson, M. 1997b. "Rewriting the Precepts of Policy Analysis." In Ellis, R. J. and Thompson, M. (eds.), *Culture Matters: Essays in Honor of Aaron Wildavsky*. Boulder, CO: Westview.

Thompson, M. 1998. "Style and Scale: Two Sources of Institutional Appropriateness." In Goldman, M. (ed.), *Privatizing Nature: Political Struggle for Global Commons*. London: Pluto.

Thompson, M. 2000a. "Global Networks and Local Cultures: What are the Mismatches and What can be Done about Them." In Engel, C. and Keller, K. H. (eds.), *Understanding the Impact of Global Networks on Local Social, Political and Cultural Values*. Baden-Baden, Germany: Nomos.

Thompson, M. 2000b. Grid-group @ uea.ac.uk, 5 December.

Thompson, M. 2001. "Clumsiness: It's as Easy as Falling off a Log." Posted on Grid-group @ uea.ac.uk, 30 July.

Thompson, M. and Ellis, R. J. 1997. "Introduction." In Ellis, R. J. and Thompson, M. (eds.), *Culture Matters: Essays in Honor of Aaron Wildavsky*. Boulder, CO: Westview.

Thompson, M. and Gyawali, D. 2001. "Transboundary Risk Management in the South: A Nepalese Perspective on Himalayan Water Projects." In Linnerooth, J., Lofstedt, R. and Sjostedt, G. (eds.), *Transboundary Risk Management*. London: Earthscan.

Thompson, M. and Rayner, S. 1998a. "Risk and Governance Part I: The Discourses of Climate Change." *Government and Opposition* 33 (2): 139–66.

Thompson, M. and Rayner, S. 1998b. "Risk and Governance Part II: Policy in a Complex and Plurally Perceived World." *Government and Opposition* 33 (3): 330–54.

Thompson, M. and Rayner, S. 1998c. "Cultural Discourse." In Rayner, S. and Malone, E. L. (eds.), *Human Choice and Climate Change*, 1. Columbus, OH: Battelle Press.

Thompson, M. and Taylor, P. 1986. *The Surprise Game: An Exploration of Constrained Relativism* (Warwick Papers in Management 1). London: University of Warwick, Institute for Management Research and Development.

Thompson, M. and Wildavsky, A. 1986a. "A Cultural Theory of Information Bias in Organizations." *Journal of Management Science*. 23 (3): 273–86.

Thompson, M. and Wildavsky, A. 1986b. "A Poverty of Distinction: From Economic Homogeneity to Cultural Heterogeneity in the Classification of Poor People." *Policy Sciences* 19: 163–99.

Thompson, M., Ellis, R. J. and Wildavsky, A. 1990. *Culture Theory*. Boulder, CO: Westview.

Thompson, M., Ellis, R. J. and Wildavsky, A. 1992. "Political Cultures." Hawkesworth, M. and Kogan, M. (eds.), *Encyclopaedia of Government and Politics*. London: Routledge.

Thompson, M., Grendstat, G. and Selle, P. (eds.) 1999a *Cultural Theory as Political Science*. London: Routledge.

Thompson, M., Grendstat, G. and Selle, P. 1999b. "Cultural Theory as Political Science." In Thompson, M., Grendstat, G. and Selle, P. (eds.), *Cultural Theory as Political Science*. London: Routledge.
Thompson, M., Warburton, M. and Healy, T. 1986. *Uncertainty on a Himalayan Scale*. London: Ethnographica.
Thompson, P. (ed.) 1995. *Issues in Evolutionary Ethics*. New York: State University of New York Press.
Thompson. N. 1992. *Existentialism and Social Work*. London: Avebury
Thomson, J. E. 1992. "Explaining the Regulation of Transnational Practices: A State-Building Approach." In Rosenau, J. N. and Czempiel, E.-O. (eds.), *Governance Without Government Order and Change in World Politics*. Cambridge: Cambridge University Press.
Thomson, J. E. and Krasner, S. D. 1989. "Global Transaction Bookss and the Consolidation of Sovereignty." In Czempiel, E.-O. and Rosenau, J. N. (eds.), *Global Change and Theoretical Challenges: Approaches to World Politics for the 1990s*. Lexington, MA: Lexington.
Thorngate, W. 2001. "The Social Psychology of Policy Analysis." *Journal of Comparative Policy Analysis* 3 (1): 85–112.
Thucydides [401 BC] 1972. *History of the Peloponnesian War* (tr. Warner, R.) (rev. ed.). Harmondsworth, Gt. Lon., UK: Penguin.
Thurer, D. 1999. "The 'Failed State' and International Law." *International Review of the Red Cross* 81 (836): 731–62.
Tidwell, A. C. 1998. *Conflict Resolved: A Critical Assessment of Conflict Resolution*. London: Pinter.
Tilly, C. 1990. *Coercion, Capital and European States, AD 990–1990*. Cambridge, MA: Blackwell.
Tollison, R. and Willett, T. 1979. "An Economic Theory of Mutually Advantageous Linkages in International Negotiations." *International Organization* 33 (3): 425–50.
Tomlinson, J. 1999. *Globalization and Culture*. Cambridge: Polity.
Tranvik, T., Thompson, M. and Selle, P. 2000. "Doing Technology (and Democracy) the Pack-Donkey's Way: The Technomorphic Approach to ICT Policy." In Engels, C. and Keller, K. H. (eds.), *Governance of Global Networks in the Light of Different Local Values*. Baden-Baden, Germany: Nomos.
Tricker, R. I. 1984. *Corporate Governance: Practices, Procedures and Powers in British Companies and their Boards of Directors*. Aldershot, Hants., UK: Gower.
Tricker, R. I. 1994. *International Corporate Governance: Text, Readings and Cases*. Englewood Cliffs, NJ: Prentice Hall.
Trivers, R. 1985. *Social Evolution*. Menlo Park, CA: Benjamin-Cummings.
Tsoukas, H. 1998. "Forms of Knowledge and Forms of Life in Organized Contexts." In Chia, R. C. H. (ed.), *In the Realm of Organization: Essays for Robert Cooper*. London: Routledge.
Turnbull, S. 1991a. "Re-inventing Corporations." *Human Systems Management* 10 (3): 169–86.
Turnbull, S. 1991b. "Socializing Capitalism." In Speeder, S. M. (ed.), *Equitable Capitalism: Promoting Economic Opportunity through Broader Capital Ownership*. New York: New Horizons.
Turnbull, S. 1993. "Improving Corporate Structure and Ethics: A Case for Corporate 'Senates'." *Director's Monthly* 17(5): 1–4.
Turnbull, S. 1994. "Stakeholder Democracy: Redesigning the Governance of Firms and Bureaucracies." *Journal of Socio-Economics* 23 (3): 321–60.

Turnbull, S. 1995. "The Need for Stakeholder Councils in Social Audits." *Social and Environmental Accounting* 15 (2): 10–15.

Turnbull, S. 1997a. "Employee Ownership: Opportunities and Threats." *Reward Management Bulletin* 1 (3): 51–52.

Turnbull, S. 1997b. "Should Companies Have External Directors." *Board Report* 2 (4): 5.

Turnbull, S. 1997c. "Stakeholder Co-operation." *Journal of Co-operative Studies* 29 (3): 18–52.

Turnbull, S. 1997d. "Stakeholder Governance: A Cybernetic and Property Rights Analysis." *Corporate Governance: An International Review* 5 (1): 11–23.

Turnbull. S. 1997e. "Corporate Governance: Its Scope, Concerns and Theories." *Corporate Governance: An International Review* 5 (4): 180–205.

Turnbull, S. (1997) 2000. "Corporate Governance: Its Scope, Concerns and Theories." *Corporate Governance: An International Review* 5 (4): 180–205 (reproduced at http: cog.kent.edu/lib/turnbull4.html, 19 October 2000).

Uhr, J. 1998. *Deliberative Democracy in Australia: The Changing Place of Parliament.* Melbourne: Cambridge University Press in association with, Australian National University, Research School of Social Sciences.

UK (United Kingdom) 1977. *Report of the Committee of Enquiry on Industrial Democracy* [Chair: Lord Bullock] (Cmnd 67060). London: HMSO.

Underhill, G. 1996. "European Parliament." In McLean, I. (ed.), *The Concise Oxford Dictionary of Politics.* Oxford: Oxford University Press.

UNDP (United Nations Development Program) 1997. *Governance for Sustainable Human Development: A UNDP Policy Document, Executive Summary.* New York: UNDP.

UNRISD (United Nations Research Institute on Social Development) 1995. *States of Disarray: The Social Effects of Globalization.* Geneva: UNRISD.

Urwin, D. 1995. *The Community of Europe: A History of European Integration.* Basingstoke, Hamp., UK: Macmillan.

Van Den Bulcke, D. and Verbeke, A. (eds.) 2001. *Globalization and the Small Open Economy.* Cheltenham, Glos., UK: Edward Elgar.

Vangen, S. and Huxham, C. 1998. "The Role of Trust in the Achievement of Collaborative Advantage." Paper presented at the 14th EGOS Colloquium, Maastricht, Netherlands, August.

Vanhanen, T. 1992. *On the Evolutionary Roots of Politics.* New Delhi: Sterling Publishers.

Vaubel, R. 1986. "A Public Choice Approach to International Organization." *Public Choice* 51: 39–57.

van Waarden, F. 1992. "Dimensions and Types of Networks." *European Journal of Political Research* 21 (1–2): 241–61.

Veries, J. de 1999. "A Trojan Horse in the Dutch Ministry of Agriculture." In Thompson, M., Grendstat, G. and Selle, P. (eds.), *Cultural Theory as Political Science.* London: Routledge.

Verweij, M. 1995. "Culture Theory and the Study of International Relations." *Millennium* 24 (1): 87–111.

Verweij, M. 1999. "Whose Behavior is Affected by International Anarchy?" In Thompson, M., Grendstat, G. and Selle, P. (eds.), *Cultural Theory as Political Science.* London: Routledge.

Verweij, M. 2000. *Transboundary Environmental Problems and Culture Theory: The Protection of the Rhine and the Great Lakes.* London: Palgrave.

Vickers, G. 1983. *The Art of Judgement: A Study of Policymaking* (2nd ed.). London: Chapman and Hall.
Vives, X. (ed.) 2000. *Corporate Governance: Theoretical and Empirical Perspectives.* Cambridge: Cambridge University Press.
Vroom, V. H. 1960. *Some Personality Determinants of the Effects of Participation.* Englewood Cliffs, NJ: Prentice-Hall.
Vroom, V. H. 1964. *Work and Motivation.* New York: Wiley.
Vroom, V. H. and Jago, A. G. 1988. *The New Leadership: Managing Participation in Organizations.* Englewood Cliffs, NJ: Prentice-Hall.
Vroom, V. H. and Yetton, P. W. 1973. *Leadership and Decision-Making.* Pittsburgh, PA: University of Pittsburgh Press.
Waal, F. de 1996. *Good Natured: The Origins of Right and Wrong in Humans and Other Animals.* Cambridge, MA: Harvard University Press.
Wagner, R. H. 1983. "The Theory of Games and Problems of International Cooperation." *American Political Science Review* 77 (2): 330–46.
Walker, R. B. J. 1988. *One World, Many Worlds: Struggles for a Just World Peace.* Boulder, CO: Lynne Riener.
Wall, T. D. and Lischeron, J. A. 1977. *Worker Participation.* London: McGraw-Hill.
Wallensteen, P. 1994. "Representing the World: A Security Council for the 21st Century." *Security Dialogue* 25 (1): 63–75.
Waltz, K. N. 1979. *Theory of International Politics.* Reading, MA: Wesley-Addison.
Waltz, K. N. 1990. "Realist Thought and Neorealist Theory." *Journal of International Affairs* 44 (1): 1–38.
Walzer, M. 1983. *Spheres of Justice: A Defense of Pluralism and Justice.* New York: Basic.
Ward, E. J. 1983. *An Exploration of the Public Interest Concept: Towards and Enhanced Theoretical and Practical Understanding.* Ann Arbor, MI: UMI Dissertation Information Service.
Warren, R. L. 1967. The Interorganizational Field as a Focus for Investigation." *Administrative Science Quarterly* 12: 396–419.
Waterman, P. 1998. *Globalization, Social Movements and the New Institutionalism.* London: Mansell.
Waters, M. 1995. *Globalization.* London: Routledge.
Weber, M. [1904] 1949. *The Methodology of the Social Sciences* (trs. Shils, S. N. and Finch, H.). New York: Free Press.
Weber, M. [1915] 1947. *The Theory of Social and Economic Organization* (tr. Henderson, A.M. and Parsons, T). New York: Free Press.
Weber, M. 1962. *Basic Concepts in Sociology.* London: Owen.
Weber, M. [1922] 1968a. *Economy and Society: An Outline of Interpretive Sociology* (eds. Roth, G. and Wittich, C.) (3 vols.). New York: Bedminster.
Weber, M. 1968b. *On Charisma and Institution Building* (ed. Eisenstadt, S. N.). Chicago, IL: University of Chicago Press.
Weick, K. E. 1995. *Sensemaking in Organizations.* Newbury Park, CA: Sage.
Weimer, D. L. and Vining, A. R. 1992. *Policy Analysis: Concepts and Practice* (2nd ed.). Englewood Cliffs, NJ: Prentice Hall.
Weiss, T. G. and Gordenkder, B. 1996. *NGOs, the UN and Global Governance.* Boulder, CO: Lynne Riener.
Weller, P., Bakvis, H. and Rhodes, R. A. W. 1997. *The Hollow Crown.* London: Macmillan.
Wendt, A. E. 1987. "The Agent-Structure Problem in International Relations Theory." *International Organization* 41 (3): 360–85.

Wendt, A. E. 1991. "Bridging the Theory/Meta-theory Gap on International Relations." *Review of International Studies* 17: 383–92.
Wendt, A. E. 1999. *Social Theory in International Relations*. Cambridge: Cambridge University Press.
Wertheimer, A. 1987. *Coercion*. Princeton, NJ: Princeton University Press.
Wheeler, N. J. and Bellamy, A. J. 2001. "Humanitarian Intervention and World Politics." In Bayless, J. and Smith, S. (eds.), *The Globalization of World Politics: An Introduction to International Relations* (2nd ed.). Oxford: Oxford University Press.
White, R. W. 1959. "Motivation Reconsidered: The Concept of Competence." *Psychological Review* 66 (5): 297–331.
White, S. K. 1991. *Political Theory and Postmodernism*. Cambridge: Cambridge University Press.
Whitehead, T. N. 1936. *Leadership in a Democratic Society*. Cambridge, MA: Harvard University Press
Whyte, W. F. (ed.) 1955. *Money and Motivation*. New York: Harper and Row.
Wijkman, P. M. 1982. "Managing the Global Commons." *International Organization* 36 (Summer): 511–36.
Wildavsky, A. 1982. "The Three Cultures: Explaining Anomalies in the American Welfare State." *Public Interest* Fall: 45–58.
Wildavsky, A. 1984. *The Nursing Father: Moses as a Political Leader*. Montgomery, AL: Alabama University Press.
Wildavsky, A. 1987a. "A Culture Theory of Responsibility." In Lane, E. (ed.) Bureaucracy and Public Choice. Newbury Park, CA: Sage.
Wildavsky, A. 1987b. "Choosing Preferences by Constructing Institutions: A Cultural Theory of Preference Formation." *American Political Science Review* 81 (1): 1–18.
Wildavsky, A. 1988. "A Cultural Theory of Budgeting." *International Journal of Public Administration* 11: 651–77.
Wildavsky, A. 1989a. "A Cultural Theory of Leadership." In Jones, B. D. (eds.), *Leadership and Politics: New Perspectives in Political Science*. Lawrence, KA: University Press of Kansas.
Wildavsky, A. 1989b. "Frames of Reference as Cultures: A Predictive Theory." In Freilich, M. (ed.), *The Relevance of Culture*. New York: Bergin and Garvey.
Wildavsky, A. 1991a. "What Other Theory Would be Expected to Answer such a Profound Question? A Reply to Per Selle's Critique of Cultural Theory." *Scandinavian Political Studies* 14: 355–60.
Wildavsky, A. 1991b. "Can Norms Rescue Self-interest or Macro Explanations be Joined to Micro Explanation?" *Critical Review* 5 (3): 301–23.
Wildavsky, A. 1991c. "Who Wants What and Why: A Cultural Theory." In Wildavsky, A. *The Rise of Radical Egalitarianism*. Washington, DC: American University Press.
Wildavsky, A. 1991d. *The Rise of Radical Egalitarianism*. Washington, DC: American University Press.
Wildavsky, A. 1993. "On the Social Construction of Distinctions: Risk, Rape, Public Goods, and Altruism." In Hechter, M., Nadel, L. and Michhod, R. E. (eds.), *The Origin of Values*. New York: Aldine de Gruyter.
Wildavsky, A. 1994a. "How Cultural Theory can Contribute to Understanding and Promoting Democracy, Science and Development." In Serageldin, I. and Taboroff, J. (eds.), *Culture and Development in Africa*. Washington, DC: World Bank.
Wildavsky, A. 1994b. "Why Self-interest Means Less Outside of a Social Context: Cultural Contributions to a Theory of Rational Choice." *Journal of Theoretical Politics* 6 (2): 131–59.

Wildavsky, A. 1998. *Culture and Social Theory.* New Brunswick, NJ: Transaction Books.
Wildavsky, A. and Chai, S.-K. 1994. "Cultural Change, Party Ideology and Electoral Outcomes." In Coyle, D. J. and Ellis, R. J. (eds.), *Politics, Policy and Culture.* Boulder, CO: Westview.
Wildavsky, A. and Drake, K. 1990. "Theories of Risk Perception: Who Fears What and Why?" *Daedalus* 119 (4): 41–60.
Wildavsky, A. and Enzell, M. 1998. "Thomas Hobbes and His Critics: Interpretive Implications of Cultural Theory." In Chai, S.-K. and Swedlow, B. (eds.), *Aaron Wildavsky: Cultural Theory and Social Theory.* New Brunswick, NJ: Transaction Bookss.
Wildavsky, A. and Lockhart, C. 1993. "The 'Multicultural' Mill." *Utilitas* 5 (2): 255–73.
Wildavsky, A. and Lockhart, C. 1998. "The Social Construction of Cooperation: Egalitarian, Hierarchical and Individualistic Faces of Altruism." In Wildavsky, A. (ed.), *Culture and Social Theory.* New Brunswick, NJ: Transaction Bookss.
Wildavsky, A. and Malkin, J. 1991. "Why the Traditional Distinction between Public and Private Goods should be Abandoned." *Journal of Theoretical Politics* 3 (4): 355–78.
Wildavsky, A. ande Polisar, D. "From Individual to System Blame: Analysis of Historical Change in the Law of Tort." *Journal of Policy History* 1(2): 129–55
Wildavsky, A., Fogerty, D. and Jeanrenaud, C. 1998. "At Once Ubiquitous and Elusive, the Concept of Externalities is Either Vacuous or Misapplied." In Chai, S.-K. and Swedlow, B. (eds.), *Aaron Wildavsky: Cultural Theory and Social Theory.* New Brunswick, NJ: Transaction Bookss.
Wilkins, M. 1970. *The Emergence of Multinational Enterprise.* Cambridge, MA: Harvard University Press.
Wilks, S. 1996. "Regulatory Compliance and Capitalist Diversity in Europe." *Journal of European Public Policy* 3 (4): 536–59.
Wilks, S. and Wright, M. 1988. "Conclusion: Comparing Government–Industry Relations: State, Sectors and Networks." In Wilkes, S. and Wright, M. (eds.), *Comparative Government–Industry Relations.* Oxford: Clarendon.
Willetts, P. 2001. "Transnational Actors and International Organizations in Global Politics." In Bayless, J. and Smith, S. (eds.), *The Globalization of World Politics: An Introduction to International Relations* (2nd ed.). Oxford: Oxford University Press.
Williams, M. and May, T. 1996. *Introduction to the Philosophy of Social Research.* London: UCL Press.
Williams, R. 1965. *The Long Revolution.* Harmondsworth, Gt. Lon., UK: Penguin.
Williamson, O. E. 1965. "A Dynamic Theory of Interfirm Behavior." *Quarterly Journal of Economics* 79: 579–607.
Williamson, O. E. 1973. "Markets and Hierarchies: Some Elementary Considerations." *American Economic Review* 63: 316–25.
Williamson, O. E. 1975. *Markets and Hierarchies: Analysis and Antitrust Implications.* New York: Free Press.
Williamson, O. E. 1979. "Transaction Books Cost Economics: The Governance of Contractual Relations." *The Journal of Law Economics* 22: 233–61.
Williamson, O. E. 1985. *The Economic Institutions of Capitalism.* New York: Free Press.
Williamson, O. E. 1986. *Economic Organisations.* Hemel Hempsted, Herts., UK: Harvester Wheatsheaf.

Williamson, O. E 1994. "Transaction Books Cost Economics and Organizational Theory." In Smelzer, N. and Swedberg, R. (eds.), *The Handbook of Economic Sociology*. New York: Russell Sage.

Williamson, O. E. and Ouchi, W. G. 1983. The Markets and Hierarchies Programme of Research: Origins, Implications, Prospects." In Francis, A., Turk, J. and Willman, P. (eds.), *Power, Efficiency and Institutions*. London: Heinemann Educational.

Willke, H. 1990. "Disenchantment of the State: Outline of a Systems Theoretical Argumentation." In Ellwein, Th., Mayntz, R., and Scharpf, F. (eds.), *Yearbook in Government and Public Administration*. Baden-Baden, Germany: Nomos.

Wilson, B. 1979. *Rationality*. Oxford: Blackwell.

Wilson, E. O. 1975. *Sociobiology*. Cambridge, MA: Harvard University Press and Belknap.

Wilson, E. O. 1978. *On Human Nature*. Cambridge, MA: Harvard University Press.

Wilson, I. 2000. *The New Rules of Corporate Conduct: Rewriting the Social Charter*. Westport, CT: Quorum Books.

Winch, P. 1990. *The Idea of Social Science and Its Relation to Philosophy* (2nd ed.). London: Routledge.

Wincott, D. 1996. "Subsidiarity." In McLean, I. (ed.), *The Concise Oxford Dictionary of Politics*. Oxford: Oxford University Press.

Witt, U. (ed.) 1993. *Evolutionary Economics*. Cheltenham, Glos., UK: Edward Elgar.

Wittrock, B. 1982. "Social Knowledge, Public Policy and Social Betterment: A Review of Current Research on Knowledge Utilization in Policy Making." *European Journal of Political Research* 10 (1): 83–89.

Wolff, R. P. 1973. *The Autonomy of Reason*. New York: Harper Torchbooks.

Wong, P. 1996. "Governance by Exit: An Analysis of the Market for Corporate Control." In Keasey, K., Wright, M. and Thompson, S. (eds.), *Corporate Governance: Economic and Financial Issues*. Oxford: Oxford University Press.

Wood, S. 1996. "Christian Fundamentalism." In McLean, I. (ed.), *The Concise Oxford Dictionary of Politics*. Oxford: Oxford University Press.

Woodfield, A. 1973. *Teleology*. Cambridge: Cambridge University Press.

Wright, M. 1977. *Systems of States*. Atlantic Heights, NJ: Humanities Press.

Wright, M. and Thompson, S. 1987. "Divestment and the Control of Divisional Firms." *Accounting and Business Research* 17 (2): 259–67.

Wright, V. 1992. "The Administrative System and Market Regulation in Western Europe: Continuities, Exceptionalism and Convergence." *Rivista Trimestrale di Diritto Publico* (4): 1026–41.

Wright, V. 1994, "Reshaping the State: The Implications for Public Administration." *Western European Politics* 17 (3): 102–37.

Wrong, D. 1979. *Power: Its Forms and Bases*. New York: Harper and Row.

Wuthnow, R. Hunter, J. D., Bergesen, A. and Kurtzweil, E. 1984. *Culture Analysis: The Works of Peter L Berger, Mary Douglas, Michel Foucault and Jügen Habermas*. London: Routledge & Kegan Paul.

Wynne-Edwards, V. C. 1986. *Evolution Through Group Selection*. Cambridge, MA: Blackwell Scientific.

Yalom, I. D. 1980. *Existential Psychology*. New York: Basic.

Yeatman, A. 1993. "Voice and Representation in the Politics of Difference." In Gunew, S. and Yeatman, A. (eds.), *Feminism and the Politics of Difference*. London: Allen & Unwin.

Young, I. M. 1989. "Polity and Group Difference: A Critique of the Idea of Universal Citizenship." *Ethics* 99: 250–74.

Young, I. M. 1990. *Justice and the Politics of Difference.* Princeton, NJ: Princeton University Press.
Young, K. 1979. "Values in the Policy Process." *Policy and Politics* 5: 1–22. Reprinted in Pollitt, C., Lewis, L., Negro, J. and Pattern, J. (eds.), *Public Policy in Theory and Practice.* Sevenoaks, Kent, UK: Hodder and Stoughton and Open University Press.
Young, L. 1995. "Communication and the Other: Beyond Deliberative Democracy." In Wilson, M. and Yeatman, A. (eds.), *Justice and Identity: Antipodean Practices.* Sydney, NSW, Australia: Allen & Unwin.
Young, M. 1958. *The Rise of Meritocracy, 1870–2033.* London: Thames and Hudson.
Young, O. R. 1979. *Compliance and Public Authority: A Theory with International Applications.* Baltimore, MD: Johns Hopkins University Press.
Young, O. R. 1982. *Resource Regimes: Social Institutions and Natural Resources.* Berkeley, CA: University of California Press.
Young, O. R. 1989. *International Cooperation: Building Regimes for Natural Resources and the Environment.* Ithaca, NY: Cornell University Press.
Young, O. R. 1992. "The Effectiveness of International Institutions: Hard Cases and Critical Voices." In Rosenau, J. N. and Czempiel, E.-O. (eds.), *Governance Without Government Order and Change in World Politics.* Cambridge: Cambridge University Press.
Young, O. R. 1994. *International Governance: Protecting the Environment in a Stateless Society.* Ithaca, NY: Cornell University Press.
Yuchtman, E. and Seashore, S. 1967. "A System Resource Approach to Organizational Effectiveness." *American Sociological Review* 32: 891–903.
Zacher, M. W. 1992. "The Decaying Pillars of the Westphalian Temple: Implications for International Order and Governance." In Rosenau, J. N. and Czempiel, E.-O. (eds.), *Governance Without Government Order and Change in World Politics.* Cambridge: Cambridge University Press.
Zacher, M. W. with Sutton, B. A. 1995. *Governing Global Networks: International Regimes for Transportation and Communications.* Cambridge: Cambridge University Press.
Zadeh, L. A. 1965. "Fuzzy Sets." *Information and Control* 8: 338–53.
Zahra, S. A. and Pearce, J. AA II 1989. "Board of Directors and Corporate Financial Performance: A Review and Integrative Model." *Journal of Management* 15 (2): 291–334.
Zecchini, S. 1996. "The Governance of a Globalizing World Economy." *Rivista di Politica Economica* 86 (6): 49–70.
Zimmerman, M. J. 1988. *An Essay on Moral Responsibility.* Totowa, NJ: Rowman & Littlefield.
Zimmerman, M. J. 1996. *The Concept of Moral Obligation.* Cambridge: Cambridge University Press.

Index

abduction, 242
active society, 130, 140
acts of will, 38
Adler, A. 109
Adorno, T. 215
adverse selection, 88
advocacy coalitions, 12
agency theory and costs, 88
agency of justice, 143
agency ontology, 7, 9, 39, 17, 101, 142, 151, 152, 153, 191, 193, 206
aggression, 213
AIDS, 183
Alderfer, C. P. 20, 29
alienation, 36, 100, 112, 141, 142, 211, 212, 230
Allison, L. 2
Altman, Y. 14
altruism, 26, 44
    reciprocal, 51
    unconditional, 52
amoral familism, 41
analytical dualism. *See* morphogenesis
anarchical society, 178
anarchism, 27, 142
anomie, 37

conformist response, 64
rebellious response, 65
retreat response, 65
ritualistic response, 65
anthropological structuralism, 21
anti-alcohol organizations, 134
anti-smoking organizations, 134
apathy, 137, 140, 142, 216, 225, 226
    implies consent, 49
    justified, 24, 42
    undesirable, 34
appreciative inquiry, 105
Archer, M. S. 9, 243, 244
Ardrey, R. 20, 29, 106, 109
Arendt, H. 2, 219
Argyris, C. 105
Aristotelian thought, 18, 139
Arrow, K. J. 44, 135
assassination, 217, 220, 222, 224
associationalists, 92, 94

assumptive world, 4, 12
attitude formation, 54
authoritarians, 18, 136, 215, 225
authority, 132
　charismatic, 139
　coercive power, 141
　definition, 2
　none legitimate, 143
　rational-legal, 136
　rejection of, 223
autonomists. *See* hermits
autonomy, individual, 7
autonomy-control balance, 132

balance of power, 178, 179, 193, 194, 203
Bandler, W. 13, 53
Banfield, E. C. 41
Barnard, C. 52, 103
Barnum, P. T. 234
Barrett, W. 247
Barth, F. 53
Baruch, Y. 14
Bauman, Z. 172
Bentham, J. 176
Benthamite thought, 51, 128
Berlin, I. 24
Bhaskar, R. 8, 52, 56, 243, 244
Biersteker, T. J. 1, 189
biopolitics, 44, 137
Blair, 78, 93
Blake, R. R. 104, 108, 110, 113
blame, 24, 28, 34, 42, 49, 91, 95, 99, 101, 105, 108, 147, 149, 153, 186, 187, 191, 193
Blanchard, E. B. 102, 104, 107, 110, 113
Blasi, J. R. 78
Blauner, R. 37

Boulder, K. 2, 23, 33, 41, 49
bounded rationality, 20
Bourdieu, P. 26, 241
Bourne, E. J. 5
Braverman, H. 113
bribery, 224, 230, 234
Brown, S. 185
Bull, H. 171, 178, 179
bureaucracy, 26, 95
Burns, T. 104, 107, 110, 112, 127
Burton, R. 13
business wrongdoing, 81

Cable, V. 183
Campbell, D. T. 186
Camus, A. 36, 37, 213
Cantor, R. 25
Caporaso, J. A. 174, 182
Carlyle, T. ix
Carr, H. E. 179
Cartesian thought, 39
categorical interests, 134. *See also* public interest, the
Catholic Church, Roman, 173
cheating, 44
child labor, 48
Christian fundamentalism, 28, 134
civic republicanism, 128, 139
civil disobedience, 218
civil society, 130
clans, 130
clumsy institutions, 246
cognitive dissonance, 56, 64, 210
cognitive pluralism, 4
cognitive system, 5, 6
Cohen, M. 101
coherentism, 7
collective action, 129
command-and-control regulatory

Index 309

instruments. *See* regulatory instruments
Commission on Global Governance, 1, 175
common (collective) good, the, 128, 133, 137, 138, 139, 140, 148, 153. *See also* public interest, the
communicative rationality, 233
communicative-value rationality, 30
communitarianism, 139, 175
community, 51
   and preference formulation, 134
community-of-assumptions, 12
community of interests. *See* interest groups
competitive cooperation, principle of, 187
compliance, 79, 89, 108.
   alienative, 42, 113, 192, 222
   coercive, 112
   cognitive commitment, 24, 99, 111, 216, 226
   culture of, 146
   instrumental, 49, 92, 105, 227
   monitoring, 179, 188
   moral commitment, 34, 94, 108, 217
   network, 145
   zero tolerance, 90, 113
confederation, 137
conflicts
   either-or, 22
   more-or-less, 22
consent, 23, 33, 97

implicit, 48
conspiracy theory, 28, 220, 230
constituency policies, 145, 146, 149, 150, 152, 181, 186, 190, 192
constructionism, 175, 183
consumerism, 128
consumption style
   cosmopolitan, 50
   isolated, 42
   naturalist, 34
   traditionalist, 25
control
   by coercion, 82
   by force, 82
   by legitimate authority, 82
   by manipulation, 82
   by persuasion, 82
   definition, 80
   ex ante, 108
   ex post facto, 102
   exercised by contrived randomness, 101, 111
   exercised by contrived participation, 105
   exercised by contrived competition or rivalry, 90
   external mechanisms, 111, 113
   hierarchical obedience and loyalty mechanisms, 109
   mutual enforcement mechanisms, 108
   mutuality mechanisms, 95
   oversight mechanisms, 98

self-control
mechanisms, 105
Coons, A. 104, 108,
110, 113
cooperative
competition,
principle of, 187
Cooperrider, D. L. 105
Cornett, L. 174, 182
corporate
accountability, 84,
86
corporate decision-
making processes
autocratic, 94, 100
constrained
institutional
autocratic, 98
constrained
instrumental
autocratic, 90
garbage-can-like,
101
group, 94
corporate decision-
making strategies
compromise, 95
computational, 98
inspirational, 101
judgemental, 90
corporate
democratization, 92
corporate directors, 78
ad hoc focused
committees, 94
and corporate
performance, 79
antagonisms, 113
authority derived
from
authority derived
from managerial
ability, 86
authority derived
from ownership,
84
authority derived
from society, 85
authority derived
from use of

coercive power,
87
collaborative, 80
compound or
multi-tier boards,
93
contractual, 97
definition, 77
election method,
makes no
difference, 100
election method,
one-share, one-
vote, 89
election method,
one vote per
shareholder or
stakeholder, 94
election method,
one-voting-share,
one vote, 97
enclavists on, 92
fatalists on, 100
governance audits,
84
governance
committees, 89
hierarchists on, 96
independent
directors, 94
individualists on,
87
nonexecutive audit
committees, 89
ownership (market
or self-
regulation)
mode, 87
political model, 88
simple finance
model, 87
stakeholder
(interactive or
codeterminant)
mode, 92
stewardship
(hierarchy)
mode, 96
supervisory board,
93

Index

unitary boards, 89, 97, 100
what is good?, 87
corporate governance failure, 95
   responses to, exit, 92, 101
   responses to, voice, 95
   responses to, loyalty, 99
   solution to, empower more and different stakeholders, 96
   solution to, leave well enough alone, 101
   solution to, more diligent drafting and enforcement of principal-agent contracts, 91
   solution to, strengthen hierarchical controls, 99
corporate governance risk, salient
   managerial elite's loss of control or trust, 99
   principal-agent problem, 91
   self-chosen isolation in vain, 101
   stakeholders, managers and sovereigns cannot agree, 95
corporate integration, 216
corporate interest, the
   definition, 83
   enclavists on, 85
   fatalists on, 86
   hierarchists on, 86
   individualists on, 83
   knowable as inclusive set of categorical interests, 85
   knowable as preferences revealed in the marketplace, 83
   knowable as the corporate good, 86
   who should determine it? 83
corporate managers, 78, 96
corporate owners, 78
corporate stakeholders, 78, 93
corporate structural complexity, 79
corporate takeovers, hostile, 215, 223, 224
corporations
   agency companies, 80
   associations, 80
   consortia, 80
   cooperative, 92
   definition, 77
   federations of companies, 80
   fraud, 82
   joint ventures, 80
   multinational business corporation, 80
   organizational fields, 80
   organizational interdependence, 80
   organizational sets, 80
   ownership transfer, 92
   public enterprises, 77
   social obligations of, 82

social
  organizations, 77
  strategic business
    units, 80
cosmopolitanists, 176
Coughlin, R. 13
coup d'état, military,
  216, 234
Cox, R. W. 169, 189
creationism, 32
criminal lawlessness,
  217, 222, 224
critical social theory,
  30, 186
Crozier, M. 95
Cultural Theory, 2
  a constructive-type
    typology, 9
  a cult theory, 14
  and international
    relations, 168
  and relational
    situations, 7
  and social theory, 9
  applications of, 6
  as a framework, 6
  crossing the *grid* or
    grip divides, 58
  despair threshold,
    64
  disillusionment
    threshold, 59
  genericity, 18
  grid-group
    typology, 13
  grid dimensions,
    10
  grid-group space,
    10
  group dimensions,
    10
  group-engagement
    process, 7, 8
  homing-in process
    of allegiance
    change, 52
  impossibility
    theorem, 13
  origins of, 6
  patterns of culture,
    9, 13
  plurality principle,
    234
  requisite variety
    condition, 234
  social-control
    space, 10
  social map, 10, 11,
    12, 13, 14, 52,
    78, 127, 168, 231
  social-control
    comfort-zone,
    54, 208, 209
  social-control
    comfort zone
    allegiance
    change process,
    52, 54
  theory of surprise,
    56
  viable social
    solidarities, 12
  See also enclavists,
    fatalists,
    hierarchists,
    individualists,
    hermits
culture
  definition, 5
Cutting, B. 4, 31, 19
cybernetic law of
  requisite variety, 234
Czempiel, E. 1, 174,
  178

D'Andrade, R. G. 4
Dahl, R. A. 185
Darwin, C. 43
Darwinian thought, 44
Davis, S. 96
Dawkins, R. 43
de Gaulle, C. 97
death-of-the-expert
  proposition, 32
demagogy, 218
democracy, 128
  associative, 140
  civic
    republicanism,
    139
  consensual, 139
  deliberative, 139

Index 313

differentiated universalism, 140
direct, 140
discursive, 139
government by discussion, 139
grass roots, 140
participatory, 139
polyarchy, 140
protective, 144
radical, 140
representative, 140
Denham, R. 78
despotism, 136
deviants, 24, 59, 99, 111, 147, 182, 225, 226, 230
dialogic methods, 105
Dickens, P. 170
Diodorus, 142
discourse coalitions, 12
dismissal, staff, 226
dissidents, 28
distribution policies, 145, 146, 149, 150, 152, 180, 186, 190, 192
Dollard, J. 213
Donaldson, I. 96
Douglas, M. x, xii, 8, 11, 12, 19, 20, 22, 28, 32, 45, 141
dramaturgical analysis, 39
Dror, Y. 141
drug trade, the, 167, 175
Dryzek, J. S. 233
du Gay, P. 26
dual consciousness, 58
Durkheim, E. 37
Durkheimian thought, 3
duties and obligations, 19

ecology, 56
economic planning, 137

economic rationalism, 83
economic regulatory instruments. *See* regulatory instruments
economica res publica, 152
egoism
    egoistic moral motivation, 46
    ethical, 46
    psychological, 46
eigen dynamics, 129
Eilstein, H. 43
Eldredge, 95
electoral system
    compulsory voting, 140
    first-past-the-post voting system, 142, 144
    limited suffrage, 137, 142
    multimember constituencies, 140
    proportional representation, 140
    single-member constituencies, 137, 142, 144
    universal suffrage, 140, 144
    voluntary voting, 137, 142, 144
elites
    global administrative, 171 180
    global ruling, 174, 180
    intellectual, 138 184
    professional, 138
    technocratic, 138
Ellis, R. J. x, 12, 52, 53, 65
empiricism, 20
empowerment, 108

enabling state, 130
enclavists
    accepts human behavior predictable, 33
    accepts human nature, capacity for moral progress, 33
    adopts commitment-based voluntary compliance, 34
    adopts communicative-value rationality, 30
    adopts hermeneutic epistemology, 30
    adopts hermeneutic-structuralist methodology, 30, 33
    adopts structuralist ontology, 30
    adopts trial-without-error learning style, 32
    adopts values-based and intersubjective reasoning, 30
    and exclusivism, 27
    and factionalism and schism, 28
    and fear of secession, 28
    and group consensus, 31
    and intolerance, 29
    and personal authority, 27
    and rejection and deflection risk-handling style, 33
    and ritual, 27
    and sense of injustice, 27
    and social action, 31
    and social norms, 29
    and value judgements, 32
    and voluntarism, 27
    and voluntary collective action, 35
    apathy undesirable to, 34
    as disillusioned, 217
    as dissidents, 28
    as governors, 226
    as instrumental rebels, 219
    as internalists, 35
    as intransigents, 218, 229
    as noninstrumental rebels, 219, 229
    as slow learners, 32
    group-engagement process preference, 8
    metalife goal, 29
    needs emphasized, 29
    on blame, 34
    on censorship, 32
    on corporate governance, 92
    on direct consent, 33
    on disengagement from any governance mode, 218
    on economic growth, 34
    on fatalists, 61
    on freedom, 34
    on global governance, 182
    on hierarchical governance mode, 217

on hierarchists, 60
on individualists, 61
on inequality and envy, 34
on information technology, 34
on leadership, 27
on management, 105
on market sphere, 35
on nature, 34
on objectives and values, 32
on organizations, 94
on problem definition, 32
on risk management, 33
on risks and risk-taking, 33
on scarcity, 34
on self-regulation governance mode, 217
on social rights and obligations, 27
on societal governance,
on societal government system, 138
on societal risks, 33
on technology and engineering, 34
on corporate interest, the, 85
on the global interests, 174
on the public interest, 134
on time and the future, 34
on trust, 28
on wants and scarcity, 34
policy instrument preferences, 186
prefer coregulation regulatory mode, 149, 186
prefer information openly and readily available, 32
prefer instructive rules, 33
prefer naturalist consumption style, 34
prefer participative organizations, 35
reality as socially constructed, 31
regulatory instrument preferences, 149
resist power and authority, 29
response of intransigent to governors' counter-responses, 229
response to governance failure, 217
salient risk, 33
salient surprise, 58
source of self-esteem, 29
engagement style, 8
enneagram, the, 19, 29, 38, 45
environmental justice activists, 219
epistemic communities, 12
epistemic defeasibility, 7
epistemic relativism, 4
epistemological hermeneutics, 30
epistemology
definition, 7
See also
hermeneutics, knowledge, naturalism,

transcendental realism
Epstein, E. J. 97, 143
equality principles
   equality before the law, 25
   equality of objective outcome, 25, 50
   equality of opportunity, 25, 35, 50
   equality of results, 34
   individual contribution, 25, 35, 50
   need and just desert, 25, 35, 50
   rank order equality, 25, 35, 50
   unachievable, 42
essentialism, 47
ethical risks, 32
ethics
   act-consequentialist, 46
   act-utilitarianism, 46
   consequentialist, 37, 46
   contractarian, 46
   deontological, 19, 27 37, 99, 111, 147, 148, 181, 216, 226
   distributive justice, 106, 112
   empirical situationism, 46
   evolutionary, 44
   moral realism, 46
   mournful realism, 46
   ordinary decency, 84
   perfectionist, 142
   personal moral code, 38, 45, 91
   pragmatic, 46
   procedural justice, 106, 109
   rule-consequentialism, 46
   rule-utilitarianism, 46
   situational, 46
   teleological, 46
ethnomethodology, 7, 39, 40
Etzioni, A. 103, 107, 109, 112, 134, 140, 141
European Commission, 94
European Parliament, 185
European Union, 168
evolutionary
   economics, 44
   epistemology, 44
   ethics, 44
   politics, 44
   psychology, 44
existentialism, 30, 36, 37, 39, 142
external environment, corporate perspective on,
   disturbed reactive, 105
   placid cluster, 108
   placid randomized, 113
   turbulent, 111
external environment, corporate response to
   analyzer, 110
   defender, 108
   prospector, 105
   reactor, 113
externalists. *See* locus of control construct

failed states, 130, 170
Falk Moore, S. 11
fallacy of composition, 52
false consciousness, state of, 225

Index

falsification, principle of, 242
fanatics, moral, religious or political, 220
fatalists
  accept human behavior unpredictable, 40
  adopt acceptance and deflection risk-handling style, 41
  adopt agency ontology, 39
  adopt alienative compliance, 42
  adopt hermeneutic epistemology, 39
  adopt hermeneutic-agency methodology, 39, 41
  adopt ingrained rules of conduct, 38
  adopt isolated consumption style, 42
  adopt trial and error learning style, 40
  and anomie, 37
  and apathy, 42
  and autonomy limited, 38
  and collective action, 43
  and conflicting social norms, 37
  and conspiracy, 38
  and detachment and disconnectedness, 36
  and fate, 37, 42
  and isolationism, 36
  and luck, 37
  as closet fatalists, 43
  as criminal capitalists, 43
  as disillusioned, 220
  as externalists, 37
  as fast learners, 40
  as fickle isolates, 37
  as intransigents, 221, 230, 234
  as isolated cheats, 43
  as noninstrumental rebels, 222, 231
  disaffected from all regulatory modes, 150, 192
  group-engagement process preference, 8
  human condition unalterable, 36
  inner-directedness orientation, 38
  instrumental rebellion pointless, 221
  metalife goal, 38
  needs emphasized, 38
  on blame, 42
  on corporate governance, 100
  on distrust, 37
  on economic growth, 42
  on enclavists, 62
  on freedom, 42
  on global governance, 191
  on hierarchical governance mode, 220
  on hierarchists, 61
  on human nature, 41
  on individualists, 62
  on inequality and envy, 42

on interactive
governance
mode, 220
on management,
111
on market sphere,
42
on nature, 42
on objectives and
values, 40
on organizations,
43, 100
on power, rules
and compliance,
41
on problem
definition, 40
on problem
solutions, 40
on risk
management, 41
on risks and risk
taking, 41
on ritual, 38
on scarcity, 42
on self-regulation
governance
mode, 221
on social action, 40
on societal
governance, 150
on societal
government
system, 141
on societal risks,
41
on technology and
engineering, 42
on the corporate
ninteres, 86
on the global
interest 177
on the public
interest 135
on time and the
future, 42
on wants and
scarcity, 42
policy instrument
preferences, 150,
192

reality as the
individual
believes it to be,
40
response of
intransigent to
governors'
counter-
responses, 230
response to
governance
failure, 220
salient risk, 41
salient surprise, 58
source of self-
esteem, *38*
fate, 38, 40, 42, 43, 60,
61, 62, 63, 64, 101,
151, 193
Fayol, H. 78, 89, 99
Fernandes, P. 78
Festinger, L. 56
Feuerbach, L. A. 36
Fisher, G. 6
flat-earth science, 32
Flathman, R. E. 2
folk devils, 225
Follett, M. P. 233
Foucault, M. 1
Foucaultian thought, 3
foundationalism, 7
Fowles, J. 36
framing, 8, 14
definition, 6
France, 96
free rider problem, 52,
189
free will, 226
freedom
a life sentence, 36
existential curse of,
38
in context of
facticity, 36
in context of
situation, 36
negative, 24, 34,
42, 49, 82, 132,
139

positive, 24, 34, 42, 50, 82, 132, 143, 144, 152
freedom fighters, 219
Freeman, R. E. 95
France, 2, 23, 33, 41, 49
Freudian thought, 213
Fukuyama, F. 170
functional structuralism, 21
functionalism, 182
fundamentalism, 28

Gambetta, D. 44
game theory, 47
garbage-can decision theory, 101, 143
Garland, D. 1
general will, 128. *See also* public interest, the
generative theorizing, 106
George, J. 186
Germany, 82, 93
Gershuny, J. L. 141
Giddens, A. 19, 172, 243, 244.
Gilpin, R. 189
global administrative elite, 171, 180
global citizenship, 176
global civil society, 176
global culture, 172
global good, 173, 193
global governance, 169, 172, 173
  antagonisms, 193
  balance-of-power (hierarchical) mode, 179
  capacity, 173
  decision-making processes dominated by more powerful member-states, 180
  decision-making processes dominated by the unknowing and untrustworthy, 192
  decision-making processes dominated by those who understand the marketplace, 190
  decision-making processes dominated by competing interest groups, 185
  definition, 168
  enclavists on, 182
  fatalists on, 191
  global society (interactive) mode, 184
  hierarchists on, 178
  international economic process (market) mode, 188
  market self-regulation, 190
  network co-governance, 186
  voluntary transnational cogovernance networks, 184, 186
  what is good? 177
global governance failure,
  response to, exit, 191, 193
  response to, voice, 187
  response to, loyalty, 182
  solutions to, empower more and different interest groups, 187

solutions to, leave
well enough
alone, 193
global governance
failure,
solutions to,
strengthen
hierarchical
controls, 182
global governance risk,
salient
interest groups
cannot agree,
186
principal-agent
problem, 191
self-chosen
isolation in vain,
193
global governors, 172
global interest, the
definition, 168
global order, 168, 187
global ruling elite, 174,
180
global society, 174,
175, 183, 194
globalism, 169
globalists, 174
globalization, 131,
167, 169, 170, 172
governability, 2, 3, 231
corporate, 83
global, 169, 170,
171
societal, 130, 170
governace
alienation due to
undiminished
cognitive
dissonance, 211,
212
alienation due to
unremitting
antagonism, 211
antagonisms,
behavior, 207
antagonisms,
philosophical,
206

antagonisms,
reasoning, 207
antagonism from
the threatened,
208
antagonism from
the trapped, 208
constructive
dialogues, 233
definition, 1
disillusionment
threshold, 210
despair threshold,
rebellion, 213
despair threshold,
withdrawal, 212
despair, 211
despairing
governed
reactions to
governors'
counter-
responses, 228
dialogues of the
deaf, 232
governors
counterresponses
to despairing
governed, 224
hierarchical mode,
208
incompatible core
values, attitudes
and opinions,
208
interactive mode,
208
self-regulation
mode, 208
unresponsive
dialogues, 231
governance capacities,
131, 148
governance failure,
131, 132
causes, 79
enclavist response,
217
fatalist response,
220

Index 321

hierarchist
  response, 214
  individualist
  response, 222.
  See also corporate
  governance,
  global
  governance,
  societal
  governance
governance without
  government, 131
governing without
  government, 131
government
  as rent seeker, 143
  benign and
  benevolent, 136
  benign in intent but
  malevolent in
  action, 141
  coercively and
  intrusively
  malevolent, 143
  intrusive but
  benevolent, 138
  private interest,
  145
government system
  definition, 127. *See
  also* societal
  government
governmentality, 1
Gramsci, A. 2
Granovetter, M. 43
Grant, W. 145
Green, T. H. 82, 175
Grendstad, G. 56
Gross, J. 10, 13, 54, 83
group boundary
  maintenance, 17
groupthink, 31
guilt, 44, 91, 151
Gundfest, J. 88
Gunn, T., 36

Haas, P. M. 174, 185
Habermas, J. 243, 244
habitus, 13
Hales, C. 2, 23, 33, 49
Hannan, M. T. 95

Harter, P. 145
Hawley, J. P. 87, 88,
  91, 98
Hay, C. 130
Hayek, F. A. 82, 130
hazardous wastes,
  dumping of, 219
Hegelian thought, 27,
  137
Heideggerian thought,
  38, 247
Held, D. 169
hermeneutic
  epistemology, 30,
  39, 96, 101, 141,
  150, 151, 186, 187,
  193, 206, 243
hermeneutic
  phenomenology, 21
hermeneutic-
  structuralist
  methodology, 30, 33,
  39, 186, 226
hermeneutic-agency
  methodology, 39, 41,
  101, 142, 151, 193
hermits, 11, 142, 212,
  225
  reaction to
  governors'
  couterresponses,
  228
Hershey, P. 102, 104,
  107, 110, 113
Herzberg, F. 102, 103,
  106, 109, 112
Herzel, L. 97
Hickson, D. J. 22, 40,
  98
hierarchists
  accept human
  behavior
  predictable, 21,
  23
  accept human
  nature sinful, 23
  adopt anticipation
  learning style, 21
  adopt functionally
  analytical
  rationality, 20

adopt naturalist epistemology, 20
adopt naturalist-structuralism methodology, 21, 23
adopt procedural rationality, 20
adopt rejection and absorption risk-handling style, 23
adopt satisficing decision-making, 22
adopt structuralist ontology, 20
adopt traditionalist consumption styles, 25
and deontological ethics, 19
and entrenched social norms, 19
and obedience, 18
and objectives and values, 22
and personal security, 18
and positional authority, 18
and predominance of collective claims, 19
and reality judgements, 22
and ritualism and sacrifice, 19
and rule-bound organizations, 26
and self-control, 18
and sense of duty, 26
apathy means consent, 24
as authoritarians, 18
as disillusioned, 215
as governors, 225
as instrumental rebels, 216, 229
as intransigents, 215, 228
as noninstrumental rebels, 216, 229
as slow learners, 21
compliance based on constrained cognitive commitment, 24
group engagement process preference, 8
heirarchical regulatory mode preference, 147
hypothetical consent, 22
metalife goal, 20
needs emphasized, 20
on corporate governance, 96
on disengagement from any governance mode, 215
on economic growth, 25
on enclavists, 59
on fatalists, 59
on freedom, 24
on global governance mode, 179
on good global governance, 178
on individualists, 60
on inequality and envy, 25
on information technology, 25
on interactive governance mode, 214
on management, 108

Index   323

on market sphere, 25
on nature, 25
on organizations, 98
on power, rules and compliance, 23
on problem definition, 22
on problem solving, 22
on regulatory compliance, 147, 181
on risks and risk taking, 23
on scarcity, 25
on self-regulation governance mode, 214
on social action, 21
on societal governance system, 146
on societal government system, 136
on societal risks, 23
on technology and engineering, 25
on the corporate interest, 86
on the global interest, 173
on the public interest, 133
on time and the future, 24
on voluntary collective action, 26
on wants and scarcity, 25
other-directedness orientation, 20
policy instrument preference, 146, 180
prone to information asymmetry, 22
reality as objective truth, 21
regulatory mode preferences, 181
response of intransigent to governors' counter-responses, 228
response to governance failure, 214
salient risk, 23
salient surprise, 58
sources of self-esteem, 20
trust in authority, 19
Higgott, R. 169
Hill, C. W. J. 93
Hirschman, A. O. 22, 56, 209
Hirst, P. 85
historical materialism, 21
historical reason moral tradition, 185
Hobbes, T. 26
Hobbesian thought, 24, 143
Hofstede, G. 104, 107, 110, 112
Hollingsworth, J. R. 148
Holsti, H. J. 179
homo economicus, 43
homo hierarchus, 18
honor, 44, 91, 151
Hood, C. 35, 99
Hoppe, R. 39
human adaptability, models of coherent individual, 55, 57, 208, 210, 211, 213

sequential individual, 55, 57, 209, 210, 212
synthetic individual, 55, 57, 209, 211, 212
human behavior, basis of
   reasoned decisions constrained by hierarchical expectations, 207
   reasoned decisions constrained by self-interest, 207
   reasoned decisions constrained by socially constructed collective expectations, 207
   reasoned decisions constrained by what is believed to be true about social reality, 207
human nature, 44
   Abraham concept of, 106
   Adam concept of, 102, 109, 112
   biologically determined, 49
   capacity for moral progress, 33
   cooperative, 105
   safety and security, 109
   self-interested and self-serving, 49
   sinful, 23
   theory X, 102, 112
   theory Y, 106
   unpredictable, 111
   unpredictably capricious, 41
human rights, 140
human temperaments typology, Burton's, 13

ideal speech situation, 246. *See also* communicative rationality
idealists, 28
ideal-types, Weberian definition, 12
identity, 17, 35, 148
ideology, 170
imprisonment, 226
income inequalities, 172
indexicality of social life, 30, 31
individualists
   accept human behavior predictable, 48
   adopt acceptance and absorption risk-handling style, 49
   adopt cosmopolitan consumption style, 50
   adopt instrumental compliance, 49
   adopt naturalisn epistemology, 47
   adopt naturalist-agency methodology, 47, 49
   adopt teleological, synoptical and instrumental rationality, 46
   and action judgements, 48
   and autonomy, 44
   and contractual relationships, 44
   and market-based social order, 44
   and materialism, 44
   and personal responsibility, 44

and objective
  truths, 21
and objectives and
  values, 47
and predominance
  of individual
  claims, 44
and rituals, 44
as disillusioned,
  222
as fast learners, 48
as governors, 227
as instrumental
  rebels, 223, 224,
  230
as intransigents,
  223, 230
as noninstrumental
  rebels, 224, 230
group-engagement
  process
  preference, 8
inner-directedness
  orientation, 45
metalife goal, 45
needs emhasized,
  45
on blame, 49
on collective
  action, 51
on coregulation
  regulatory mode
  preferences, 190
on corporate
  governance, 87
on detachment
  from any
  governance
  mode, 223
on economic
  growth, 50
on enclavists, 63
on fatalists, 64
on freedom, 43, 49
on global
  governance, 187
on hierarchical
  governance
  mode, 222
on hierarchists, 63

on human nature,
  49
on inequality and
  envy, 50
on interactive
  governance
  mode, 222
on management,
  102
on market self-
  regulatory mode
  preference, 152
on market sphere,
  51
on nature, 50
on power, rules
  and compliance,
  49
on problem
  definition, 48
on problem
  solutions, 48
on risk and risk
  taking, 48
on risk
  management, 48
on scarcity, 50
on social action, 47
on societal
  governance, 151
on societal
  government
  system, 143
on societal risks,
  49
on technology and
  engineering, 50
on the corporate
  interest, 83
on the public
  interest, 135
on the global
  interests, 176
on time and the
  future, 50
on wants and
  scarcity, 50
organizations, 51,
  89

policy instrument preference, 152, 190
reality as objective truth, 47
response of intransigent to governors' counter-responses, 230
response to governance failure, 222
salient risk, 49
salient surprise, 58
source of self-esteem, 45
industrial democracy, 92
information, statutory freedom of access to, 144
information regulatory instruments. *See* regulatory instruments
information technology, 25, 34, 42, 50
information, statutory right of access, 138, 140
inner-other directedness dichotomy, 20, 29. *See also* locust of control construct
interest groups, 176
  defined, 134
  global, 171
  government, business and labor interaction, 145
  rogue, 220
intergovernmentalism, 184
internalists. *See* locus of control construct.
international anarchy, 174
international governmental organizations, 168, 170, 184, 188
international law, 178
international order, 179
international public 'goods', 168
international regimes, 168, 169, 180, 186
international relations
  communitarianists, 175
  constructionists, 175, 183
  cosmopolitanists, 176
  critical social theorists, 186
  functionalists, 182
  neofunctionalists, 174, 176
  neoliberals, 174, 187, 189
  neorealists, 173, 174, 178, 179
  public choice theorists, 188
  realists, 173, 178, 179
international society, 173, 174, 178, 179, 180, 181, 193, 194
international trade and investment, 172, 188
interpersonal relationships
  entrenched social norms, 19
  personal moral codes, 45
  sanctioned social norms, 38
intersubjectivity definition, 5
Islamic fundamentalism, 28, 134
issue networks, 12
Italy, 93

Index

iterative mixed scanning model, 141

Jackson, R. H. 169, 170, 171
Jacobson, H. K. 180
Janis, L. L. 31
Japan, 93, 97
Jaques, E. 26
Jensen, L. 24, 42
job hygiene work environment factors
  money, 103, 106, 109
  status, 103, 106, 109
  security, 103, 109
  administration, 109, 112
  supervision, 109, 112
  working conditions, 109, 112
Jones, C. 93, 98, 169
judgements
  action, 48
  normative, 30
  reality, 22
  value, 32
judicial policy-making, 138, 140, 142, 144
judicial review, 138, 140, 142, 144
judicial system, focus of
  human rights, 140
  law and order, 137, 142
  property rights, 144
Juvenal (Decimus Junius Juvenalis), ix

Kakabadse, A. 78
Kaplan, A. 2
Katsh, S. M. 81
Keohane, R. O. 168, 169, 171, 189
Kester, W. C. 97
Kierkegaardian thought, 7, 39
Knight, W. A. 179
Knoke, D. 82
knowledge.
  a posteriori, 7, 20
  a priori, 20
  tacit, 3
  verifiable, 21
  narrative, 31
  propositional, 47. *See also* naturalism, hermeneutics, transcendental realism, true beliefs
Koestler, C. O. 219
Kooiman, J. 1, 127, 129
Korac-Kakabadse, N. 78
Korea, North, 97
Kouzmin, A. 4, 19, 31
Krasner, S. D. 168
Kratochwil, F. 186
Kuhn, T. S. 242
Kymlicka, W. 134

labeling of people, 225, 226, 229, 230
labor unions, 219
language
  as representation, 47
  games, 21, 30
Lasswell, H. D. 2, 81, 128
Latin America, 192
Laumann, E. O. 82
Laurence, P. R. 90
law and order, 137, 140, 142, 144
leadership style
  charismatic, 139
  coach, 107
  country club, 108
  developer, 104
  driver, 113
  impoverished, 104
  parent, 110
  task, 113
  team, 110

learning style
  anticipation, 21
  luck, 47
  trial and error, 40
  trial witout error, 32
legitimation crisis, 130
Leonardi, R. 43
Lerry, W. 32
LeVine, R. A. 3
Lewin, K. 4
Lewis, O., 36
life space, 4
linguistic philosophy, 30
linguistic structuralism, 21
lobby groups. *See* interest groups.
localism, 169
Locke, E. A. 144
Lockean thought, 144
locus of control construct, 14, 35, 37, 213
logical positivism, 20
Lorsch, J. W. 90
Louis XIV, 97
loyalty, 19, 91, 129, 136, 137, 226
luck, 44, 47, 49, 91, 105, 153, 191
Luxembourg, 93

Maassen, G. F. 78
Mace, M. L. 97
Mahler, G. 36
Mamadouh, V. 23, 33, 49
man
  economic, 102
  hierarchical, 109
  isolated, 112
  social, 106
management
  definition, 78
  enclavists on, 105
  fatalists on, 111
  hierarchists on, 108
  individualists on, 102
  by wandering around, 107
  for inclusion, 105
  for results, 102
  for survival, 111
  purpose of, 102
  what is good?, 102
management buyouts, 215
management process
  command and control, 111, 113
  creating incentives and disincentives, 105
  inspiring performance consciousness, 108
  solving task-related problems, 104
  supporting *quid pro quo* individual exchanges, 104
management system
  benevolent authoritarian, 110
  consultative, 104
  exploitative authoritarian, 113
  participative group, 107
March, J . G. 21, 32, 40, 48, 111
market characteristics of, 25
market failure, 189
Mars, G. 43
Marshall, G. 37
Marxism, 37
Maslow, A. 20, 29, 38, 45, 103, 106, 109
materialism, 47

matrix organizations, 89
Mayntz, R. 79, 127, 132
Mazrui, A. A. 172
McCelland, D. C. 20, 29, 106, 109
McGregor, D. 102, 106, 109, 112
McKinney, J. P. 9
McNeill, W. H. 179
meritocracy, 51
Merton, R. K. 3, 64
metanarratives, 3
metaphors, 5
methodological families, 21
methodological individualism, 45
methodology.
    definition, 21. *See also* hermeneutic-agency methodology, hermeneutic-structuralist methodology, naturalist-agency methodology, and naturalist-structuralist methodology
Milgram, S. 219
millenarianism, 28, 220
Millsian thought, 133
Millstein, I. M. 81
minimal state, 130
Minnow, N. 77, 81
Mintzberg, H. 107, 110
Mitchell, D. 82
mixed scanning model, the, 141
mob behavior, 217, 220
modernists, 47
monarchism, 136
Monks, R. A. G. 77, 78, 81
moral community, 175

moral hazard, 88
moral tradition
    historical reason, 185
    universal moral order, 185
Moran, M. 128
Morgan, G. 103, 105 107, 109, 112
morphogenesis, 9, 244
Morrow, P. 103, 106, 109
motivation
    approval of authority figures, 109
    commitment through goal setting, 106
    finacial incentives, 103
    group recognition and acclaim, 106
    group-constructed understandings, 105
    organizational satisfaction of needs, 109
    self-interest, 102
Mouton, J. S. 104, 108, 110, 113
multiculturalation of meaning, 31
multilateral organizations. *See* international governmental organizations
multinational business, 171, 172. *See also* corporations: multinational business corporations
Murdoch, I., 36
Murray, R. 152
mutualism, 92
mythology, 103
myths of nature, 25

Mytilenian Debate of 427 BC, 142

Nadelmann, E. A. 175
Nader, R. 82
Napoleon, 97
narcissism, 45, 227
national governing elites, 184
natural selection, 52
naturalism, 20
naturalist epistemology, 91, 138, 144, 152, 153, 181, 182, 191, 205, 241, 242. *See also* epistemology
naturalist structuralist methodology, 21, 23, 99, 147, 181, 225
naturalist-agency methodology, 47, 49, 91, 152, 191, 227
naturalized epistemology, 7
negotiated order, 35. *See also* social order
neoclassical economic theory, 176, 189
neocorporatism, 145
neofunctionalism, 174, 176
neo-Kantian thought, 46
neoliberal institutionalism, 174
neoliberalism, 170, 176, 187, 189
neorealism and international relations, 173, 174, 178, 179
neostates, 170
nepotism, 51
network community, 176
network governance. *See* societal governance: co-governanace
network society, 130

network theory, 141
networks
    definition, 129
    role of state, 148
new global order, 175
Ney, S. x, 22, 28, 32, 141
Nietzchean thought, 38, 39, 242
nihilism, 39, 221
nihilistic rebellion, 231, 234
nomologicality, 8, 23
nonconformists, 225, 228, 229, 230
non-governmental organizations, 134. *See also* interest groups. See also interest groups
norms
    and group boundaries, 17
    conflict and confusion, 37
    constitutive, 10
    felt injustices, 25
    hierarchical group behavior, 23
    jointly affirmed, 29
    normlessness, 37
    regulatory, 11, 33
    rules of equality, 27
    sanctioned social, *38*
Nye, J. S., Jr. 168

obedience, 18, 136, 137, 226
obligation, 91
Olli, E. x, 13, 14, 55, 57, 208, 210, 211
Olsonian thought, 188
ontological synthesis debate, 9
ontology
    definition, 7. *See also* agency, morphogenesis,

stucturalism,
structuration.
Onuf, N. G. 11
opportunism, 88, 91,
  152
opportunism for guile,
  28
optimal rational
  decision-making
  model, 141
order, 1, 127
  organized or made,
    130
  social, 129, 130
  spontaneous or
    grown, 130
organizational culture
  club culture, 110,
    112
  definition, 103
  individualism, 104,
    107, 110, 112
  masculinity, 104,
    107, 110, 112
  person-centered,
    107
  power centered,
    112
  power-distance,
    104, 107, 110,
    112
  quid-pro-quo
    exchange-
    centered, 104
  role-centered, 110
  task-centered, 104
  uncertainty
    avoidance, 104,
    107, 110, 112
organizational decline,
  response to
  exit, 105, 113
  loyalty, 111
  voice, 108
organizational ecology,
  95
organizational
  engagement
  coercive alienative,
    112

normative moral,
  107
remunerative
  calculative, 103,
  109
organizational
  orientation
  bureaucratic, 109
  controlling, 112
  missionary, 107
organizational social
  systems
  cooperative career,
    104, 107, 110
  formal authority,
    104, 107, 110
  political, 104, 107,
    110
organizational
  structure
  definition, 80
organizations
  adhocracy, 107
  clan, 94
  cooperative, 112
  diversified, 110
  entrepreneurial,
    103
  formal authority,
    112
  holonic, 90, 94
  innnovative, 107
  J-type, 98
  matrix, 94, 99, 100
  multi-divisional
    (M-form), 89,
    90, 94
  network, 35
  organized anarchy,
    111
  personnel
    bureaucracies, 98
  pictured as a brain,
    109
  pictured as a
    machine, 109
  pictured as
    configuration of
    cultures, 107
  pictured as in a
    state of flux and

transformation, 103
pictured as instruments of domination, 112
pictured as living organisms, 103
pictured as political systems, 107
pictured as psychic prisons, 112
political, 107, 112
professional, 110
rational bureaucratic, 35
sequestered egalitarian, 35
transactional market, 35
under unfettered political control, 77
workflow bureaucracies, 98
Ortega y Gasset, J., 36
Ostrom, V. 6

Packard, V. 45, 103
paranoia, 225, 228, 230
Parsons, T. 98
passive resistance, 223
path-goal theory, 106
Pearce, F. 78
perspectivism, 31
Peters, B. G. 107, 137
phenomenology
  hermeneutic, 30
  transcendental, 30
philosophico-historical reductionism, 31
piracy, 175
Platonian thought, 19, 137
Polanyi, K. 153
policy argument, 141
policy communities, 12
policy instruments
  enclavists on, 149
  fatalists on, 150, 192
  hierarchists on, 146
  individualists on, 152.
  See also constituency policies, distribution policies, redistribution policies, regulatory policies
policy networks
  global, 184
political émigrés, 242
political metanarrative
  supremacy of collective over the individual, 137
  supremacy of the individual over the collective, 143
  existential preoccupation with the human condition, 142
  group bonding against outsiders, 139
polyarchy, 185
Porter, M. E. 78, 189
positivism, 20
postmodernism, 21, 31, 142, 183
postmodernity, 183
poststructuralism, 21, 30
poststructurationism, 9, 21, 243, 244, 245.
  See also morphogenesis
Pound, J. 88
poverty, 172
Powell, W. W. 19
power, 88
  and sovereign, 173

and unequal
  relations, 138,
  182
check and balances
  on, 144
coercive, 42, 83,
  87, 100, 101,
  112, 131, 132,
  135, 141, 151,
  154, 174, 177,
  180, 195, 225
definition, 2
delegation of, 140
deliberative, 140,
  184
economic, 49, 103,
  132, 174, 188,
  227
exchange, 1, 49,
  82, 103, 132,
  188, 227
expert, 23, 82, 109,
  132, 147
in international
  relations, 173
integrative, 33, 82,
  106, 132, 185,
  227
knowledge, 23,
  109, 132
legitimate
  authority, 23, 82,
  109, 132, 180,
  225, 226
manipulative, 151,
  180, 225
needs, 106, 109
normative, 33, 98,
  106, 132, 185
of corporations, 85
of global networks,
  184
of global ruling
  elite, 181
of management, 96
of network, 141
of policy
  argument, 141
of state, 130, 137,
  174, 183, 189

personal, 33, 106,
  132, 185, 227
persuasive, 151,
  180 185, 188,
  227
physical, 41, 83,
  112, 132, 192,
  225, 229
political, 96, 140,
  141, 178
positional, 82, 132,
  147, 180
referential, 82,
  106, 132, 185
resource, 49, 82,
  103, 132, 188
reward, 49, 82,
  103, 132, 188,
  227
seizure of, 216,
  229
structure, 104
threat, 41, 23, 83,
  112, 132, 192,
  240, 244
veto over, 234
void beyond, 241
Power, M. 2, 131
pressure groups. *See*
  interest groups
primitivism, 32
principal-agent
  problem, 91, 152
private interests, 128
private property, 143
privateering, 175
probabilism, 7
problem definition, 22,
  32, 40, 48
procedural rationality,
  20
property rights, 25, 44,
  136, 137, 140, 142,
  143, 144
protests, acts of, 218
psychological
  contracts, 103, 106,
  109, 112
public enterprises, 77
public interest,

as displaced
private interests,
81, 128
as the common
good, 133, 137
as will of the
people, 132
knowable as an
inclusive set of
'categorical
interests,' 134
knowable as an
inclusive set of
categorical
interests, 138,
139
knowable as
preferences
revealed in the
marketplace, 13
definition, 81, 128
enclavists on, 134
fatalists on, 135
hierarchists on,
133
individualists, 135
premises of, 132
protected by the
state, 146
traditions, 128
unknowable, 135,
143
who should
determine it?,
132
public policy analysis
communicative
value, 141
communicative-
value, 185
functionally
analytical, 138,
180
nonrational, 142
synoptic and
instrumental, 144
public policy decision-
makers
represetives of
categorical
interests, 141
rule-based, 138
self-interested, 144
societal governing
elites, 138
unknowing and
untrustworthy,
142
public policy decision
making
collective, 141
satisficing, 138
garbage-can-like,
143
optimal, 144
public policy process
a decision-making
system, 138
balancing
competing
interests, 140
garbage-can-like
decision
processes, 142
uses synoptic and
instrument policy
analysis, 144,
190
public services,
provision of
bureaucratic, 137
central (national),
131
communal, 131
managerialized,
131
market, 131, 143
nature of
irrelevant, 142
partnership, 139
public, 131
supra-national, 131
Pugh, D. S. 22, 40, 98
punctuated equilibria,
95

rational choice theory,
39, 47
rationality
communicative-
value, 106
definition, 8

fatalistic, 39
functional
    strategic, 47
inspirational
    strategic, 39, 111
instrumental, 102
neo-Kantian, 46
nonrational, 38, 111
teleological, synoptical and instrumental, 46.
See also reason, reasoning
Raven, B. 2, 23, 33, 41, 49
Rawlsian thought, 143
Rayner, x, 10, 13, 52, 54
realism, 20
    and international relations, 173, 178, 179
reason
    definition, 3
reasoning
    communicative-value, 207
    constrained rational calculation, 20
    functional-analytical, 207
    individal beliefs basis of, 39
    instrumental-strategic, 207
    mutual understandings, basis of 105
    nonrational, 207
    practical, 46
    self-interest based purposive decisions, 46
    scientific method, 47
    sense-making, 40
    sociological, 40
    teleological, 46

values-based and intersubjective, 30
See also rationality
rebellion
    instrumental, 213
    noninstrumental, 213
reciprocity, 129
redistributive policies, 147, 145, 149, 150, 152, 181, 186, 190, 192
reductionism, 47
Reeve, A. 37
reflexivity, 40
regulatory compliance
    alienative, 150, 192
    cognitive commitment, 147, 181
    instrumental, 152, 190
    moral commitment, 149, 186
regulatory instruments, 145
    command-and-control, 145, 147, 149, 150, 181, 186, 190, 192
    economic, 146, 147, 149 150, 152, 181, 186, 190, 192
    information, 146, 147, 149, 150, 152, 181, 186, 190, 192
regulatory policies, 145, 146, 149, 150, 152, 180, 186, 190, 192
    definition, 145
regulatory regime
    compliance culture, 146

enforced self-regulation, 145
expert-determined, 145
negotiated rule-making, 145
regulatory takings, 143
Reich, S. 169
Reinicke, W. H. 80, 83, 171, 184, 185
relativism, 31
reliabilism, 7
religious moral crusades, 134
religious sectarian movements, 134
rent seeking behavior, 143, 188
responsibility
    Cultural Theory of, 24
retroduction, 244
revealed preferences, 48 83, 176
Rhodes, R. A. W. 1
Riesman, D. 20, 29, 38, 45, 103
Righter, R. 179
rights, 221
    as justified claims, 139
    as justified practices, 139
    individual, 139
Riker, W. H. 135
riotous behavior, 220
risk management, 23, 146
risks taking, 23
Riso, D. R. 20, 29, 38, 45
ritual, 19, 216, 222, 226
Robinson, 81, 84
rogues, 49, 91, 105, 153, 191, 216
Rorty, R. 185
Rosaldo, M. Z. 4
Rosenau, J. N. 131, 168, 173, 179, 183, 184, 188, 191

Rousseauian thought, 24
Ruggie, J. G. 186, 189
rule of law, 44, 51, 151
rules
    categories of, 11
    commitment, 49
    definition, 10, 11
    directive, 23, 42
    ingrained, *38*
    instructive, 33
Rushton, J. P. 26
Rustow, D. A. 170

sabotage, 217, 220, 222
sacrifice, 19
Salacuse, J. 189
Sartre, J.-P. 36, 38, 39, 41
scalar chains, 109
Scharpf, F. W. 27, 28
Schein, E. H. 5, 103
Schmidt, W. H. 105, 108, 113
Schmitter, P. C. 129, 134, 145
Schmutzer, M. A. E. 13, 53
Schön, D. A. 105
Schwarz, M. 11, 13, 14, 35, 46
scientific method, 47, 206
secret enemies within, 96, 149, 150, 186, 187
self-control, 18, 19
self-determining self, 43
self-fulfilling prophecy, 3, 225, 228
self-governance
    autopoietic systems of, 129
    actor constellation systems of, 129
self interest, 26, 46, 47, 49, 51, 52, 84, 102,

135, 152, 227, 229, 230. *See also* egoism
selfish genes, 43
self-regulation, 151, 188, 189
Selle, P. 56
Selznick, P. 90, 102
sense-making process, 40
September 11, 2001, ix 167. *See also* terrorism
shame, 44, 91, 151
shared meaning system, 2
Shareef, R. 98
shareholder democracy, 94
Shepro, R. W. 97
Shostakovich, D. 36
Shweder, R. A. 5
Simon, H. A. 22, 90
skepticism, 39
Skinner, B. F. 226
Smith, A., 135
social constructionism, 3, 4
social control, 151, 225, 226
social contructivism. *See* social constructionism
social market, 93
social movements, 35, 134, 171, 172. *See also* interest groups.
social order, 24
  competitive and volatile, 44
  contractual market-based, 44
  ingrained rules, 38
  personal authority, 27
  positional authority, 18
social phenomenology, 39
socialism, 142
societal governance antagonisms, 153
  associations, 130
  authority derived from mutual agreement, 134
  authority derived from positional authority, 133
  authority derived from use of coercive power, 135
  co-governance, 128, 129, 145, 148, 149
  definition, 127
  democtratic corporatist, 129
  enclavists on, 148
  fatalists on, 150
  hierarchical, 128 145,
  hierarchicists on, 146
  individualists on, 151
  interest governance, 129
  market self-regulating, 129, 145
  organic, 127
  self-governance, 129.
societal governance failure
  response to, exit, 151, 153
  response to, voice, 149
  response to, loyalty, 147
  solutions to, empower more and different interest groups, 150
  solutions to, leave well enough alone, 151
  solutions to, more stringent drafting and enforcement of principal-

agent contracts, 153, 191
  solutions to, strengthen hierarchical controls, 147
societal governance risk, salient
  interest groups cannot agree, 149
  self-chosen isolation in vain, 151
  societal governing elites' loss of control or public trust, 147
  principal-agent problem, 152
societal governing elites, 131, 174
societal government
  deliberative-style, 139
  guardian-style, 137
  bicameral legislature, 140, 144
  centralized, 142
  devolved political system, 140
  enclavists on, 138
  executive dominance of, 137
  executive subservient to, 140, 142
  fatalists on, 141
  hierarchists on, 136
  individualists on, 143
  multitier political structure, 144
  separation of powers, 144
  unicameral legislature, 137, 142
  unitary political structure, 137
  unwritten constitution, 142
  written constitution, 144
societal risks, 23, 33
sociobiology, 43, 49, 51
sociopolitical governance. *See* societal governance
solipsism, 39
Somit, A. 137
Sorensen, G. 169, 170
Sorrentino, R. M. 26
sovereignty
  definition, 171
  individual, 7
  national, 171, 174, 178, 183
Spiro, P. J. 5
Srivastva, S. 105
standpoint epistemologies, 5
Starr, P. 20
state, the
  active society, 130, 140
  as a spiritual entity, 137
  communitarian view of, 140
  cooperative, 140
  definition, 82
  elitist theories of, 138
  enabling state, 130
  governance role of changing, 131
  knowledge capacity of, 133
  minimal state, 130
  modes of public services delivery, 131
  network society, 130
  New Right theories of, 144

pluralist and neo-pluralist theories of, 141
stateless society, 142
strong societies, weak states, 143
surveillance and direction, 131
Stern, N. H. 168
Sternberg, E. 77, 81, 84, 89
Stirner, M., 223
Stogdill, R. M. 104, 108, 110, 113
stoicism, 47
Strauss, A. 35
Streeck, W. 129, 134, 145
structural unemployment, 172
structuralism, 7, 9, 21, 17, 20, 21, 30, 33, 96, 99, 147, 150, 181, 182, 187, 206
structuration, 9, 243, 244, 245
subsidiarity, 140, 183, 194
suckers, 52
suicide, 37
superstition, 3
supranationality, 184, 185
Sutton, B. A. 169
symbolic interactionalism, 21, 30
systematic empiricism, 47
Sztompka, P. 37

takeovers and mergers, 80
Taket, A. 32
Tannenbaum, K. 80, 105, 108, 113
Tansay, J. 234
technostructure, 103, 109
teleology, intrinsic, 46

terrorism, 81, 167, 217, 220, 222, 224
Thomas, W. I. 2
Thompson, M. x, xii, 4, 10, 11, 12, 13, 14, 18, 35, 46, 52, 53, 54, 56, 65, 90, 95, 98, 101, 135, 234, 246
Thompson, J. D. 90
Thomson, J. E. 174
Thorngate, W. 54
Thurer, 130
totalitarianism, 136
transcendental realism, 243, 244, 245
transaction costs, 25, 51, 88, 189
transnational moral entrepreneurs, 175
transnationalists, 174
trench warfare, 113, 153, 193
Tricker, R. I. 81
true beliefs, 7, 111. *See also* knowledge
trust, 19, 27, 37, 41, 44, 93, 99, 129, 130, 131, 141, 147, 181, 185, 226
Turnbull, S. 91

Underhill, G. 185
United Kingdom, 81, 82, 131
United Nations, 127, 179, 185
United States of America, 81, 82, 88, 91, 97
unity of command principle, 89
universal moral order tradition, 175
utilitarianism, 46, 49, 128
utopians, 27

Van Vliet, M. 129
veil of ignorance, 46

Vickers, G. 22, 32, 41, 48
violence, 217, 220, 222
Vroom, V. H. 18, 44

Waltz, K. N. 174, 178
war, 179, 226
　civil, 216
　cold, 216
　guerrilla, 216, 219
　limited, 178, 216
　of liberation, 219
　total, 216
Waterman, R. H. 107
Waters, M. 169
Weber, M. 139
Weick, K. E. 40
whistle-blowing, 218
White, R. W. 20, 109
Whitehead, T. N. 110
Wildavsky, A. x, xii, 141
will, the general, 128. *See also* public interest, the
will of the market, 151
will of the people, 132
Williams, A. T. 87, 88, 91, 97, 98
Williamson, O. E. 89, 90, 94
Wilson, E. O. 43
Wordsworth, W., 12
work commitment, based on
　careers, 103
　organizatiuonal loyalty, 109
　work satisfaction, 107
worker directors, 92
worker self-management, 92
workers' control, 92
works councils, 92
world community, 176
world government, 172, 179
world order, 179
world organizations. *See* international governmental organizations
Wuthnow, R. 9, 10

Young, O. R. 127, 169, 188

Zacher, M. W. 169, 175, 191
Zahra, S. A. 78
zealots, 220
Znaniecki, F. 2
zone of indifference, 52, 65. *See also* Cultural Theory: social-control comfort zone

About the Author

JOHN DIXON is Professor of International Social Policy in the Department of Social Policy and Social Work at the University of Plymouth in the United Kingdom. Among Professor Dixon's 30 books are *The State of Social Welfare: The Twentieth Century in Cross-National Review* with R. P. Scheurell (Greenwood Press, 2002), *The Marketization of Social Security: International Perspectives*, with M. Hyde (Quorum Books, 2001) and *The Chinese Welfare System: 1949–1979* (Praeger, 1981).